With All Deliberate Speed

With All Deliberate Speed

Implementing *Brown v. Board of Education*

EDITED BY BRIAN J. DAUGHERITY
AND CHARLES C. BOLTON

The University of Arkansas Press
Fayetteville • 2008

Cloth
ISBN-10: 1-55728-868-2
ISBN-13: 978-1-55728-868-4

Paperback
ISBN-10: 1-55728-869-0
ISBN-13: 978-1-55728-869-1

12   11   10   09   08   5   4   3   2   1

Text design by Ellen Beeler

⊗ The paper used in this publication meets the minimum requirements of the
American National Standard for Permanence of Paper for Printed Library
Materials Z39.48-1984.

Library of Congress Cataloging-in-Publication Data

With all deliberate speed : implementing Brown v. Board of Education / edited
   by Brian J. Daugherity and Charles C. Bolton.
      p. cm.
   Includes bibliographical references and index.
   ISBN 978-1-55728-868-4 (cloth : alk. paper) — ISBN 978-1-55728-869-1
   (pbk. : alk. paper)
   1. Segregation in education—Law and legislation—United States—History.
   2. Discrimination in education—Law and legislation—United States.
   3. African Americans—Civil rights. I. Daugherity, Brian J., 1972– II. Bolton,
   Charles C., 1960–
   KF4155.W58 2008
   344.73'0798—dc22

                                                              2008000753

July 31, 2008

Contents

Introduction

The United States Supreme Court's *Brown v. Board of Education* decision of May 1954, which declared segregated schools unconstitutional, stands as one of the most important legal pronouncements of the twentieth century. The decision helped spark more than a decade of civil rights protest, ultimately toppling the American system of racial apartheid, dismantling "separate but equal" in public accommodations, and removing suffrage restrictions on black Americans. In 2004 Americans of all backgrounds celebrated the fiftieth anniversary of this historic ruling and its impact on American society.

Despite an increasingly vast literature on the history of the civil rights movement in the United States, relatively little of this work has explained how the mandate of the *Brown* decision—ending school segregation— was fulfilled. Some of the most notable recent scholarship related to the *Brown* decision and its implementation has highlighted the national scope and importance of the decision and has focused on the role of government officials, segregationist organizations, white liberals or moderates, and a handful of influential black attorneys.[1] African Americans and the campaign to implement *Brown*—especially at the state and local level—has remained somewhat neglected, resulting in a skewed discussion related to the importance of *Brown* and a limited understanding of the early years of the civil rights movement more broadly.[2]

The implementation of *Brown* was a central component of the early civil rights movement. Throughout the 1950s, African American efforts, both within the South and beyond, were largely concentrated on implementing *Brown*. Even in the 1950s, these efforts fueled the expansion of *Brown* into other realms of life, and sometimes included marches and street demonstrations—signs of direct action protests to come. The era also witnessed growing black frustration with efforts to achieve school integration, which helped fuel the larger movement of the 1960s. In these ways and others, a better understanding of the state and local campaigns to implement *Brown v. Board of Education* sheds crucial light on the early years of the civil rights movement in the United States.

With regards to the history of school desegregation, current scholarship suggests that the rise of southern resistance in the mid-1950s came about largely because white southerners objected to the federal encroachment on their rights that *Brown* represented. This portrayal, however, understates the school desegregation efforts of African Americans and their supporters. Several essays in this collection suggest that supporters of school integration strongly influenced the actions of state government officials and segregationists throughout the region. In other words, many elements of southern massive resistance appear to be more closely related to the actions of blacks and black organizations than previously noted. A better understanding of the black efforts directed toward school desegregation in the years after *Brown* will help provide us with a better understanding, and perhaps a revised portrayal, of the civil rights era as a whole.

It is important to remember that African Americans initially fought to implement the *Brown* decision with little help. Limited guidance and support from the Supreme Court, congressional resistance, and presidential hesitation made the endeavor a difficult one, particularly in the late 1950s and early 1960s. Complicating the process was growing white southern opposition, including the revival of white supremacist organizations such as the Ku Klux Klan, the birth of segregationist organizations such as the White Citizens' Councils, and government-organized resistance. In the North, housing segregation and white indifference limited the implementation of *Brown*. African American organizations struggled to bring about the implementation of *Brown* in the face of enormous obstacles.

The Supreme Court itself recognized the potential problems involved in implementing its 1954 decision. The Court wrestled with the implementation question for another year, before issuing instructions in May 1955 that became known as *Brown II*. In this decree, the Court announced that the initial action for implementation would be left to local federal district courts, meaning native white southerners in the segregated South. The Court also offered an ambiguous timetable for action, urging a vague pace for change with the oxymoron, "with all deliberate speed."[3]

After *Brown II*, black leaders remained cautiously optimistic about eliminating segregated education. The lukewarm embrace of the *Brown* mandate by President Dwight D. Eisenhower was one concern; another was the rapid growth of segregationist opposition. Most black leaders recognized that change would not come overnight, despite initial optimism and the euphoria that accompanied having the highest court in the land rule that racial segregation was unlawful. *Brown II* made it necessary for black plaintiffs to attack segregated schools on a case-by-case basis.

Throughout the struggle, the National Association for the Advancement of Colored People (NAACP) and its members and supporters were the primary force pushing for school integration. Their campaign, directed by the national office of the NAACP and also the NAACP Legal Defense and Educational Fund, involved the coordination of thousands of representatives across the nation. The story represents an integral, but essentially unknown, aspect of NAACP history.[4] Of course, African Americans did not uniformly support the integrationist goals of the NAACP, especially as the struggle to effect school integration moved into its second decade and as African Americans realized the enormous costs whites inflicted on black children and black education in their efforts to resist school integration.[5]

Black attorneys like Thurgood Marshall, the lead attorney for the NAACP's Legal Defense and Educational Fund, and Robert L. Carter recognized that local conditions would necessitate a variety of strategies in implementing the *Brown* decision.[6] Two days after *Brown II*, Thurgood Marshall told Carl Murphy, president of the *Baltimore Afro-American,* that the NAACP's strategy would be to seek implementation of the decree "state by state, that's what I hope. For example, we're going to treat Georgia one way, we're going to treat Maryland another way." Recognizing that the *Brown* decision ultimately required blacks to press for the implementation of the ruling all over the South, Marshall told Murphy that he believed "those white crackers are going to get tired of having Negro lawyers beating 'em every day in court. They're going to get tired of it."[7]

Marshall, Carter, and other black leaders in the struggle worked long and hard to ensure enforcement of the historic decree they had successfully convinced the U.S. Supreme Court to adopt. School desegregation litigation slowly overcame legal obstacles adopted by most southern states, leading to initial and then token desegregation throughout much of the region. African American pressure also led to the adoption of school desegregation plans in many nonsouthern locales. Well into the 1960s, however, only small numbers of black students attended formerly white schools, despite enormous efforts by African Americans and African American organizations such as the NAACP.

Over time the executive and legislative branches of the federal government became more involved in the school desegregation campaign. Following a decade of relative inaction, Congress passed major civil rights legislation—with presidential support—in 1964 and 1965. The 1964 Civil Rights Act proved the most important piece of federal legislation for advancing the desegregation of public schools. Title VI of the act provided a mechanism whereby federal funds could be withheld from school districts that failed to eliminate racial discrimination. With increasing sums of federal education money flowing into the nation's schools after passage of the Elementary and Secondary Education Act of 1965, Title VI became a stick used by the federal government, through the Department of Health, Education, and Welfare (HEW), to push states to make at least some effort toward dismantling their dual school systems. In many cases, states turned to the mechanism of freedom of choice to satisfy federal demands, but the procedure often limited rather than promoted school integration.[8]

Although Title VI allowed HEW to step up its oversight of the school desegregation process, increasing federal efforts to force compliance with the *Brown* mandate, dual school systems persisted throughout much of the nation. In the end, it was litigation undertaken by black attorneys and parents that actually led to the dismantling of dual school systems nationwide. Starting in 1968, the Supreme Court issued a series of three school desegregation rulings that transformed the definition of what was acceptable related to the implementation of *Brown*. In 1968, in *Green v. New Kent County, Virginia,* the Court ruled that freedom-of-choice plans were ineffective and generally not an acceptable method of ending public school segregation. The following year, the Court handed down *Alexander v. Holmes,* which declared that unitary school systems had to be established "at once." Finally, in 1971, the Court's ruling in *Swann v. Charlotte-Mecklenburg County Board of Education* decreed that busing was an acceptable method to achieve school integration.

Over time, federal courts also increasingly recognized that northern states had often deliberately perpetuated school segregation, via district zoning patterns, the placement of schools, and other methods. Though not overtly as in the South, these measures deliberately promoted racial segregation, and federal courts ordered northern districts to comply with its new school integration rulings in the late 1960s and 1970s. Throughout the nation, school districts were ordered to abandon dual school systems in favor of racially integrated schools. The *Swann* decision was a particularly important decision because it suggested a method to end the de facto school segregation in northern urban areas with racially segregated housing patterns.

In many locales, school integration occurred only under duress, leading to the establishment of unitary school systems without undermining the beliefs in white supremacy that had demanded separate educational institutions. As a result, when school integration finally occurred, it sometimes impacted public education in ways that adversely affected those black Americans for whom such action had been designed to assist. Indeed, whites throughout much of the nation never embraced the idea that blacks and whites should be educated together. As a result, continued, widespread white opposition to school integration meant that the period of federal support for dismantling segregated schools would be a relatively brief one. By 1973, the Nixon administration and an increasingly conservative U.S. Supreme Court began a federal retreat on supporting the goal of ending segregated schooling, a reversal of federal policy largely complete by the 1990s.[9]

•   •   •

The story of how the *Brown* decision was implemented in the United States is the subject of this book. Each chapter within this collection examines a different state in the post-*Brown* years, focusing on how African Americans and their supporters sought to bring about school desegregation, generally in the face of white opposition. Key questions include the role of the state NAACP, state government actions and policies, key judicial proceedings and rulings, ties to national events, the time frame of desegregation, and analyses as to why desegregation proceeded as it did. Together, the essays highlight many commonalities within the school desegregation process, including the crucial role of the NAACP and its attorneys, determined state government opposition, the impact of white segregationist organizations, and the important role played by the federal government, particularly in the 1960s.

The key variable is location and how it impacted the implementation process. States controlled their respective education policies and were determined to respond to the wishes of their citizens, shaping responses appropriate to their racial make-up, history, and vision for the future. As pressure from the NAACP, black parents, and the federal government increased, the southern states fought to preserve what many considered a way of life. Although white resistance to school integration was not initially as pronounced in states outside the South, black advocates for an end to segregated education in the North and West also found the road to successfully carrying out the *Brown* mandate to be a long and arduous one. While the various state and local stories examined in this collection reveal both common themes and distinctive local developments, we hope that by examining the same period and themes in different localities around the nation, greater light will be shed on the school desegregation process and the early years of the civil rights movement nationwide.

• • •

The 1957 school desegregation crisis in Little Rock was one of the first confrontations over the implementation of the *Brown* decision to garner national attention. Still, as Johanna Miller Lewis shows in "Implementing *Brown* in Arkansas," there is a great deal more to the desegregation story in the state. While some Arkansas districts desegregated in 1954, others resisted strongly—a product of the varied geography of the state. Statewide, desegregation proceeded erratically for much of the decade after *Brown*. Federal government pressure, particularly the efforts of the HEW in the mid-1960s, was key to increasing the pace of desegregation in Arkansas and bringing about true integration near the end of the decade.

Although Arkansas received the early headlines, the school desegregation struggle unfolded across the South in the late 1950s and early 1960s. Each state waged its own unique battle against the *Brown* decision, but even within individual states, local conditions typically dictated the details of compliance with the school desegregation decision. In "The Cost of Opportunity," J. Michael McElreath examines school desegregation in North Carolina, focusing on the Research Triangle region. There, four school districts followed different paths of compliance with *Brown*. North Carolina generally eschewed outright resistance, and token desegregation occurred fairly quickly in areas around the state. In the Research Triangle region, a combination of NAACP and federal government pressure fulfilled the promise of *Brown*. But as

McElreath points out, the process was strongly influenced by local considerations, including the stance of local school officials. Where school officials worked for the benefit of all students, the costs of opportunity were tolerable; where traditional race relations dominated the process, African Americans bore a disproportional burden.

North Carolina's Upper South neighbor, Virginia, represented an early battleground state in the struggle over school desegregation, as the state emerged as a leader of southern white resistance to the *Brown* decree. In "Keep on Keeping On," Brian Daugherity examines the NAACP and the campaign for school desegregation in Virginia. State NAACP leaders actively sought better educational opportunities for blacks starting in the 1930s, working closely with the national office of the NAACP in New York. After *Brown,* the state NAACP initiated widespread litigation to overcome white resistance, enshrined in the state's massive resistance laws, and began the desegregation process in the 1950s. In the 1960s, support from the federal government aided the implementation process, culminating in 1968 with the *Green v. New Kent County, Virginia,* U.S. Supreme Court decision. From its role in the original *Brown* litigation, to its victory in *Green,* the Virginia NAACP played a key role in attempting to fulfill the promises of *Brown v. Board of Education.*

School desegregation proved most difficult to achieve in the Deep South states of South Carolina, Georgia, Alabama, Mississippi, and Louisiana, yet in each of these states, local conditions affected the outcome. In South Carolina, as Vernon Burton and Lewie Reece describe in "The Palmetto Revolution," the relationship between politics and school desegregation proved key. Burton and Reece interweave the story of growing black political involvement and southern political realignment, arguing that greater black political strength helped bring about the implementation of *Brown* in South Carolina. Considering the state's role as a southern leader and its involvement in the original *Brown* case, the story of African American efforts to implement *Brown* in South Carolina is an important one.

Thomas O'Brien's chapter on school desegregation in Georgia, "Defiance, Protest, and Compromise," highlights the determination of NAACP leaders as well as government officials and segregationists who opposed them. O'Brien, however, also considers the role of white moderates, who opposed school desegregation in principle but supported the maintenance of free public education throughout the state. Although

NAACP litigation forced the state to act, it was white moderates who convinced Georgians to accept token desegregation rather than abandon the state's public school system. Actual school integration in Georgia arrived in the late 1960s, following more insistent court orders, but, as O'Brien notes, the achievement was not universally beneficial to African Americans.

Mississippi proved to be the most difficult state in which to enforce the *Brown* ruling. As Charles Bolton explains in "The Last Holdout," the Magnolia State successfully resisted desegregation for a decade after *Brown*, despite efforts by African Americans and the NAACP to force compliance. State leaders and segregationists—including the leaders of the Mississippi-based White Citizens' Councils—utilized a variety of mechanisms to thwart black attempts. Even more so than in other southern states, the increased dedication of the federal government to school desegregation proved crucial to the school desegregation effort. As Bolton notes, the Civil Rights Act and guidelines issued by HEW were critical to bringing about desegregation in Mississippi. Still, it was only continued pressure by the NAACP—and rulings from the federal courts—that led to true integration in the late 1960s and early 1970s. Even then, white resistance continued in the form of segregated private schools and white oversight of the integration process.

Another southern state, Florida, followed a much different development path in the twentieth century than its southern neighbors, and this divergence influenced how the *Brown* decision was implemented in Florida. In "A State Divided," Caroline Emmons deftly examines the impact of modernization on the school desegregation process in Florida, suggesting that post–World War II economic and population growth moderated the state's allegiance to white supremacy and aided efforts to implement *Brown*. Still, the struggle was not easy. Like its neighbors, Florida's state legislature adopted a variety of laws to slow the desegregation process and intimidate the proponents of integration. Turning to the federal courts, NAACP officials fought back against state-sponsored coercion and pushed the state to comply with the Supreme Court's mandate in *Brown*.

School desegregation in the border South proceeded more rapidly than in the former states of the Confederacy, but as Bradley Skelcher discusses in "Promises of *Brown*," regional differences within Delaware played an important role in the school desegregation process in that state. Some have described Delaware as the most northern southern state, and especially in southern Delaware, spirited public resistance challenged the implementation of *Brown* for years. As in other states, NAACP litigation, initiated after *Brown II,* began the desegregation process, but token desegregation remained the norm until the late 1960s. Following new school integration decisions by the U.S. Supreme Court at the turn of the decade, the state integrated its schools via consolidation, at great cost to Delaware's African American population.

In border states such as Delaware, the dedication to segregated schools was not as fierce as the massive resistance campaigns that consumed their southern neighbors, but the commitment to integrated education in these border locales remained lukewarm. Peter Moran's "Border State Ebb and Flow," notes that Missouri maintained state-sponsored school segregation in 1954. Following the high Court's decision, Missouri moved quickly to comply—state officials and the public supported desegregation, and many localities were happy to rid themselves of the financial liability that segregated schools represented. Still, compliance in Missouri generally meant eliminating segregation, not bringing about integration, and particularly in the cities this compliance meant little change because of residential segregation, transfer policies, and white flight to the suburbs. Pressure by HEW and federal courts in the 1970s initiated busing in the state's urban centers, where most African Americans resided, but only controversial and expensive court initiatives in the 1980s and 1990s brought about significant integration. Today, because of shifting viewpoints on the desegregation process, resegregation is the dominant trend.

School desegregation outside the South became an important issue in the late 1960s and early 1970s, but as Jayne Beilke demonstrates in "The Complexity of School Desegregation in the Borderland," segregation was an issue in many northern states even before 1954. In Indiana, black pressure both before and after *Brown* worked to bring about school integration, in the face of de facto segregation related to housing patterns and district policymaking. This pressure included lawsuits and, in the mid-1960s, the involvement of HEW. Busing, though contested by both blacks and whites, achieved a modicum of integration in the 1980s and 1990s, though not without some cost to African Americans. Achieving integration in Indiana, as Beilke points out, involved challenges similar to those in the South and also urban areas throughout the nation.

Because the twentieth-century migration of blacks from the South concentrated African Americans in northern and western cities, some of the most notable school desegregation struggles outside the South occurred in urban school districts. Jack Dougherty offers a localized examination of how desegregation proceeded in one of these northern urban centers in "Northern Desegregation and the Racial Politics of Magnet Schools in Milwaukee, Wisconsin." As Dougherty notes, African Americans in the North sought to utilize *Brown* to improve their educational opportunities in the 1950s. With help from the NAACP, blacks initiated litigation and also direct action campaigns to overcome residential segregation and other obstacles thwarting integrated schools. In Milwaukee, white flight, black in-migration, and residential segregation left the city increasingly black in the 1960s. Litigation pressured city officials to bring about integration, primarily through the use of magnet schools in the 1970s. Thereafter, African Americans focused increasingly on preserving black institutions in lieu of white control over the integration process.

Another urban area with a growing black population in the twentieth century was Las Vegas, Nevada. In "*Brown*, Integration, and Nevada," Michael Green shows that Nevada's small black population during the civil rights era was as determined to secure equal educational opportunities as blacks elsewhere. As in Indiana, de facto segregation prevailed both before and after *Brown* in Nevada. Centered in Las Vegas, black Nevadans utilized direct action as well as litigation to bring about school integration. This achievement led to busing in the early 1970s, in a pattern decidedly similar to black efforts elsewhere in the United States.

Brown v. Board of Education has been hailed as perhaps the most important U.S. Supreme Court decision of the twentieth century. Some point to its role in spurring renewed black efforts in the long black freedom struggle. Others have noted that the decision crystallized white opposition to the black effort to secure civil rights. Although the *Brown* decision undoubtedly played a major role in the civil rights movement of the 1950s and 1960s, the Court's mandate that separate schools were unconstitutional and had to be ended proved to be a problematic proposition. As the essays in this volume demonstrate, segregated schools were eventually destroyed through a combination of sustained black protest and litigation, and uneven federal support. Even so, replacing the old dual educational arrangements with unitary school systems proved difficult to achieve.

Implementing *Brown* in Arkansas

Johanna Miller Lewis

Arkansas is home to the first public school in the former Confederate States of America to implement racial desegregation, as well as the high school where arguably the most infamous moment in school desegregation occurred in the 1950s. While Arkansas's history contains two extreme outcomes with regard to school desegregation, across most of the state the process occurred in much the same way it did across the nation. That is to say, some local school boards in Arkansas desegregated their schools voluntarily, some under court order, and others only when the U.S. Department of Health, Education, and Welfare's Office of Education threatened to withdraw funds from segregated districts under the auspices of the 1964 Civil Rights Act.

The differences in school desegregation cannot be tied to a single source. However, a number of factors influenced how desegregation proceeded in Arkansas. First and foremost is that Arkansas is a notoriously poor state and labors under lower income averages and higher educational loads.[1] Other factors influenced the progress of desegregation, including the ratio of black students to white students in any given district; the geographic location of the district; the National Association for the Advancement of Colored People's local involvement or lack thereof; and the size and financial stability of the district.[2] The historian John Kirk demonstrated the NAACP's failure to encourage civil rights activism at the grassroots level in Little Rock in *Redefining the Color Line*. However, the records of the NAACP clearly show that, in the mid-1950s as the legal battle for desegregation escalated, the national office experienced numerous problems dealing with the Arkansas State Conference of Branches, as well as lawyers and branches throughout the state.[3] In all probability these difficulties had less to do with ideology or strategy than the major gap represented by the national office's apparent wealth, sophistication, and education in comparison to Arkansas's poverty, ignorance, and simplicity. Nonetheless, such differences resulted in a problematic relationship between the Arkansas State Conference and the national office.

This essay traces the history of desegregation in Arkansas's public schools following the *Brown* decision and sheds new light on the school districts lost in the shadow of Little Rock Central High School. As is the case with most states, no comprehensive history of school desegregation exists in Arkansas. Therefore, the sources for this essay are drawn from academic journals and books, records of the Arkansas Department of Education and the national office of the NAACP, newspaper and magazine accounts depicting the various stages of desegregation, as well as some local school district histories.

For the most part, the issue of racial desegregation in Arkansas is a black and white one. Groups such as Native Americans, Hispanics, and Asians did not exist in large enough numbers to threaten the European American population and, in most cases, were more easily subsumed into the dominant culture.[4]

Eliminating the dual system of education for blacks and whites was further complicated by the 1949 consolidation of Arkansas's school districts. After the state created a funded system of public education in 1868, the number of school districts grew irregularly until peaking in the 1920s with more than 5,000 districts. Rural out-migration that began in the 1930s and accelerated greatly in the 1940s reduced the number of districts to just over 3,000 by the end of World War II. The first state-supported consolidation effort came in 1948 with an initiated act and later became Amendment 40 to the constitution. This act/amendment became effective for the school year 1949–1950 and, using attendance as the standard to maintain a district, reduced the number of districts to 423. The next consolidation effort (state initiated) came in 1969, and another followed in 2004, further reducing the number of districts to 254.

In a state where school districts never receive "enough" funding, the issues of equality and consolidation have dominated educational law and politics in Arkansas. Consolidating the number of school districts in Arkansas holds the promise of spending fewer funds on administrative costs and more on education. Debates have centered not so much on desegregation but on equal funding and facilities for the existing districts, at a time when funding formulas are based on student enrollment and "white flight" has decreased the number of students in districts with large minority populations.[5]

Before the complicated story of how Arkansas handled desegregation in public education can be adequately explored, however, some background information on race and education in the state will be helpful.[6] *Plessy v. Ferguson* demanded from a federal level that, if separate, facilities must be equal. In reality this rarely occurred. Funding was barely enough for one system of education, let alone two; education for blacks suffered as a result. Throughout the mainly rural South, white school boards spent little on African American facilities and curricula, frequently relegating blacks to single-room, frame buildings with only one teacher to instruct students of all grades.

More specifically, in a state as poor as Arkansas education for white students was insufficient, but it was still considerably better than for black students. Black students often had a shorter academic year, inadequate or nonexistent supplies and equipment, few teachers, and badly maintained buildings. While black students comprised approximately 30 percent of the total enrollment in Arkansas public schools, the state spent only 10 percent of the entire school fund on black children. In short, education for African Americans reflected their contemporary political, economic, and social status and state allocations to black schools reflected that inferior status.

A state as rural as Arkansas, albeit with some urban areas, differed from other places in the South in that while the ratio of white high schools to students was 1:2,255; the ratio of black high schools to students was 1:24,469. In 1920 that meant 160 high schools for whites and 6 for blacks. All the black high schools were located in urban areas with significant black populations: Little Rock, Pine Bluff, Hot Springs, Helena, Fort Smith, and Texarkana. Unfortunately, 85 percent of black students lived in rural districts.[7]

In Little Rock, for example, the black community rallied to build a new high school in the late 1920s when the student body outgrew the M. W. Gibbs School and the frame portions of the building burned in a suspicious fire. The lack of space forced black students on to a "split-shift" schedule in the remaining brick portions of the building in which high school students attended class in the morning, and the elementary and junior high students attended in the afternoon.[8] Even the Little Rock School Board realized the African American population needed a new high school; unfortunately money for a segregated black school "had been diverted to create superior facilities for white children."[9] That school was Little Rock High School built in 1927. An impressive, 600,000-square-foot, four-story, buff-colored brick building with arches featuring sculptures over the front doors that would later find fame as Central High School, the facility cost the Little Rock School Board $1.5 million to build. The school, called "the most beautiful high school in America," housed the four high school grades and had enough classrooms for three thousand students. When there were not enough students to fill the building when it opened, the school board opened the facility to a new junior college they operated (Little Rock Junior College) from 1927 to 1931.[10]

Little Rock did not get its new black high school, named for Negro poet laureate Paul Laurence Dunbar, until the fall of 1929 and at a cost of $400,000. The Little Rock school system received aid in financing the building from John D. Rockefeller's General Education Fund, the Julius Rosenwald Foundation, and numerous private donations, many of which came from the black community. To save money the school was built on land the school board already owned, and the design was derived from the plans for Little Rock High School. Similarities exist between the two schools, but Dunbar is considerably smaller and has a less ornate exterior design. The 200,000-square-foot, three-story building featured red brick, concrete, and stone native to Arkansas.[11]

Arkansans reacted to the Supreme Court's 1954 decision in *Brown v. Board of Education of Topeka* in a myriad of ways. Governor Francis Cherry proclaimed that "Arkansas will obey the law," and had no intention of approaching desegregation "with the idea of becoming outlaws."[12] But former Arkansas governor (1970–1974) and U.S. senator

(1975–1999) Dale Bumpers (Democrat-Arkansas) remembered that southerners felt "that the court wasn't really serious and that somehow the whole thing could be finessed given a little time."[13] Nonetheless, two school districts in northwest Arkansas—Fayetteville and Charleston (Fort Smith School District #9)—and one district in central Arkansas—Sheridan—took immediate steps to desegregate their schools with varying degrees of success. A lawyer in Charleston, Arkansas, at the time, Dale Bumpers, advised the local school board to comply with *Brown* immediately. As he noted in his memoir, *The Best Lawyer in a One-Lawyer Town,* "I knew the decision had to be honored sooner or later, and I knew sooner would be easier . . . Better to do it [desegregate] voluntarily than under a court order."[14]

Five days after the Supreme Court handed down *Brown,* the Fayetteville School Board voted to admit nine black students to Fayetteville High School for the 1954–55 academic year. Financial reasons primarily motivated the board. It previously sent the district's handful of black secondary students to segregated schools in Fort Smith and Hot Springs, nearly 60 and 150 miles southwest of Fayetteville, and the resulting tuition and transportation expenses totaled nearly five thousand dollars a year.[15]

In the summer of 1954 Charleston, Arkansas, school superintendent Woody Haynes informed a local civic club that the school board planned to desegregate both white schools at the beginning of the next school year. On July 24, the school board unanimously voted to close its black school and admit eleven black students to the white school, with its enrollment of about 480. When Charleston schools opened on August 23, 1954, the district became the first in the former Confederate states to hold desegregated classes following the *Brown* decision (Fayetteville High School did not open until September 13, 1954). The Charleston School Board kept their activities surrounding desegregation quiet to prevent backlash from white citizens in the state. In fact, Superintendent Haynes denied rumors that the school had integrated its classes.[16] Not until after news surrounding Fayetteville's desegregation, as well as the state's attorney general's decision to provide the Supreme Court with a report on segregation in Arkansas's schools, did the Charleston board president finally reveal the school's activities.[17]

Neither of the two towns in the northwest corner of the state reported any problems with their initial desegregation efforts.[18] Only Sheridan, in central Arkansas, failed to succeed. In late May 1954, the board of the Sheridan School District, located east of Little Rock, unanimously voted to send its twenty-one black students to the local high school with six hundred white students. Once again the school board acted to save the approximately $4,000 required to send black students to a segregated school each year. Unlike Fayetteville and Charleston, opposition from white residents caused the school board to rescind its decision the following day. A week later, three hundred parents held a meeting to petition the school board to resign, and four members promptly acquiesced. When fall rolled around, Sheridan continued to bus twenty-seven black students to a black school in a neighboring district.[19] What was the difference? Located on the edge of the Arkansas delta with a higher population of blacks, white residents of Sheridan exhibited the racial prejudice common in the Deep South, where Jim Crow and the inferiority of blacks were foundations of society. Nevertheless, in April 1955 NAACP Legal Defense Fund (LDF) field worker Vernon McDaniel told the Little Rock NAACP that the state, "represents perhaps the brightest prospect among the southern states for integration, and it is expected to follow its previous pattern of pioneering."[20]

McDaniel had reason to be optimistic about Arkansas. Of the state's seventy-five counties, fifteen of them did not have black students in public schools, and twenty-two others had black student enrollments of less than 10 percent. The remaining thirty-seven counties had black student enrollment ranging from 11 to 60.5 percent, with the higher percentages located in the southeastern portion of Arkansas.[21] When the state board of education met in September 1954, the chair of the West Memphis School Board exaggerated that *Brown* would "tear our school system all to pieces." However, the majority of board members supported a strategy of minimal compliance with *Brown*, not outright defiance. In the end, the state board of education instructed school districts to wait for the implementation directions coming in *Brown II* before desegregating—a position the Arkansas State Conference of Branches of the NAACP deplored. Even so, Arkansas attorney general Tom Gentry warned the board that *Brown* was "the law of the land and we are going to have to abide by it."[22]

On May 31, 1955, the Supreme Court further defined the *Brown* order to desegregate in its *Brown II* decision, calling for school districts to desegregate with "all deliberate speed." The decision did not provide a hard and fast deadline for southern schools even to begin planning, let alone achieve, any level of desegregation, devastating advocates of *Brown I* and overjoying segregationists. *Brown II* had an immediate impact in Arkansas. School districts and politicians around the state, but especially in eastern Arkansas, could now stall, postpone, or drop excuses for desegregation. *Brown II* had a secondary impact on Arkansas and the South, too, in providing racists and die-hard segregationists the false hope that actively challenging desegregation through protests and the courts might result in overturning *Brown*.[23]

The Little Rock School District was the largest district in the state, and had the highest percentage of black students. Whatever happened in Little Rock would have a major impact on how the rest of the state implemented the Court's decision. In late 1954, Superintendent Virgil Blossom announced plans to gradually desegregate Central High School, as well as two new high schools, Hall High School (in a traditionally white neighborhood) and Horace Mann High School (in a traditionally black neighborhood), through colorblind attendance zones in September 1957. Elementary schools would begin the desegregation process around 1960. The local chapter of the NAACP responded to Blossom's plan by calling it "vague, indefinite, slow-moving and indicative of an intent to stall further on school desegregation." After the Supreme Court handed down *Brown II*, Arkansans who intended to barely comply with desegregation rejected it altogether.[24] In Little Rock, Superintendent Blossom and the school board quickly cut back their plans. By placing an all-black teaching staff at Horace Mann and allowing white students (but not black students) "exceptions" to the attendance zones, Mann would be black, Hall would be white, and Central High School would be the focus of desegregation.[25] Where Little Rock led, other large school districts in the state followed: Fort Smith, North Little Rock, Pine Bluff, and Hot Springs all postponed their desegregation plans until Little Rock acted.[26]

In the summer following *Brown II*, the school board for District No. 46 of Hoxie, in northeastern Arkansas, abolished its dual education system. Superintendent Kunkel Edward Vance stated the decision was "right in the sight of God," in compliance with the Supreme Court's ruling, and more cost efficient.[27] On July 11, 1955 (the school year began in midsummer to allow farm children time off in autumn to help with harvesting), Hoxie schools opened with twenty-one black students attending classes alongside approximately eight hundred white children. The next issue of *Life* magazine covered the events, stating, "By the end of the day the children were behaving as if they had gone to school together all their lives." Entitled "A 'Morally Right' Decision," and illustrated by photographs of white and black children playing together, this article brought increased attention from inside and outside of the state to the school board's decision.[28]

Within a short time, racist literature and letters from segregationist organizations in Tennessee, Alabama, Georgia, and Mississippi inundated the townspeople and school board members of Hoxie.[29] Three weeks into the term, a newly formed local citizen's committee against integration empowered by *Brown II* decided to boycott the schools beginning August 4. However, the longer that both black and white students in any number successfully attended the Hoxie schools, the more and more inflammatory racist organizations such as the newly formed Little Rock chapter of White America, Inc., and the White Citizens' Council of Arkansas became in their crusade to influence the local citizens' committee and end integration. Upset and harassed by the outside interference over what they perceived as a strictly local matter, Hoxie School Board members dismissed the agitators' actions and brought the school term to a close two weeks early to carefully consider "a solution to the present . . . problem" and allow everyone to calm down.[30]

Viewing this action as a weakening of the board members' resolve, segregationists from near and far rallied in Walnut Ridge (the town next to Hoxie) on September 17 to hear inflammatory speakers warn that, following school integration, the next step would be the "mongrelization" of the white and black races.[31] This action served to intimidate school board members and parents to the point that, by October 24, when the school term resumed with integration still in place, attendance fell by nearly 60 percent. After segregationists filed a suit charging mismanagement against the school board, attorneys for the school board filed suit in the United States Court for the Eastern District of Arkansas: *Hoxie School District No. 46 of Lawrence County, et al., v. Herbert Brewer, et al.* The Hoxie Committee for Segregation, the White Citizens' Council of Arkansas and White America, Inc., were among the segregationist organizations listed as defendants. The school board petitioned the court for a restraining order to prevent the defendants from interfering with racial integration in the public schools. The judge initially granted a temporary injunction and, in January 1956, granted a permanent order.[32]

While segregationist forces did not abandon Hoxie, integration nevertheless proceeded and by October 1957, approximately twenty-two black students, in grades 1–12, attended classes with nearly nine hundred white students.[33] Despite the stirrings of what would later be termed "massive resistance" to school desegregation, the Hoxie School

Board held firm on the issue of racial integration. While the board easily could have acceded to public demands and withdrawn its plans for desegregation, as the Sheridan School Board previously had done, members clearly resented the outside interference with "their problem" and refused to alter their course, thereby continuing Arkansas's record of successful public school desegregation.[34]

At the same time of the Hoxie School Board suit, on October 28, 1955, the NAACP brought its first suit against an Arkansas school district (Van Buren) in *Carolyn Jane Abernathy, et al., v. J. J. Izard as board president, et al.* Attorneys Thurgood Marshall of New York City, chief counsel for the NAACP; U. Simpson Tate of Dallas, regional NAACP attorney; D. L. Grace of Fort Smith and Robert L. Carter signed the complaint. With only 2.2 percent black population, the Van Buren School District segregated black elementary students in their own school and bused high school students to Fort Smith. The suit called for twenty-four black students (out of eighty-seven total) to be integrated into the white school system. On January 18, 1956, Judge John Miller ordered the Van Buren district to "make a prompt and reasonable" start toward racial integration and to submit a progress report on August 15, 1956.[35] Other districts in the state such as DeVall's Bluff, Dumas, Forest City, Stuttgart, Union County, Cleveland County, and Hempstead County either had no plans to desegregate, preferring to put additional funds into both black and white schools, or kept their plans private.[36]

By 1956, three more school districts had desegregated all or part of their programs. In northwest Arkansas, the Bentonville School District desegregated all twelve grades beginning in the 1955–56 academic year without a problem. The small district of about fifteen hundred students included only two black students. Following the example set in Charleston, school district officials did not reveal the desegregation until December 1956. The nearby Lincoln School District in Washington County near Fayetteville also integrated its one black student to the white high school in fall 1956 without notice. University of Arkansas sociology professor A. Stephen Stephan revealed the action in the winter 1957 issue of the *Journal of Negro Education*.[37] In May 1956 the Hot Springs School District, in the central part of the state, decided to desegregate its high-school-level auto mechanics' class in September.[38] School officials admitted black students to the program on a pro-rata basis according to their percentage of total enrollment. By 1960, this class contained fourteen white students and four black students.[39]

The apparent success of this "gradual" approach to integration led three additional school districts to prepare plans to desegregate their schools in the fall of 1957. Van Buren and Fort Smith School Districts, both in northwest Arkansas, began a "grade-a-year" plan. In Fort Smith's case, the district began desegregating from the first grade and by the 1959–60 school year had four black students (out of about one thousand in the district) attending classes with white students in grades 1–3. Under court order, the Van Buren School District produced its integration plan on August 21, 1956. The plan called for integrating the high school in 1957, and then desegregating its classes from eighth grade down at the rate of one a year. By the fall of 1960, approximately twenty-three black students (out of seventy in the district) attended desegregated classes in grades 6–12. In 1963, the district closed its Negro school and integrated all fifty-five black students into the twelve grades.[40]

As mentioned earlier, Superintendent Virgil Blossom drastically changed the Little Rock School District's desegregation plan after *Brown II*. The new plan drew criticism from the city's black citizens for not ending segregation more quickly. Working-class white citizens complained that Blossom's plan favored Little Rock's elite whose children would attend the newly completed Hall High School.[41] While the school board's desegregation plan was presented to numerous civic and community organizations prior to the fall of 1957, when desegregation was set to begin, Blossom appeared to perceive the issue simply as a school concern, rather than a larger city, state, and even national problem.[42] Tired of waiting for change, on January 23, 1956, twenty-seven black students appeared at four white Little Rock public schools (two high schools, one junior high, and an elementary school) and requested transfers for the spring semester. The principals referred the students to Superintendent Blossom, who denied their requests based on set policy.[43]

In February 1956, attorneys for the NAACP's Legal Defense Fund, including Pine Bluff attorney Wiley Branton, along with Thurgood Marshall and Robert L. Carter of New York, and U. Simpson Tate of Dallas filed suit on behalf of those black children who attempted to register in white Little Rock schools over a period of sixteen days but were denied admittance in *John Aaron, et al. v. Dr. William G. Cooper, board president, et al.* Realizing that under the district's plan "all deliberate speed" could mean that complete desegregation possibly would take up to eleven years, an unidentified spokesperson for the NAACP stated, "[segregation] is no longer the law of the land and we are . . . adamant in observing the LAW now as we were before, so our next step . . . will not be in any appeal to Blossom, but in the federal courts."[44] On August 28, 1956, federal judge John Miller dismissed the suit, stating that the Little Rock School Board's gradual desegregation plan was adequate and would "lead to an effective and gradual adjustment of the problem." Nonetheless, Miller said the court would retain jurisdiction over the case in the event "further orders . . . may be necessary to obtain the effectuation of the plan."[45] A month later, NAACP lawyers filed a notice to appeal the decision with the district court clerk's office and were granted a hearing on March 11, 1957, at which time the court took the matter under advisement. In late April, the Eighth Circuit Court of Appeals upheld Judge Miller's ruling that Little Rock's desegregation plan was sufficient.[46]

North Little Rock and Pine Bluff, two school districts that delayed any meaningful plans for desegregation until the court ruled on Little Rock, finally announced their plans in September 1956. North Little Rock proposed a system identical to the Blossom Plan. Pine Bluff, the city with the second-largest African American population (next to Little Rock), decided to wait a year and implement its grade-a-year plan beginning with first grade in the fall of 1958.[47] In January 1957, William Dove attempted to enroll his five children in the all-white Dollarway School just outside of Pine Bluff but was rebuffed by school superintendent Hazel Watkins and school board president Lee Parham. Dove's children regularly attended Townsend School, an all-black school in the Dollarway area.[48]

As a result of the national attention Arkansas received from the Hoxie case in 1955 and 1956, Governor Orval Faubus worked with the state legislature to provide school districts with some assistance in remaining segregated. In February 1957 the Arkansas General Assembly passed four bills designed to maintain segregation in public schools. The measures (1) created a state sovereignty commission with investigative powers; (2) required persons and organizations working for integration to register and provide reports of their actions; (3) relieved students of compulsory attendance in desegregated schools; and (4) authorized school districts to hire legal counsel to defend school board members and officials. Earlier in the school year, Arkansas voters approved a constitutional amendment in the November 1956 election supporting nullification, interposition, and pupil assignment in hopes of skirting the Supreme Court's decision to desegregate public schools.[49]

As the 1957–58 school year and the planned desegregation of four large school districts around the state (Little Rock, North Little Rock, Van Buren, and Fort Smith) approached, tensions between pro-integration and pro-segregation groups heightened. One small school district in northwest Arkansas, Ozark, took advantage of all the commotion in the central part of the state to try and desegregate without much notice in September. In early July Superintendent R. L. Graves announced that three black students would attend the previously all-white high school at the beginning of the school term.[50]

Meanwhile, attorneys for the Little Rock School Board and the Capitol Citizens' Council clashed over the circuit court's endorsement of the gradual desegregation plan, while white opposition to desegregation escalated as it spread throughout the state. Segregationists argued that the Supreme Court lacked the authority to compel local school districts to integrate because, in their opinion, the Court decision affected only the involved litigants. Not until Congress passed a law to the same effect would the decision be applicable nationwide. They maintained that the governor could "interpose" the state's sovereign power between the federal government and its citizens to prevent implementation of the *Brown* decision. While interposition lacked authority under constitutional law, many people believed the doctrine could negate or delay the Supreme Court's ruling.[51]

The Mothers' League of Central High School formed on August 22, 1957, and announced its intention to prevent integration at Central. Closely aligned with the Capitol Citizens' Council (itself a branch of the White Citizens' Council), the Mothers' League served as a vehicle through which segregationists could align their cause with the respectability of "motherhood."[52] On August 27, the league's recording secretary, Mary (Mrs. Clyde) Thomason, filed a petition seeking a temporary injunction against school desegregation. The injunction was initially granted by Pulaski chancellor Murray Reed, but subsequently nullified by federal district judge Ronald Davies, who ordered the school board to proceed with its integration plans.[53]

The conflict reached crisis proportions when Arkansas governor Orval Faubus, citing the potential for violence, called on the Arkansas National Guard to prevent the nine black students (who actually had registered to attend Central) from entering the school. Foreshadowing later events, Faubus noted, "There is the possibility that this action could develop into a test of authority on any unwilling people."[54] In a televised address on September 2, Faubus told Little Rock's citizens that local gun and knife sales had risen dramatically and he had received threats of impending violence at the school. Many residents were astounded by Faubus's action. Although most white citizens opposed integration, they had resigned themselves to comply with the Court's decision.[55]

Following Faubus's order, school officials asked the nine students not to attend school the following day. Concurrently, Judge Davies ordered the board to continue with its desegregation plan. On September 4, the nine students attempted to enter Central only to be turned away by the National Guard.[56] The next day, Governor Faubus sent a telegram to President Dwight Eisenhower, explaining his position and asking for the president's cooperation. He stated: "The situation in Little Rock . . . grows more explosive by the hour. This is caused . . . by a federal judge who decreed 'immediate' integration . . . without hearing any evidence whatsoever as to the conditions now existing in this community."[57] On September 20, Judge Davies ordered Faubus to stop preventing the nine black students from entering Central High School. Faubus removed the Guard and left the Little Rock Police Department to control the unruly mob in front of the school the following Monday. As the morning progressed, the police could not control the crowd and removed the nine black students through a side door for their safety.[58] President Eisenhower responded by sending in the 101st Airborne from Fort Campbell, Kentucky, and federalizing the Arkansas National Guard. Two days later, under federal troop escort, the nine black students entered Central High School. A military presence remained for the duration of the school year.

Citing the turmoil from the previous fall, in January 1958 the school board petitioned the court to delay implementation of its desegregation plan. While initially granted by federal district judge Harry Lemley, the Eighth Circuit Court of Appeals overturned the stay and the United States Supreme Court upheld its ruling. Governor Faubus, acting under the authority of recent state legislation, ordered all four of Little Rock's high schools closed, pending a public vote on the immediate integration of all of them, or against integration. Little Rock residents voted nearly three to one against integration, and the schools remained closed for the rest of the school year. The situation escalated in May 1959, when three segregationist school board members attempted to fire forty-four teachers and administrators whom they accused of being "integrationists."

Led by the Women's Emergency Committee to Open Our Schools (WEC), an organization of white women dedicated to preserving public education, male business and civic leaders finally formed Stop This Outrageous Purge (STOP) and rallied to reinstate the affected faculty and staff. Later that month, STOP and the WEC succeeded in removing the three segregationist board members, and the county election commission replaced them with three "moderate" members. The board then voted to reopen the schools in the fall of 1959, while continuing with their desegregation plan.[59]

During the following decade, the Little Rock School Board continued to implement its plan of gradual desegregation. Citing the state's Pupil Placement Law, which established sixteen criteria for accepting transfer students to previously all-white schools, including such factors as the academic ability and psychological stability of the black students and the effect on established programs, space, faculty, and transportation, the school board limited the number of black students attending classes with whites to a minimum.[60] Again, however, the federal appeals court criticized the board for its use of the placement laws and ordered it to devise a more objective procedure for assigning students.[61]

In 1965, the Little Rock School Board abandoned the state pupil-assignment law and adopted a freedom-of-choice plan. Under the plan, students entering the first grade, junior high, or senior high for the first time could state a preference to attend the school of their choice.[62] This plan, however, still did not result in substantial desegregation, and in 1966, in *Clark v. Board of Education* black parents sued the district, arguing that their children were denied the opportunity to enroll in white schools. This case has remained active in both the federal district court and the Eighth Circuit Court of Appeals, with a number of decisions handed down in the ensuing fifteen years.[63]

Following the turmoil at Little Rock and wanting to avoid problems in their own schools, few districts attempted desegregation between 1959 and 1963. Of the six districts that implemented some form of desegregation, two, Gosnell and Pulaski County, did so because their districts incorporated U.S. Air Force Base schools, which lost federal funding if they refused to desegregate schools. In the case of Gosnell, the majority of the district's students included children of military personnel stationed at Blytheville Air Force Base in northeast Arkansas. The only Pulaski County school to desegregate was the elementary school at Jacksonville Air Force Base near Little Rock. By 1962, the district opened the Jacksonville Junior and Senior High Schools to three black students from the air base.[64]

Also in 1962, tiny Mansfield School District, near Fort Smith, opened all twelve grades to about fourteen black students in the district. Previously, the students traveled eighty miles per day to attend segregated schools in Fort Smith. Mansfield officials also followed the lead of Fayetteville and Charleston and became the third district in the state to desegregate its athletic activities as well.[65]

By the last year of this period, 1963, two more school districts announced plans to voluntarily desegregate. Hot Springs, which previously only allowed black students to participate in an auto mechanics class, announced during the summer that the district would desegregate the first and second grades under a "stair-step" plan. During the first year, approximately ten black students attended desegregated classes.[66] The school board in Pine Bluff, southeast of Little Rock, originally planned to begin voluntary desegregation in 1958. The turmoil in Little Rock the previous year, however, caused the board to delay implementing its plan for another five years. In late 1960, attorney Wiley Branton told a rally of about three hundred members of the NAACP that black parents in the Pine Bluff School District had asked him to pursue steps to enroll their children in desegregated schools. Several days later, the Pine Bluff branch of the NAACP filed a petition signed by sixty-six parents requesting a special meeting with the school board.

The board met with the black parents but advised them that it was not ready to announce definite desegregation plans. Branton asked the board members if they intended to force black parents to sue the district for desegregation, but the board stood by its original statement and refused to comment further. In 1963, calling its decision voluntary and not appearing as a result of pressure from any particular organization, the board voted to implement its plan.[67] Like Hot Springs, Pine Bluff decided to begin desegregation in the first and second grades upon request for assignment to a formerly all-white school by the students' parents. The plan called for desegregation to proceed by two grades each year. In September, six black students enrolled in four elementary schools without incident.[68]

During the five-year period following the crisis at Little Rock, the only district to implement a desegregation plan as a result of litigation was Pine Bluff's neighbor, the Dollarway School District. In 1958 the Dollarway School Board denied three black high school students admittance to the all-white Dollarway School. Pine Bluff attorney George Howard Jr. filed suit (*Dove v. Parham*) on behalf of the students in federal district court in February 1959.[69] While the district court initially ordered the school board to enroll the three plaintiffs, the Eighth Circuit Court of Appeals overturned the decision. In 1960, the district announced it would consider applications from black students to enter the first grade at Dollarway School. Attorneys for the board argued before the court that it was acting within Arkansas's Pupil Placement Law by considering only first graders for assignment to the white school.[70] Judge J. Smith Henley of the circuit court approved the district's plan and in September 1960, one black first grader, Delores Jean York, became the first to attend Dollarway School.[71]

The case made headlines when the Dollarway School District received five thousand dollars from the state to assist with its legal expenses in fighting the lawsuit. This payment was the first made under Arkansas Act 358 of 1959, in which the state legislature appropriated funds to the state board of education to assist local school districts in their fight against desegregation.[72]

Attorneys for the black plaintiffs continued to challenge the district's policy of disallowing lateral transfers (those other than in the first grade), and in 1963, the federal court ordered the district to admit its first black secondary student (and attorney George Howard's daughter), Sarah Howard, to Dollarway High School. On the second day of classes, racial violence broke out as Sarah Howard reported harassment by several of her fellow students, and her uncle, William Howard, became involved in an altercation with a white youth when he attempted to pick up the black children from school. After the school board sent home a notice to all parents indicating that it would not tolerate physical violence at the school and would punish perpetrators, the black students returned and reported no additional incidents of violence.[73]

In 1964, Congress passed the Civil Rights Act and, as the Department of Health, Education, and Welfare began devising guidelines for compliance, 11 more Arkansas school districts announced desegregation measures, bringing the total number of desegregated districts to 24 out of the approximately 228 districts with students of both races. While some, mainly smaller districts with few black students, desegregated all twelve grades, others implemented freedom-of-choice plans that largely maintained separate attendance zones for black and white children but allowed a few black students the opportunity to request transfers to previously all-white schools. Black leaders maintained that other pressures—economic or even physical threats—could be placed on students and their parents to prevent them from applying to all-white schools and that these plans continued to place the burden of desegregation on the black students.[74] Statewide by the fall of 1964, approximately 930 black students attended classes with whites, representing just over 3 percent of the total black enrollment for the 24 districts.[75]

In early 1965, the federal Office of Education announced it would require school districts to file statements of compliance detailing their desegregation efforts in accordance with Title VI of the Civil Rights Act or forego federal aid. The office additionally set its target date for full desegregation in public schools as the fall of 1967. According to Francis Keppel, federal commissioner of education, for a district to meet the federal guidelines it needed to file an assurance that the district is already in compliance and either submit a final federal court order or an acceptable plan for desegregation.[76] By 1965–66, only four districts in the state were still involved in active litigation: Little Rock, Fort Smith, El Dorado, and West Memphis.

Plaintiffs in West Memphis agreed to dismiss their case in 1966 after the school district agreed to open all-white West Memphis Senior High to black students wishing to transfer from Wonder High School. In 1963, black plaintiffs in Fort Smith, represented by attorney George Howard Jr., demanded that black students be transferred to Fort Smith Northside High School. The United States Supreme Court ultimately decided the case in 1965. The Court ordered the district to immediately integrate its high schools, in effect invalidating the stair-step desegregation plan used by many districts across the state. Howard also represented the plaintiffs who sued the El Dorado School District in 1964. The parents of six black high school students sued on behalf of their children for admission to all-white El Dorado High School from their former school, Washington High. In amending the district's plan to desegregate all grades within three years, the Eighth Circuit Court of Appeals ordered the district to modify its freedom-of-choice plan to eliminate dual attendance zones based on race. The court further stated, "the bell was tolled for segregated schools more than a decade ago . . . after 11 years of deliberation, discussion and delay, the Court should turn a deaf ear to arguments that now is not the earliest practicable date [to integrate the schools]."[77]

Other districts across the state, perhaps seeing the writing on the wall in the rulings of the circuit court and the Supreme Court, and unable to give up federal funds, joined districts across the South in devising and implementing desegregation plans. By 1966, the number of black students attending classes with whites in Arkansas increased almost 700 percent over the previous year. However, this still represented only about 5.5 percent of black students in the state. The South, as a whole, averaged nearly 16 percent.[78] In March, the federal Office of Education announced several changes to its guidelines. Expressing reservations about freedom-of-choice plans, the agency advised districts to enact the plans in such a way as to eliminate dual education systems. In addition, the guidelines mandated faculty desegregation, elimination of unequal facilities and programs, and standardized reporting procedures.[79]

By late 1966, only four school districts in the state refused to comply with the agency's guidelines and faced the loss of federal aid. In one case, the Justice Department stepped in and filed suit against the Junction City School District. This district, with an almost 50:50 ratio of black students to white, eventually faced a federal court order to file a desegregation plan. Bright Star, a district with no black students, still refused to comply with federal guidelines and accepted the loss of federal funds.[80]

Elsewhere in the state, the pace of desegregation continued slowly, mainly through the use of freedom-of-choice plans. In 1970, following the U.S. Supreme Court's decision against such plans two years earlier in *Green v. New Kent County, Va.*, the district court found Little Rock's freedom-of-choice plan unacceptable and required the district to implement a plan to achieve racial balance in all schools. As in other areas of the nation (and later across the state), busing became the method for distributing white and black students proportionately throughout districts in the early 1970s, and public schools in Arkansas most likely achieved the most racial desegregation at this time.[81]

In 2007 many Arkansas school districts continue to struggle with problems of declining enrollments and racial resegregation due to "white flight." A shrinking student population in any district results in a decrease in state funding, while private and parochial schools grow by leaps and bounds. The dual system of education that *Brown v. Board* declared unconstitutional may have been effectively eliminated but the state's failure to further consolidate districts means that money that could be spent on improving instruction and curriculum in districts identified as underperforming by the federal No Child Left Behind Act, is paying superintendents in districts with fewer than one thousand students instead.

An economic and population boom in wealthy northwest Arkansas (the fastest-growing area in the state and home to Wal-Mart) has led to the mainly white school districts there receiving increased funding while the mainly black school districts in the poverty-stricken Delta are losing state money. While 254 school districts in a state with only seventy-five counties continue to absorb precious financial resources for administration, the smaller districts cannot provide the quality education and wide-reaching curriculum that the large districts can and state law now requires. In addition, the last round of school consolidation (which continues to play out), unleashed a new series of legal challenges over the inequality of the state funding formula for education. Unfortunately, these facts demonstrate that issues of racism in education are far from over in Arkansas.

The Cost of Opportunity

SCHOOL DESEGREGATION'S COMPLICATED CALCULUS IN NORTH CAROLINA

J. Michael McElreath

Painful as it may be to admit, perhaps the school desegregation experiment has failed. Incompetent efforts (whether halfhearted or ham-fisted) to mix the races in schools engendered tremendous animosity from those who both supported and opposed desegregation.[1] If the intent was to guarantee all children an equal opportunity for quality education, persistent gaps between the achievement levels of different racial groups suggest that something went seriously awry.[2] Even at the most basic level of measuring success, over fifty years after *Brown v. Board of Education*, most African Americans attend schools that are largely segregated by race, and resegregation is growing.[3] What can we learn from what many see as a quixotic enterprise or a lost cause?[4]

One place to search for answers to this question is the Triangle region of North Carolina. The region's experience helps us to see that desegregation's success was determined, in the end, by particular local factors. In a small geographic area, three school districts, by different paths, maintained most of their white enrollments during desegregation. Their stories, and the alternative outcome in the fourth district, offer evidence that desegregation did not have to fail, but also that genuine *integration* was rarely achieved.[5]

I. Numerous Paths

The segregationists said, "You can't legislate morality," and they were right. Those who supported integration responded that, even though hearts might not change overnight, eventually experience would win over all but the most committed racists. Blacks and whites, given the opportunity to grow up as equals in schools, would get to know each other as human beings rather than as stereotypes. They would sit together in class, play on the same teams, learn to cooperate. The vast majority of white girls would not end up having black babies. The sky would not fall, and people would just get used to living together in integrated school communities.[6]

In many ways, North Carolina's experience of desegregation vindicated the integrationists' predictions. Unlike many public schools elsewhere, those in North Carolina mostly weathered the desegregation process and avoided the worst effects of white and middle-class flight. But desegregation—the mixing of different races within the same school buildings—proved far more feasible than real integration.

The utopian dream of racial harmony has proved the exception rather than the rule, even in North Carolina. The varied experiences of students in the Triangle region (encompassing the cities of Durham and Raleigh, the college town of Chapel Hill, and the rural areas surrounding them) demonstrate that desegregation was achieved in many places, but widespread integration happened almost nowhere.

Achieving truly integrated education depended on numerous factors, with at least most of them working in the same direction. It required the cooperation of actors from the executive, legislative, and judicial branches of the federal government down to individual students. Given the obstacles that integration had to overcome, it should not be surprising that the stars so seldom aligned. Still, the fact that it did occur in some instances offers some insight about what sorts of factors proved most useful in the desegregation process.

Demographic differences played an important role in aiding or thwarting desegregation, as a comparison between western and eastern school districts within North Carolina would show. Eastern districts with heavy concentrations of black students dealt with strong opposition to desegregation and witnessed the creation of many all-white (or nearly so) private segregation academies. Many whites in western North Carolina, home to far fewer African Americans, also reacted negatively to desegregation. But once they failed to preserve segregation through legal schemes, they generally gave up further efforts and accepted the small numbers of blacks into overwhelmingly white schools. In short, desegregation's effectiveness always depended on the wider context in which it occurred. But even a conducive context, based partly on racial demographics, could not guarantee a positive outcome.

The primary determinant of desegregation's efficacy was the quality of local leadership. A willingness to lead positively rather than in reaction or fear could go a long way toward ensuring positive results. Those districts and schools where desegregation achieved the most positive outcomes were those where local officials—especially school boards, superintendents, and principals—provided real leadership. Such leaders helped to prepare their communities to see school desegregation as a positive change, rather than as a negative obligation they had to accept. Unfortunately, such leadership was in relatively short supply.

II. Token Times

At the beginning of the school desegregation process, the Triangle region seemed relatively well placed to meet the challenge of such a major feat of social engineering. During the decade prior to 1954, partly in an attempt to avoid the *Brown* ruling, North Carolina had rapidly increased funding for its black schools. Disparities between school facilities had diminished.[7] Also, the initial response of state political leaders to the *Brown* decision was cautious and measured. They never promised to defend segregation forever. Though they deplored *Brown* as an unconstitutional foray of federal courts into states' rights, North Carolina's leaders did relatively little to uphold that prerogative.

After *Brown II* required that schools desegregate with "all deliberate speed," Governor Luther Hodges asked blacks voluntarily to continue using segregated schools. With Hodges's backing, however, the state's legislators also produced the Pearsall Plan. This plan delayed significant desegregation for a decade, but it also helped whites accommodate themselves slowly to the idea of mixed-race schools. Either because or in spite of the delays in desegregation caused by the plan, the public schools of North Carolina largely did survive. Many saw the Pearsall Plan as a success both for the supporters of public schools and those who supported gradual, peaceful desegregation.[8]

Perhaps different political and civic leadership in the decade after *Brown* could have prepared North Carolina more effectively for the transition to desegregated schools. For a decade, no state leaders called on white North Carolinians to view desegregation as a change they should embrace as consistent with the values of a democratic society.[9] Absent strong pro-integration leadership from the state level, desegregation's success depended on the quality of local leaders.

Token desegregation began in North Carolina in 1957 in three school districts (Charlotte, Winston-Salem, and Greensboro), following secret consultations among the members of their school boards. The Pearsall Plan made such tokenism feasible, and cross-racial assignments spread to Durham in 1959, Raleigh and Chapel Hill in 1960, and the surrounding counties in 1963. By 1966, when a federal court ruled the Pearsall Plan unconstitutional, only about 5 percent of the state's African American students attended schools with whites. In the Triangle, only Chapel Hill had more than token numbers attending schools across racial lines.[10]

In every case, the first cross-racial assignments followed pressure by African American parents. The general pattern of delay and tokenism obscures significant differences among the districts, however. In the Triangle, Durham City's desegregation was the most contentious. There, black complaints over unequal school facilities dated back to the 1920s.[11] Following the *Brown* decision, new federal cases filed on behalf of hundreds of Durham children led to the first desegregation in the district in 1959.[12] The massive activism in Durham was less present elsewhere, for several reasons. Durham was home to a substantial black middle class that was more independent of white employers, less subject to potential retaliation. The leaders of desegregation efforts elsewhere were more vulnerable. In Raleigh, an effort among black parents to begin a class-action suit to press for desegregation never materialized, and the father in the first family that tried to gain a cross-racial assignment for his son lost his job.[13] In Chapel Hill, despite many early requests for desegregation, no litigation was filed until 1960.[14]

In the Triangle's county districts, desegregation moved even more slowly.[15] The counties began tokenism in 1963 after small numbers of African American parents in each district sought transfers for their children to all-white schools. In each case, the county school boards approved at least some of the transfers, usually in a fairly quiet manner. Several possible factors explain the difference from the city schools, each of which began desegregation only after court action. The relative success of tokenism in the city districts probably prepared the way for the counties' acquiescence.

Most school boards' openness to desegregation depended on keeping the numbers at token levels, however. As in the city districts, Wake County's board used confusing, sometimes contradictory logic in selecting black students for transfer to white schools. In 1963, with about twenty black applicants for cross-racial transfer, the board rejected all but those of six high school girls. The board denied the others for various reasons, including overcrowded conditions, low achievement records, and "best interest of student." Though the board turned down some applicants because of poor academic performance, it also denied one student because her excellent record "could qualify [her] for a scholarship." The board rejected a request from one student partly because it did not have his transcript. One board member said also, "I think to put one [black boy] alone [in the Cary school] is bad." She did not elaborate.[16]

Though belated, Durham County's desegregation efforts moved rapidly. The black community there organized to seek a desegregation *plan* in addition to simply token levels of student transfers. In July 1963, parents of sixty-one African American children filed a class-action lawsuit in federal court. Unlike in each of the Triangle's city districts, the plaintiffs and the Durham County School Board were able to agree on a desegregation plan without going to trial. A federal judge issued a consent order in 1964, and the parties were to confer again to work out acceptable plans for future years. The plan accomplished "freedom of choice," a pattern it had taken years to develop in Chapel Hill by persuasion and in Durham City by coercion. On paper, the plan was ahead of the desegregation programs in Raleigh, Wake County, and Orange County, but the numbers of students granted cross-racial transfers remained low.[17]

By the end of the 1963–64 school year, token desegregation was widely accepted by white Triangle residents. But no Triangle school district had dismantled segregated patterns. Under the aegis of the Civil Rights Act of 1964 and broadened federal enforcement efforts, however, the second decade after *Brown* brought real desegregation to the Triangle and the rest of North Carolina.

III. The Free-Choice Experiment

The provisions of the Civil Rights Act (CRA) of 1964 gave federal bureaucrats in the Departments of Health, Education, and Welfare and Justice power to force general desegregation. North Carolina's state leaders reluctantly advised local districts to comply with the CRA's requirement that "dual school structures" be abolished. Though Governor Dan Moore complained that the CRA was an unwarranted intrusion into local matters, he agreed with his attorney general's assessment that the act contained no wiggle room. State deputy attorney general Ralph Moody added that a school system could not escape the act's reach simply by abstaining from the use of federal funds, for under Title IV of the act, the attorney general of the United States could bring suit to force desegregation anyway. "In short," he wrote, "the whole Act contemplates total and complete desegregation of public schools whether federal funds are received or not."[18]

Following the state's lead, the six school districts in the Triangle all assured HEW that they would comply with the new federal desegregation guidelines. For most of them this meant considerable changes in assignment policies. Under North Carolina's pupil assignment law, black parents were supposedly given a fair chance to transfer their children to predominantly white schools. In fact, only a tiny percentage of North Carolina's African American students attended schools with white children before the CRA provided a federal battering ram to knock down state and local customs supporting school segregation. The year before the HEW regulations took effect, 3 percent of the Triangle's African American pupils attended predominantly white schools.

Chapel Hill was the only Triangle district to claim that it had already eliminated what HEW called the "dual school structure," and it was certainly the only one that could advance this position with a straight face. Beginning in 1962, the district had started assigning elementary students based on geography, and the following year allowed all students to transfer to the school of their choice. In 1964, the district had also started asking students entering junior high school to choose their school rather than making initial assignments based on race. Taken together, these assignment provisions were the most liberal in the state, but HEW was not satisfied. Rather than continuing race-based promotion patterns, HEW required the district to offer all parents an annual chance to choose their children's schools. After several other minor revisions, HEW approved the Chapel Hill desegregation plan in August 1965.[19]

Unlike Chapel Hill, which was fairly far along with its development of free-choice procedures by 1965, most districts across the South complied with the HEW regulations by submitting plans that substantially changed their pupil assignment policies. Raleigh City, Wake County, and Orange County all developed plans to allow parents to choose their children's schools. Following clarification and fine-tuning, HEW agreed that these plans constituted acceptably free choice for African American parents to send their children to desegregated schools.[20]

Durham City and Durham County were both in the midst of desegregation plans overseen by the federal district court, and they attempted to use their court orders as the basis for meeting the requirements of the CRA. In Durham County, the consent order was modified in the summer of 1965 to allow for the phasing in of freedom of choice in initial assignments to all grades over a three-year period. The plan granted liberal transfer policies for all students in the meantime. HEW accepted the consent order.[21] In Durham City, however, HEW pressed for, and achieved, more than the federal courts had required. The new plan provided for annual "complete freedom of choice" (limited only by school capacity), more conspicuous and timely notice to parents of the plan's features, and greater publicity of the plan among school personnel and the wider community.[22]

Despite the considerable effort that went into providing truly free choice to parents to choose desegregated schools, the plans were largely failures. With the onus still on them to request transfers, most black parents did not avail themselves of the opportunity of (or subject themselves to the consequences of) choosing desegregated schools. The year after most freedom-of-choice plans went into effect, HEW revised its guidelines for implementing the desegregation requirements under the CRA. The new guidelines spelled out how much progress would be acceptable in districts using free choice, for the first time suggesting specific numerical targets for compliance.[23] Underlying the new guidelines was the assumption that, given a truly free choice, African Americans would not choose to remain in segregated schools.

North Carolina's leaders howled that the HEW guidelines demanded more than the CRA had intended. Much of the dispute between these leaders and HEW over the guidelines derived from white southerners' conviction that the terms of the Civil Rights Act were completely satisfied once a bona fide free-choice plan was in operation. Judge John J. Parker, sitting on the Fourth Circuit Court of Appeals, had interpreted *Brown* in 1955 to mean that, "The Constitution . . . does not require integration. . . . It merely forbids the use of governmental power to enforce segregation."[24]

Ever since then, southerners committed to maintaining segregation had trumpeted what came to be known as the Parker Doctrine, often by adopting racially "neutral" assignment plans that worked, nevertheless, to prevent all but token desegregation. HEW's initial acceptance of freedom-of-choice plans in its first set of desegregation policies had emboldened the state's leaders to think that free choice was the ultimate solution. From HEW's perspective, however, freedom of choice had always been a means rather than an end. Its position was that the CRA imposed an affirmative duty on school districts that had segregated on the basis of race to eliminate segregation. For HEW, "eliminating segregation" meant "achieving desegregation."

There was some irony involved in the southern school boards' response to the new guidelines. Many boards that had shown themselves extremely sensitive to race while making assignments before the CRA suddenly claimed that anything less than colorblind administration was downright distasteful to them. In the first year of HEW oversight, Wake County superintendent Fred Smith said, "We do not at this time know the racial composition [of each class]. I hate to count noses, but this looks like what the Commissioner [of Education] wants." In that year, with 93 of the district's seventy-seven hundred black students in schools with whites, Smith claimed, "We don't list or label a school, they're just listed alphabetically, and you can't tell which is a Negro or white or inte-grated or not integrated."[25] HEW had no patience for such professed naïveté. Until larger numbers of black students were attending schools with whites, most schools would remain racially identifiable.

IV. Desegregation for Real

HEW demanded greater student and faculty desegregation in 1966–67, though its demands varied with each district. The more cooperation the HEW regulators perceived, the more favorably they were likely to view a district's efforts. Under heightened scrutiny, Chapel Hill's school lead-ers moved fastest to eliminate dual school structures. In 1966–67, the district desegregated all students in grades 6–12, and the following year it introduced attendance zones to desegregate its elementary schools as well. One HEW official told the Chapel Hill superintendent Willard Swiers that the attendance reports the district had sent indicated that "you have completed the elimination of the dual system of schools."[26] Very few southern districts could make such a claim in 1967.

HEW officials communicated their expectation that every district would move quickly to eliminate all vestiges of segregation in the assign-ment of students and staff. At first, some districts were able to placate

HEW without great difficulty, but others came in for serious interventions. The most aggressive of these occurred in Wake County, where HEW officials recommended numerous specific changes in school assignment patterns designed to increase cross-racial assignments from ninety-three students the previous year to somewhere between nine hundred and one thousand students in 1966.[27] In the end, the district's leaders rejected most of the suggested changes as too much, too soon. In some cases, they argued, the suggested changes were nonsensical.

The Wake County School Board's willingness to compromise with HEW may also have been affected by the glare of publicity. At the board meeting in which Superintendent Fred A. Smith reported on his meeting with federal officials, a large crowd of white school patrons appeared, anxious about potential upheavals in student assignment. Smith wrote HEW later that, "Due in part to the seemingly overbearing pressure implied in your suggestions and to the extensive news coverage given to a nearby school system in which a team from your office had recently visited, some 50 to 55 school patrons were present and, unfortunately, created a rather unfriendly atmosphere in which the Board of Education was to deliberate. . . . To say the least, the entire setting was hostile."[28] In the meeting, Mary Gentry, a school patron who would later be elected to the school board, said the board should give HEW the "white" position on desegregation. Whites in some sections of the county, she said, "will never take their children to integrated schools. I think they [HEW] are only interested in our color, not our schools." Board member Ferd L. Davis said that he "felt Washington's plan for transporting Negro children to the white schools and white children to the Negro schools was ridiculous."[29]

In the end, the sole action of the board relative to desegregation that evening was a resolution that beginning in 1967–68, new schools would be desegregated. "This may not be enough," Davis said, "but let them tell us. A pair of aces don't always win the pot, but they're good for openers." Here Davis made explicit the often unstated, game-like relationship between HEW and local districts. Superintendent Smith said he doubted HEW would be satisfied with the board's limited plan. Nevertheless, despite all the noise it had made, HEW did not make any attempt at that time to cut off federal funds to Wake County, or any other Triangle district.[30]

Over the next three years, HEW moved with more or less urgency to push every Triangle district to dismantle its old patterns that perpetuated the use of racially identifiable schools. With community support behind it, Orange County's board adopted a plan to eliminate dual structures by the fall of 1969. Its plan, like Wake County's, relied heavily on the construction of new schools to avoid requiring whites to attend formerly black schools.[31] In Raleigh City, a protracted battle with the HEW's Office for Civil Rights over the pace of desegregation finally ended in 1971. A federal judge, relying partly on a precedent set that year in *Swann v. Charlotte-Mecklenburg,* the most important North Carolina school desegregation case to reach the Supreme Court, ordered the Raleigh City schools to use whatever means were necessary to create representative racial mixes of students and faculty in all district schools. The district's solution to segregated residential areas was a massive use of busing and four sixth-grade centers, attended by all the district's sixth graders.[32]

The most dramatic shift based on the newly aggressive federal court efforts to end segregation came in Durham County. There, ongoing court consent orders provided a quick means for plaintiffs to demand revision of the orders in light of new court decisions. When the Supreme Court ruled in 1969 that school districts must "terminate dual school systems at once and . . . operate now and hereafter only unitary schools,"[33] the Durham County plaintiffs won an immediate application of the rule in their district. The practical effects seemed extraordinary: about twenty-five hundred elementary pupils were reassigned to new schools in the middle of a marking period in January 1970. The immediate impact of the reassignments on students' interracial schooling was unclear, however, since entire classrooms of children, white as well as black, were simply moved along with their teachers to new schools.[34]

By the early 1970s, as in the rest of North Carolina, each of the Triangle districts removed barriers that had maintained racially identifiable schools. Most schools' student bodies saw a fair amount of racial mixing. At various times, educational and civic leaders in each district had taken courageous steps to move the process forward, but at other times each district had demonstrated some degree of timidity, recalcitrance, or defiance. School leaders' initial response to *Brown* was uncertainty and trepidation, and these were eventually overcome only by a combination of local pressure and federal coercion. Although federal oversight continued, thereafter the state's districts increasingly faced issues related to desegregation that federal power could not solve.

V. Affirmative Actions

Placing students in the same school is no guarantee that they will actually learn together or much about one another. In Durham and Raleigh, true desegregation in the early 1970s was followed by middle-class flight into Durham and Wake County schools. School patrons in both counties were asked to approve merger of the districts, partly to help maintain the schools' ability to desegregate meaningfully, but in both counties, the voters demurred. Hostility to merger in Durham City came from both county whites and African American leaders. The latter group hoped that, as the city district lost whites, they would have a good chance of controlling the city school board for the first time. They were right—the board had its first majority-black membership by 1975. The cost of this electoral victory in the long run, however, was high. The Durham City schools gained a reputation for sinking standards and discipline problems. By 1992, when the two Durham districts were finally merged by county commissioners without voter approval, the city schools were over 90 percent African American, while the county schools were only about a third black. The difficulty of merging the systems is still apparent in 2007 on a school board bitterly divided on many issues along racial lines.

In the early 1970s, Raleigh and Wake County witnessed the same demographic trend of mostly white patrons leaving the city for the county. Whatever the underlying causes, many of Raleigh's political, civic, and business leaders thought the ultimate impact of the trend was clearly negative. They had watched urban school districts around the country suffer as middle-class families left for suburban districts, taking their interest, commitment, and resources with them. They only had to look down the road at Durham to see the development of a racially identifiable district that was increasingly thought of as failing its students and undermining its city's economic well-being. Robert L. Farmer, who served as a Wake County delegate to the North Carolina House of Representatives at the time, said the Raleigh business community supported merger because "the tax base was decaying and property values were going down in the inner city. Business folks didn't want downtown Raleigh to rot."[35]

Following a failed merger vote in 1972, a coalition of Raleigh's political and civic leaders began to discuss an alternative strategy for merging the school systems without the consent of voters. North Carolina law allowed for school district mergers without a popular vote as long as both school boards supported it. The Raleigh School Board supported merger after the late 1960s when, because of a change in the county board's policies, the city school district could no longer annex new portions of the county into its system. Unable to grow, the Raleigh system began to wither as many young families bought homes outside the city. Those that remained were increasingly poor and African American. The city board chair Casper Holroyd said it was poverty more than race that spelled trouble for the city schools; because comprehensive education of children from low-income families took more resources than the education of kids from affluent homes, the city desperately needed more money for its schools.[36] On the other hand, many Wake County residents were either hesitant or openly hostile to merger. Wake schools primarily served attendance areas centered on small incorporated towns, and many fretted about a "feeling of loss of identity in individual communities, a loss of community pride and a loss of local initiative."[37]

In the end, merger of the Raleigh and Wake school systems was very much connected to the local question of political power. In 1974, three new seats were added to the Wake County Board of Education, ostensibly to provide additional representation to outlying county areas. The new seats had a profound impact on merger, however. Until 1974, according to new board member A. Roy Tilley, "most of the members were in that donut around Raleigh." Cary, Garner, and Millbrook were closer to the city and had direct representation on the board, while other areas of the county were farther out and had no direct voice. Further exacerbating the underrepresentation of some county areas, there were two members on the county board who were residents of Raleigh.[38]

According to Tilley, the outlying county areas had suffered with older schools. They were not growing like the suburbs, and residents there felt the school board often ignored their interests. The addition to the board of members was meant to remedy this situation.[39] But the additions also added members more likely to support merger. Though a merger vote had failed in Wake County in 1972, some of the anti-merger arguments had been rendered moot. Wake County commissioners had since equalized school taxes in the two districts, for instance. The only substantial remaining argument against merger was uncertainty about what merger would mean for school assignments and busing.

Parents of children attending schools in the outlying areas of Wake County were fairly certain merger would not affect them; their kids were too far from Raleigh to be bused into the city, and their schools already had more than their share of black students. It was the whites in the county areas closest to Raleigh who worried that merger would mean drastic changes for their children, since they were near enough to the city to make the busing of their white students into town (and blacks out of town to their schools) perfectly feasible. The strong opposition to merger came from these areas that did not want to take on the task of Raleigh's desegregation.[40]

Fearing that they would never overcome white county residents' opposition, pro-merger forces began to ask the General Assembly to intervene. Members of the General Assembly from Wake County, however, were very reluctant to act on so controversial a topic without the political cover that support from both school boards would provide. The political winds shifted in April 1975 when the new eight-member Wake board signaled that it might be ready to support merger.[41] The Raleigh board unanimously supported merger, but it took some last-minute wrangling to convince the Wake board to agree.

When the Wake board met on April 14, 1975, an anti-merger member objected to taking a vote on merger since the matter had not been placed on the board's official agenda a week before. Samuel S. Ranzino, a Wake board member but a resident of Raleigh who supported merger, voted with merger opponents on the technicality, and the board adjourned without acting on merger. Merger proponent Roy Tilley of Fuquay later recalled, "The Millbrook group got to Sammy Ranzino the night we were supposed to vote for merger and said, 'We need more time.' I got home that night probably around midnight and I was about as dejected as I have ever been." Around 2:30 that morning, Walter Painter of East Wake, a parent who came to all the board meetings and also supported merger, called Tilley to console him. They spoke for half an hour, and Painter encouraged Tilley to find a way to overcome the opposition.

> The only thing to fix it was for Ranzino to change his mind. I called him at 6 am and said that I knew he supported merger as much as I did, and we had to get it done quickly while the current legislature was in session. I pointed out that he and Danielson would be leaving the board, and no one else from old Raleigh would be coming on who would support merger. I said the legislature was going out of session in three weeks and if we didn't get it done before then, no one would be able to be

elected who would support merger now that it had become so controversial.

Ranzino understood Tilley's reasoning and never wavered in support of merger again. At its next meeting, the Wake board voted 5–3 in favor of asking the Wake legislators to effect merger.[42]

From that point on, despite some heated public meetings and various legal maneuvers to try to block it, merger was a foregone conclusion. The most controversial aspect of the merger plan was that it denied Wake County's residents a chance to vote on it, and hundreds of them protested this undemocratic expedient. From the perspective of most of Raleigh's political, business, and civic leaders, however, merger of the Raleigh and Wake school systems saved both the schools and Raleigh's economic viability. As Tilley put it, "Had merger not happened [in 1975], we would have been just like Durham."[43] Instead, Wake County's merged school system is a model of the possibility of desegregation's success to this day.

VI. Stories from Three High Schools

Chapel Hill was among the first districts in the South to desegregate its secondary schools entirely. In 1966, all 10–12 graders were assigned to a new high school building. All sixth graders would attend the formerly all-black Lincoln Junior-Senior High School. There had been token desegregation without turmoil in Chapel Hill's secondary schools since 1961, and the district did not expect complete desegregation to be a problem.

Except for moving all the students into the new high school simultaneously, however, the district did nothing to ensure that black and white students would feel an equal sense of ownership or belonging. Every symbol for the new school—including the name, the mascot, the colors, the school song, the names of the yearbook and newspaper—was adopted from the old (white) Chapel Hill High School (CHHS). CHHS's principal retained her position, while Lincoln's principal was her assistant. Lincoln's head football coach was made defensive coach under the less successful head coach of CHHS. Only a handful of Lincoln's teachers taught in the new school, and all but one of these taught in nonacademic subjects. Lincoln's excellent band disappeared, and its trophies were actually thrown away.[44] Ed Caldwell, an African American community leader, remembered later: "Everything they had been proud of at

Lincoln—the band, the newspaper, the football tradition, the customs—meant nothing at Chapel Hill High." Steven Scroggs, a white high school student at the time, remembers, "There was a perception—particularly by the upperclassmen—of *them* coming to *our* school. I think the adults of the world at that time felt: New school, everybody comes together at one time—it's a level playing field. It was nowhere close to being a level playing field. It was still Lincoln was moving in on Chapel Hill High territory. . . . The kids from Lincoln lost a great deal more than the kids from Chapel Hill High."[45] The pain and anger over the disrespect shown Lincoln simmered for three years before erupting near the end of the 1968–69 school year.

On Monday morning, May 19, 1969, nearly one hundred black students at Chapel Hill High School barricaded themselves in the lobby, chained one door and blocked another. They were angry over the results of an election for junior marshals to serve as honorary ushers during graduation ceremonies. Five whites and two blacks were elected for the seven positions. Though the racial breakdown of the marshals closely approximated the racial percentage of the student body, to many African American students the election outcome represented a pattern they could no longer tolerate. In demanding *equal* rather than *proportional* numbers of marshals, they were demanding an acknowledgment that the school valued them as much as their white peers.[46]

The school's principal and district superintendent Wilmer S. Cody met with the students and worked out a compromise whereby four black runners-up in the election would be made marshals as well. Many students felt it was unfair to alter the results of a fair, democratic election. One of the students phoned the chair of the school board, and he agreed to put the students on the agenda for that night's meeting if black student representatives could be present as well to express their views.[47]

The school board meeting was packed with both students and parents. Following heated debate about the marshals controversy and the frustration that lay behind the sit-in, the board voted to eliminate marshals altogether. The majority of the board members believed they could not simply reverse the compromise agreed to by the principal, since to do so would severely undermine her authority, but they also would not endorse the compromise outright since they believed it had resulted from the use of force to overturn a democratic election.[48]

The Solomonic decision was extremely unpopular—it gave neither side exactly what it wanted. White students and some of their parents were probably the most upset, but many blacks who favored the compromise were also unhappy, and a delegation of about thirty blacks walked out of the board meeting in protest. The next day black students marched through town and met at the Roberson Street Community Center, listening to militant speakers as well as black community leaders who counseled more cool-headed negotiation. Some whites blamed the turmoil on outside agitators like Preston Dobbins, a leader of UNC's Black Student Movement who had advised the high school students.[49]

Tensions remained high in the school for the remainder of the school year. There was "a minor slugfest in the hallways" three days after the sit-in, but for the most part the animosities did not lead to blows. Black students in Chapel Hill presented a list of grievances and asked for more black teachers, greater attention to black history and literature in courses, greater acknowledgment of Lincoln's traditions at CHHS, and a disciplinary board made up of community members to review cases of suspension or expulsion. Superintendent Cody said many of the concerns the students raised were already being addressed.[50]

If tempers abated in the school, however, the matter lingered within the community. Hundreds of white parents signed a petition supporting the validity of the original marshal election and deploring "the use of the school ground as a place for social confrontation." The school board agreed to hear arguments in favor of changing their decision about marshals, and over three hundred people packed a school auditorium for the hearing. At that meeting it became clear that the students and the town had, for the most part, moved beyond the marshal issue. There were some angry words, but also some sincere searching for honest dialogue. Don Fuller, the outgoing white student body president, said, "The real issue is 'why was there so much anger in the first place . . . why were the parents and School Board oblivious to so much tension?' Democracy has served 70 percent of the school, but one third [African American students] has felt blocked out." Several black and white students blamed the tensions partly on the warnings they had heard from parents before the schools were desegregated. One parent agreed, "We are guilty if we taught our children to disrespect." Board member Guthrie expressed the belief that "high schools all over the state and the nation are going to be facing similar situations in the next few years. We just happen to be a few years ahead in facing some of the problems that are coming for others."[51] Chapel Hill's secondary schools struggled through several years of tense race relations and intermittent conflicts.

Desegregation did not have to turn out that way. Wayne Bare became the principal of predominantly white Garner High School in Wake County in 1967–68, a year before the opening of a new facility that would house all the area's students in grades eleven and twelve, black and white. He came to the district from the Winston-Salem/Forsyth County School District, a large district created through a city-county merger in 1963. As school desegregation would a few years later, the district's creation led to the merging of different school cultures. The experience taught Bare that merging different school traditions involved serious concerns over power, even when consolidation was not complicated by issues of race.[52]

Bare brought that perspective to Garner, and when the Wake County Board of Education planned to merge the black and white Garner-area schools in 1968, he prepared carefully:

> We made a fairly concerted effort starting early in the calendar year 1968 to involve people from the previous two schools to talk about student activities—everything from whether we were going to do plays, how many cheerleaders we were going to have, what's going to be the mascot, school colors and all of that, some of which ought to be common sense. We also began to have training of personnel which for lack of a better name were called human relations workshops.

Bare convened groups of student leaders from the rising junior and senior classes at the two schools during the semester before the merger. They discussed the coming change and made suggestions to ease the transition, including the adoption of an entirely new mascot and a new combination of the colors of the old schools. They also said there should be some representation of each race on the cheerleading squad, but left it to the school administration to decide how many "representative" would be.[53]

Bare also showed concern for black students by assembling a biracial staff. His assistant principal had served as the acting principal at the former Garner Consolidated School (GCS), as had one of the two school counselors, a woman well known and trusted by the black students. Coaches, black and white, were assigned based on merit, and the band director was black. In general, Bare tried to select teachers regardless of race with a good deal of experience with juniors and seniors. The students recognized Bare's efforts to make desegregation a positive experience for everyone. At the end of the first year in the new school, they dedicated their yearbook to him.

Unlike high schools in Chapel Hill and Garner, Durham's Hillside High essentially lost its chance to offer all of its students a desegregated education. There were simply too few whites. By the time Beth Levine attended Hillside in the 1980s, the school was over 90 percent black. Levine, the youngest daughter of a Duke professor, was among the minority of white students who remained in the Durham City Schools after full desegregation. From third grade on, she attended mostly majority black schools. She attended Hillside High School and thrived socially, making many close black and white friends. She got to know many black athletes in class and became the trainer for both the varsity football and basketball teams. But she knew she was unusual in the ease with which she moved between racial groups. She remembers feeling pulled at lunchtime, deciding whether to sit with her white friends or with the black players. She often got flak from her white friends for hanging out with her black friends, though never similar pressure from the blacks. Perhaps because of the unconditional acceptance she experienced with the players, Levine says, "I realized I was more comfortable with blacks, and that's true to this day."[54]

Neither the Supreme Court nor HEW caused Levine's revelation, but school desegregation gave her opportunities to know and like her black friends. Even students who did not embrace this opportunity as much as Levine had the chance to become acquainted and interact with one another in classrooms, hallways, auditoriums, clubs, and athletic teams. Those opportunities made it possible to get past fear and antipathy engendered by ignorance. Desegregation, even accomplished against the wishes of many and even done in ways unfair to many black students, provided a chance for students to change their own views about race based on direct experience.

VII. The Ledger

The great variety of experiences North Carolina students, teachers, and administrators had with desegregation demonstrates that both outside pressure and local initiative were necessary for school desegregation to work. Federal intervention and oversight was a prerequisite to force local school boards and superintendents to implement assignment plans that were truly desegregated, but once that had been accomplished it was up to principals, teachers, and students to determine to what degree their school experience and their lives would be integrated.

In most obvious ways, and more so than many other parts of the country, the Triangle region of North Carolina today is desegregated. It is impossible to conceive of the changes that have taken place in race relations had the schools not been desegregated also; the significance of the schools would have mocked the sincerity of the other transformations had they gone unchanged. The extended battles over school desegregation also gave the people of the region a chance to practice negotiation and compromise over power formerly held entirely by whites.[55]

Those welcome changes came at a high price for African Americans. Blacks (and many whites, especially conscientious educators) are justified in feeling disappointment at the disparities that still exist between black and white students. It is also understandable that some older black leaders unfavorably compare aspects of today's large, often impersonal high schools to the supportive, tight-knit communities that used to flourish at schools like Lincoln. Some wonder if their grandchildren would be better off in community schools with black teachers, coaches, counselors, and administrators who might better challenge them and nurture their sense of self-worth.

Though many African Americans in the Triangle share fond memories of the segregated schools, there are few that really wish for a return to segregation. For some it is a matter of practical necessity: they are willing to continue bearing the costs of desegregation "out of fear that resegregation would be worse." David Forbes, pastor of the Christian Faith Baptist Church in Raleigh, who led civil rights sit-ins and marches as a Shaw University student in the 1960s, says, "If I could find a political model that would guarantee equal distribution, then I would not romanticize about integration for one moment. But I don't know what that model would be." Black school board members in Durham County, the one Triangle district that has given up on desegregation as a priority, say that racially segregated schools *can* work, but they still wish all their schools were more diverse.[56]

In addition to practical concerns, and despite all the attendant costs, many black Triangle residents have faith in the more transcendent goals of school desegregation. A 1994 survey revealed that only 3 percent of African Americans (and 9 percent of whites) in North Carolina supported separate schools. Jermaine White, the Hillside High School student body president that year, said, "We have to overcome that this isn't all about race. We have to come through this thing positively and make the transition [to desegregated schools in Durham County] smooth like we did with merger. We're all one race and that's the human race."[57]

Bill McNeal, Wake County Schools' second African American superintendent, says the district's citizens would be wrong to allow the schools to resegregate. When asked about the achievement gap between black and white students in 2001, McNeal said, "People will look at that and think integration is a failed experiment. They'll turn it into a whipping boy. But the decisions we made in the past have also helped to produce this region's prosperity. You can't ignore that. You can't separate the two."[58] McNeal is right about that, and the region's prosperity has benefited black residents also. Ultimately, the accounting on school desegregation is extremely complex. Large debts incurred over generations are never paid without great sacrifice. Those struggling to make our schools truly democratic institutions will be paying down this debt for the foreseeable future.

"Keep on Keeping On"

African Americans and the Implementation of Brown v. Board of Education in Virginia

Brian J. Daugherity

The fiftieth anniversary of the *Brown v. Board of Education* decision (1954) resulted in an outburst of publications and scholarly activity related to the history of U.S. school desegregation. Conferences, journals, books, and films examined the many stories behind *Brown* and critically examined the decision's legacies and impacts. Much of this scholarship shed new light on the decision and its results, but an important part of the *Brown* story remains largely untold—how African Americans and predominantly black civil rights organizations worked to implement the Supreme Court's decision after 1954.[1]

This chapter examines African American efforts to implement the *Brown* decision in Virginia. While considering how government officials, segregationist organizations, and white supporters influenced the implementation process, this study focuses on how the National Association for the Advancement of Colored People and its supporters in Virginia sought to bring about school desegregation in the state. Blending African American, southern, legal, and civil rights history, the story sheds new light on the school desegregation process and the early years of the civil rights movement in Virginia.[2]

The NAACP had a strong record in Virginia long before *Brown*. Created in the 1910s, the state's earliest branches were among the first in the South. The Virginia "State Conference," created in 1935, was the first in the nation. Its successful implementation of NAACP policies and rapid growth encouraged the national office of the NAACP to create State Conferences throughout the nation.[3] In 1947, the Virginia State Conference was the first in the country to hire a full-time executive secretary, W. Lester Banks, and by the 1950s the State Conference boasted a membership of twenty-five thousand in more than one hundred branches around the state, making it the largest in the South.[4]

The NAACP's principal opponent in the school integration battle in Virginia was the state's Democratic political machine, the Byrd Organization. As governor in the 1920s, Harry Flood Byrd Sr. had consolidated government positions and used patronage to create a political oligarchy that ruled Virginia for the middle years of the twentieth century. He ran the organization from Washington, D.C., representing Virginia as a U.S. senator from 1933 to 1965. A southern Democrat known for his fiscal conservatism, Byrd regularly clashed with the national Democratic Party on spending issues and the party's growing support of civil rights. Though not virulently racist, the Byrd Organization's leadership strongly supported states' rights and opposed efforts to limit its authority over the commonwealth, including the right to maintain segregated schools.[5]

Virginia's schools had been racially segregated since their founding just after the Civil War. In 1902, a new, post-Reconstruction state constitution required segregated education as well. During the debate over its adoption, Paul Barringer, chairman of the faculty at the University of Virginia, argued that educational opportunities for African Americans be limited to "'a Sunday-school training,'" because the principal function of black Virginians was as a "'source of cheap labor for a warm climate.'"[6] By the 1920s, state legislation had expanded segregation to include virtually every aspect of life, and clarified how segregation would affect Virginia's public schools.

The results were devastating for black education. In 1925, Virginia spent an average of $40.27 per year on each white public school student, but only $10.47 on each black.[7] Facilities for blacks, teacher salaries, course offerings, and educational resources suffered as a result. In 1940, L. P. Whitten of Abingdon pleaded with national NAACP director of branches William Pickens: "If you will see that it is carried in the *Pittsburgh Courier,* I can secure pictures of all schools here so that the public may know of the deplorable conditions."[8]

In the 1930s, the Virginia NAACP brought legal attacks against these inequities. Staff attorneys, including Oliver White Hill and Spottswood

Robinson III, played leading roles in the national NAACP's equalization campaign of the 1930s and 1940s. The national NAACP focused its equalization efforts on Virginia, and by the late 1940s equalization lawsuits had been filed against over a hundred districts throughout the state.[9] Working closely with Special Counsel Thurgood Marshall, the association's head attorney, Hill and Robinson helped develop legal techniques that led to the improvement of black educational opportunities throughout the South.[10] Oliver Hill's personal relationship with Thurgood Marshall, begun as classmates at Howard Law School, developed into a professional partnership.[11]

World War II broke out in the midst of the equalization campaign. Oliver Hill, W. Lester Banks, S. W. Tucker, and a number of other civil rights leaders from Virginia entered the military, slowing down the push for educational equality. At the same time, World War II increased African American aspirations for equal treatment. In Virginia and elsewhere, postwar activism revitalized the equalization campaign and set the stage for an even greater legal assault—on segregation itself.[12]

It was yet another World War II veteran, L. Francis Griffin, who connected the NAACP to one of its most important anti-segregation cases in Virginia, *Davis v. Prince Edward County*. Griffin, from Farmville, served in the army for four years during World War II, and then returned to Prince Edward County and took over as minister of his father's Baptist church. Recognizing the injustices of the county's educational system, Griffin and other black leaders pushed county officials to equalize the schools until the spring of 1951, when students at the all-black Moton High School walked out of school in protest.

Initially the students sought only a new black high school. State NAACP leaders, however, explained that the association no longer filed equalization lawsuits and would only file a lawsuit challenging segregation in the county's public schools. With some reservations, the black community agreed, and *Davis v. Prince Edward County* was filed in federal district court in May 1951. Later, the case became one of the five cases bundled together by the U.S. Supreme Court in *Brown v. Board of Education*.[13]

As might be expected, Virginia's political leaders reacted negatively to the *Brown* decision. Over the previous three years, the state's legal team had presented an extremely vigorous defense of segregation before the courts involved in *Brown*. Following the decision, Senator Byrd called the ruling "the most serious blow that has been struck against the rights of the states."[14] When some state officials offered less provocative responses, Byrd reacted angrily, and officials around the state noticed. By midsummer, Governor Thomas B. Stanley—who had initially spoken of compliance—declared, "I shall use every legal means at my command to continue segregated schools in Virginia."[15]

Virginia's outcry clearly demonstrated that few of the state's public officials had previously entertained the idea of abandoning segregation in the public schools. Though federal courts had ordered the commonwealth to begin desegregating its institutions of higher learning, and also interstate transportation, those changes were resisted by most white Virginians. The state's clear and extensive defense of segregation in the litigation leading to *Brown,* and state officials' negative reactions to *Brown,* suggest that segregation was still a remarkably solid, and enthusiastically embraced, institution within the commonwealth. The historian Robbins Gates—discussing the period before *Brown*—noted, "There is no reason to assume that any responsible, white, public official in Virginia envisioned that state's governmental policy as moving 'gradually' toward a time when white and Negro children would attend integrated public schools."[16]

Following the decision, state officials rapidly developed the means to preserve segregated education. In August 1954, Governor Stanley appointed a thirty-two-man board, known as the Gray Commission, to study the *Brown* decision and recommend a course of action.[17] Its leader, Garland Gray, was a state senator from Southside, Virginia, and a Byrd Organization stalwart. In October, Gray proclaimed, "'I have nothing against the Negro race as such, and I have lived with them all my life, but I don't intend to have my grandchildren go to school with them.'"[18]

Governor Stanley also organized a meeting of southern governors in Richmond to rally resistance to *Brown.* Nine attended the June 1954 gathering, with three others sending representatives. After a daylong closed-door session, nine of the states resolved "not to comply voluntarily with the Supreme Court's decision against racial segregation in the public schools."[19] The remaining states—Kentucky, Maryland, and West Virginia—decided their problems of adjustment were surmountable. That these three states bordered Virginia seemed of little concern— Virginia aligned itself with states further south.

In fact, the meeting of southern governors suggested that Virginia was prepared to help lead the South in opposition to the Supreme Court's ruling. As former state legislator Benjamin Muse put it in the

Washington Post, "Virginia, with its glorious role in the early history of the republic and again in the struggle for the great Lost Cause—also with its genteel and honored political leadership of the day—was surely indicated to carry the banner of the South in this latest conflict."[20]

At the same time, the NAACP geared up to force implementation of the historic decision. Its national office, located in New York City, traditionally made the major policy decisions for the association, and the implementation of *Brown* would be no exception.[21] The national office included the NAACP's board of directors, executive secretary and staff, and the association's many departments.[22] It also worked closely with the NAACP's Legal Defense and Educational Fund, a separate but related organization that handled much of the litigation involved in the implementation of *Brown.*[23] Clearly, the association's school desegregation efforts would be directed from New York City.

In the association hierarchy, State Conferences made up the level below the national office. By 1954 a State Conference existed in every southern state. Their responsibilities included the implementation of national office policies and the establishment and oversight of local branches. Branches, sometimes referred to as "chapters," were the lowest level of the NAACP hierarchy. Their objectives and policies were strongly influenced by the national office, which also assigned annual branch membership and fundraising goals.[24]

The weekend following the *Brown* decision, the national NAACP held a conference on school desegregation in Atlanta, Georgia. At the gathering, staff from the national office outlined a previously developed program for implementing *Brown* to the association's southern State Conference presidents.[25] The southern leaders adopted resolutions— proposed by the national office—emphasizing the importance of national and state oversight of the implementation process.[26] In a form letter sent to southern branches shortly after the meeting, the national office emphasized, "It is imperative that all of our units act *in concert as directed* to effectively implement this historic decision."[27]

The conference delegates also adopted the Atlanta Declaration, which set forth the NAACP's implementation program for the immediate future. The declaration asked NAACP branches to collect signatures from black parents who favored immediate desegregation in order to press school boards in local communities for compliance. Rather than initiate widespread litigation to force desegregation, however, the national office instructed its branches to negotiate and cooperate with their local school boards.[28] Branch leaders were encouraged to gather the support of various black and white community organizations to effectuate this process. As the Atlanta Declaration explained, "We are instructing all of our branches in every affected area to petition their local school boards to abolish segregation without delay and to assist these agencies in working out ways and means of implementing the Court's ruling."[29]

A month after the Atlanta Conference, the NAACP's annual convention in Dallas, Texas, solidified the implementation program and tried to spur its branches into action. Focusing on the process whereby *Brown* would be implemented, the convention provided guidance to branches during the interim between *Brown* and the Supreme Court's ruling on the implementation of *Brown*.[30] Daylong workshops explained the national office program and the prospective role of the branches. A key goal was building community support among whites as well as blacks to bring about desegregation. Local branches were again encouraged to seek support from ministers, labor unions, educational organizations, and social and civic groups for desegregation.[31] Litigation, effective but abrasive, was to be avoided. Conference delegates resolved that "the enjoyment of many rights and opportunities of first class citizenship is not dependent on legal action but rather on the molding of public sentiment and the exertion of public pressure to make democracy work."[32]

Looking back, it is clear that NAACP leaders initially were overoptimistic about the implementation of *Brown*. A number, including Thurgood Marshall, expected the decision to bring about rapid and profound change.[33] The historian Alfred Kelly, who worked closely with Marshall and other NAACP attorneys, later noted, "'In a sense, these men were profoundly naïve. They really felt that once the legal barriers fell, the whole black-white situation would change.'"[34] Oliver Hill, head of the Virginia State Conference legal staff, explained that his optimism was based on the belief that southern whites respected the law. When *Brown* declared segregation unconstitutional, however, Hill noted that "many Negroes experienced a rude awakening as white folks' reputed great respect for the law disappeared."[35]

While its legal staff worked with national office lawyers on arguments for the Supreme Court's implementation decision, the Virginia State Conference directed its branches to begin working toward school desegregation. On May 26, 1954, executive secretary Lester Banks sent a letter to the officers of the conference's eighty-eight branches announcing a "State-wide Emergency Meeting" to discuss carrying out the national office's implementation program in Virginia.[36] The meeting took place in Richmond on June 6, 1954, and more than three hundred NAACP representatives from around the state attended. The delegates unanimously endorsed the recommendations of the Atlanta Conference, but noted that additional planning would be needed to implement the national office's program in Virginia. They decided that the State Conference, with branch input, should develop a statewide program that would allow the Virginia NAACP to operate with both "uniformity and efficiency." In the meantime, the delegates agreed to refrain from desegregation activities.[37]

State Conference leaders also called upon the Virginia government to comply with *Brown*. In June, Oliver Hill and a small delegation of other African American leaders met with Governor Thomas B. Stanley. During the closed-door session, the black leaders suggested that Stanley position Virginia to lead the South in compliance with the ruling.[38] Several months later, Hill and fellow NAACP attorney W. Hale Thompson, along with several white liberals and other African Americans, attended a public hearing on the *Brown* decision sponsored by the Gray Commission. Hill implored the commission, "Gentlemen, face the dawn and not the setting sun. A new day is being born."[39]

The public hearing, however, symbolized the challenges facing the supporters of integration. Most of those who addressed the commission, including a number of public officials, called for the continuation of segregation. After Sarah Patton Boyle, a native white Virginian, spoke in favor of integration, an audience member accused her of supporting the mongrelization of the white race.[40] One leading white newspaper, the *Norfolk Virginian-Pilot,* called the event a "'field day for [white] extremists.'"[41]

By then, segregationists had organized and developed plans for the post-*Brown* era. The state's leading segregationist organization, the Defenders of State Sovereignty and Individual Liberties, was established in October 1954 and grew rapidly. In the tradition of Virginia paternalism, the group denounced violence and outright intimidation, focusing instead on political persuasion and social and economic pressure to bring about its goals. Based in Southside, the group rallied Virginians to oppose *Brown* on the basis of both white supremacy and states' rights.[42]

Though only a small percentage of white Virginians joined the Defenders or other segregationist organizations, the vast majority did support the preservation of segregation.[43] Only white liberals, who made up a small percentage of the population, openly supported racial equality, and as they came under attack from segregationists, fewer liberals publicly expressed support for integration over time.[44] Another segment of Virginia's population—white moderates—strongly favored segregation, but encouraged compliance with *Brown* rather than openly defying the Supreme Court or abandoning the state's public schools.[45] Unfortunately for the NAACP, Virginia's segregationists initially dominated the debate over school desegregation in Virginia, and they opposed integration, the NAACP, and the Supreme Court.[46]

The high court announced its ruling on the implementation of *Brown*, commonly referred to as *Brown II*, on May 31, 1955. The decision, because it failed to establish a time frame for school desegregation and allowed federal courts to accept delays in desegregation, was widely viewed as a setback for the NAACP.[47] The following month, the national office sponsored an "Emergency" Southwide Conference on Desegregation in Atlanta. At the conference, and again at the NAACP's annual convention in June, the association reiterated its commitment to the national office's original implementation program established in the spring of 1954. Perhaps underestimating the additional hurdles posed by *Brown II*, the national office maintained that, "In the overwhelming majority of instances it can be expected that compliance *without legal action* will be the rule, perhaps grudgingly and reluctantly in some areas, but compliance, nevertheless."[48] Southern branches were requested to engage local school boards and community organizations to press for desegregation that fall.[49]

The Virginia State Conference dramatically increased its desegregation efforts following the implementation ruling. On June 12, 1955, the State Conference sponsored another statewide meeting to explain how to carry out the NAACP program in Virginia. NAACP officials told branches in communities that were acting in "good faith"—where school boards were making a "prompt and reasonable" start toward desegregation—to work with school officials and community organizations to bring about desegregation at the earliest practicable date. Branches in communities with recalcitrant school boards, however, were ordered to formally petition their school boards for the admittance of black students into the white schools.[50]

Virginia's branches undertook the petitioning process with vigor. Association members convinced black parents in many communities to support their desegregation efforts, despite growing white opposition. By the end of the summer, NAACP branches had submitted petitions to school boards in Alexandria, Arlington, Charlottesville, Isle of Wight County, Newport News, and Norfolk. Others were in preparation. The first real steps toward bringing about desegregation in Virginia had been taken, laying the groundwork for possible litigation. Still, each school board flatly refused to desegregate its schools that fall.[51]

At the same time, examples of growing defiance in Virginia troubled the State Conference. In June, the state board of education ordered the continuation of segregation for the 1955–56 school year. In November, the Gray Commission suggested ways the state could negate or minimize the impact of *Brown*. The Defenders of State Sovereignty spoke of abandoning the state's public schools completely, and a growing number of political leaders supported the indefinite maintenance of school segregation statewide.

Virginia's segregationists were fortified by the lack of support for integration shown by President Eisenhower and a strong axis of opposition in the United States Congress. The president supported gradual change and compliance with the law but declined to play a leading role in the school desegregation process.[52] Roy Wilkins later commented: "President Eisenhower was a fine general and a good, decent man, but if he had fought World War II the way he fought for civil rights, we would all be speaking German today."[53] In Congress in March 1956, 101 representatives and senators adopted the Southern Manifesto, pledging to use all legal means to prevent the integration of schools in the South. Virginia's Harry Byrd helped draw up the measure.[54]

In the midst of this rising opposition, the national office of the NAACP became increasingly skeptical about the prospects for voluntary compliance with *Brown*. Federal district court rulings in the summer of 1955—involving two of the cases that were part of the original *Brown* decision—failed to bring about school desegregation that fall, as the NAACP had requested.[55] Growing racial violence in the South, including the harassment of NAACP members and the murder of Emmett Till, also influenced NAACP leaders.[56] A growing number in the national office believed that widespread litigation might be the only method to force the South to comply with *Brown*.[57]

In January 1956, abandoning its initial implementation plan, the NAACP announced a massive increase in southern school desegregation lawsuits.[58] The national office set up a timetable for filing the suits at a southwide conference in Atlanta in February. It chose to proceed state-by-state, filing litigation based on local circumstances (the level of commitment within the black community and the likelihood of community resistance), available legal aid, and the case histories of federal judges, some of whom were more liberal than the general white southern public.[59] Legal action began that spring in eight southern states, including Virginia, which had completely resisted desegregation thus far.[60]

The Virginia NAACP filed lawsuits in four communities in April and May 1956. The chosen locations were Newport News, Norfolk, Charlottesville, and Arlington—all moderate urban areas. In addition, litigation against Prince Edward County was renewed. Without exception, the class-action lawsuits sought to bring about school desegregation by September 1956.[61] As Oliver Hill explained, "The reasonable time has passed."[62]

As might be expected, the new NAACP litigation brought tensions in Virginia to the exploding point. Animosity toward the association, already obvious, skyrocketed. Harassment of association members and supporters increased, and even white liberals urged the state NAACP to reconsider its approach.[63] Looking back in 1961, Benjamin Muse wrote, "It is difficult to describe the intensity with which the NAACP was hated by white Virginians."[64]

The NAACP litigation also prompted the state of Virginia to react. Historians of the civil rights era often portray the rise of state-sanctioned massive resistance as a reaction to the growth of federal power represented by the *Brown* decision. In this interpretation, massive resistance represents a manifestation of states' rights, and most southern resistance is aimed at the federal government and the federal court system. This portrayal, however, minimizes the influence of African American agency in the post-*Brown* milieu. Clearly the NAACP's shift toward widespread litigation, and the filing of lawsuits in early 1956, fueled the rise of massive resistance. The state of Virginia—and the South as a whole—was responding to its greatest threat.[65]

In February 1956, following a series of inflammatory editorials in a leading Virginia newspaper, the Virginia state legislature adopted a Resolution of Interposition, pledging to oppose the implementation of *Brown*.[66] The resolution resembled statements adopted by other southern legislatures that spring, as well as the Southern Manifesto adopted by the U.S. Congress in March.[67] The Virginia resolution's leading supporter, *Richmond News Leader* editor James Jackson Kilpatrick, had previously written to Senator Byrd, "I would toss an old battle-cry back at the NAACP: Hell, we have only begun to fight."[68]

In the summer of 1956 Governor Stanley called a special session of the state legislature to deal with the unfolding situation. During a month-long session starting in late August, the General Assembly adopted twenty-three laws dealing with school segregation. Together the measures defended school segregation statewide and provided new powers to the governor to deal with unfavorable court decisions.[69] Seven of the bills were developed to impede the work of organizations promoting school desegregation in the state. Referring to the NAACP, delegate James Thomson of Alexandria declared, "With this set of bills . . . we can bust that organization . . . wide open."[70] The state of Virginia had declared war on the NAACP.

As its school desegregation lawsuits wound their way through the court system, the State Conference worked to minimize the effects of the state's new "massive resistance" laws. For several years it sparred with legislative committees set up to investigate the supporters of school integration in Virginia.[71] The State Conference also initiated litigation against the Virginia attorney general with the goal of overturning the General Assembly's new legislation. These legal efforts quickly bogged down in the courts and the legislation reduced the effectiveness of the Virginia NAACP's school desegregation campaign. Publicly, the association argued that the anti-NAACP legislation united the black community behind the NAACP, but, when pressed, NAACP officials conceded that the attack had cost the association members, money, and valuable resources.[72]

Massive resistance, however, did not shut down the NAACP in Virginia or force the abandonment of its desegregation campaign. To counteract the loss of members and funding, the State Conference asked its branches to increase membership drives and fundraising. One letter in early 1957 entreated, "Never before has our NAACP needed the support of every Negro citizen as it has today."[73] To protect its finances, the State Conference transferred its "principal monies" to New York.[74] And perhaps most important, the association tried to maintain morale with a stream of pronouncements and memorandums. One, written by executive secretary Lester Banks in early 1957, urged members to "keep on keeping on" until the NAACP's objectives had been achieved.[75] Under the circumstances, it is doubtful Banks could have asked for more.

In the meantime events unfolded in Virginia's courtrooms. In the summer of 1956, federal courts ordered desegregation in Charlottesville and Arlington to begin during the coming school year. With help from the state, both localities appealed, temporarily suspending the court orders, but the victories by the NAACP helped fuel state legislators' anger that summer. Several of the state's new massive resistance laws, including a pupil placement provision, established additional school desegregation roadblocks, forcing NAACP attorneys to spend much of 1956 and 1957 in court.[76] By early 1958 the state's pupil placement law had been ruled unconstitutional, and federal judges in Virginia renewed orders calling for school desegregation the following September.[77]

In September 1958, rather than allow federal courts to force Virginia to integrate, Governor J. Lindsay Almond Jr. closed nine public schools in Charlottesville, Norfolk, and Warren County.[78] Many of the affected white students enrolled in private schools funded by state taxpayer money and created with help from segregationist organizations. Moderate whites, on the other hand, spoke openly against the school closings and worked to protect public education in the commonwealth. The NAACP filed suit immediately. Earlier that spring, Oliver Hill noted that if school closures were needed to "bring Virginia to its senses, then the sooner we reach that crisis the better."[79]

In January 1959, federal and state courts declared the cornerstone of massive resistance—Virginia's school-closing law—unconstitutional. Though extreme segregationists encouraged the state to adopt new legislation to continue massive resistance, Governor Almond gave in. During a special session of the state legislature, Almond prevented the passage of additional massive resistance legislation and secured the repeal of the school-closing law.[80] Shortly thereafter, authorities reopened the closed schools in the affected localities, and on February 2, 1959, twenty-one black students entered formerly all-white public schools in Virginia. Nearly five years after *Brown*, the Virginia NAACP had achieved one of its most cherished goals.[81]

Following this historic event, Virginia's public officials worked to minimize the amount of school desegregation that would take place in the coming years. Shifting from absolute defiance to token compliance, the General Assembly adopted new legislation in the spring of 1959. A new pupil placement law centralized the assignment process under the authority of the state Pupil Placement Board (PPB) and modified the process. The state also allowed school districts to adopt Virginia's first freedom-of-choice plans, which allowed parents to choose which schools their children would attend. A new tuition grant law supported white students who chose to attend segregated schools.[82] Explaining the result of this new legislation, historians Andrew Lewis and Matthew Lassiter write, "the policies which supplanted massive resistance—private school tuition grants, discriminatory pupil placement laws, freedom-of-choice plans, and incessant legal delays—thwarted substantial progress toward meaningful school integration throughout the 1960s."[83]

Substantial progress would have taken even longer without the efforts of the State Conference. Its attorneys continued to press for desegregation in the federal courts, handling dozens of cases from many parts of Virginia in subsequent years. Its efforts forced additional localities to admit African American students into their formerly all-white schools, and pressured districts which had already begun desegregation to admit greater numbers of black students.

Over time, the pace of school desegregation increased. Under judicial pressure, the state's Pupil Placement Board—which continued to reject most black applications for transfer—slowly increased the number of blacks admitted, and even forced some districts to begin desegregation.[84] Other localities chose to assign pupils on their own and voluntarily increased the number of black students in formerly white schools.[85] At the same time, Virginia's federal courts ordered token desegregation throughout the state. Still the U.S. Supreme Court, which accepted token desegregation, expressed disappointment with the pace of southern school desegregation in 1963—a sign of what was to come.[86]

Other branches of the federal government also placed increasing pressure on the white South. In 1964 Congress passed the Civil Rights Act, which threatened to cut federal funding to localities that refused to integrate their schools. An increase in federal public school funding the following year, coupled with compliance guidelines from the Department of Health, Education, and Welfare (HEW), offered additional incentives for southern districts to desegregate.[87]

Fearful of losing federal funding, districts throughout Virginia notified HEW of their plans to comply in 1965. The most popular route involved adopting freedom-of-choice plans, which allowed students to choose which schools they would attend. Although these plans placed the burden of desegregation on African Americans, and minimized desegregation in other ways, they were initially accepted by the federal government.[88] By the summer of 1965, approximately 90 of the state's 130 public school divisions had experienced some desegregation, and the process was scheduled to begin in most others that fall.[89]

Still, the NAACP's efforts had failed to bring about widespread school integration in the state. HEW's desegregation guidelines promised to increase the pace of integration, but the department's acceptance of freedom-of-choice plans continued to place the burden of desegregation on African Americans, who—because of intimidation, community ties, and other factors,—often favored the status quo.[90] At the same time, federal courts, including the U.S. Supreme Court, refused to require school boards to undertake more active, and effective, integration efforts.[91] In 1965, fewer than 12,000 of the approximately 235,000 black students in Virginia went to desegregated schools.[92]

In response to the slow pace of change, the NAACP launched a new wave of school desegregation litigation in the mid-1960s. Multiple lawsuits in Virginia attacked freedom-of-choice plans, which Lester Banks called "a continuation of Virginia's 11-year effort to stave off school integration."[93] The NAACP also sought the nondiscriminatory assignment of personnel and the abandonment of potentially discriminatory construction plans.[94] Arguing that the burden of school desegregation belonged to local school boards, as opposed to African Americans, the NAACP asked federal courts to force local boards to take the initiative in integrating the public schools.[95]

The most important new lawsuit in Virginia was based in New Kent County, just east of Richmond.[96] Rural and conservative, the county had seen little racial change in the years since *Brown v. Board of Education.* The president of the local NAACP, Calvin Coolidge Green, had pressed the county to begin desegregation in the early 1960s to no avail. In response to the board's refusal, Green met with attorneys from the state NAACP and in early 1965 helped develop a lawsuit to force the school board to integrate the county's schools. *Charles C. Green v. County School Board of New Kent County, Virginia,* filed in Green's youngest son's name, was filed in March 1965. In the suit, NAACP attorneys pointed out that the county's schools remained 100 percent segregated eleven years after *Brown.* Faced with the NAACP lawsuit and pressure from HEW, the county adopted a freedom-of-choice plan in the summer of 1965, but the number of student transfers remained small.

The lawsuit fared poorly in the lower federal courts. The U.S. District Court for the Eastern District of Virginia ruled against the NAACP in 1966, as did the Fourth Circuit Court of Appeals. Both ruled that the county's hastily developed freedom-of-choice plan fulfilled its requirement to integrate the county's schools. These decisions were disappointing but not surprising, as other NAACP suits at this time suffered the same fate.[97]

After the ruling by the Fourth Circuit Court, NAACP attorneys debated their course of action, eventually choosing to take the *Green* case to the U.S. Supreme Court. As a test case to show that current desegregation programs—including freedom of choice—were not working, *Green* had a lot to offer. County demographics showed that school segregation prior to 1965 had been a deliberate policy, and the county's freedom-of-choice plan hadn't substantially altered the racial makeup of the schools. "We had all these school cases, and we wanted to get a case to be the pilot case so the Supreme Court could really break the log-jam," former State Conference attorney Henry L. Marsh III explained. "New Kent was the logical choice."[98] The NAACP petitioned for, and was granted, certiorari by the Supreme Court.

At the same time, the federal court system exhibited signs of a new attitude on the issue of school integration. In 1965 Judge J. Skelly Wright of the Court of Appeals for the District of Columbia predicted that the Supreme Court would eventually rule de facto school segregation unconstitutional.[99] In 1967, Judge John Minor Wisdom of the Fifth Circuit Court of Appeals wrote that "boards and officials administering public schools have the affirmative duty under the Fourteenth Amendment to bring about an integrated, unitary school system in which there are no Negro schools and no white schools—just schools."[100] The Supreme Court itself was also increasingly forceful in its denunciations of non-compliance. In *Griffin v. County School Board of Prince Edward County* (1964) the Court declared, "There has been entirely too much deliberation and not enough speed in enforcing the constitutional rights which we held in *Brown v. Board of Education*."[101]

On May 27, 1968, the Supreme Court issued its ruling in *Charles C. Green v. County School Board of New Kent County*. The Court found that the county was operating a dual system of schools, down to "every facet of school operations—faculty, staff, transportation, extracurricular activities and facilities."[102] This finding undermined the Court's 1954–55 desegregation decisions, which put an affirmative duty on school boards to establish a "unitary, non-racial system of public education." With regard to the county's freedom-of-choice plan, the Court noted, "it is relevant that this first step did not come until some 11 years after *Brown I* was decided and 10 years after *Brown II* directed the making of a 'prompt and reasonable start.'" Furthermore, "rather than further the dismantling of the dual system, the [freedom-of-choice] plan has operated simply to burden children and their parents with a responsibility which *Brown II* placed squarely on the School Board."[103]

Echoing Judge Wisdom's ruling, the Court ordered the county school board to develop a plan to "convert promptly to a system without a 'white' school and a 'Negro' school, but just schools." Though it did not rule that freedom-of-choice plans were necessarily unconstitutional, the Court found that, where other plans could be more effective, they were preferable. Justice William J. Brennan, writing for the unanimous Court, wrote: "The burden on a school board today is to come forward with a plan that promises realistically to work, and promises realistically to work now."[104]

The impact of the *Green* decision spread far beyond the borders of New Kent County. It was *Green* that announced the duty of school boards to affirmatively eliminate all vestiges of state-imposed segregation, transforming *Brown*'s prohibition of segregation into a requirement of integration and prompting Supreme Court Justice William H. Rehnquist to refer to *Green* later as a "drastic extension of *Brown*."[105] Federal courts, recognizing that northern school segregation was related to discriminatory policies, also increasingly required northern school boards to re-fashion their desegregation plans to eliminate dual school systems as well.[106]

Across Virginia, school boards adjusted their policies to achieve the new mandate. In most cases, this meant abandoning freedom-of-choice plans in favor of more substantive measures.[107] The NAACP pushed those who hesitated, filing and renewing litigation in federal courts around the state. By the early 1970s, most districts had integrated their black and white student populations. In urban areas, this oftentimes meant busing students, which was angrily contested by whites. In rural areas around the state, geographically based attendance zones usually eliminated racially identifiable schools.[108]

Within only a few years, aided by follow-up Supreme Court decisions in 1969 and 1971, the nation witnessed the culmination of a key goal of the civil rights movement—the integration of southern public schools.[109] A National Park Service study of school desegregation in the United States explains: "The results were startling. In 1968–69, 32 per cent of black students in the South attended integrated schools; in 1970–71, the number was 79 per cent."[110] Acknowledging the decision's impact, the historian and legal scholar Davison Douglas calls

Green "the Court's most important school desegregation opinion since *Brown*."[111]

Integration, unfortunately, did not come without a cost to African American communities, in Virginia or around the nation. In the South, integration was generally carried out under the control of white public officials, and decision making was not always even-handed. Many black schools in Virginia were closed or converted to lower-level schools during the process, and African American educators and administrators were demoted and sometimes fired.[112]

The battle over school desegregation in Virginia represents a key aspect of the struggle for black equality. The long-lasting campaign started in the 1800s, when Jim Crow schools were established in the state. In the twentieth century the NAACP initially fought to improve black educational opportunities in the commonwealth, before filing litigation designed to overturn segregation in the early 1950s. Between 1954 and 1959, as African Americans in the state fought to overcome massive resistance and bring about initial school desegregation, they also laid the groundwork for broader civil rights activism in the 1960s. While the NAACP continued to focus on educational opportunities, the larger black community worked to eliminate Jim Crow in other aspects of life. Federal government aid in the 1960s, along with growing support within the judiciary, aided the campaign for school desegregation, culminating in the late 1960s with the desegregation of public education in Virginia. As the twenty-first century opens, attention remains focused on how to ensure equal educational opportunities for minority students throughout the state.

The Palmetto Revolution

SCHOOL DESEGREGATION IN SOUTH CAROLINA

Vernon Burton and Lewie Reece

A popular movement for civil rights reform swept the United States in the mid-twentieth century, in the process dramatically reshaping U.S. society and culture. In the South, the civil rights movement marked an opening of the political, educational, and social systems in a way not seen since disfranchisement. These efforts were marked by local, state, and regional distinctions that created unique civil rights movements that were often as different as the myriad of organizations and individuals that became involved in the freedom struggle. Nowhere was that more true than in the efforts of black South Carolinians to desegregate the public and private school systems and to become participants in the political system. Throughout this process an entrenched white political elite actively opposed efforts to open up the system, before grudgingly accommodating themselves to political reality. This surrender to the power of the federal courts has assumed a mythic quality in both memory and in contemporary politics in which white South Carolinians have assured themselves that integration occurred with "grace and dignity," largely ignoring and forgetting years of resistance to basic human rights and the active campaigns of persecution that they waged against civil rights workers. The story of how African Americans and some whites transformed the political system and desegregated education, often against tremendous odds, is less well known. In the end it was the process of continual African American pressure in the streets and in the courts, battering down official intransigence, that transformed the political system.[1]

When historians and nonhistorians alike think of the civil rights movement, they imagine marches, protests, and courageous people working against impossible odds, daring to be free. It is not wrong to think this of the civil rights movement, for truly the individuals involved were noble pioneers shining aloft a lantern of hope for the future. We fail, however, to appreciate the meaning and purpose of the civil rights movement by ignoring the way in which it was a focused movement centered on transforming the legal, educational, and political system. Historians rarely think of the civil rights movement as being interested in law, public policy, and shaping political discourse in the local communities from whence it came. In many ways such an approach does a disservice to those southern states that never attracted national governmental and media attention, and had their own civil rights movement that time has obscured.

In seeking to use the legal, educational, and political system, the civil rights movement was operating in a context in which public institutions were weapons of oppression. The civil rights movement was reacting against and seeking to tear down the legal, political, educational, and economic structures that had been imposed in the era of segregation. The disfranchisement constitutional conventions and the legal system that emerged from the state houses and courts were a tyrannical system meant to create a neo-slavery that would be applied to African Americans. In seeking to shape a new political society then, the larger goal of the civil rights movement was to shape new public policies that would support an integrated society. In many ways the very breadth and depth of the civil rights movement makes it important to not compartmentalize the various elements of shaping a new society. That was particularly true in South Carolina, where the freedom struggle was focused not simply on educational policy, but on a broader reformation of South Carolina society. Moreover, desegregation was never possible unless the political and legal order was reformed at the same time. This was reflected in the ways that political, educational, and legal supporters of the *ancien regime* sought to use all of their power to preserve white supremacy. The final demise of segregated education was only possible when the political system was forced to change. In comprehending how South Carolina desegregated, it is essential to see the connection between education, law, public policy, and the larger political culture of race that had long dominated its history.

Although U.S. society has long struggled with the problem of race relations, such questions took on a special meaning in South Carolina. Prior to the Great Depression, South Carolina had a large black majority. Even after the Great Migration of the early twentieth century, the African American minority remained significant and exerted a powerful influence on the state's politics. In the antebellum period this was reflected in the constant fear of slave revolts and a concern for the political stability in a slave society. No southern state underwent a more radical transformation under Reconstruction and, from the perspective of white elites, the need to control the political environment was paramount. Relying on the force of law, political power, and racial violence to maintain white supremacy, these efforts culminated in the 1895 constitutional convention that officially disfranchised African Americans in the state. Disfranchisement as a political event was of profound importance in shaping the way that white Democrats envisioned their larger society. It eliminated a large group of voters that had been seen as a political threat and seemed at last to provide a mechanism of social control that had eluded white elites since the institution of slavery was abolished in 1865. It is no coincidence that shortly after they successfully disfranchised African Americans, South Carolinian politicians adopted legally enforced segregation as a means of preserving the racial status quo by maintaining racially separate schools.[2]

Disfranchisement did far more than simply remove African Americans from the political process; it also secured political power for an entrenched political elite who dominated county and state politics for decades. This was particularly true of the Barnwell Ring, personified by state senator Edgar Brown, which long dominated the legislative politics of South Carolina. Even when political outsiders such as Cole Blease and Olin Johnston were able to achieve victory, they did so as political reformers whose racial reactionary views were little different from their factional opponents. Race remained the central issue of white South Carolinian politics, with all sides committed to protecting the racial status quo, especially including segregated schools.[3]

Although African Americans were socioeconomically disadvantaged and effectively kept out of the political process, their numbers within the state continued to arouse concern among those who could vote, and they became scapegoats in a political environment that invited shallow demagoguery. From "Pitchfork Ben" Tillman and Cole Blease through "Cotton Ed" Smith, South Carolina demagogues rode the race issue to political prominence. As Congressman James F. Byrnes, who eventually became a senator, Supreme Court justice, secretary of state, and governor of South Carolina, cautioned in 1920: "It is certain that if there was a fair registration [African Americans] would have a slight majority in our state. We cannot idly brush the facts aside. Unfortunate though it may be, our consideration of every question must include the consideration of this race question." Even in the Dixiecrat South of 1948–49, when race was clearly the dominant issue in every southern state, political scientist V. O. Key, in *Southern Politics in State and Nation,* singled out South Carolina, entitling chapter 7, "South Carolina: The Politics of Color."[4]

As long as segregationist politicians controlled the political processes, educational opportunities for African Americans were limited. Benjamin Mays, an African American educator from Ninety Six, summarized the situation: "We can never have justice in education under a segregation law." Discrimination in schooling was blatant. In his 1911 inaugural address, Governor Cole Blease explained, "I am in favor of building up the free school system so that every white child in South Carolina may be given a good common school education. . . . I am opposed to white people's taxes being used to educate Negroes. I am a friend of the Negro race. . . . The white people of the South are the best friends to the Negro race. In my opinion, when the people of this country began to try to educate the Negro they made a serious and grave mistake, and I fear the worst result is yet to come. So why continue?"[5]

Those white Carolinians that held political power offered African Americans minimal participation in the public life of their communities. William Watts Ball, a Laurens native and longtime editor of the *Charleston News and Courier,* perhaps best reflected these attitudes in 1914 when he answered a query about African American education from a resident of Nebraska. Ball suggested that most whites viewed the whole subject of African American education with "aloofness and indifference," reflecting the common white attitude that blacks were better off without access to the schoolhouse. Ball went on to express an almost universal belief that if "they must be trained, training should be of the manual kind." Those African Americans who did attend schools were severely disadvantaged when compared to their white contemporaries: African American teachers were paid considerably less than white teachers to teach more children and were, according to Ball, "usually ignorant persons." In 1915, Ball again defended his state's education policies, declaring northern philanthropists' support for improving black education to be "the most insidious attack that has ever been made upon the sentiment and civilization of the South." That Ball's observations on expenditures reflected reality are confirmed by examining the levels of public spending on African American children during the age of segregation. According to the historian Louis Harlan, in 1915 the state of South Carolina spent $13.98 on the education of a white child, and only $1.13 on an African American student. In rural areas this discrepancy was even greater. Benjamin Mays's home county of Greenwood, for example, spent $6.29 for each white child attending school in 1901 but the risible expenditure for each black child was only 23 cents. Such disparities never ceased, even in urban areas. In 1933, Charleston County spent four times more on white schools than black. Twenty-five years later, white schools' expenditures still exceeded black schools by a margin of almost 4 to 3. (See Table 1 for the ratio of white/black pupil expenditures from 1896 to 1960, the first and last years for which figures for segregated expenditures are available.) The discrimination in the state's segregated institutions of higher education was even more flagrant.[6]

In 1945, ten of forty-six counties in South Carolina had no accredited high schools for African Americans and twenty-five had only one. Three years later, South Carolina's superintendent of education estimated that 62 percent of African Americans in the state were totally or functionally illiterate. Three in four had received less than an elementary education; the school year was often only three or four months long in many rural schools; and students often missed school so that they could work in the fields. These problems reflected the larger white racial view that dominated South Carolina politics in the early twentieth century. As South Carolina was influenced by the Great Depression and the changes brought about by the New Deal, the larger question became one of how educational opportunities for African Americans could be improved while preserving white supremacy.[7]

Although the New Deal certainly had an important role in the politics of South Carolina, race still had a large impact. South Carolina had its share of economic liberals who managed to build successful political careers as supporters of President Franklin Delano Roosevelt. Congressman, and later Senator, James F. Byrnes was a key administration ally;

Table 1: Racial Discrimination Ratios of Educational Expenditures in South Carolina, 1896–1960

Year	South Carolina
1896	1:2
1900	4:2
1905	4:3
1910	5:4
1915	8:7
1920	8:5
1925	8:4
1930	7:4
1935	5:0
1940	4:4
1941	4:5
1942	4:2
1943	3:7
1944	3:6
1945	3:2
1946	2:9
1947	2:6
1948	2:5
1949	2:6
1950	2:4
1951	2:2
1952–1953	1:6
1953–1954	1:7
1954–1955	1:6
1955–1956	1:3
1956–1957	1:4
1957–1958	1:6
1958–1959	1:5
1959–1960	1:5

Source: Annual Reports of the South Carolina Department of Education (South Caroliniana Library) in named years.

Note: Ratios were obtained by dividing (total education expenditures on whites divided by white public school average attendance) by (total educational expenditures on blacks divided by black public school average attendance). For a few years, enrollment figures had to be substituted for attendance.

Governor Olin Johnston pushed through an ambitious reform agenda; and Senator Burnet Maybank was a stalwart supporter of the Roosevelt administration. But the limits of that agenda were always evident and became more so as the issues of civil rights became a more pressing concern later in the decade. An example of the power of race was the 1938 senatorial election, in which conservative senator Ellison "Cotton Ed" Smith easily turned back a challenge from Governor Johnston. Smith had supported only those New Deal programs that he believed benefited South Carolina and wrapped himself in the racial legacy of white supremacy, vigorously tarring the cotton mill worker Johnston as a contemporary carpetbagger. Although Johnston defeated Smith in the 1944 elections, South Carolina politics had by then gravitated increasingly toward issues centered on the preservation of white supremacy. The South Carolina House of Representatives passed a resolution in 1944 denouncing "indignantly and vehemently" any and all "amalgamation of the White and Negro races by a co-mingling of the races upon any basis of equality." It further resolved an affirmation of "White Supremacy as now prevailing in the South" and pledged "lives and our sacred honor to maintain it, whatever the cost, in War and Peace." The year 1944 proved critical in the history of the state, not simply owing to the forced retirement of Senator Smith, but the beginnings of increased African American activism and the return of Second World War veterans, both black and white, to the state. Moreover, the dichotomy between the national and state parties, as separate entities, became harder to maintain in the aftermath of an important national convention.[8]

African Americans tried without success to interest the state Democratic Party in allowing them to participate in state and local party primaries. As a result African American civil rights activists John McCray and Osceola McCaine helped lead the drive to create a semi-independent organization known as the Progressive Democratic Party (PDP). Their larger goals in 1944 were support for President Roosevelt's bid for a fourth term, pushing for African American voter registration, and recognition by the national Democratic Party. Despite the PDP's affiliation with the state Democratic Party, McCray, as leader, was just as eager to develop ties and connections with the state Republican Party. In May, writing to J. A. Mason, a South Carolina Republican, McCray assured Mason that he had put together a "long list of prominent names in the republican parties to cast their votes with us," and as late as 1948 he was cooperating with J. Bates Gerald, who ran in 1948 as the Republican candidate for the U.S. Senate.

Efforts to receive recognition from the national Democratic Party were unsuccessful. A PDP delegation was sent to the 1944 Democratic National Convention in Chicago and the national party was prepared to offer support for increased African American participation in party affairs, but not national recognition. Similar efforts in 1948 to position a PDP delegation as the true Democratic Party in the state met with failure. Nonetheless, the PDP remained focused on increasing African American voter registration, which reached 50,000 by 1950. But the increased pressure of African American Carolinians perhaps helped to prevent James Byrnes from being selected as the vice presidential candidate in 1944. The key factor may have been the objections of labor leaders to Byrnes's labor record and as a result the nomination went to Senator Harry Truman of Missouri. The defeat of Byrnes's nomination for the vice presidency ultimately led to repercussions within the state party, but for the moment the increasing concern for the political establishment was federal court cases that sought to force African American participation in the Democratic primary.[9]

South Carolina political leaders were certainly aware of the possibility that the federal courts might invalidate all-white primaries in the state, which had first been established in 1896 when the state Democratic Executive Committee prohibited all African Americans from voting in primaries. The annual state poll-tax requirement never applied to these primary elections, probably because party rules already excluded African Americans. When the U.S. Supreme Court overturned the all-white primary in 1944, in the Texas case of *Smith v. Allwright,* Governor Olin D. Johnston called a special session of the South Carolina legislature to repeal all laws relating to primary elections. "After these statutes are repealed," Johnston told the legislature, "we will have done everything to guarantee white supremacy in our primaries." After the South Carolina legislature erased all mention of primaries from the state convention, the Democratic Party adopted rules excluding African Americans from its "private" primary elections. When the National Association for the Advancement of Colored People challenged the "private" primary in federal court, Judge J. Waties Waring of Charleston ruled, on July 12, 1947, in their favor because, acting "solely for the purpose of preventing the Negro from gaining the right to vote," the governor and legislature violated the Fourteenth and Fifteenth Amendments. State officials reacted to the decision by declaring that they were prepared to allow African American voters to cast ballots only if they swore on oath: "I believe in and will support the social and educational separation of the races." Waring struck this provision down as unconstitutional as well and the General Assembly in 1950 adopted new state regulations for primary elections. Along with a literacy test, electoral devices restored to the primary election laws were statewide full-slate and majority vote requirements, all of which were designed to dilute the vote of African American citizens.[10]

At the local level, however, it was not so much legal and constitutional requirements, but the power of local officials that prevented minorities from being able to vote. As had been the case since the passage of the disfranchisement constitution in 1895, local officials decided which African Americans could cast ballots and under what circumstances they could do so. Reverend Joseph DeLaine, the leader of a voter registration drive in Clarendon County, noted that local officials refused to count poll taxes and often took real pleasure in humiliating school principals by suggesting they did not "read well enough" to qualify. Meanwhile, "white men could register without being questioned or wait their turn and register their wives who were absent." In 1940, the Cherokee County Democratic Executive Committee graphically described one of the measures by which they ensured that the number of registered African American voters in their county could be counted on the fingers of one hand: "If a coon wants to vote in the primary, we make him recite the Constitution backward, as well as forward, make him close his eyes and dot his t's and cross his i's." That these practices were not confined to one county is evidenced by the fact that only fifteen hundred African Americans in South Carolina were registered to vote in 1940. Over time the pressure of the federal courts changed this process and African Americans slowly gained access to the ballot. African American voter registration was less difficult in urban areas—in rural regions of the state such as Clarendon County it would take the Voting Rights Act of 1965 to transform the political environment. Voter registration, however, was just one area in which state officials sought to suppress African American rights; an equally pressing concern for them was the question of the preservation of segregation in the public schools. This was enshrined in the state's constitution, article 11, section 7, which stated that "separate schools shall be provided for children of the white and colored races, and no child of either race shall ever be permitted to attend a school provided for children of the other race."[11]

Segregated education in the state, however, was wretched for black students. Schools meant for African American students were woefully underfunded and students had to make do with facilities that in no way could be considered adequate. James Hinton, head of the state NAACP, remembered "very vividly one school where they had 35 gallon oil drums with 2 by 8's sitting on them, and that was the seating facility." Students who testified about the schools recalled no science labs or math instruction, and the lessons in English were of a very poor quality. Although African American teachers did their best with these meager resources, they received significantly lower pay than their white counterparts, leading a group of teachers from Charleston to sue for equal pay in 1943. The case was argued before Judge J. Waties Waring, but before he could rule on the issue the local school board met the teachers' demands. This success was followed by similar efforts from outside of Charleston and, in February 1944, Judge Waring ordered the equalization of teacher pay throughout South Carolina. The state formed a committee to study this issue and, after it was realized that black teachers generally scored lower on the National Teacher Exam, the South Carolina General Assembly adopted a policy of basing salaries on performance in this exam, thereby ensuring that African American teachers continued to be paid less than whites.[12]

A common complaint of both students and parents in Clarendon County, a county in which 91.4 percent of its residents lived in rural areas and 70.8 percent were black, was the refusal of local officials to provide a bus system for African American children to get to school, even though the school board ran some thirty buses for the county's white children. As a result, students would often have to walk several miles, some as many as nine each way, to school. Despite ever-increasing agitation from an African American community led by Reverend Joseph DeLaine, local government officials continued to turn a deaf ear to demands for equalization. The NAACP, which had been composing a comprehensive strategy to slowly whittle away at segregated education, had little difficulty persuading this community that their best option was to file suit. The NAACP had been trying without evident success to get 50 one-dollar memberships in Clarendon County, but on June 8, 1949, at the first meeting to discuss joining a lawsuit, a large audience declared themselves ready to fight segregation "all the way up to the Supreme Court of the United States" if necessary, so long as Reverend DeLaine became their leader. *Briggs v. Elliott* argued that the education system in Clarendon County failed to meet the "separate-but-equal" standard that had long been held as the legal justification of segregation and demanded that African American children of school age be provided with "similarly situated educational advantages and facilities equal in all respects to that which is being provided for whites." It went further, however, by maintaining that segregation deprived the children of Clarendon County of their constitutional rights to equal protection under the Fourteenth Amendment. The suit was filed despite an immediate policy of harassment that local whites exacted on those members of the African American community who signed petitions of protest or agreed to participate in the lawsuit, and included calling in mortgages, firing teachers, denying credit to landowners, and even threatening DeLaine with violence, eventually forcing him to flee the community.[13]

By 1950, it was clear that it was only a matter of time before the U.S. Supreme Court would once again review the constitutionality of segregation. The effort African American parents in Clarendon County mounted to integrate the public schools attracted considerable public attention from within and outside South Carolina and, in an attempt to head off the growing demands to end segregation, James Byrnes agreed to end his retirement and was elected governor in 1950. Experienced in national politics and in the judiciary, Byrnes brought a sophisticated and subtle approach to resisting racial integration, urging legal devices to counter the court rulings. He counseled, for instance, that local school districts gerrymander. "The Washington administration and the United States Supreme Court cannot regulate the area or boundaries of our school districts. We must investigate to see if it is practical to establish school districts to include the sections where most of the Negro population resides and other school districts to include sections where most of the white people reside." He wanted local school boards to use waivers for children who needed to go to school outside their district, "a Negro child residing in the school district for whites," or "a white student residing in a preponderantly Negro district." Byrnes thought that "this Gerrymandering of districts" could be used effectively in cities, but less so in rural areas. In later years, South Carolina education leaders and politicians used Byrnes's suggested gerrymandering to preserve as much of segregated schools and school districts as possible.[14]

To forestall integration, Byrnes used a significant portion of a new $75 million sales tax for the education of African American children, and white leaders throughout the state began equalizing the facilities of white and black schools in a deliberate attempt to salvage segregation. By 1962, South Carolina had spent over $210 million attempting to match the "equal" in "separate but equal." In 1951, Byrnes urged the creation of a so-called segregation committee and staffed it with some of the state's leading legal minds "to study and report on the advisable course to be pursued by the State in respect to its educational facilities in the event that the federal courts nullify the provisions of the State Constitution requiring the establishment of separate schools for children of the white and colored races." Chaired by state representative L. Marion Gressette, this special school committee coordinated efforts to maintain the racial status quo. Byrnes even recommended that South Carolina eliminate from its constitution the provision for public schools, an amendment passed in the 1952 general election by a vote of 187,345 to 91,823 and was subsequently ratified in 1954 by the state's General Assembly. During this time, new schoolhouses were built, African American teacher's salaries raised, and brand-new buses were bought; although no effort was spared in making educational facilities for blacks and whites appear equal, they remained separate. These developments, however, were but a prelude to the coming decision from the Supreme Court and the rising tide of African American activism in the state. That such efforts originated in Clarendon County could only be ironic and a testimony to the ability and heroism of people in desperate circumstances attempting to seek justice.[15]

For the next several years, the full array of Jim Crow terror and repression played out in rural Clarendon County. For their heroic efforts, Reverend Delaine and his wife lost their jobs and received death threats signed "KKK." Their house burned to the ground while the all-white fire department stood by and watched. When Delaine fired his gun in self-defense against whites, he was charged with a felony and forced to flee the state. When World War II veteran Harry Briggs, the black mechanic for whom the case was named, stubbornly resisted white pressure to remove his name from the list of plaintiffs, he and his wife lost their jobs and they too had to leave the county. All forty of the unacknowledged heroes of Clarendon County who made up the list of plaintiffs in *Briggs v. Elliot*, having challenged the South's racial codes, suffered. Whatever elements of white paternalism or leniency had existed, quickly faded.

Long-standing debts, an everyday occurrence in the southern agriculture economy, were called in, and whites refused to sell black plaintiffs seeds or supplies. Equipment usually loaned willingly to help African Americans with harvests or plowing was refused and crops rotted in the fields. Nevertheless, despite all these injustices, the African American community remained steadfast and continued to be the motivating force behind the lawsuit.

When the case was argued before the federal district court in late May 1951, the facts were so overwhelming that the state of South Carolina made no attempt to deny them, instead asking the justices to give them time to equalize the facilities. Ignoring evidence presented to them documenting the psychological damage caused by segregation, the court, in a split decision, ruled that segregation was constitutional. Citing the legal precedent of *Plessy v. Ferguson,* they declared that, "so long as equality of rights is preserved," educational segregation was a matter for legislative policy, over which they had no power. They agreed to give South Carolina six months to demonstrate that the state was implementing Byrnes's equalization policies. In a scathing dissent, however, Judge Waring became the first federal judge to issue an opinion stating that the *Plessy* "separate-but-equal" ruling was in fact unconstitutional. Attacking his colleagues for evading the true issues at the heart of the case, Waring argued that his colleagues' reliance on *Plessy* was flawed and indeed irrelevant to the matter at hand. He also rejected South Carolina's request for time to equalize the segregated schools as a ploy to distract attention from the issue at hand, concluding his opinion by bluntly stating that *"Segregation is per se inequality."* Although seemingly a setback for the NAACP, *Briggs* was in fact one of a series of suits it was bringing from Delaware, Kansas, Virginia, and the District of Columbia. South Carolina, however, was the first and the only one from the Deep South.[16]

Brown v. Board of Education represents a key turning point in the history of race relations in the United States. The decision was a momentous event and suggested a country prepared to deal at last with its racial past. History, however, has invested it with a romantic glamor that obscures in many ways the limits that *Brown* imposed as a court decision. The very fact that the famous case is *Brown* rather than *Briggs* is suggestive on many levels. The Court deliberately chose to make the case that undermined segregation from Kansas, where only elementary schools in towns of ten thousand or more were segregated—and then only if the community elected to do so—rather than from a Deep South state such as South Carolina, where segregated schools were required by law. The Supreme Court's choice of the Kansas case was part of a conscious strategy to make this an American, not a southern, problem.

Brown and *Brown II* were also something of a compromise in which the Court achieved unanimity, but at the price of not speaking clearly about how southern educators were to achieve desegregation. This led men such as George Bell Timmerman Jr., who replaced James Byrnes as governor of South Carolina in 1955, to believe that, regardless of the Supreme Court's ruling, it would be possible to maintain separate schools within the state. The larger question of what the desegregation process was to look like was one that the Supreme Court left to the lower courts, which was either a gesture of moderation or an act of cowardice, depending on how charitable one is in evaluating the Supreme Court's ruling. It also allowed many southern politicians to claim a victory, as they had argued that the district courts were best suited to make such decisions "based upon local conditions and attitudes of both races."

Speaking for a unanimous court, Chief Justice Earl Warren did find that segregation was "inherently unequal." Yet the grounds for that decision seemed to rest less with constitutional objections to segregation and more on the importance of education in formulating good citizenship and the negative social impact of segregation on African American children. In 1955's *Brown II* decision, which specifically dealt again with Clarendon County, the Court declared that the whole subject of when, where, and under what circumstances desegregation would occur was best left to educators to decide and the courts would then decide whether they had exercised "good faith." In the infamous closing of *Brown II,* however, the Court ordered that school districts were to move to a "racially nondiscriminatory basis with all deliberate speed." As a consequence, the state of South Carolina would have plenty of wiggle room in maneuvering, delaying, and doing all in its power to preserve segregation, a fact South Carolina's political leadership realized once the revolutionary shock of *Brown* had worn off.[17]

Following the remanding of *Briggs v. Elliott* to the federal district court, Judge John Parker did as many white South Carolinians anticipated and narrowly interpreted *Brown.* He ruled that although the decision forbade the government from enforcing segregation it did not actually require integration, stating that the court had decided only that "a state may not deny any person on account of race the right to attend any school that it maintains. . . . [The Constitution] does not forbid such segregation as occurs as the result of voluntary action. It merely forbids the use of governmental power to enforce segregation." Such logic was certainly convoluted but it also meant that next to no pressure would be exerted on South Carolina to integrate as Judge Waring had retired from the bench in 1952 and was therefore not in a position to dissent against Parker's pronouncement. Most civil rights cases in South Carolina came before the new governor's father, George Bell Timmerman Sr., whose standard tactic was to throw them out. This scheme prevented the NAACP from appealing his rulings to the U.S. Fourth Circuit Court of Appeals and forced the return of these cases to his court, where he was able to employ further delaying tactics. So successful were these tactics that plaintiffs could graduate from high school before their case was heard. Compounding this situation, parents were forced to sue as individuals, and their cases could not therefore be recognized as a class-action suit. If a family did manage to navigate their way through this legal labyrinth, there was still the possibility that the school would lose state funding by admitting their child, thereby hurting the entire community. Consequently, the schools in Clarendon County remained strictly segregated and even in urban centers such as Charleston, Columbia, and Greenville local officials succeeded in maintaining the racial status quo.[18]

Emotionally and intellectually, white Carolinians were ill prepared to accept the larger purpose of *Brown*. Although some were ready to accept that it was now time to move toward an integrated school system, or at the very least to meet African Americans halfway, such a view was held by the minority. Most saw the Court decision as being illegitimate for a variety of important reasons: they viewed it as a political decision imposed by politicians rather than a matter of law; they resented the implication that they had not dealt with African Americans fairly; and they accused outside agitators of stirring up racial issues. In the context of the Cold War, it was hardly surprising that South Carolina senator Strom Thurmond, who had run for president as the Dixiecrat candidate in 1948, and the *Charleston News and Courier* would engage in red baiting and portray desegregation as nothing more than a Communist plot designed to destabilize U.S. society. Many white Carolinians had only a limited sense of what segregated life was like for African American Carolinians. In *South Carolinians Speak* (1957), moderate whites articulated a vision of what course of action the state should follow. For some this meant explaining in graphic terms why whites and African Americans should never attend school together. Robert Herbert, a lawyer expressing more conservative views, suggested that whites ought not to be asked to have their children exposed to "crime and venereal disease and illegitimacy," which he considered common among African Americans but evidently unheard of among whites. Helen Christensen, a retired librarian and representative of the more liberal sentiment, suggested that African Americans should realize that "equality cannot be bestowed; it must be earned," while Andrew Peeples, a director of information services for the state board of health, suggested that he knew fully well that "the responsible Negro leaders in South Carolina are aware of the impossibility of integration without mass violence." When one considers that these were the more "enlightened" voices of white South Carolina, it is no surprise that little progress toward desegregation was made in the 1950s. The desire for a way of protecting white supremacy and subverting the Supreme Court's ruling thus drew on popular support and reflected a profound commitment to the existing racial order.[19]

Although Governor Byrnes and the state of South Carolina had been preparing intellectually for the possibility of segregation being struck down as unconstitutional, it was quite another matter to be prepared to face a new reality. While some hotheads, such as H. R. E. Hampton, the associate editor of the *State,* could complain that too many voices were counseling to remain calm, the reality was that the political establishment's plan was a well-thought-out strategy. After all, few would accept Hampton's judgment that defeat in the Civil War did not preclude the possibility of a second secession in order to preserve the existing racial order. Three of the more important individuals who helped shape the immediate response to these matters were state senator Edgar Brown, who as president of the state senate operated as a legislative kingpin, Governor James Byrnes, and J. Heyward Gibbes, Columbia superintendent of education. Byrnes believed that in the present situation it was best for people to keep their wits about them; South Carolina had no need to "proceed with undue haste." Brown counseled a similar strategy in suggesting to Columbia attorney Irvin F. Belser that the best course was to simply delay and force the Court to intervene. Brown noted to Belser that "we [South Carolina] appeared there not as a class but representing the Clarendon County School District." Accordingly, the best strategy would be to force the NAACP to "take up every other district, because each is a separate district, and with separate conditions, it would take a life-time to ever substantially uproot our present public school system." Delay, however, was but part of a conscious strategy of public policies that sought to protect segregation and make it difficult for integration to ever take place. The role played by local educational officials was clearly critical and the influence played by J. Heyward Gibbes in the capitol city of Columbia was of vital importance.[20]

Gibbes served for many years as Columbia's superintendent of education and was the personification of the thoughtful racial "moderate" whose attitudes on racial questions were reflective rather than emotional. Like many white Carolinians, Gibbes disapproved of integration and the efforts of "do-gooders" to force whites and African Americans together. He especially feared the dangers of miscegenation and the idea that both races would "lose their identity." But in the 1940s, Gibbes was evidently on good terms with Judge J. Waties Waring, who suggested that they were co-laborers in the cause of justice. "It is fortunate for Columbia to have you in charge of its school system," noted Waring, who expressed a hope that together the two of them could play a part in engaging in "moderate, gradual, and understanding action" to improve race relations. Reflective of Gibbes's own views of the proper way to meet the challenge of *Brown* was a lengthy memorandum that he sent to Byrnes in 1954 outlining the proper strategy to follow. Governor Byrnes evidently found it useful, for he commended it in a letter and suggested it was the best piece of advice he had ever received on integration.[21]

In a single-spaced two-and-a-half-page letter Gibbes presented to Byrnes what he believed were the various choices and options that South Carolina faced in the immediate situation. Gibbes's own preferences were for maintaining a segregated system with no change, although he did recognize that it seemed "impracticable" to simply defy the Court. Gibbes then discussed the possibility of simply doing away with the public school system, but he doubted it "can be effectively done." A more compelling suggestion was to operate the schools "in a manner that will be technically within the law," but in reality would maintain a segregated system. "Our aim should be to minimize the mixing, to discourage it by one means or another" and that would have the effect of keeping a segregated system in place. Gibbes believed it essential the state assume a "temperate and reasoned nature" toward the court system as a means of generating good will. Gibbes suggested that South Carolina should implement a series of measures, all racial in nature, to preserve the segregated system: the use of district lines in urban areas to restrict African Americans to segregated schools; the introduction of intelligence tests that could be used "as a consideration in assigning pupils to various schools;" and the decentralization of the state's "public education as much as it can." Gibbes believed the last point to be of prime importance as it would allow individual school boards to be responsible for educational decisions at the local level and to perhaps, on their own, challenge "one phase or another of the court's rulings." Gibbes's thoughts on the subject were prescient, but they reflected the attitude of someone who was responsible for the educational system in the capitol city of the state. The enactment of his ideas in Columbia and the development of an educational consensus reflected a conscious strategy that would preserve segregation for the next fifteen years.[22]

Columbia's experience in mapping out a racial strategy for not implementing *Brown* may be said to have fit into a larger pattern of experience throughout the state. Gibbes's records of conversations with state education officials reveal a deep commitment to the preservation of a segregated system. Gibbes's own view was that the state of South Carolina should show public deference to Court orders, while privately they should "continue to segregate [and] let the Fed. Gov't try to stop it." He believed that by taking "advantage of every legal technicality," the state would be able to "bend instead of break" on matters of integration. The state legislature gladly took up the challenge, enacting numerous pro-segregation measures that were found in "everything from the state budget to resolutions commending the State of Virginia for its stand against segregation." Compulsory attendance laws were also repealed, allowing white parents to withdraw their children from integrated schools.

Educational institutes, from the elementary to the college level, were informed that they would have state funding withdrawn and were ordered to close their doors if they were forced to admit any student by a federal court. Furthermore, if any attempt was made to desegregate any state-funded college, it and the all-black South Carolina State College in Orangeburg would also be closed until the applicant withdrew their name. School officials were given the power to order the transfer of a student from one school to another if they believed that "enrollment of certain pupils in a certain school may threaten to result in riot, civil commotion, or may in any way disturb the peace of the citizens of the community." Formal requests were required of all African American parents who wished to send their children to a white school and they were forced to submit to a humiliating evaluation of their homes and their offspring's abilities. Even the NAACP was targeted, with one resolution petitioning the U.S. attorney general to place it on the list of subversive organizations. These institutional obstacles certainly played a role in limiting the ability of African American parents and children to achieve an equal education. Playing an equally important role, however, were the larger weapons of intimidation and coercion that were unleashed on the African American community.[23]

It did not take long in the aftermath of the promulgation of *Brown* for white supremacy hate groups to interfere with African American efforts to achieve equality. In the mid-1950s white supremacists had congregated throughout the South in White Citizens' Councils that advocated preservation of segregation and hostility toward African American voting. Many members were also prepared to use violence to stem the civil rights movement in their communities. One historian described the purpose of the Citizens' Councils as the same as "other white supremacy groups. . . . Its members wear business suits instead of bedsheets," a description echoed in the deposition of former Charleston state senator Charles Gibson. When asked about the Citizens' Council of Greater Charleston of 1967, Gibson replied, "I know generally citizens' councils around the south were . . . I always considered they were members of the Klan and has [*sic*] suits on instead of sheets." Compared to other southern states, the impact of the White Citizens' Councils was fairly modest in South Carolina, although their petty persecutions of local African Americans severely restricted the ability of local communities to desegregate. Many of those African Americans who filed petitions seeking access for their children to white schools lost their jobs or farm leases and suffered boycotts if they owned their own business. The Ku Klux Klan also became more active, after a period of relative inactivity. Threatening phone calls and letters were commonplace. In Clarendon County, trying to prevent the Citizens' Councils and other hate groups "from putting us out of business" sometimes took precedence over pushing for integration.

An obviously attractive target for many white Carolinians was the state NAACP, which was seen in the rhetoric of the time as a subversive organization that had to be crushed. In 1955 then-lieutenant-governor

Ernest Hollings proclaimed, "If there's one thing against our way of life in the South, it's the NAACP. And if the U.S. Supreme Court can declare certain organizations as subversive, I believe South Carolina can declare the NAACP both subversive and illegal." South Carolina made it illegal for schoolteachers to be members of the organization, and dedicated teachers like civil rights activist Septima Clark lost their jobs and retirement benefits when they would not deny they were members of the NAACP. In Columbia this requirement caused something of a quandary for local education officials, as they were unsure how aggressively they should ferret out NAACP members. Yet state policies did dampen public support for the organization. By 1960, little progress had been made toward integration with only three schools in the state integrated—a U.S. Department of Defense operated elementary school at the Marine Base on Parris Island, St. Anne's Roman Catholic School in Rock Hill, and the Lutheran Seminary in Columbia. Racial opinion on the part of white leaders had clearly hardened, and only renewed pressure from the growing civil rights movement and the federal government broke through these barriers. But although progress had been stymied on education, a larger number of African Americans had been able to qualify to vote in 1960 and their influence on the political system would prove to be significant. It spoke to a larger political restructuring that was beginning to take shape at the dawn of a new decade.[24]

The 1950s would usher in a revived Republican Party in the state, albeit a party that had turned its back on its civil rights heritage, and which became increasingly the spokesperson of racial conservatism. Key to this changed political institution was the success of the lily-whites who were eventually able to expel African Americans from the party's counsels. Their triumph, however, was delayed until 1956, owing to "Tieless" Joe Tolbert's long tenure as chairman of the Republican Party. Tolbert, from Ninety Six, was the heir to a Republican political tradition in which his family became Republicans during Reconstruction. As party chairman, Tolbert remained committed to African American leadership in the state Republican Party. One lily-white discovered this in 1922 when his efforts to create a white Republican Party in the state were flatly turned down by national Republicans. When Sigfrid L. Blomgren, who had run unsuccessfully for Congress from a Charleston district, asked one Republican official whether they wanted a white party in the state, he was told *"no, only white controlled, the negro must be counted in."* Before leaving Washington, Blomgren, who believed

Tolbert to be an opportunistic crook, could but ruefully note that "every nigger doorkeeper, elevator man, porter in the administration offices looks on him with tremendous respect." Throughout the 1920s and early 1930s Tolbert fought a rear-guard action against aggressive lily-whites, a factional hostility that would only be partly broken by the coming of the New Deal and a long Republican winter. Conservative whites took control of the South Carolina Republican Party following the death of Tolbert in 1946 and continued to appeal to African American voters while seeking to minimize segregation as an issue. A state of relative political inactivity was effectively broken by the strong public connection many southerners made with Dwight D. Eisenhower's campaign for the presidency.[25]

The 1952 presidential campaign brought with it considerable enthusiasm for the Republican ticket in South Carolina, although it proved to be a temporary phenomenon rather than the start of permanent Republican strength. Despite strong support from Governor Byrnes, Democratic candidate Adlai Stevenson held off the Republicans, winning 50.7 percent of the popular vote to Eisenhower's 49.3 percent. By 1956 support for Eisenhower had appreciably cooled, with many white voters considering northern Republicans to be as unreliable on race as northern Democrats, given the administration's failure to oppose desegregation. In the presidential election that year Eisenhower (25.2 percent) ran a distant third behind both the Democrats (45.4 percent) and an Independent ticket headed by Walter Burgwyn Jones from Alabama (29.5 percent) that appealed to the White Citizens' Council vote. Nonetheless, Eisenhower split the black vote with Democrats and carried a number of African American majority precincts.

Although African Americans were prepared to vote for a national party candidate, they increasingly found state Republicans an uncongenial home, as increasing numbers of conservative whites came to join the GOP. In the 1960 presidential election Republican candidate Richard Nixon was unable to build on Eisenhower's 1956 success with African American voters. Nevertheless, the result was quite close (48.8 percent of the popular vote to Kennedy's 51.2 percent), suggesting the increasing success state Republicans were having in drawing white voters into their ranks. As South Carolina became more closely contested between the two parties, Democrats would draw increasingly on African American voters. Nevertheless, developing a relationship across the racial divide was not easy, and many African Americans found that the state party was continuing to practice harassment and refused to treat black party members as equals.[26]

Despite the association of the civil rights movement's success with support from the Kennedy and Johnson administrations, relations between African American and white Democrats in South Carolina improved only marginally from the earlier period as the local party leadership remained as imperious as ever toward the place of African Americans in South Carolina. Even so, the national Democratic Party's support of desegregation and other civil rights issues eroded the support that the party had traditionally enjoyed in South Carolina. Conversely, with the end of the Eisenhower administration, South Carolina Republicans were no longer encumbered by the problem of a party perceived as too friendly toward African Americans. A large influx of conservative whites, many hardcore segregationists, therefore began flocking toward the GOP, allowing the development of a two-party system. The national Democratic Party's association during the Kennedy and Johnson years with civil rights made it increasingly difficult for Democrats to campaign as economic liberals and reactionaries on race relations. Olin Johnston reflected this change fairly dramatically as he began to moderate his private relations with prominent African Americans. In the 1940s, Johnston had done all he could to prevent African Americans from voting or participating in the Democratic Party. Now Johnston developed a personal relationship with John McCray, and both began to view each other as political allies. Clear limits obviously existed as Johnston still insisted on opposing all civil rights laws, but his behavior marked something of a modification to his earlier attitude. In 1962, when Johnston ran for reelection to the Senate he was strongly challenged by William Workman, a conservative journalist and Republican convert, who was able to hold Johnston to under 60 percent of the two-party vote. The split vote demonstrated the growing support for the Republican Party within the state. Simultaneously, Republicans for the first time elected state legislators and built a party organization that would be able to challenge the Democrats. As the pace of social change increased in the 1960s, race relations in the state moved beyond simply legal responses and on to more direct challenges to the political system.[27]

This was particularly true of the concerted desegregation efforts mounted in Charleston. The modern civil rights movement in Charleston wrought lunch counter sit-ins, regular demonstrations, and protests by African Americans. Beginning on April 1, when African American students sat down at an all-white counter in the Kress Department Store, the spring of 1960 saw at least eight separate protests involving more than seventy-five students, all of whom were charged with trespassing. During the next three years a concerted effort by the local African American community endeavored to end segregated lunch counters. On June 5, 1963, the NAACP announced that Charleston, the last large South Carolina city still to have segregated lunch counters, was to be targeted for demonstrations. The state and Charleston NAACP directed a campaign to "eliminate all state imposed and state upheld racial segregation and discrimination." The first arrests began June 13, 1963, and included Reverend I. DeQuincey Newman of the state NAACP. By the Fourth of July, over 500 African Americans were arrested in Charleston and 229 had already been tried and convicted. Fifty-five African Americans were also arrested trying to integrate Hampton Park and Colonial Lake. When African Americans protested in front of the *Charleston News and Courier* because of its reactionary editorial policy, violence broke out between angry whites and blacks and rioting ensued, causing the National Guard and the South Carolina Law Enforcement Division to occupy Charleston. On September 11, a bomb was tossed at Canaan Baptist Church and a Molotov cocktail at an African American social club. By the summer of 1963 Charleston police had arrested 600 African Americans; bail bonds were reported to be $1.4 million. Events in Charleston, however, were but part of an increasing pattern of African American activism, which included tensions within the African American community as a whole.[28]

One can exaggerate the disagreements that existed across generational lines and between the various civil rights organizations. The state NAACP had been involved in these issues for decades, and yet they cannot be categorized as simply "conservative legalists" opposed to "movement activists." Instead, the NAACP was deeply involved in the protests mounted in Charleston and, in general, black Carolinians avoided the factional disputes that wracked other southern states. For John McCray, however, the intervention of new organizations had no other purpose than to "take over our organization." Casting aspersion on Martin Luther King Jr.'s Southern Christian Leadership Conference, McCray described it as little more than a "money-making adventure of certain preachers." From McCray's perspective it was a case of non-Carolinians who failed to appreciate the sacrifices of an earlier generation. In fact, McCray had a particularly idiosyncratic view of the civil rights movement's struggle. He became all but consumed with the bizarre notion that the Congress of Racial Equality (CORE) volunteers were actually

Republican activists bent on signing voters for the GOP. Even so, most African Americans in the state saw legal, political, and movement protests as being linked together as different tactics for different situations. Key issues included finding ways to break down segregation in public accommodations and education and to properly secure the ballot. By the early 1960s such efforts acquired a momentum that was manifested by a number of important breakthroughs in the courts.[29]

Harvey Gantt, a determined African American veteran from the Charleston protests, wanted to return from Iowa State University to attend school at Clemson. Clemson College had received previous requests for admission from African Americans but had been able to fend them off. Gantt, however, was more determined. After his first request for transfer in 1960 was denied, he set in motion a two-year legal process that overcame numerous appeals from Clemson in the federal courts. The college's defense centered on its argument that Gantt was not denied admission because of his race, but because he had failed to meet admissions requirements. Although the district court accepted these arguments and dismissed the case, the U.S. Fourth Circuit Court of Appeals overturned it in January 1963, finding that Clemson College had made no efforts to desegregate since the *Brown* ruling of 1954 and ordered that the school admit Gantt immediately. It furthermore rejected South Carolina's policy of not prohibiting segregation, but instead discouraging integration as unacceptable and unconstitutional. Following this decision, other colleges in the state began to desegregate, including the University of South Carolina, which in the fall of 1963 admitted its first black students since Reconstruction.

South Carolinians had seen the violence and rioting that had accompanied the enrollment of James Meredith at the University of Mississippi in 1962, and officials determined that these scenes could not be repeated in their state; even staunch segregationists such as the editors of the *Charleston News and Courier* urged moderation in the citizenry's response to the decision. As the case moved toward it dénouement, the rhetoric of South Carolinian politicians became increasingly resigned to the inevitable. Businessman Charles E. Daniel, a trustee at Clemson and former state senator, typified this mood when he declared that although he did not agree with desegregation, "it is the law and we must abide by it. We want to avoid any tragedy like Mississippi. . . . We are a great state and we don't want to get in the ditch now." Even though Gantt was able to matriculate at Clemson College without incident, some politicians remained defiant. Senator Gressette, for example, declared after the judgment was announced that "There will be no surrender. . . . We may lose a battle but we are engaged in a war. . . . If I thought [desegregation] was the best thing for Clemson—the best thing for South Carolina—I would advance a different course."[30]

As the Gantt case was moving through the courts, similar attempts were being made to force the desegregation of elementary and second-ary schools. In April 1960, at a time that no school district in South Carolina was fully integrated, parents of forty-three African American children in Clarendon County filed suit seeking an injunction against "the operation of a dual school system, against pupil assignment on a basis of race or color and against the application to Negro students of assignment criteria not applied to whites." The case was set back in June 1962 when district judge C. C. Wyche, who later that year dismissed the Gantt case, ruled that the case could not be tried as a class-action suit and ordered that all but one of the forty-two litigants be removed. In his opinion, Wyche declared that "It is the individual who is entitled the equal protection of the laws . . . He alone may complain that his consti-tutional privilege has been invaded." Since the one remaining litigant had already graduated from the segregated school by this time, it appeared as though the case had reached an impasse. Wyche's ruling was overturned by the Fourth Circuit Court of Appeals, however, and the case was allowed to proceed as a class-action suit. The state house of representatives responded by passing a bill eliminating class-action suits in school segregation suits brought before the state courts, but admitted that this action was largely symbolic and would have little effect on desegregation cases. When the Supreme Court refused to hear the case it effectively allowed the continuation of class-action suits against South Carolina.[31]

A similar action to the Clarendon case was brought by Arthur Brown, head of the Charleston NAACP, in May 1962 to desegregate Charleston schools. During the course of this case, Thomas A. Carrere, school superintendent, "expressed his own belief that genetic differences accounted for Negroes' poor scores on achievement tests" as a rationale for the continued state of segregated education in the state. On August 22, 1963, Judge Robert Martin, however, rejected the defendant's stance and ordered that children be admitted without reference to their race. Later that year, District 20 in the city of Charleston became the first school district in the state to desegregate when eleven African American children enrolled in these white schools. Despite Judge Martin's order, however, the school board reaffirmed that segregation was in the best interests of all students and instructed its attorney to try to reverse the order. In the 1964–65 school year, the Charleston School District was again told it had to totally desegregate, leading to increased white flight from local public schools to lily-white segregation academies.[32]

Progress in achieving desegregation remained slow despite this judicial order as South Carolina adopted a variety of tactics to delay integration for as long as possible. In early 1962, Governor Ernest Hollings advocated a plan that would see the state dropping its threats of denying funds to schools that were forced to desegregate, instead allowing the local school boards to decide how to allocate the money. Since the boards favored schools that resisted integration, parents of African Americans would have no choice but to file individual lawsuits in all 108 districts, stretching the NAACP's meager resources. The state legislature adopted another plan in May 1963 when it passed a measure that provided state funds that should have been targeted at public education to children who wished to attend private, segregated, schools. This measure was ultimately struck down in court, but not before dozens of new private schools appeared in the state.[33]

By the end of 1965, only eighteen school districts in South Carolina were desegregated and even in those districts desegregation affected only a small proportion of the black community. For example, only 185 African American students attended desegregated schools in Charleston in 1966. Much of the myth about "integration with dignity" is untrue, as ultimately state and educational officials were forced to accept political reality. The positive coverage the state received from the national media, especially in light of the violence in Mississippi, no doubt helped make it more palatable for the political establishment to avoid overt racial hostility. Even so, the horrors and daily indignities that faced African Americans as they attempted to desegregate South Carolina's public accommodations are difficult to ignore. For example, on February 8, 1968, in an event that became known as the Orangeburg Massacre, some 200 African American students attempted to desegregate their local bowling alley. Following some minor altercations with the protestors, the South Carolina Highway Patrol fired into the crowd, killing 3 and wounding an additional 27. Cleveland Sellers, a native South Carolinian and leader of the civil rights movement, was charged and convicted of rioting as a result of these protests; he served time in prison and did not receive a pardon until a quarter century later. In contrast, the nine patrolmen who faced federal charges as a result of the shootings were all acquitted. The NAACP leader Reverend I. DeQuincey Newman protested that South Carolina "is just about in the same boat as Alabama and Mississippi." Newman continued, "The perpetrators of the tragedy and those who have covered up for them have rendered a great disservice to sometimes heroic efforts that have been made in the area of race relations and interracial cooperation." One of the last states to integrate education, South Carolina did so only under court order; it was not done voluntarily. South Carolina chose to not close the public school system and set in motion what would become its strategy throughout the next decade—resist all efforts at desegregation, engage in dilatory maneuvers for more time, and, when at last compelled to do so by the courts, submit in the end.[34]

The increasing two-party system in South Carolina made it more palatable for Democrats to accept integration. The emergence of moderation, however, took place at the same time as a revived Republican Party was showing increasing strength and as the national government at last passed the 1964 Civil Rights Act. Prior to 1963, the Kennedy administration had shown largely a reactive posture toward civil rights issues; such issues had never been a priority. The Birmingham, Alabama, protests, however, were so graphic in their violence and attracted such considerable national attention that Kennedy could not fail to see the coming relevance of a new Civil Rights Act that would eliminate segregation. Kennedy's death occurred before the passage of the act, but his successor, Texas politician Lyndon Johnson, pushed through the legislation. In 1965, Congress passed the Voting Rights Act, which guaranteed to all U.S. citizens the right to cast a free ballot and undermined disfranchisement.

South Carolina was the first state to challenge the 1965 Voting Rights Act, maintaining that it subjected the state to unnecessary intrusive supervision without proof of intentional discrimination. In denying its challenge, and affirming the constitutionality of the act in *South Carolina v. Katzenbach,* Chief Justice Earl Warren stated, "Congress felt itself confronted by an insidious and pervasive evil." He noted the long history of racial discrimination in the voter registration process in South Carolina, directly quoting some of the more outrageous remarks of Governor Benjamin Ryan "Pitchfork Ben" Tillman at the 1895 disfranchising convention as evidence of its discriminatory purpose. Warren stated that "the constitutional propriety of the Voting Rights Act of 1965 must be judged with reference to the historical experience which it reflects." Its history of racial discrimination was finally catching up to South Carolina. The effects of such events were stiffly resisted by South Carolinians and yet the passage of both the Civil Rights Act of 1964 and the Voting Rights Act of 1965 allowed the political system to gradually accommodate itself to both. Title VI of the Civil Rights Act gave real force to *Brown v. Board* in that it denied federal funding to institutions that practiced racial discrimination. The Elementary and Secondary Education Act of 1965 raised the amount of money at stake to unprecedented levels. Progress would prove to be slow, but these developments represented a small movement of reconciliation between African Americans and whites. Nevertheless, it would require the willingness of the courts to enforce the new civil rights laws to make them a reality.[35]

In the aftermath of the 1964 Civil Rights Act, local school districts often seized upon parental choice as a way of preserving a segregated system. Freedom-of-choice plans required African American parents to get the school board's approval to send their children to a desegregated school. In South Carolina, such requests were frequently denied on the basis of the catch-all pronouncement that the child's best interests would be served by keeping them in the black school. Even if permission was granted, parents remained responsible for transporting their children to and from the school—an often insurmountable obstacle when one considers that African Americans were significantly less likely to possess their own cars or other means of transport. Furthermore, this tactic left the racially segregated infrastructure intact and delayed further the rate of change. An example of how freedom-of-choice plans worked in the aftermath of the 1964 Civil Rights Act is found in Horry County. In 1965, T. W. Anderson, the county superintendent for Horry, suggested that parents had the "absolute right to choose each year the school the pupil will attend." Such programs allowed school districts to engage in token integration in which a few African American students were selected and thus maintained the racial status quo, while claiming that this reflected parental choice. In that same year the superintendent of Bamberg, South Carolina, admitted that transfers were rarely accepted and that "there could be only one Negro in a class section."

With the election of Republican president Richard Nixon in 1968, many white southerners expected the administration to bring an end to efforts at integration, as evidenced by newspaper headlines such as that in the October 24, 1968, edition of Clarendon County's *Manning Times:* "Nixon Raps Hew on Schools, Favors 'Freedom of Choice.'" Nixon's Southern Strategy was in effect a desire to help build up a Republican Party in the South. Nixon never saw that process as meaning southern Republicans would have a veto over desegregation, however, and these same southerners were often ignored in implementing policy. Litigation remained the preferred method Nixon envisioned for desegregation. It had the value of giving the administration broad discretion for intervening, while at the same time being able to claim innocence with southern Republicans who might object to the radical direction of court intervention. This plan seemed to reach fruition when the Supreme Court, in a case originating from Virginia, *Green v. New Kent County,* declared most freedom-of-choice plans illegal in 1968, but federal district courts initially allowed South Carolinia school districts to eliminate their dual systems gradually. In early 1970, however, the Fourth Circuit Court of Appeals ordered the immediate desegregation of Darlington and Greenville Counties. In the middle of the academic year, these two districts were given less than one month to transfer thousands of students to new schools; the rest of South Carolina was ordered to follow suit that fall.

White South Carolinians did not allow desegregation to occur without one final show of defiance. Although Governor McNair urged moderation against threats of school closures, many politicians—most prominently Republicans Senator Strom Thurmond and Congressman Albert Watson—demanded that the state defy the court order and preserve freedom-of-choice plans. Nixon, however, ordered an immediate federal intervention to ensure that desegregation went ahead, sending numerous attorneys and federal marshals to monitor the situation and file lawsuits against districts that continued to resist the court order. Even so, with desegregation came pickets, school closures, armed guards in school hallways, and bomb threats. In Darlington County, three thousand white students boycotted the desegregated schools while the situation there continued to escalate until, in a highly symbolic moment, two buses carrying students to a newly integrated school were overturned by a mob in Lamar. At the same time, many African Americans lost the individual gains that they had fought hard to win: principals were demoted to assistant principal status; black athletic coaches became assistants to whites. There was also a loss of community identity as schools were forced to give up such distinguishing features as mascots, team colors, and school newspapers in favor of those from traditionally all-white institutes.[36]

In 1971, most South Carolina school districts were finally desegregated, although racial inequalities in the quality of education would linger for years to come. African Americans came to participate more fully in the politics of the state, but as Republicans came to increasingly dominate state politics it could often seem as though the gains of the civil rights movement were elusive. It would be foolish to suggest that little progress has been made for the better, but even some fifty years after *Brown,* there remain ample opportunities for improvement. Although white South Carolina had been forced by the federal government to integrate, the white political elite did not want to give up control of the schools, even when those schools were primarily populated by African American students. County and city governments, as well as local school boards, changed their method of elections from districts and wards to at-large voting in an effort to dilute the African American vote and maintain practically all-white elected bodies. When the Voting Rights Act was passed in 1965, the U.S. Bureau of the Census reported that nineteen South Carolina counties elected at least some members of the county governing body from single-member districts that helped ensure predominantly African American areas would be represented by a candidate of their choice. By 1973, the bureau's survey indicated that eleven counties had switched entirely to an at-large election system, thereby undermining the African American vote.[37]

The example of Charleston County clearly demonstrates how local jurisdictions used the laws to control integration and the schools. In 1967, Charleston senator Charles Gibson introduced a bill to consolidate the Charleston County School districts. Debate over this bill dominated the South Carolina Legislature, set off a record filibuster, and divided both the Charleston legislative delegation and the people in the County. The discussion of the act included issues of race, busing of children, and transfer of teachers to different districts. The bill was approved June 8, 1967, as Act No. 340. The Gibson School Bill was amended by the same house delegation that amended senate bill S131 to change the method of electing county council to at-large from districts. The motivation behind the amendments to the Gibson School Bill has been carefully researched by the historian R. Scott Baker, who concludes, "The Act of consolidation was a fitting conclusion to a quarter century of shrewd white resistance, testimony to the ability of whites to limit the impact of NAACP litigation. By equalizing expenditures and maintaining constituent district boundaries, consolidation stymied the NAACP's attempt to achieve meaningful desegregation in Charleston." Baker shows that "Equalization was always a means to a larger end: the maintenance of racial separation in education. . . . By blocking desegregation across district lines, consolidation embedded schools in racially segregated and economically unequal social environments."[38]

The racial motivation for this change is all too obvious when one considers that the trustees were to be an elected board, except in the four districts (20, 23, 9, and 1) where African Americans had the opportunity to elect representatives. Thus, in the Gibson School Consolidation Bill, Act 340, in 1967 this racial distinction was incorporated, denying African Americans the vote where they might have the majority and determining vote for school trustees. In these four predominantly African American districts, trustees would instead be appointed, thereby allowing the racial makeup of the board to be predetermined. It was not until 1974 that these predominantly African American school districts were allowed to elect their trustees in the same manner as did the predominately white districts.[39]

Since the mid-1970s, little progress has been made toward ensuring the continuation of equal, desegregated schooling in the state. In many districts, attempts at enforcing integration were accompanied by white flight to private schools once the student body was more than one-third African American. State-sanctioned segregation may have ended, but segregated education remained, and remains, the normal experience for most African American students in South Carolina. In 2004, 36.5 percent of Lee County's residents were white, but only 6.5 percent of the student population in public schools was white; in Hampton County, the figures were 45.5 percent and 1.5 percent. Making matters worse was a growing disparity between the level of funding available to the richest (predominantly white) and poorest (predominantly black) counties, since almost one-third of funding for public education in each district came from local property taxes. With fewer funds available, schools in districts such as Summerton and Turbeville in Clarendon County could not afford to make the improvements necessary to maintain the standard of teaching achieved in the richest districts. This shortcoming was partially addressed by the 1977 Education Finance Act, which increased the share of state money from 50 percent to over 70 percent and established a minimum statewide salary for certified teachers, and by the

1984 Education Improvement Act, which targeted funding deficits in an effort to equalize spending. In 1998, the Education Accountability Act attempted to set standards for achievement and allocated funding to schools designated as unsatisfactory in these measures. These efforts, however, have been seriously hampered by cuts to the state budget that have resulted in the loss of hundreds of millions of dollars from education. The worst-performing districts, and those that most require this additional funding, remain those that are predominantly African American.[40]

In 1993, eight school districts sued the state of South Carolina for failing to provide an adequate level of education to all students in the state. The plaintiffs in *Abbeville, et al. v. The State of South Carolina, et al.* point to statistics showing that over 50 percent of students in their districts cannot read, write, or do math at a basic level and dropout rates that average 54 percent and ask that each "child in the state of South Carolina should receive the opportunity [to] read, write and speak the English language, and knowledge of math and physical science. Further each child should understand history and how our government operates, so that they can be informed members of society and actively participate in elections that affect their future. Finally, each child should possess vocational and academic skills that allow them to be productive members of their community." The case was originally thrown out by the circuit court in 1996, but three years later the state supreme court ruled that the state must "provide the opportunity for each child to receive a minimally adequate education." The case is still ongoing, however, and the emphasis has shifted to an effort to ensure that the poorest districts are provided with sufficient funds to meet these requirements.[41]

Tragically, the revolution that began in the Palmetto State and helped transform the United States into a more tolerant society has had little impact on the lives of those parents brave enough to take a stand for what they knew to be right. Although African Americans in Clarendon County won the 1954 Supreme Court decision, Clarendon continued to maintain separate schools until 1965. In that year, the state allowed students to select the schools they would attend, and four black students attended a previously all-white school in the fall of 1965. In reaction, whites established a private academy, Clarendon Hall, and in 1969 only 281 white students were left in the Summerton public school system. One year later, when the schools officially desegregated, there were only 16 white students left. In 1991, of the 1,274 students in

Summerton's public schools, only 23 were white. Even so, in an article on Summerton published that year, the *New York Times* reported, "Whites and blacks coexist with an easy surface sociability that is far more amiable than can be found in many Northern cities." Today the Summerton public schools are still overwhelmingly black (the school superintendent is white) and almost 97.5 percent of them come from poor households. The situation has begun to improve—a new high school was built and the period 1995–1999 saw a marked improvement in the district's performance in statewide tests, even exceeding scores from other nearby districts for the first time—but there is still much progress to be made.[42]

In sharp contrast to Summerton is the nearby town of Manning, the county seat. Manning has integrated successfully, as have many schools throughout the South. Some southern whites in the Summerton School District oppose racism and want their children to attend integrated public schools. They find themselves with a dubious choice—to send their children to a segregated private academy or to an underfunded black school. Some have opted instead to send their children to the integrated public schools in Manning. (South Carolina law allows parents to send children to schools in any school district where they own property.) Of course, most African Americans do not have even this limited choice.[43]

Defiance, Protest, and Compromise

THE STRUGGLE TO IMPLEMENT
BROWN IN GEORGIA, 1950–1973

Thomas V. O'Brien

This chapter examines the struggle to desegregate schools in the state of
Georgia between 1950 and 1973. Georgia's blacks had long struggled to
secure learning for their children. After World War II and before the U.S.
Supreme Court handed down *Brown v. Board of Education* in 1954,
black Georgians pushed state and school officials to live up to the equal
component of the separate-but-equal doctrine. These leaders in the state
were guided by a series of U.S. Supreme Court cases brought to court by
the Legal Defense and Education Fund, the litigation arm of the
National Association for the Advancement of Colored People that had
pressured the educational establishment to live up to the separate-but-
equal doctrine.[1]

The NAACP in Georgia before *Brown*

In September 1950 attorney Austin T. Walden, a leader in both the
Atlanta and Georgia NAACP, consulted with NAACP Legal Defense
Fund chief Thurgood Marshall and filed *Aaron v. Cook,* a suit filed on

behalf of two hundred children and their parents that challenged segregated public schooling in Atlanta. *Aaron* was the first suit of its kind to be filed in a large southern city.[2] Theoretically, Walden and other members of the Georgia NAACP were opposed to segregated schooling. Operationally, however, they worked within the separate-but-equal doctrine enunciated in *Plessy v. Ferguson*. The *Aaron* case had a second prong; it called on Atlanta school officials to remedy its system of unequal schools by equalizing teacher pay, facilities, per pupil expenditures, and other tangible factors. *Aaron's* desegregation prong operated only as a distant reminder to whites that the black community was serious about equalization.

Under pressure from *Aaron,* state leaders finally adopted plans to equalize the state's schools. The threat contributed to unprecedented reform that pumped revenue into schools statewide.[3] Between 1945 and 1955 the average per-pupil expenditure increased 300 percent from 65 to 194 dollars. In the same period the state contribution to public schooling increased from 37 to 69 percent. A year after *Aaron* was filed Governor Herman E. Talmadge used the threat of racial mixing to push through the legislature a record-breaking $208 million appropriations bill, which targeted more than half of new expenditures on black schooling. Under the gubernatorial administrations of Talmadge and his successor, S. Marvin Griffin, state support for public schooling increased significantly and the black-white funding gap shrunk.[4] *Aaron* continued to pressure Georgia's politicians to equalize the schools, but the NAACP took no action and the case laid dormant on the docket until 1956 when it was dismissed for lack of prosecution.[5]

Massive Resistance, 1954–1961

Despite the move to equalize, few Georgians of either race were able to fully comprehend an end to segregated schooling. The state's older black leaders for the most part were cautious, aware of the kind of anger and violence a militant reaction might provoke. Generally supportive of the *Brown* decision, but cognizant of growing white defiance, the old guard proceeded with measured caution. Atlanta's blacks, in particular, with the power of the ballot, had made significant headway toward equality with the separate-but-equal paradigm. Their leaders had won fights to get blacks on the city police force, to equalize teacher salaries, and to get sewers and streetlights installed in black neighborhoods.[6] In 1955, after the Court ordered desegregation to begin with "all deliberate speed," the old guard signaled that it would not file additional lawsuits. Rufus Clement, president of Atlanta University and newly elected member of the Atlanta School Board, noted the decision offered a chance for the races to work together constructively. William Boyd, state president of the NAACP, saw *Brown II* as taking the middle road, but still offering the South an honorable way to comply. As massive resistance crystallized, attorney A. T. Walden favored a flexible strategy to effect change: "We do not want to rush precipitously," he cautioned, "until we have time to consider the whole situation."[7] Significantly, Walden indicated that he would not push the desegregation prong of the *Aaron* case.

When it came to integration, white Georgians, like many others across the South, generally had their collective heads in the sand. Georgia politicians and school officials were every bit as committed to resisting *Brown* as their counterparts in Virginia and the Deep South. White reaction to *Brown* ranged from silence to violent resistance, with political leaders encouraging resisters. In the months after *Brown,* state politicians outdid themselves in insisting that segregation remain the law of the land. To align this position with the state constitution, however, required the state to expunge its fiduciary responsibilities to public education. For that to occur, an amendment to the state constitution was necessary, a process that required a referendum. During the autumn of 1954 a proposal was drafted that would give the legislature the power to discharge itself from the obligation of providing an "adequate education" for the state's 800,000 children. The proposal also called for the provision of vouchers from state and local governments to be awarded to children for educational purposes.[8]

The "private school plan," as it became known, ignited the school-race issue statewide. The state superintendent, teachers' associations, a number of daily newspapers, and voter and civic groups—both black and white—came out strongly against the amendment. The League of Women Voters, for instance, asserted there was "unshakable confidence" in the public schools, and that they would continue to be called on to "produce intelligent and productive citizens."[9] The Democratic Party, however, which held the balance of power in the state, threw its weight behind the amendment and secured its placement on the November ballot. The debate escalated in the weeks before the election, but in the end segregationists claimed victory as the amendment passed with 54 percent of the popular vote.[10] The outcome gave the governor and legislature a mandate to preserve segregation at all costs if necessary. "Come hell or high water," declared Governor Griffin, the schools of Georgia would not be desegregated.[11]

Between 1956 and 1958, lawmakers passed an avalanche of legislation to maintain segregation and defy the U.S. Supreme Court. In February 1956 Governor Griffin signed six bills into law, including two that allowed public school plants to be used for private educational purposes, one that made it a misdemeanor to enter a closed public school, and another that extended state retirement benefits to private school teachers. The marquee pieces of legislation were bills that required the public schools to close if ordered to desegregate, provided vouchers to students, and directed state and local governments to collect taxes to facilitate the conversion to a private system.[12]

White state leaders, such as Governor S. Marvin Griffin and political boss Roy V. Harris, continued warnings and threats to convert the public school system to a private one if the color line was breached. Harris, a native of Glascock County near the South Carolina border, had served in both houses of the state legislature between 1937 and 1946. He gained the reputation in the state and region as the "king-maker" because of his uncanny ability in leading five successful gubernatorial campaigns. In 1947 Harris left the legislature and began publishing the *Augusta Courier,* a weekly newspaper that covered Georgia politics and allowed the fiery segregationist to continue to exert his influence.[13]

As long as there were no legal challenges to the status quo, resisters could continue their posture of defiance and encourage legislators to pass state laws against racial mixing in the schools, which they did forthwith. Changes in local and state NAACP leadership in the middle 1950s, however, pushed desegregation litigation to the fore. Old-guard leaders handed over the campaign to less conciliatory litigators, among them Donald Hollowell and Eugene E. Moore of Atlanta, and C. B. King of Albany. King handled most of the work in South Georgia, while Hollowell took the lead in Atlanta and north Georgia with Moore usually in the second chair. Hollowell was an articulate, soft-spoken man in his forties, but his gentle presentation did not impede his measured persistence and determination to end the reign of Jim Crow. Working with Constance Baker Motley from the NAACP's national office, Hollowell took on segregation head-on. In 1956, 1958, and 1960 he filed three suits to desegregate public education in the state. Two of the cases, *Calhoun v. Latimer,* which sought the desegregation in the Atlanta public schools, and *Holmes v. University of Georgia,* which sought desegregation at the public flagship university in Athens, reached fruition, and soon precipitated a crisis.[14]

The crisis culminated in 1961 during the administration of Governor Ernest S. Vandiver when federal courts ruled in favor of the NAACP in both suits. Although Vandiver had campaigned on a slogan that "not one" black would attend school with whites, the governor was considered more moderate in his views than his predecessors. Still, there was no sense of how he would react to federal orders to desegregate.[15]

The fight over desegregation was anticipated in Atlanta during the fall of 1961, but speedy rulings in *Holmes* by federal district court judge William T. Bootle and appeals court judge Elbert Tuttle abruptly transferred the showdown to Athens in February of 1961.[16] State lawmakers, who came primarily from rural sections of the state, were poised to take their stand in Atlanta and implement massive resistance legislation requiring the state to abandon the city's public schools in favor of continued segregation. But with the change of venue, implementing the same legislation meant abandoning the University of Georgia (UGA), the state's revered land-grant institution. For rural lawmakers, with constituents loyal to UGA, the choice between segregation and the state's flagship was far more difficult. Abandoning "progressive," Yankee-influenced urban schools in Atlanta could be viewed as defensible, even admirable. But closing down UGA was another matter. Moreover, state interference with the university system's flagship over the issue of segregation had backfired once before, in the 1940s during Eugene Talmadge's governorship, and led to the defeat of the conservatives.[17]

Plaintiffs in the *Holmes* case were Atlantans Charlayne Hunter and Hamilton Holmes, top-notch students from the city's black middle-class community. The case was tried in 1960 and won just in time for Holmes and Hunter to be admitted to the university for the spring semester in February 1961. When Judge Bootle stayed his own order to admit the students, however, it appeared that NAACP efforts had been foiled. On appeal, as Governor Vandiver threatened to cut off university funds, appellate judge Elbert Tuttle set aside Bootle's stay, allowing Holmes and Hunter to matriculate. After two nights of rioting on campus, the two enrolled, marking the start of desegregation in the state.[18]

The Showdown over Desegregation in Atlanta

Although Holmes and Hunter were routinely harassed, they persevered and graduated from UGA, helping lay the foundation for a relatively peaceful transition to token desegregation in higher education. Still, in the spring and summer of 1961 there were no guarantees that school desegregation would proceed smoothly in Atlanta. In the *Calhoun* case, federal district court judge Frank Hooper had directed the Atlanta School Board to submit a desegregation plan by December 1959, signaling to Georgia's General Assembly that that body would have time to change state laws to bring them in compliance with federal law. Atlanta School Board president John Latimer said that he would not defy the order, and directed superintendent Ira Jarrell to develop a desegregation plan. Jarrell's plan purported to admit pupils to the city school "without regard to race or color," but beyond its rhetoric it discouraged even the smallest effort to bring about desegregation. Referred to as a pupil-placement plan, it required extensive standardized testing of black pupils who sought transfer to white schools. The plan also called for placement to begin at grade 12 and to proceed one grade each year.[19] These features ensured that token desegregation would be carefully controlled and take place over the decade. In effect, its design rejected wholesale desegregation. The NAACP, of course, took issue with the plan, as did a number of black parents who pointed out that the plan failed to comply with the order to commence desegregation. Notwithstanding these concerns, Hooper approved it on the condition that pupil placement be administered without racial bias.[20]

As Hollowell, Constance Baker Motley, and other NAACP lawyers pushed forward in court, individuals who favored the continuation of public schooling organized. The most effective of these organizations was Help Our Public Education (HOPE), a coalition of mostly white middle-class Atlanta women and parents of school-age children. Fearful that Atlanta would become "the next Little Rock," Muriel Lokey, Frances Breeden, and Maxine Friedman chartered HOPE in 1958 to give "direction, guidance, information, and program to all citizens in Georgia who desire the continuation of the public schools in the state."[21] Within a year HOPE had hired activist Frances Pauley as executive secretary and opened up chapters in Gainesville, Marietta, Jonesboro, Rome, Athens, Macon, and Savannah. Pauley, who had contacts with the state League of Women Voters, used her influence to start chapters in Brunswick, Valdosta, and Columbus by 1960.[22] HOPE initiated a lecture series on the public schools, lobbied legislators and journalists, and organized public demonstrations in support of continued public schooling. Although the overwhelming majority of state legislators were opposed to their efforts, HOPE was backed by powerful members from the Georgia business community and a small group of lawmakers at the capitol known as the "Sinister Seven." HOPE also had support from a number of state journalists including Sylvan Meyer from the *Gainesville Times,* C. A. Scott, from the *Daily World,* Atlanta's black newspaper, and Ralph McGill, editor of the *Atlanta Constitution* and arguably the South's most influential columnist.

Judge Hooper's ruling to back the Atlanta School Board's desegregation plan also carried with it an expectation that the state would repeal massive resistance legislation or abandon the state's school system. Hooper's decision did not set a starting date, but signaled to the state that it was its turn to act. Vandiver responded by establishing the General Committee on Schools, later referred to as the Sibley Commission after its chairman, John A. Sibley. In his eighties, Sibley had an impressive resume as a judge, banker, lawyer, and businessman. He had come of age in Baldwin County, in the rural Black Belt, and by 1950 had established a reputation as one of the preeminent leaders and visionaries of the New South. Vandiver sensed that Sibley had what it took to appeal to segregationist rural white elites, as well as pragmatic urban capitalists. More than anyone else, Vandiver felt that Sibley could navigate the crisis and keep Georgia moving forward economically.

In the spring of 1960 the Sibley Commission canvassed the state, holding hearings in each of Georgia's ten congressional districts to see how the people felt about continued public schooling and racial segregation. Testimony came from blacks, whites, young, and old, and rural and urban dwellers. Organizations like HOPE were quick to see that the commission's findings would have a bearing on how politicians would handle the school crisis. HOPE organized its membership and other pro-school groups to testify at each hearing. By early May the commission had completed its work and filed its report and recommendations. A minority report called for the state to continue resisting desegregation, even if it meant abandoning the public school system. Sibley authored the majority report, however, which carried the most weight. Reflecting contemporary white southern thought, the report began with a negative appraisal of the *Brown* ruling and of the federal judiciary's "usurpation of the legislative function." But breaking with proponents of massive resistance, Sibley called for alternatives to closing the schools and converting the public system to a private one. As rear-guard actions to preserve both the schools and the fundamentals of segregation, it recommended freedom-of-choice and pupil transfer options, and tuition voucher programs where no "suitable" (e.g., segregated) schools were available. This route would require two constitutional amendments to repeal the state's segregation laws and allow the legislature to align state law with Hooper's federal ruling in the Atlanta case.[23] If white Georgians kept their cool, Sibley advised, ceased open and rigid defiance, and allowed for some flexibility, legal and otherwise, they could have public schools and continued segregation. Moreover, elites could maintain control over the state's major institutions and continue their pursuit of the New South economic program.

While the Sibley report gave confidence to organizations like HOPE, it was a disappointment to the NAACP. Although the lawyers took some relief in its recommendations against abandonment and privatization, they correctly viewed the report as a signal that the power brokers of the white South were shifting to more subtle forms of resistance. In May 1960, only days after the Sibley report was released, Hooper ruled from the bench in *Calhoun* that due to a conflict between federal and state law, Atlanta city schools would have a grace period of one year to implement a desegregation plan. In rebuttal, Hollowell and Motley of the NAACP stated they would appeal the ruling, arguing that an order that gave the legislature a last chance to act had no legal precedent in the high courts. As tempers flared, A. T. Walden, the old-guard lawyer, sitting in the third chair, intervened. The patriarch suggested that an appeal would be unnecessary if Hooper wrote in his formal order that the effective date of implementation would be May 1, 1961, regardless of state action. But because the school year ended in May, the actual implementation date would be September 1961. Walden's recommendation carried, and gave Georgians their first concrete time and place for public school desegregation to commence.[24]

With a deadline in place, the ball was now in Governor Vandiver's court. Caught between calls to compromise from business elites and urban progressives, and demands to continue massive resistance from die-hard rural legislators, Vandiver declined to call a special session of the legislature to act on the Sibley Commission's recommendations.[25] This choice set the stage for a sixteen-month debate on the merits of abandoning the public school system to avoid desegregation, or changing desegregation laws in order to keep the public schools operating. The debate featured a nationally televised CBS documentary entitled "Crisis in Atlanta," hosted by Edward R. Murrow and Fred Friendly. Over the summer and fall of 1960, due in large part to the efforts of HOPE and like-minded groups, and behind-the scenes moves by business elites, white public opinion began to shift toward continuing public education and allowing token desegregation. As the moderates surged to support open schools, Gainesville newspaper journalist Sylvan Meyer declared that it was "mind changing time in Georgia." The notion of breaching the color line, which in 1958 had been so distant and incomprehensible, began in 1960 to appear almost inevitable.[26]

In an attempt to counter what was becoming a mood for compromise, segregationists retaliated by forming their own grass-roots groups, such as the Georgians Unwilling to Surrender (GUTS) and the Metropolitan Association for Continued Segregated Education (MASCE).[27] Curiously, however, private organized resistance to desegregation in Georgia had not gained the influence that it had in Mississippi, Alabama, and other parts of the Deep South. Efforts to establish a state Citizens' Council began in 1955, but in spite of an all-star cast of firebrand segregationists, such as Harris, Griffin, and Talmadge, the State's Rights Council of Georgia (SRCG) never got off the ground. Even at its peak in the mid-1950s, the SRCG could claim only 10,000 members, less than 10 percent of the total in the Deep South.[28] The Ku Klux Klan was also less potent in Georgia than elsewhere in the South. The "Invisible Empire" which recruited from the white working class, had its share of members in Georgia, and periodically held rallies on Stone Mountain near Atlanta. Still, after a surge in membership shortly after *Brown,* the Klan faltered. Although the Georgia Klan remained an intimidating force of violence—and carried out a number of bombings, beating, lynchings, cross-burnings, and rallies—factional rivalry and disorganization lessened its impact.[29] One of the more potent efforts to resist desegregation came from the Georgia attorney general, Eugene Cook. In a deliberate effort to weaken and distract the NAACP, Cook used his office to broaden his investigative power, and refine and tighten the common law offenses of barratry, champerty, and maintenance. His efforts led to a $25,000 fine against the NAACP and the jailing of the president of the Atlanta chapter.[30]

In spite of actions to stall the start of the desegregation process, the NAACP persisted. By May 1961, under the court-approved plan, black students in grades 11 and 12 were eligible to apply for transfers to any of the previously all-white Atlanta public schools. By June, although more than 124 blacks had applied for transfer, only 10 had been approved by the superintendent's office. Although school officials assured they were screening the transfers on a nonracial basis, the numbers told the real story. A third of those denied transfers appealed the decisions, citing race as a key factor in their rejections.[31]

As blacks sought transfer into the all-white high schools, a number of whites demanded transfer out of schools due to be desegregated. One case involved Sandra Melkild, a twelfth grader who petitioned to transfer from Northside, one of the three white high schools scheduled for desegregation, to Dykes. Sensing the case would lead to massive chaos and loss of funds, Atlanta officials denied her transfer, only to be overruled by the state board of education.[32] The state board policy allowed whites to transfer to public and private schools. Over the next fourteen months the state board approved $206,640 in tuition grants for 1,148 students who were attending a number of private schools in the Atlanta metropolitan area.[33]

As these cat-and-mouse games of compromise and avoidance played out, black college and high school students throughout the state were increasingly annoyed by the snail's pace of desegregation, moderates' acceptance of tokenism, and the state's continued resistance. Joining groups such as the Student Nonviolent Coordinating Committee (SNCC) and the Congress of Racial Equality, both headquartered in Atlanta, they participated in a series of organized and sustained direct-action campaigns in opposition to all forms of segregation. Led by student activists such as Julian Bond, the students first published a powerful statement demanding full citizenship rights in the spring of 1960. The statement, which was carried in the three Atlanta dailies, insisted on immediate rights, pointed out inequalities in education, jobs, housing, hospitals, businesses, and more, and announced that students across the state would enlist in the sit-in movement.[34]

By February 1961 the students staged sit-ins at Atlanta's downtown lunch counters. As the students persisted, Atlanta's old-guard black leaders, at the request of Mayor William B. Hartsfield, intervened. The protests, argued old-guard blacks, would impact negatively on the Atlanta school crisis, and possibly lead to the state's abandonment of public schooling. Mayor Hartsfield, through the city's old-guard leaders, passed along the promise that Atlanta's business community would desegregate their retail operations at the time the public schools were desegregated in the city.[35]

Preparing for Tokenism

The summer of 1961 was a time of preparation for what many hoped would be a peaceful beginning to desegregation. HOPE and sister organization Open All Schools in September (OASIS) led a publicity campaign and coordinated efforts with the mayor's office, Atlanta newspapers, and police department. A number of the city's religious and civic leaders joined the open schools groups to ensure a peaceful transition to tokenism. As a precautionary move, the Atlanta police barred anyone not directly involved with the desegregation process from entering a one-mile radius of the city's white high schools. An information center in the mayor's office, operated by OASIS, was arranged for the press corps to cover the event. On August 30, 1961, nine students entered the previously all-white public high schools without incident. It was the first peaceful high school desegregation event in the Deep South. School officials and the city fathers were pleased and enjoyed praise from President John F. Kennedy.[36] In the wake of tokenism, Georgia political leaders abandoned massive resistance and supported an all-out public school equalization campaign, freedom-of-choice plans, and the establishment of all-white academies.

Token Desegregation Begins in Georgia

Although blacks in Georgia had won two important victories in the courts (*Calhoun* and *Holmes*) and crossed the race line, the decisions technically pertained only to the public schools in Atlanta and the flagship university in Athens. *Calhoun,* the Atlanta case, nevertheless, was a particularly important ruling, and it became the prototype for desegregation plans for other school districts throughout the South.[37] What followed was an uphill struggle by blacks and liberals to bring about meaningful integration in the midst of passive resistance. Over the next decade the fight for school integration was to be fought school-by-school, county-by-county, college-by-college.

The struggle had many dimensions. At times it was part of an effort by white moderates to preserve the public school system, at other times it was on the agendas of activist organizations such as the Student Nonviolent Coordinating Committee, Congress of Racial Equality, or Martin Luther King Jr.'s Southern Christian Leadership Conference (SCLC). Liberal regional, state, and local biracial organizations, such as the Southern Regional Council (SRC), Georgia Council on Human

Relations, and the Greater Atlanta Council on Human Relations, also participated in the struggle to implement *Brown*. Throughout the decade local and national lawyers of the NAACP—Donald Hollowell, C. B. King, and Constance Motley—were central to the effort, litigating local cases, defending protesters who had been arrested, conferring with judges, plaintiffs, and adversaries.

The pace of desegregation continued for the next six years at a snail's pace, in large part, because pupil placement plans placed the onus of transfer on black applicants. The Atlanta plan's second feature—the grade-a-year mechanism—also served to keep the rate of change at a near standstill. By the summer of 1962, Motley, Hollowell, and E. E. Moore Jr. were back in Hooper's courtroom, asserting that the token desegregation of Atlanta did not constitute a good faith effort to end the dual systems of public education. As part of their protest the lawyers demanded that the entire system, including faculties and extracurricular activities, be reorganized on a nonracial basis. In the meantime, they urged Hooper to order Atlanta to accelerate the grade-a-year plan. The pressure pushed Atlanta school officials, grudgingly, to desegregate seven more high schools, admitting forty-four students by the summer of 1962.[38]

Meanwhile that summer, events in Albany, Georgia—a fast-growing city of almost 77,000 residents in the Black Belt, and the county seat of Dougherty County—captured the nation's attention. The Reverend Dr. Martin Luther King Jr., who had been arrested in an Albany protest in December 1961, appeared in court to accept a forty-five-day jail sentence.[39] Upon his release in August, King announced his support of a plan to bring about the desegregation of Albany's white high school. White Albanians, however, had well-established credentials for resisting desegregation and refused to allow the process to commence. As word of the plan became public, displays of graffiti appeared on the white school, including a large daub on the front of the building reading "No Niggers Please." Days before the start of the school year, the Ku Klux Klan staged a rally at the superintendent's office to block blacks from applying for transfers. A group of blacks, however, managed to avoid the mob and entered the building. School officials told the group that school assignments had been made for the year and could not be changed. Black leaders C. B. King and W. D. Anderson countered that they would not acquiesce and promised to file a suit in federal court. A year later King had secured a federal court order for Dougherty County and the city of Albany to submit desegregation plans by mid-August for the 1963 school year. When local blacks tried to accelerate the process, however, the federal court turned them away, ruling that the grade-a-year plan sufficiently met the letter and spirit of the law.[40]

In the early 1960s the NAACP legal campaign in Georgia pushed for desegregation in the most populated centers in the state, particularly the urban-suburban counties and cities of Atlanta, Macon, Savannah, Brunswick, Columbus, and Albany. Blacks in Bibb County, home of the city of Macon, filed suit in 1963, and after a long fight, won token entry into Macon's schools. With the start of tokenism in the junior high and high schools, Bibb County school officials took the novel step to segregating affected schools by gender. Black demands also led to token desegregation in Albany and Americus in 1965, but in spite of these gains, racial diversity in Georgia's schools in the early and middle 1960s proceeded at a pace that is best described as a slow, glacial crawl.

Local officials, with the consent of state lawmakers, ignored the law and circumvented court directives. By December 1964 only 11 of Georgia's 196 school districts had admitted blacks and were thus considered desegregated. Still, less than one-half of 1 percent of the black student population—1,337 students—was in schools with whites.[41] These numbers provided evidence that if *Brown* was to be enforced as the law of the land, a more forceful approach was needed.

A good example of this foot-dragging occurred in Dougherty County. At first it appeared that school officials would follow the example set earlier that year in the city of Albany, the county seat, but they decided to resist implementing a gradual plan and appealed an order to submit a plan. When the case reached the U.S. Supreme Court in September 1964, Justice Hugo Black refused to stay the lower court order, and nine blacks finally entered the county's previously all-white high school.[42]

The onus of implementation could not be left solely to black Georgians, who had long been short-changed by the system. In this regard, the NAACP and black activists viewed the passage of Title VI of the Civil Rights Act of 1964 as "late but better than never." Written into law in the summer of that year, and over intense opposition from Richard B. Russell, Georgia's senior U.S. senator, Title VI aimed to increase the number of blacks in previously all-white schools by denying federal dollars to schools if they failed to dismantle dual systems. After five years of enforcement the numbers told the story of how resistant the state had been to school desegregation: by April 1969 Georgia ranked second from the bottom in violations for noncompliance with federal law, and had forfeited seven million in federal aid.[43]

There were also black efforts underway to desegregate the private and parochial schools in the state, notably a handful of Roman Catholic schools in Albany and Savannah, and Lovett Academy, an Episcopal preparatory school in northwest Atlanta. The Lovett case gained widespread attention in 1963 when, after the son of Dr. Martin Luther King Jr. and two other black students were repeatedly denied admission, Bishop Claiborne withdrew church support from the school and suspended the headmaster. Claiborne's action drew the contempt of an acting headmaster, who resigned under protest.[44]

Making matters worse for integrationists, a number of academics weighed in on the alleged damage that integration caused blacks. The first instance of this in Georgia occurred in 1963 in the city of Savannah, when the psychologist Henry E. Garrett from Columbia University, the social philosopher Ernest van der Haag, and others challenged psychologists Kenneth and Mamie Clark's famous studies in the 1950s and testified in court that Savannah-Chatham County blacks would be damaged by integration if the dual system were terminated. Siding with the academics, federal district court judge Frank Scarlett dismissed the local NAACP's desegregation petition, holding that both races were damaged by integration. On appeal, the circuit court overruled the district court, noting that Scarlett's actions were an "abuse of discretion." The circuit court then ordered him to direct the Savannah-Chatham County district to submit a desegregation plan for at least one grade each year for the upcoming school year. That September, twenty-one black students entered two previously white public high schools in the district.[45]

Although overruled in Chatham County, Scarlett also had jurisdiction in neighboring Brunswick-Glynn County district. Brunswick school officials had quietly negotiated a plan with local black leaders to voluntarily desegregate that city's schools in 1963. Temporarily foiling the plan, Scarlett barred the agreement, reasoning that another hearing was required in order to proceed "with all deliberate speed." To alleviate the standoff before the start of classes, the school board called on Governor Carl E. Sanders to intervene, but to no avail. Finally, at the start of the year in September, the appellate court vacated Scarlett's order and cleared the way for the voluntary plan.[46]

The 1964 school year brought more resistance, more token desegregation in the urban and suburban areas, and increased black pressure to make Georgia live up to the letter and spirit of *Brown*. It also was a turning point in the desegregation of southern schools, due to the unprecedented involvement of the federal courts and federal executive in the process. President Lyndon B. Johnson, responding to pressure from the larger civil rights movement, directed the Justice Department to encourage the federal court to speed up the desegregation process in the *Calhoun* case. Johnson's actions prompted appeals, and the U.S. Supreme Court took on the case. Atlanta officials testified that the grade-a–year/transfer plan was working and urged the court to stay the course. Representing the plaintiffs, Constance Baker Motley and Donald Hollowell countered that the program failed to bring about a unitary system and called for a "redrawing of attendance zones based on school capacity and geography."[47] The U.S. Supreme Court ruling pleased neither party. The Court conceded that the grade-a-year program was progressing too slowly but was unwilling to agree that the scheme was itself flawed. The justices remanded the case to the lower courts and ordered that by September 1964 Atlanta must accelerate the process by desegregating grades 1, 10, 11, and 12, and add at least two more grades each successive year until all grades were desegregated. The high Court also weighed in on *Stell v. Savannah Board of Education* in Savannah-Chatham County. The defendants in *Stell,* backed by a number of leading social scientists as well as officials from seven southern states, called for a return to the segregated system, due to the "fact" that blacks and whites had inherent mental differences. Siding with the lower court, the high Court dismissed the argument, and ordered that the process of desegregation continue.[48]

Black Persistence

Throughout 1964 and 1965 blacks in Georgia, supported by the NAACP, the SNCC, the SCLC, and CORE, rallied against white resistance. The litigation effort worked closely alongside the direct-action campaign. Protesters in Moultrie, a small city in the southwest corner of the state, thought they had succeeded at getting the school board to meet their major demands for school improvement, including a deadline to submit a desegregation plan. But by winter, foot-dragging by the board to submit a plan spawned more protests, including a march by some 500 people on the county courthouse that resulted in the arrest of 150 high school students. These arrests then spawned a school boycott by most of the remaining students, leading to another 400 arrests. The boycott finally ended in late February 1965 when Moultrie school officials reluctantly submitted a desegregation plan, agreeing to hire more teachers, to seek reaccreditation, and to put in a sewer system and pave streets near the high school.[49]

If some whites begrudgingly conceded to black demands, others were determined to resist and evade. The city of Newton, in Baker County, was the site of some of this resistance. When a group of blacks attempted to enroll their children in the white school, the county sheriff and his deputies blocked their entrance, reasoning that the children had not been formally accepted at the school. Undeterred, the parents asked the federal government for protection so that they could register peacefully. Clearing the path to register, however, did little to bring about compliance. Although more than fifty students sought admission under the freedom-of-choice plan, only seven were placed in the city's white high school. When a white mob gathered at the school on the first day of classes, the students (under escort from members of the SNCC) chose not to risk making their way through the hostile mob. Other black students in Baker County, organized by the SNCC, responded by boycotting their segregated schools, but ended the boycott when token desegregation began. Events in Baker County drew the attention of the Department of Health, Education and Welfare's Office of Education, which investigated the district to determine if the county was in compliance. The federal officials were timid, however, and even amidst protests by the SNCC and the SCLC, did little to enforce a plan. Eventually, in 1966, as protests continued, HEW took action and denied federal aid to the county schools because of violations in their desegregation plans.[50] Although details differed, the pattern in Baker County was common in Georgia in the mid- to late 1960s: white resistance, black protest, and federal intervention.

All major strands of the civil rights movement were drawn to the adjacent counties of Warren, Taliaferro, and Green in the fall of 1964. Dr. Martin L. King Jr. and the SCLC arrived in the area to demonstrate their disgust with evasion tactics and impatience with token integration. Hours after a march in Crawfordville (Taliaferro), King arrived in Warrenton (Warren) to support a student protest to end their enrollment at the segregated high school and force their matriculation at the white high school. The students' parents, however, disagreed with the tactic and urged their children to stay put. The episode ended when roughly half of the students withdrew from the black high school and enrolled in a freedom school set up by the SNCC. The NAACP then sought an injunction against school officials in the three counties for delaying compliance vis-à-vis white designs.[51]

Taliaferro County was the site of the most intense school desegregation struggle in Georgia in 1964. White resistance and counter-actions by local activists, the SCLC, and the NAACP led the federal court to quickly review the hot spot. Earlier, county officials had put in place a policy that provided white students with transfers to neighboring schools, but severely restricted the number of transfers available to blacks. The scheme limited desegregation to a trickle, and encouraged massive white flight. In October, the court declared Taliaferro County bankrupt and appointed Claude Purcell, the state superintendent, in charge of the system. The ruling cleared the way for Purcell to offer a desegregation plan of his design. Activists had anticipated that the plan would forbid whites from fleeing Taliaferro for neighboring schools, but Purcell's plan took a different direction. Applying a "you can run but you can not hide" strategy, it granted blacks the same opportunities to win transfers to schools outside the county. For two months, as black students risked travel on school buses en route to the white schools, many whites boycotted and stayed home.[52]

Local white officials meanwhile used reading skills assessments, psychological tests, and other more subtle efforts to deny blacks entry, prompting the U.S. Justice Department to file a suit against Taliaferro, Wilkes, Warren, and Greene Counties for discriminating in their school operations. By January 1966, with federal aid cut off, school officials in Taliaferro responded by closing the county schools. Such hardheaded resistance and avoidance came at a high price; by 1986 Taliaferro County enrolled only 171 students in its public schools, having relinquished its responsibility for educating its students to Greene County. Meanwhile 12 percent of the students in Greene County and 17 percent of those in Warren County avoided desegregation by attending private schools.[53]

Despite protests and federal intervention, resistance to a unitary, biracial state school system continued. In 1966 a handful of systems in Georgia were found to be in violation of Title VI, and funds were cut off. By 1969, 36 school systems in the state had been denied federal aid for noncompliance. By the turn of the decade 119 of the state's 194 districts had not updated desegregation plans to bring about racial balance. Save Mississippi, Georgia led the South in the number of cases of noncompliance. Local officials and school boards complained that the HEW guidelines, which had changed a number of times since 1964, were confusing and unrealistic.[54] Indeed, during the decade, the guidelines had become increasingly prescriptive. By 1966 HEW had established time scales, regulations about school choice and geographic student assignment, program and facility equalization, and the integration of teachers and staff. "Significantly, student assignment guidelines were aimed at removing state-imposed restrictions limiting choice and moving toward a true freedom of choice policy."[55] For those who declined to make a choice, geographic proximity, not race, would be used to determine the placement.

In the late 1960s the federal courts closed loopholes in the law that allowed for evasion. In 1966 the Fifth Circuit in *U.S. v. Jefferson County School Board of Education* ordered the end of dual systems, and in 1968 the U.S. Supreme Court in *Green v. County School Board of New Kent County*, declared the county had an "affirmative duty" to desegregate and to create a "unitary system in which racial discrimination would be eliminated root and branch."[56] A year later in *Alexander v. Holmes County Board of Education* the high Court ruled that the *Brown II* standard of "all deliberate speed" was no longer constitutionally permissible. Every district, the Court held, had an obligation to "terminate dual school systems at once" and to operate "only unitary schools . . . [—] schools in which no person is to be effectively excluded . . . because of race or color."[57] These decisions undercut key provisions of Georgia's passive resistance strategy.

As the numbers of students desegregating schools in the state increased, school officials turned to academic performance to resist implementation. Specifically, resisters turned to achievement tests and grade-level performance as a means of justifying and delaying desegregation. The school board in Douglasville, for example, passed a policy to admit black applicants to white schools so long as admission "did not jeopardize the academic standing" of any of those schools. The most obvious example of "academic rationale" occurred in February 1965 when 79 pupils who sought admission to Murphy High School in Atlanta were denied admission and sent to all-black Howard High. School officials had set up special classes at Howard, allegedly to help the students improve reading skills, despite the fact that white students with equally weak skills remained at Murphy. Later, when schools were forced to desegregate, IQ and "aptitude" tests were used to separate students by race into different academic tracks and ability groups. School officials also used differences in behavior to justify segregating students by race in schools and classrooms.[58]

The Growth of Private White Academies

Perhaps the most egregious tactic of resistance used by many local whites was to flee the public schools by establishing all-white private academies.[59] By 1970, of the 34,000 students in private schools in the state, 20,000 were estimated to be there to avoid desegregation.[60] A decade later, as federal enforcement curtailed other forms of resistance, over 80,000 students attended 366 private schools. By 1989, there were 527 private schools, many of them white flight academies. Georgia historian Donald Grant reported that fewer than 20 percent of the state's private schools were accredited. In addition to modeling a means of resistance, white flight from the schools led to a decrease in support for public education. The most disturbing example of this occurred in Sumter County. Sumter school officials had ignored protests, court orders, and a lawsuit for more than twenty years. In the face of a ruling to desegregate in 1970, the school board evaded the order by lowering taxes and establishing the all-white Southland Academy. The school board was composed largely of county landowners, and these elites and others of their class sent their children to Southland. In its first year Southland enrolled 1,100 students, leaving the county's public schools 80 percent black. By 1986 nearly one in five students in Sumter County attended private school. Grant reported that prior to the founding of Southland the millage rate for county property taxes was 19.5, but by 1983 it had dropped to 7.[61]

The Georgia story, however, was not completely gloom and doom. *Southern School News,* a liberal periodical, reported in late 1964 that nearly fifteen hundred blacks had desegregated eleven districts and ten units of the university system. The year 1966 also brought faint glimmers of hope that the spirit of integration might be realized. In Augusta, a bastion of resistance, Mrs. A. M. Williams became the first black principal of a previously all-white high school, as the city announced that fifty-two black students would also be transferred to the school as required by federal guidelines. In Atlanta a football schedule was reworked so that sixteen mainly white high schools would now compete against seven mainly black schools. Breaches in the color line were underway across the region. Throughout the South, the percentage of black students in mostly black schools (90 percent or more), dropped from 63 percent in 1968 to 35 percent by the late 1970s. Within the decade, the region that had the most racially segregated schools in the country was now the most integrated.[62]

Lester Maddox and the Politics of Resistance

Despite these glimmers of light, implementing *Brown* in Georgia in the late 1960s and early 1970s remained arduous. Implementation took a turn for the worse in 1967 when an Atlanta restaurant owner, Lester Maddox, was elected governor. Maddox was a "born showman who never asked forgiveness for his segregationist stands." He first gained national attention in 1964 when, on the day after the Civil Rights Act was signed into law, blacks who attempted to enter his Pickrick chicken restaurant were turned away. With supporters behind him wielding ax handles, Maddox stood in the door of his restaurant with a pistol. Ax handles became his symbol of defiance, and to avoid integration he later closed his restaurant. As his popularity soared among segregationists, Maddox announced he would run for governor. Finishing a close second in the 1966 Democratic primary, Maddox forced a runoff with front-runner Ellis Arnall. By Georgia law the runoff was open to all voters, and Republican strategists urged their members to turn out the vote for Maddox, believing that in the general election their candidate, Howard Callaway, could more easily beat Maddox than Arnall. The strategy to defeat Arnall worked, but on Election Day neither Callaway nor Maddox received a majority of the votes (due to write-in votes for Arnall), and the decision was thrown to the state legislature dominated by Democrats. The legislature proceeded to install Maddox as governor.[63]

By April 1967 Governor Maddox was urging all of Georgia's school districts to fight the tightened HEW desegregation guidelines, proclaiming that the federal government had no right to dictate to state and local authorities how school funds should be spent. Encouraged by Maddox, Lowndes County school officials removed black teachers from a previously integrated school. Although officials in Lowndes County stood to lose $360,000 in federal funds, Maddox and his supporters remained defiant. The governor threatened he would take steps to allow for additional public funds to be spent on private schools. The actions of Maddox and Lowndes County officials drew the attention of U.S. commissioner of education Harold Howe, who warned school officials to reinstall the teachers or face the consequences.[64]

By the late 1960s inroads had been made in desegregating the larger cities and towns in Georgia. In rural sections of the state, however, as blacks sought entry into previously all-white schools, a pattern of harassment designed to discourage transfers to all-white schools had developed. Despite these dangers, blacks organized and protested. The town of Social Circle, fifty miles east of Atlanta (named because of its "exuberant hospitality"), was the site of one such struggle. In February 1968 fifty demonstrators lay down in the path of a school bus to protest the deplorable conditions at the town's black high school. State troopers arrived on the scene and dragged off the protesters, arresting all but six of them. Four teachers, two black and two white, also joined the protests by refusing to report to the high school for their teaching assignments, claiming the facility was substandard. When the school board fired the teachers, more protests ensued, as demonstrators marched to city hall and demanded the teachers be reinstated. As school officials and local whites resisted the demands, the number of demonstrators multiplied. When state police escorted the buses to the white schools by back routes, protest organizers threatened to block school entrances.[65]

That same year in Sylvester, Worth County, 175 miles south of Atlanta, the county's first two black students transferred to the nearby previously all-white high school under a federal district court order. Yet even before they had settled at their desks, they were removed by the local sheriff and held indefinitely on charges of delinquency. The children's "delinquency" stemmed not from their behavior, but from the activities of their parents, who were civil rights activists working in the area. If incarcerating the pupils was supposed to intimidate protesters, it seemed to have the opposite effect. While the sheriff's office continued to detain one of the pupils, a girl, an extensive boycott of three predominately black schools ensued, as protesters demanded the girl's release and presented the school board with a list of demands. By week's end the girl was still in police custody and the school board ordered the schools closed. After the federal district court ordered the schools to open in January 1969 on an integrated basis, the school board appealed, but the circuit court rejected the plea for a rehearing of the case, and ordered the board to open all its schools by the January deadline, or abandon them all together. When the schools opened in January the student was still in police custody. Her continued detention spurred more protests and attracted to the scene the NAACP, the SCLC, and the national media. During January and February more than 100 protesters were arrested and detained at a makeshift county prison farm. Finally, after ten weeks in jail, the federal district court ordered the girl's release. In victory, Ralph Abernathy of the SCLC led a march of 750 activists, including the recently freed child, through downtown Sylvester.[66] In the face of blatant resistance, the direct-action movement had succeeded in drawing attention to the bare facts of separate and unequal school opportunities in even the most rural parts of Georgia.

Although the desegregation strategy of the NAACP and other activists had the best of intentions—opportunity, social justice, and first-class citizenship for blacks—it did not always yield results that benefited black communities. Desegregation sometimes led to blacks receiving inferior instruction. A study by Horace Tate, head of the Georgia Teachers and Education Association (GTEA), reported that the desegregation effort in Atlanta led to the transfer of the most experienced black teachers to previously all-white schools and the least experienced white teachers to the previously all-black schools. Also, desegregation sometimes worked to take jobs away from black teachers and principals and to undermine the coherence and traditions in the school community. Black principals and teachers, who had served as advocates and role models for students in the schools before implementation, were often demoted or replaced with the advent of desegregation.[67] Such unintended results no doubt impacted the dropout rate and how black students learned and were disciplined.

The Order to Bus in Richmond County

The most important U.S. Supreme Court decision affecting the implementation of *Brown* in Georgia at the start of the 1970s was *Swann v. Charlotte-Mecklenburg Board of Education*. *Swann* in many ways represented the high point of the Warren Court's judicial activism, forcing the hand of state and local school boards and educators to live up to the letter of the law. Decided in 1971, *Swann* built on the logic of the 1964 Civil Rights Act, as well as the *Green* and *Alexander* decisions. *Swann* held that busing was permissible to achieve desegregation. In Georgia, *Swann* had an immediate impact in five districts, and set the stage for a revolution in desegregation that many thought was impossible in a deep southern state. Within days after the decision, a group of white parents in Athens unsuccessfully challenged a busing order, claiming that local school officials had violated their Fourteenth Amendment rights to "equal protection" by making racial assignments to achieve racial balance. The *Calhoun* case was also impacted when the Fifth Circuit Court of Appeals ordered the Atlanta School Board to design a new pupil-assignment plan complying with *Swann*. Savannah school officials had hoped that *Swann* would outlaw busing and had postponed implementing a federal court busing order to transport some three thousand additional students. But in *Swann's* wake, the local chapter of the NAACP pressed for implementation. Legal appeals reached the U.S. Supreme Court, where Justice Thurgood Marshall refused the defendants' request to halt the busing plan. The NAACP also used *Swann* effectively to bring Muscogge and Clayton County school officials into court and compelled them to redraft plans that were found in violation of federal law.[68]

The most publicized story surrounding *Swann's* acceleration of desegregation in the state unfolded in 1972 in the piedmont city of Augusta in Richmond County, near the South Carolina border. Augusta had long been a city of resistance, in large part as a result of the presence of Roy V. Harris, an outspoken segregationist editor and powerful state political boss. By the 1970s Harris's power in the state had waned, but his influence in Richmond County remained strong. When the Fifth Circuit Court of Appeals and the U.S. Supreme Court refused the school board's request to block an extensive busing plan, officials organized a county-wide boycott of the schools. On the first day of the boycott, more than one-half of the county's students stayed home. Over the week the protest narrowed, involving mostly the white students at the seven schools directly affected by the order. Augusta school officials continued to hold out on implementing the plan into the spring of 1972 as Congress debated a bill that reexamined racial balance. The bill would have required desegregation plans to be put on hold until all defendants' appeals had been exhausted. Although the bill was signed into law in June, Justice Lewis F. Powell of the U.S. Supreme Court ordered Augusta to proceed with busing without delay on the grounds that the purpose of the plan was not to achieve racial balance but to uproot illegal segregation.

Powell's action led to the first test of congressional law that aimed to weaken the requirement of racial balance and busing to achieve a unitary system.[69] Powell's ruling, based on *Swann*, was a key blow to the new federal law.

On the eve of the Richmond County boycott, state legislators called for a statewide boycott of the public schools to protest racial balance and busing. At first it appeared that Governor Jimmy Carter would support the boycott, but when the protest failed to materialize, Carter backed off his promise. It was a critical turning point for the new governor, who had national political aspirations. From that point forward Carter was able to cast his lot with forward-leaning moderates, as he worked to neutralize the racist and socially conservative stances of the Maddox administration and secure support for public education, an effort which upgraded the state's foundation program and established preschool and kindergarten education throughout Georgia.[70] Carter's efforts to "overcome race," and the Warren Court's rulings in *Swann* and *Green*, helped usher in a decade-long period of rapid desegregation in the state, making Georgia and the rest of the South the least segregated region in the country.

The Atlanta Compromise

Although efforts to resist busing in Augusta were blocked by Justice Powell, busing in Georgia's largest city remained controversial through the late 1960s and early 1970s. By January 1969 the *Calhoun* case marked its twelfth anniversary. Over that period there were 292 legal moves in the case, an average of two a month. Atlanta's integration plan had changed dramatically over the years, beginning cautiously as a pupil placement and a grade-a-year plan, then to a freedom-of-choice plan, and finally to a hard-hitting racial balance design. The adjustments were made to accommodate revised federal laws and court decisions that had been spurred by protest and relentless white resistance. Judge Hooper had been with the case from the start, and in late 1968 he ordered the system to merge the faculty and student bodies and to achieve racial balance. The racial composition of the faculties at each school were to reflect the racial ratio of the city as a whole, 57 percent black and 43 percent white. As teachers organized to protect themselves from transfer, the main question was whether Hooper would follow a recent ruling handed down by U.S. Supreme Court justice Hugo Black that required exact racial balance ratios, or whether he would follow a ruling by the circuit court that gave schools more flexibility by allowing for a ratio range. If Hooper's order was designed around Black's ruling, it would require the transfer of 1,800 of the city's 5,000 teachers. With Lester Maddox's support, 1,500 white students and teachers marched in downtown Atlanta to protest the impending transfers.[71] Meanwhile, a group of 500 parents came together to protest and to attempt to influence Hooper's impending ruling. The *New York Times* reported that 120 teachers resigned.[72]

Teacher transfers dominated local news coverage for most of the year. Hooper persisted in following federal precedent, but perhaps in response to Maddox's actions, allowed for flexibility in his order. Hooper approved a design that transferred 1,400 teachers, mostly whites, to predominately black schools. Despite some protest, Atlanta's teachers accepted transfer under a lottery system. The transfers started in March 1970 and were completed the following year.[73] With the transfer process underway, Hooper turned to the second feature of his ruling, that the district merge its white and black schools into a unitary system. Achieving racial balance among the student body—in a system involving 150 schools, 39,000 whites and 70,000 blacks—would prove far more elusive.

By 1970, as other states responded to federal pressure and experimented with busing as a means to bring about racial balance, some observers in Atlanta warned that such a move would result in white flight from the city and school privatization, leaving in its wake an all-black school system. Even the idea of busing led large numbers of whites to threaten to boycott the schools.[74] "[L]et it be known, in no uncertain terms," declared Maddox, who was elected lieutenant governor after his term as governor expired, "that you will not be an accessory to these crimes against our children."[75]

Such posturing and worries were in the forefront among Atlanta's school officials, who in January 1970, sat down to piece together a no-busing, neighborhood school plan for the Hooper court. The plan, which created attendance zones to honor the neighborhood school concept, fell far short of moving Atlanta toward a unitary system. Only forty-three schools would undergo any change, increasing white enrollment in twenty-two predominately black schools by 12 percent, and black enrollment in twenty-one predominantly white schools by 9 percent. The plan would reassign thirty-five hundred students, roughly 3 percent of Atlanta's students, and leave untouched fifty-six schools that were either all-white or all-black. The plan contained a resolution that any significant desegregation would have to be accompanied by open housing legislation—new laws that would address discriminatory practices in home rentals and purchases. Hooper tentatively approved the plan and postponed the starting date until the 1970–71 school year.[76]

Motley, Hollowell, and the other NAACP attorneys had supported Hooper on the teacher transfers but were disappointed with his ruling to achieve racial balance. The NAACP joined forces with the ACLU and proposed an alternative plan, a mega school district design that would merge all the urban and suburban systems into one massive regional system. Hooper ruled against the proposal, pointing out that much of the segregation in metropolitan Atlanta was de facto and therefore beyond the reach of the Atlanta School Board.[77] Hooper's ruling was a prelude to what would become a shift away from judicial activism by the Warren Court. Within two years' time, the U.S. Supreme Court, under the newly appointed chief justice Warren Burger would rule in *Milliken v. Bradley* (1974) against busing students across district lines in metropolitan Detroit to achieve integration. The decision exempted suburban districts from assisting in desegregating urban schools and was the first to limit the use of busing as a remedy.

During the fall of 1972 the NAACP appealed Hooper's ruling, and proposed a plan that called for busing 18,400 students to desegregate 106 predominately black schools. For a while it had appeared that a massive busing plan would prevail, but speculation began that the plan would accelerate white flight to the suburbs and leave the Atlanta schools virtually all-black. Opponents to busing, as they had done before, intensified their protests. At a city school board meeting one woman voiced her opposition in the form of a threat: "The whites would leave [Atlanta] and let the blacks have it."[78]

It was in this context that Benjamin E. Mays (along with other local leaders) made what was and continues to be a highly controversial decision that changed the course of implementing *Brown* in Georgia. Just before Thanksgiving, the retired president of Morehouse College, NAACP member, and newly elected Atlanta School Board president, called for a settlement of the *Calhoun* case. As school board president, he then collaborated with the local chapter of the NAACP to develop an alternative plan.

Given that Mays was a revered leader in the black community and had been steadfast in his support for integration and civil rights, his actions seem out of place.[79] What might explain his decision to "throw in the towel" on desegregation? Was it based on threats of white flight—and a subsequent decline of the school tax base (and later public school support)—as the evidence above suggests? Was it due to pressure from a number of local blacks who were opposed to extensive busing of their children to achieve racial balance? Was it a pragmatic realization that it would be futile to continue channeling resources into litigation for busing and racial balance? Or was it related to a larger goal of providing children of color with quality schooling regardless of a school's racial composition, as some timely research had revealed?[80] A definitive answer to these questions, like true racial integration, remains elusive. What is known is that Mays was a well-informed and thoughtful leader. Thus, in the autumn of 1972 he undoubtedly had conferred with other old-guard leaders in the NAACP and the SCLC and concluded that for all intents and purposes white flight was a moot point. As many observers were arguing that an extensive busing plan would drive whites from the city, the pattern of white flight, in fact, had been occurring for more than a decade. By the early 1970s it was nearly complete. When *Calhoun* was first filed in 1958, 70 percent of the student body was white. In the intervening years thousands of white families and scores of businesses fled the city for suburban schools, leaving behind a student body that was, by 1973, 80 percent black.[81] As Mays put it sanguinely, "Massive busing at this point would be counter productive. We'd end up with no whites to bus."[82] Also, Mays, like a number of black intellectuals before and after him (notably W. E. B. Du Bois), had come to understand that integration was not an end in and of itself, but rather one of several strategies to be deployed as needed to help bring about racial uplift. Two decades earlier, in explaining his support for plaintiffs in the *Aaron v. Cook* case, Mays stated his position as to why desegregation would be useful. To argue that black children "want to go to school" with whites, he wrote, "is to miss the point entirely." "Mixed schools are not at the heart of the [Atlanta] suit." Separate-but-equal, he continued, is "a myth" because it is part of a larger system that disproportionately empowers whites. "[I]f one racial group makes all the laws and administers them, holds all the power and administers it, and has all the public money and distributes it, it is too much to expect that group to deal as fairly with the weak, minority, non-participating group as it deals with its own."[83] In 1972, one year before the official "compromise," Mays pinpointed why integration had failed: "Atlanta may have had a chance to preserve [the quest to work for] interracial schools as recently as 10 years ago, . . . but it chose to fight integration."[84] Mays, thus, was willing to "compromise" on desegregation for at least two reasons: He saw few (if any) tangible benefits in pursuing a busing strategy, and saw black administrative control of the district as an opportunity for black empowerment.

Led by Mays and local NAACP director Lonnie King, Atlanta's black leaders abandoned the strategy of busing. Instead, a *quid pro quo* was negotiated. *Calhoun* was dropped in exchange for control of the city's school system. Dubbed the "Second Atlanta Compromise" (the first being Booker T. Washington's 1895 speech), the agreement was a decisive move away from integration and marked the end of the effort to implement *Brown* in Georgia. The merits of Mays's choice notwithstanding, 1973 proved to be a watershed year for the NAACP in Georgia. After fifteen years of litigation that sought to bring about a unitary system of schools, the local chapter, ostensibly with the approval of the national chapter, accepted a proposal for minimum integration in exchange for maximum control of administrative positions. The plan left a majority of Atlanta's black students in majority black schools. In exchange the Atlanta School Board was given the flexibility to hire a black superintendent who would in turn bring black leadership to a number of the top administrative positions until there was a 50:50 racial balance within the administration. The agreement also called for 30 percent of the teachers in majority white schools to be black and required busing 2,000 students, 16,400 fewer than the previous plan. Although it appeared that the federal law would have been on their side, and that "integration was still a goal," commented Roy Wilkins, the NAACP's executive secretary, achieving quality education for black children in the South's largest cities was the primary objective.[85]

Behind the scenes there was far less consensus on the shift in strategy. As Ronald Bayor has found, local NAACP leaders thought they had the support from the national office, but Wilkins, who was under considerable pressure from integration strategists in New York and elsewhere, reversed his position and "ordered the Atlanta chapter to reject the settlement."[86] The disagreement was not quickly resolved and those in the Atlanta chapter who supported the settlement were suspended.

Conclusion

If the story to implement *Brown* in Georgia could be compared to a prizefight, there was no knockout blow that settled the score. At the end of the long battle, one could, at best, judge the victor to have won by decision. One judge might award the decision to those who argued in favor of *Brown* and those who put life and limb on the line in an effort to bring about a modicum of desegregation, and thus some degree of racial justice. This judge might take note of breaches of the color line, not only in Georgia's schools, but also in other previously all-white public areas in the state such as libraries, golf courses, restaurants, and shopping establishments. These developments, small as they were, no doubt helped pave the way for more tolerance, understanding, and social decency in the state and region. From this viewpoint, the struggle to implement *Brown* in Georgia was a set of incremental but nonetheless critical steps in the larger struggle for racial equality in the second half of the twentieth century.

Others who review the evidence will draw a different conclusion. In the end the will to defy *Brown,* though perhaps humbled by a highly intelligent and scrappy opponent, outlasted the contender's demands to install the letter and spirit of the landmark decision. The fighter with the most power in the wake of *Brown* was the segregationist, and it was he who consistently used that power to foil efforts to desegregate in good faith. As LDF attorney Constance Baker Motley said, referring to Judge Hooper in the *Calhoun* case, "I have never been convinced that he believed blacks had rights that whites were bound to respect. I sized him up not as one of the worst federal judges we had to confront (he was always dignified and courteous) but as one who believed that you make promises to black people and do not keep them—a typical segregationist view."[87]

Since 1973 a disturbing set of patterns and beliefs continue to undermine the quest for quality schooling and social justice for blacks in Georgia. By the late 1980s the Atlanta public school system was found to be one of the eleven most segregated urban systems in the nation and *the* most segregated urban system in the South. Moreover, between 1994 and 2001 Georgia as a whole experienced a slight *increase* in school segregation statewide.[88] Meanwhile, black children in so-called integrated schools in Georgia and elsewhere have been far more likely to be identified as less capable and intelligent than their white peers. They are also far more likely to be labeled as "exceptional learners" and placed in the lower ability groups and tracks in the academic program. Intraschool racial segregation is rampant. Compared to their white peers, black students are far more likely to be held to lower expectations and to be disciplined more harshly by teachers and principals.

Sadly, the only category where black children seem ahead of their white peers is in the dropout rate.[89] Even though we are more than five decades beyond *Brown*, the public schools in Georgia that blacks worked so hard to desegregate in the 1950s and 1960s continue to play a key role in structuring racial inequality and preserving white privilege.

The Last Holdout

MISSISSIPPI AND THE *BROWN* DECISION

━━━━━━━━━━━━━━━━━━

Charles C. Bolton

Mississippi resisted the *Brown v. Board of Education* decision longer than any other southern state; for ten years after the landmark case, public schools in the Magnolia State remained strictly segregated. Finally, after persistent prodding from black parents and grudging support for an end to segregated education from the federal government, in the fall of 1964 small groups of black children began attending formerly white schools in three Mississippi school districts. Between 1965 and 1969, most of the state's formerly all-white public schools experienced at least some school desegregation, although no black schools were desegregated. Throughout the late 1960s, the state stubbornly clung to as much of its dual school system as possible; the federal government increased pressure on the state for an end to segregated education; and thousands of black parents and children defied white attempts at intimidation and humiliation to attend a white school under the inaptly named freedom-of-choice mechanism. The real effort to desegregate Mississippi's public schools did not occur until 1970, following another U.S. Supreme Court decision, *Alexander v. Holmes.* This 1969 case, which directly involved over thirty Mississippi school districts but ultimately spoke to the entire South, ended *Brown*'s "all deliberate speed" timetable, which Mississippi had effectively used as a delaying tactic for sixteen years. *Alexander* required school desegregation "at once," and within twelve months the state's system of dual education was completely eliminated, although the transformation was accomplished largely on white terms, with often draconian costs for black Mississippians.

The fact that Mississippi fought so long and hard against implementing the *Brown* decision is especially tragic in light of the fact that the state's creation of a segregated public school system had proved disastrous for both white and black education in Mississippi. Like many southern states, Mississippi had only the most minimal public education system for either race prior to the twentieth century. During the progressive era, poor white champions James K. Vardaman and Theodore Bilbo succeeded in increasing spending on white education and consolidating the myriad and far-flung white educational operations. The result was a significant, but gradual, upgrade to white public education, fueled by increases at both the state and local levels in educational appropriations during the first half of the twentieth century. Despite spending increasing sums of money on white public schools, in the early twentieth century Mississippi was so poor that public schools for blacks in neighboring Tennessee were better funded than Mississippi's white schools. Politically disfranchised, black Mississippians were able to secure only minimal support from the state's expanded budget for education, but even these small diversions of public funds ensured that white public education in Mississippi remained decidedly mediocre. Despite the shortcomings of white education, as measured by per pupil expenditures, teacher salaries, or other typical gauges of educational quality, white Mississippians perceived their schools as top-notch, since the main quality they sought to preserve in their schools was their status as one-race schools. For their part, blacks remained disgruntled about the inequities of school funding, but with no opportunity for recourse through political or legal channels, they persevered, building a school system that provided education for their children by taking the minimal state support and adding generous offerings of northern philanthropists and a second tax on those of their race who had property to tax.[1]

By the 1940s, the inequalities of the state's dual education system became an increasing topic of conversation among both blacks and whites. Indeed, because of its recent transformation through increased spending on white education and the consolidation of white schools, the public education system in Mississippi became perhaps the most glaring refutation of the notion that separate could ever be equal in the state. By the 1940s, the amount of money spent on black elementary and secondary education in Mississippi remained ridiculously low, even by the standards of the rest of the Deep South. In 1942–43, Mississippi spent an average of $47.95 on each white child but only $6.16 on each black one. The corresponding numbers for neighboring Alabama were $48.92 and $14.91. In 1945 black teachers in Mississippi made on average about 36 percent of what white teachers earned. Hundreds, perhaps thousands, of black children did not attend school in the 1940s because of a lack of adequate school facilities.[2]

For a decade following World War II, blacks pressed for changes in the educational status quo, and white leaders offered a limited, and ultimately insufficient, response. In 1945, black teachers urged their professional organization, the Mississippi Association of Teachers in Colored Schools (MCATS), to initiate legal action if the legislature did not address the problem of salary inequities. The following year, a statewide meeting of black leaders called on the state's political leaders to tackle not only that matter but also the related issues of inadequate school facilities and a lack of teacher training opportunities. Over the next decade, in part as a response to black complaints but also in an effort to preserve segregation, the state legislature passed a series of equalization measures designed to ensure a more equal distribution of state resources between black and white education.[3]

The so-called equalization campaign in Mississippi, however, never managed to bridge the chasm that had been created between white and black schooling during the first half of the twentieth century. One problem was a simple lack of funds. Mississippi had barely been able to finance the upgrade to white education over the previous half century. Any efforts to continue improvements in that system, while essentially starting from scratch to construct a suitable school system for black Mississippians, entailed sums of money the state simply did not have. In 1945, Mississippi already spent a considerable part of its citizens' earnings on public education, ranking ninth among all states in percentage of income expended on education. Because of the state's relative poverty, however, Mississippi remained dead last in terms of actual tax dollars used for public education.[4] Quite simply, Mississippi did not have the money to equalize black and white education.

The equalization project also foundered because although state political leaders saw the equalization program as a bulwark against challenges to segregation, local leaders did not always agree about the imminent danger to segregation and frequently failed to implement equalization policies. A good example is efforts to equalize black and white teacher salaries in the years before the *Brown* ruling. State officials did not get serious about this issue until a Jackson teacher, Gladys Noel Bates, who was secretly backed by MCATS and publicly supported by the National Association for the Advancement of Colored People, sued the Jackson Public Schools in 1948. Although Bates and her husband were fired from their school jobs and their house mysteriously burned down, Gladys Bates saw her lawsuit through to the end. When a federal court dismissed Bates's lawsuit in 1950 on a technicality, the court did note that unequal teacher salaries had resulted from racial discrimination. To discourage further challenges on the issue of unequal teacher salaries, the state legislature approved, in both 1950 and 1952, special salary supplements for black teachers, but less than half of the $2.24 million allocated for this purpose in 1952 actually reached the hands of black teachers. Local officials took the money but failed to disperse it to the intended recipients. As Bolivar County superintendent A. H. Ramsey reasoned at the time, "Our negro teachers are getting all they are worth." Since local officials controlled the funding that made up at least half, and sometimes more, of the total education budget, the reluctance of local officials to accept equalization as a way to fix "separate-but-equal" education doomed the already flawed effort.[5]

Although *Brown* outlawed segregated schooling, white Mississippians refused to abandon the practice. Indeed, a number of Mississippi's political leaders urged resistance to the decree. The first signs of black activism on the issue of school desegregation were quickly squelched. Although some white Mississippians thought blacks would not attempt to undermine the dual school system, several black groups during the summer of 1954, in Amite and Walthall Counties and the town of Columbus, asked for a beginning of school integration. Each of these efforts were met by white threats and intimidation. After members of the Walthall County NAACP branch submitted a school desegregation petition in August 1954, local officials closed the county's black schools for two weeks and fired school employees thought to be involved with the NAACP.[6]

After the *Brown II* ruling in May 1955, which called for school desegregation to proceed on a timetable of "all deliberate speed," black Mississippians renewed their assault on segregated schools, while white Mississippians redoubled their efforts to preserve the dual school system by any means necessary. Shortly after the decision, the NAACP called for black parents to file school desegregation petitions with their local school boards. Approximately sixty of these petitions were filed across the South in the summer of 1955, including in five Mississippi communities: Vicksburg, Natchez, Jackson, Yazoo City, and Clarksdale. In all five locales, the names of the petition signers, anywhere from 42 to 342 individuals in the five areas, were published in the newspaper and the signers were subjected to various forms of social and economic intimidation, which caused the vast majority of the petitioners to remove their names from the documents. At the same time, the five school boards simply ignored the petitions, pretending that they had never been received.[7]

The experience of the black petitioners in the summer of 1955 was the fate that befell all those who challenged the dual school system for the next ten years. In Mississippi, violence and intimidation had long played a major role in suppressing black efforts to force a change in the racial status quo. The post-*Brown* era would be no different. In 1954, a group of private white citizens in the Delta had organized the White Citizens' Council, which quickly spread throughout the state and the rest of the South. The council was composed of the elite of Mississippi communities, and the organization encouraged its members to use its financial clout to intimidate blacks calling for school desegregation, by firing black employees, evicting black tenants, and refusing to do business with black merchants and landowners. Although officially opposed to violence, the council created an atmosphere in which racial violence flourished. In 1956, the state created the Mississippi State Sovereignty Commission, initially endowed with a $250,000 appropriation and charged with maintaining segregation through a network of spies and informants.[8]

While wielding the stick of intimidation and violence, white Mississippians also offered black Mississippians a carrot to maintain their loyalty to segregated education. Even after the *Brown* decision, a number of Mississippi leaders continued to advocate an equalization program as the best alternative to ending the dual school system. Governor Hugh White, who had pushed through a comprehensive (though unfunded) equalization program during a 1953 special legislative session, tried to get black support for funding his equalization plan in exchange for a pledge of fealty to segregation. White failed to secure such a commitment when he met with almost one hundred black leaders (one-fourth were teachers) on July 30, 1954. Following that meeting, state leaders resolved to continue the equalization program as a way to avoid school desegregation, but only after securing an amendment to the state constitution that allowed the public schools to be abolished in any district where school desegregation occurred. Whites in a number of white-majority areas of the state, such as south and northeast Mississippi, opposed the school closure amendment. The opponents formed an organization known as the Friends of Segregated Public Schools, which suggests that they clearly supported the continuation of the dual school system. But the Friends argued that the school closure amendment was both unnecessary and perhaps dangerous in the hands of Delta whites, who had traditionally opposed most measures supporting state-funded public education for anyone, black or white. A number of whites were convinced by the Friends' arguments, but not enough to defeat the amendment, which Mississippi voters ratified by a two-to-one margin in a December 1954 ballot.[9]

With the school abolition amendment in place, state officials moved forward with their equalization program. Unlike the pre-*Brown* equalization program, the post-*Brown* plan put some major funds into upgrading black school facilities and equalizing black and white teacher salaries. Between 1956 and 1960, the state government and local Mississippi communities spent approximately $127 million upgrading school facilities. Almost 70 percent of these funds went to improve black schools.[10] Many white Mississippians supported the state's equalization efforts as a "practical" way to preserve segregated schools. For instance, Erle Johnston Jr., public relations director for the Mississippi State Sovereignty Commission in the early 1960s, argued that "the only way we can retain our separate school system is through the cooperation of the colored race." Johnston thought this cooperation would be forthcoming by providing black Mississippians with "consideration and recognition and an honest attempt to make certain that colored people have adequate facilities to which they are entitled." Like many other whites in the state, Johnston believed that the state's black population did not want school integration, an intent that was clear because of "the fact that they have not tried to integrate our public schools . . . since the Supreme Court decision."[11] Johnston's claim conveniently ignored the black demands for school desegregation since *Brown*, as well as the state and private efforts that had silenced those requests.

Despite spending millions of dollars, Mississippi's effort to substitute a truly separate-but-equal school system for *Brown*, which declared such arrangements unconstitutional, was ultimately a failure. For one thing, black efforts for school desegregation, despite widespread intimidation, never abated entirely. Indeed, although many black Mississippians applauded the equalization campaign as a way to upgrade their underfunded schools and teachers, most saw equalization as a complement, rather than an alternative, to school desegregation. Such had been the message conveyed by black leaders in their meeting with Governor White in 1954, and many black leaders, such as C. R. Darden of Meridian, continued to support both the state's equalization program and the NAACP's drive to promote an end to the dual school system throughout the late 1950s and early 1960s. The state's equalization campaign also failed because it never actually equalized funding. Although by the early 1960s state appropriations had largely been equalized, local funding, which comprised roughly half of all education spending, continued to go disproportionately to white schools. For example, in the Jackson public schools (the state's largest district), which had a black enrollment of 42 percent, state funding by 1959 roughly mirrored the district's racial breakdown. Local spending, however, continued to slight the black schools; in 1959, black schools received less than 30 percent of the district's local school funds. In many rural districts, the disparity was even greater, especially in some of the Delta districts, where the vast majority of local monies were used to finance schools for a white minority. Although state leaders seemed committed to creating a real equalization program, many local leaders did not have the same dedication, and their actions proved decisive in undermining the effectiveness of the equalization effort. The most serious flaw in the state's equalization strategy, of course, was that the program tried to preserve an educational arrangement that had been outlawed by the highest court in the land. For ten years, however, the fact that black Mississippians had the law on their side mattered little, as the federal government did little to enforce the *Brown* ruling.[12]

The first implementation of the *Brown* decision in Mississippi came in 1964 in three school districts: Biloxi, Jackson, and the Harmony community in Leake County. In late August and early September of that year, sixty-one first graders entered previously all-white schools in the three districts. This first crack in the wall of Mississippi's segregated educational structure occurred largely because of the perseverance of black parents in the three locales. All were communities where the civil rights movement had sunk roots in the years since *Brown*. All three had launched school desegregation lawsuits in the early 1960s, as part of the larger campaign against segregation and also because of the continuing inequalities between black and white education. In Biloxi, the school desegregation effort was spurred by Gilbert Mason, a medical doctor who had led the first direct-action protest in the state in 1959 (a wade-in on the Gulf Coast's segregated beaches). Mason and his wife, Natalie, had also been disturbed by the substandard facilities and course offerings available to their son in the city's black public schools. The lead plaintiff in the Jackson suit was Medgar Evers's son. The elder Evers led the Jackson civil rights campaign until he was assassinated in 1963 by a white Mississippian. The parents who joined Evers in the Jackson litigation, launched just before his death, were in part motivated by a desire for what Medgar Evers called "equal school opportunities for our children." Among the complaints of the Jackson parents were more new buildings (the black schools remained seriously overcrowded while the white schools operated below capacity), better libraries, and better-trained teachers. In Harmony, the Hudson sisters, Dovie and Winson, had been recruited to the civil rights movement by Evers in the early 1960s. Part of the struggle in this isolated hamlet of independent black landowners in east-central Mississippi became a fight for desegregated schools. Although Harmony residents had been quite happy with their local school, built largely by the black community in the 1920s, they filed a lawsuit asking for school desegregation after the school was closed by the county as part of its equalization program.[13]

Despite fears that this initial desegregation would spark violence or a massive exodus from the public schools, neither occurred. Although both state and federal police forces stood ready to enforce the court orders in the three districts, no one sought to stop the black first-graders from entering the previously white schools. Pressure, however, had been applied to black parents in all three districts in the days and weeks before school began, diminishing the numbers that ultimately crossed the color line. In fact, in Leake County, only one student remained to desegregate that district's schools, although the children of fifty-two families had initially been named in the Leake County school desegregation lawsuit. A campaign of intimidation and harassment, however, had deterred all but A. J. and Minnie Lewis, who enrolled their daughter Debra at the formerly all-white Carthage Attendance Center. In Jackson, the Citizens' Council had launched a crusade to establish a system of white council schools to shield local whites from the arrival of school desegregation, but their efforts attracted relatively few takers. Apparently, most whites in Jackson were not as exorcized about the token integration of 1964 as local Citizens' Council leaders. More successful in the capitol city was the campaign by a group of moderate white women, Mississippians for Public Education. The women did not offer support for school desegregation, but they did successfully urge compliance with the court order and support for the maintenance of a public education system.[14]

In the early 1960s, it appeared that only through courageous black activism would any desegregation of Mississippi's schools be accomplished, since the only way to force compliance with the *Brown* decision was through individual lawsuits in every school district. While black dissatisfaction with segregated education continued to grow throughout the 1960s, as the failures of equalization became increasingly obvious, relying on lawsuits in every Mississippi school district to bring about the most minimal of school desegregation would have required both many years to accomplish and the willingness of black plaintiffs to come forward in every locale, many of which did not have the leadership of a Gilbert Mason, a Medgar Evers, or a Dovie and Winson Hudson. District-by-district lawsuits were not required, however, as the school desegregation landscape began to shift.

Although largely ineffectual in enforcing *Brown* in the late 1950s and early 1960s, the federal government increased pressure on Mississippi (and other southern states) to begin the process of school desegregation after 1964, largely through the passage of two key pieces of federal legislation. Title VI of the 1964 Civil Rights Act allowed for the cutoff of federal funds to any entity that practiced racial discrimination. That provision became especially important for Mississippi school officials after the U.S. Congress passed the Elementary and Secondary Education Act (ESEA) in 1965. This measure provided unprecedented levels of federal funding for public education. No state benefited from ESEA money more than Mississippi, since the funds granted were based on state poverty levels. Dangling millions of much-needed education dollars in front of Mississippi officials, while also threatening to take away the largess for violating Title VI, proved to be key in altering the stance of Mississippi segregationists. In fact, the state quickly moderated its position on school desegregation from "never" to "maybe a little."[15]

The Department of Health, Education, and Welfare had oversight of determining whether school districts receiving ESEA funds satisfied the requirements of Title VI. The initial guidelines adopted by the HEW were relatively modest, requiring school districts, beginning with the fall of 1965, to permit freedom of choice within a school district in at least four grades and to begin faculty desegregation. The freedom-of-choice mechanism was designed to allow all parents to choose any school in a district for their children. Mississippi officials, however, sought to negotiate an even less ambitious start to school desegregation. Citing the recent success of the 1964 school desegregation in the state, Mississippi school administrators asked commissioner of education Francis Keppel to allow the state's school districts to implement school desegregation on a grade-a-year schedule rather than the four grades a year proposed by HEW. The agency ultimately compromised with the state, allowing it to extend freedom of choice to only two grades per year to satisfy the guidelines, as well as delaying faculty desegregation until 1966. Despite this special consideration, one-third of Mississippi school districts initially refused to submit a HEW compliance plan, as state politicians convinced many local officials that either the U.S. Congress or the president would intervene to stop the HEW. When no such reprieve arrived, most of the districts agreed to submit some form of a plan, although many of them were filed only to avoid a cutoff of federal funds and did little to start the process of school desegregation. Although the HEW tightened its Title VI compliance guidelines in 1966, this change did little to expand school desegregation in Mississippi. In the fall of 1966, after two years of freedom-of-choice desegregation, fewer than 3 percent of the state's black children had moved into the previously all-white schools; over one-third of the state's school districts had made no move to desegregate their schools; and no white child had chosen to attend a black school.[16] In effect, freedom-of-choice school desegregation became merely another mechanism to avoid eliminating the state's dual school system.

Obviously, freedom of choice placed all the onus of eliminating dual schools on black parents and teachers, and many white Mississippians initially believed that few blacks would take advantage of the system and request transfers to the white schools. Thousands of black Mississippians, however, decided to take up the burden. Some saw school desegregation as part of the larger freedom struggle being waged against Mississippi's system of racial apartheid. Others recognized that as long as the state's segregated school system continued to exist, black education would continue to be shortchanged. Mary Blackmon, one of two black students to desegregate the white high school in Canton in 1965, remembered that she did not "feel like I had to be with a certain group of people, that was not the point. The point was that we didn't feel like our schools were equal. We didn't feel like we got equal equipment, or textbooks, or anything."[17]

The numbers of black parents who exercised their "choice" and selected a white school for their children in 1965 and 1966 did remain relatively small, because whites worked hard to sidetrack the procedures. For one thing, although one requirement of the freedom-of-choice program was that school districts mail their patrons instructions about the new procedures, one study found that fewer than 3 percent of black parents ever received any notification. In addition, whites, once they realized some blacks would indeed choose to send their children to white schools, responded with a campaign of intimidation and violence. Black students seeking transfers were frequently required to take achievement tests in order to "qualify" for a move to the white schools. Black parents who chose to transfer their children into the white schools faced a variety of white pressure. To cite just a few of the hundreds of instances that occurred in 1965 and 1966, in Clay County, Johnnie Thomas lost his job and had his welfare aid discontinued; in addition, his nine children, who typically chopped cotton in the summer months for area farmers, could not find employment the summer after they entered the white schools. In Tallahatchie County, local whites harassed the families of two black girls who entered a previously all-white school. The father of one was summoned to town by a group of whites, who told him "he better keep his girl from going to the white school." In the same county, whites visited the home of the other girl, beat up her father, and shot him in both legs. In Rankin County, many of the black parents who came to register their children at the white schools—which was held on a separate day than the white registration—were intimidated by the presence of local police and the state highway patrol. Despite the law enforcement presence, two of the parents were physically threatened during the registration process. One of the other parents lost his credit after registration, while another group of parents were sent a letter by their landlord after registration day asking them to sign a pledge to withdraw their children from the white schools.[18]

The black children who did enter the white schools under freedom-of-choice plans also frequently faced harassment and intimidation from white students and sometimes even from white teachers. In most cases, there would only be a handful of black students at a white school. The newcomers were greeted with insults and jeers from the white students, as well as other forms of indignity and danger, such as being spit on or having rocks thrown at them. Black students were also oftentimes segregated at lunch, on the playground, and, in some cases, in their classrooms. White teachers were sometimes as rude and unkind toward the black students as the white children, although many of the black students desegregating the white schools reported respectful and fair treatment at the hands of the white teaching corps. The worst instances of white harassment typically occurred in the first year or two of desegregation. Although the harassment of black parents and students declined somewhat after 1967, the two years of pressure had its intended effect. Only the most dedicated black parents subjected themselves and their children to a system of school desegregation that whites continued to resist with passion. Not surprisingly, the number of black students crossing over to the white schools under the freedom-of-choice system continued to remain quite small: fewer than 7 percent by the 1968–69 school year.[19]

Even as Mississippi officials claimed that they had eliminated the state's dual school system by agreeing to freedom-of-choice plans, the state continued to champion its equalization program as a way to improve the black schools, where the vast majority of Mississippi's black children continued to receive their education. As in the past, however, the state's equalization program fell short of actually equalizing black and white education, because the state still did not have the necessary funds to construct two quality school systems. When additional federal money became available under the ESEA (much of it through the Title I program, which was designed to supplement the instruction of disadvantaged children), the state used these new federal funds to help with equalization expenses, such as upgrading black schools or hiring additional teachers at black schools to relieve overcrowding, items that should have been covered by the regular state budget. Even more problematic, some districts used the Title I money to upgrade white schools, and in a few instances, to supply the needs of private, segregation academies.[20]

So, while white hostility to school desegregation kept the number of black transfers to the white schools down, the state continued to only half-heartedly make the necessary investments to improve conditions in the black schools. Leake County, one of the first three locations to experience school desegregation in 1964, is a good example. In 1967, fewer than ten blacks had enrolled in the previously all-white Carthage High

School, primarily, according to one observer, because "the experience of the Negro students at the white schools have not been encouraging and as a result people are quite apprehensive about sending their children to formerly white schools." At the same time, the local black high school, Jordan High, was seriously overcrowded, with many classes of forty or more, well above the state-mandated maximum class size. One parent of a Jordan student complained that conditions at the school were so bad that on some days classes were not even held; students would spend a good part of the day in extended recess.[21]

Ultimately, freedom-of-choice schools represented merely a new way to delay abolishing the South's dual system, a fact increasingly recognized by the federal courts. In 1968, the U.S. Supreme Court, in *Green v. County School Board of New Kent County, Virginia,* characterized freedom-of-choice plans as a beginning, not the end, of a process to end the South's dual school system and ordered school boards to adopt plans that led to real school integration. The following year, in a Mississippi case, *Alexander v. Holmes,* the Supreme Court ruled that "'all deliberate speed' for desegregation is no longer permissible. . . . The obligation of school districts is to terminate dual school systems at once and to operate only unitary schools." A judgment on whether or not a school system had actually created a unitary school system would be based on whether or not individual schools remained racially identifiable as "black" schools or "white" schools.[22]

As the *Alexander* litigation worked its way through the federal court system, white Mississippians lamented the possible abolition of freedom of choice. They could not really envision a system that truly integrated the public schools; indeed, for over fifteen years, they had managed to evade the *Brown* mandate, and they urged their leaders to find some way to preserve their treasured system of segregated schools. Lana Booker in east Mississippi told Senator John C. Stennis in August 1969 that "I can not go along with this mixing the races. I will not permit my child to be taught that its allright. I can see it in the Army and college but not my little 7 year old. Never! All negros study is sex." Mr. and Mrs. Rudolph Harrison of Meridian believed that school integration was "Communist inspired from beginning to end to promote marriage between the Negro and White races in order to weaken the high standards of education we now have, our morals, and every phase of our way of life." They told Senator Stennis that they "appreciate your efforts in endeavoring to keep our school segregated, and believe we can count

on you to do everything within your power to keep on doing so." Mrs.
Lavon Wade of Clarke County lamented the *"total integration of our
schools* and doing away with the freedom-of-choice plan. Maybe even
putting our white children in negro schools in negro communities." She
reminded Senator Stennis to use his influence with President Nixon: "We
know you have the power and are in a position to *Bargain* with him.
Please do this for our *white schools of Mississippi.*"[23]

Senator Stennis and other Mississippi politicians did indeed try to
preserve freedom of choice as a way to forestall the actual integration of
the public schools. These efforts, however, secured only the most limited
of delays. Rather than beginning the massive integration of the state's
schools in the fall of 1969, that process was forestalled only until after
the *Alexander* ruling came out in October 1969, with some Mississippi
districts forced to combine their two school systems in the winter of
1970, while the remainder had to make this transition in the fall of
1970.[24] Although finally forced to end its dual school system in 1970,
white Mississippians did not end their resistance to school integration.
In the early 1970s, they made one last stand to resist the *Brown* decision, either by completely abandoning the public schools or by looking
for ways to keep the now-mandated unitary systems as "white" as possible. Black Mississippians welcomed the end of segregated education
but soon recognized that the costs of the victory were high.

In most of the Mississippi Delta and other black-majority areas of
the state, the arrival of school integration in 1970 was accompanied by
a massive white exodus from the public schools. In some districts, such
as Canton, Tunica County, Holmes County, Noxubee County, Anguilla,
and Wilkinson County, practically every white left the district, moving
to often hastily constructed private schools. In other districts with a
similar demographic profile, smaller groups of whites stayed with the
public schools after integration, although these whites often faced
harassment and isolation from their white neighbors. In the Kemper
County schools, which had a black school population of about 60 percent in 1970 but that became almost 90 percent black after white flight
in 1970, those whites who stayed with the public schools became,
according to one observer, "social outcasts. No one talks to them and
they are eliminated from all county social functions."[25] In much of the
state where blacks significantly outnumbered whites, a new dual school
system emerged after 1970: a public system for blacks and a private system for whites, a situation that continues into the twenty-first century.

Fewer private schools developed in the white-majority sections of Mississippi, in part because the white population had fewer resources to construct a parallel school system and in part because whites in these areas of the state had fewer fears that their schools would lose their identity as white schools. In white-majority districts, the creation of unitary school systems mandated by the *Alexander* decision did occur, but the details of how that transformation proceeded were generally set by whites. While some communities created biracial committees to fashion plans to eliminate the dual school system, most Mississippi school districts utilized the time-honored practice of having whites make all the decisions. As a result, the creation of unitary schools in these areas often involved efforts to preserve as much racial segregation as possible within the new integrated systems or to ensure that schools remained as white as possible.[26]

The tactics used to accomplish these aims varied from district to district. Some schools initially tried to segregate classes by race within a school. This practice was usually overturned after some minimal complaining, since it so obviously violated the requirement for a unitary school system. A more covert and subtle way to segregate the school population by race was the adoption, by a number of school districts, of ability grouping practices. While such tactics perhaps had some educational value, they generally were not applied fairly when whites, most of whom readily assumed that all blacks were intellectually inferior, were making the determination of who the "slower" students were. Aaron Henry, longtime NAACP leader in Mississippi, noted he could level the playing field if he or other blacks designed the tests used to segment students by intellectual ability. The conversion to a unitary school system also required a reduction of school assets and personnel, both of which had been essentially duplicated because of the dual school system. With whites designing the plans, it is not surprising that blacks shouldered most of the reductions. More black schools than white were closed, though the numbers would have been even more lopsided had the state not recently invested millions of dollars in black school plants. Those black schools that were utilized in the new unitary systems were typically cleansed, fumigated, and remodeled to prepare them to accept white children. In the area of personnel, blacks clearly shouldered the lion's share of reductions. After integration, only a handful of black principals, coaches, and counselors remained, and the black teaching corps declined substantially while the number of white teachers increased.[27]

After a period of adjustment to the new reality of integrated education during most of the 1970s, in the last twenty-five years black and white children in many Mississippi communities—typically those where blacks do not outnumber whites and in rural areas outside the Delta—have attended school together on something more than a token scale. Given Mississippi's long and strident resistance to any school desegregation, this development is itself quite significant. In addition, the end of segregated schools has allowed state politicians to support improvements to public schools rather than focus all their energies on the education front on how to maintain an unaffordable, and after 1954, illegal dual school system. A good example of this change is the passage of the Education Reform Act in 1982, which raised teacher salaries, created a system of public kindergartens, reinstated the compulsory attendance law abolished after *Brown,* tightened teacher certification requirements, and reorganized the state department of education.

Despite these positive changes, school integration in Mississippi has not been a total success. Whites continue to shun the public schools in the Delta, and the exodus of whites there has meant a decline in the resources available for black education. In other parts of the state, racial tensions continue to flare up occasionally in those schools that are substantially integrated. In addition, many of the state's city school systems have become increasingly resegregated over the last twenty-five years, as whites have fled the city limits for nearby county systems that are more white than the city systems they have left behind. These lingering problems are perhaps not surprising, given Mississippi's long resistance to the *Brown* decision. The state ended its dual school system only under pressure from the federal government. The transformation was carried out by the same segregationists who had long battled the *Brown* mandate. As a result, the new unitary schools were crafted in ways that adversely affected black students and teachers. The legacy of that long resistance and the way the dual school system was finally abolished continue to haunt Mississippi public education into the twenty-first century.

A State Divided

IMPLEMENTATION OF THE *BROWN* DECISION IN FLORIDA, 1954–1970

Caroline Emmons

Despite its geographical location, debate has long raged over whether or not Florida is "really" a southern state. Observers have devised various methods by which Florida's southernness could be measured, arguing that Florida became more or less southern depending on where in the state one focuses, or on which era of Florida history. Florida's growth in the twentieth century, from a bona fide frontier wilderness to one of the largest and wealthiest states in the United States, makes it challenging to develop sweeping generalizations. In many respects, Florida serves as one of the best examples of the rise of a second New South after World War II, with a more diverse population and economy and, as a result, more pressure to reconsider older models for race relations. This transition was both a challenge and an opportunity for black Floridians seeking political and civil rights.

One issue in particular serves to bring into focus these debates about Florida's identity as a southern state: the *Brown v. Board of Education* decision of 1954. At the same time that Floridians were struggling to understand the implications of the *Brown* decision, the state's population also had begun to see itself as less southern and more Sunbelt. Of course, the demographic, economic, and political changes in Florida that followed World War II and the U.S. Supreme Court decision in *Brown* are not unrelated. Many historians of the period have observed that the war triggered an intensification of the struggle for equal rights. And in order to maintain the extraordinary population and economic growth of the post–World War II years, Florida's political and business leaders would have to moderate and eventually shed the state's traditional hierarchical structure based on white supremacy.

Florida's African American population had, of course, long had to confront the reality of a society based on white supremacy. Beginning with Reconstruction, black Floridians had resisted the inferior schools and facilities which were imposed on their children.[1] By the turn of the twentieth century, blacks in Florida had begun to form organizations whose purpose was to demand better treatment from their government. In 1915, the first branch of the National Association for the Advancement of Colored People in Florida was established in Key West, and by 1920, branches existed in Tampa and Jacksonville as well. From the beginning, these branches protested the substandard school facilities available to black children throughout the South.

In the 1930s, the Florida NAACP was one of the first in the South to join the battle to equalize the salaries of black and white teachers. Led by Harry T. Moore, a schoolteacher himself until he was fired by the Brevard County School Board for his organizing activities, the NAACP in Florida initiated lawsuits in counties from Pensacola in the far northwestern Panhandle all the way down to Miami. By the early 1940s, these suits had resulted in federal court orders to equalize salaries. The Florida cases helped create precedents in challenging the separate but equal dictum that would ultimately be used in the *Brown* case.[2] And perhaps even more important, the experience of local NAACP branches in mobilizing support for these suits enabled the members of those branches to see that segregation was vulnerable to legal attack.

Despite recognition by black Floridians that these victories were an important achievement, the pace of change remained maddeningly slow. As in other parts of the country, World War II served to accelerate the process dramatically. During the war, Florida's population growth began to surge, a trend that continued after 1945. Many of these new immigrants were liberal Jews who were appalled by the degree of racism they encountered in Miami and other regions where they settled. Indeed, anti-Semitism was also a significant problem in Miami.[3] In the early 1950s, there was a series of bombings of Jewish synagogues in Miami and Jacksonville, as well as other bombings targeting black activists. In 1951,

Harry T. Moore and his wife were killed when a bomb placed under their home in Mims, Florida, detonated.[4]

Moore's death outraged the black community, as well as the growing community of white northern transplants. The circumstances of the Moores' murder, as well as other racially motivated attacks against African Americans and Jews, offer evidence that Florida was indeed "southern," at least in terms of the willingness of white racists to use violence to preserve the status quo. But after the murder of the Moores, a flood of telegrams and letters inundated the offices of the state's leaders from tourists threatening to boycott the state, which naturally created concern among the state leaders.[5] The susceptibility of Florida to such outside pressures made it somewhat unique among southern states in the early 1950s.

As Raymond Mohl has described, Jewish activists in Miami were an important source of support for civil rights activities in the state. The alliance between Jews and blacks was not unique to Miami but that city does provide an excellent example of this collaboration. Mohl quotes Matilda "Bobbi" Graff, who was part of the Jewish influx into Miami after the war, as saying, "Miami in 1946 was a strange world to us. To the tourist, it was a fantasy land. But it was also a growing metropolis where segregation, discrimination, and blatant racist terror were the law. To a concerned human being, it was a challenge."[6] Graff was one of a number of Jews in Miami who sought, with other black and white Miamians, to create a less repressive climate in the city.

By the early 1950s, blacks throughout Florida were increasingly politicized and mobilized. In large part due to the efforts of Moore, the number of black voters had skyrocketed, and they were recognized as a growing political force (despite the fact that the percentage of African Americans within the overall population was declining).[7] Blacks increasingly had important allies in south Florida, with its growing population of transplanted northerners. And Florida was experiencing dramatic economic and industrial growth, especially in the field of tourism and aeronautics. Cape Canaveral's development beginning in the late 1950s spurred an additional influx of educated, northern whites who rejected the white supremacy of the traditional South.[8] These conditions helped set the stage for the unfolding drama surrounding the *Brown* case.

As *Brown* began its journey through the court system in the early 1950s, Florida's political leaders watched with alarm but little public comment.[9] The primary concern Florida politicians faced when dealing with education was the extraordinary overcrowding resulting from rapid population growth. A critical issue for these politicians was to figure out how to try to equalize school facilities in hopes of heading off court orders to integrate and how (sometimes whether) to build new, segregated schools to accommodate the growing population. The Florida legislature had, in fact, appropriated a larger proportion of resources for black students than white students beginning in 1940.[10] Some African American activists continued to protest the construction of segregated schools.[11] However, the African American community remained split over the issue of integration. In the spring of 1954, Constance Baker Motley of the NAACP Legal Defense Fund noted that some black teachers she met in south Florida were not in favor of integration and wanted to keep the focus on equalization of facilities. She advised the national office that more attention needed to be paid to educating the black population on the importance of integration rather than equalization.[12]

One of the first official reactions by the state government regarding *Brown* came from Florida attorney general Richard Ervin, who prepared an *amicus curiae* brief for the United States Supreme Court's deliberations on implementation of *Brown* (which resulted in *Brown II*). Ervin argued that the diversity of the state required different solutions for different regions and urged the court not to use "coercive measures" to force the state to move too quickly.[13]

The preliminary skirmishing in Florida over the reaction to *Brown* took place during a special election for governor because of the sudden death of Governor Dan McCarty. There was not much debate over school desegregation during the campaign, probably due to the fact that the Court's decision lacked a clear implementation schedule. Most of the candidates took the position that the state was not obliged to take any immediate action, and all of the major candidates criticized the decision. But the winner of the election, LeRoy Collins, would have to devise a better-articulated position quickly.

Collins was the product of the so-called Old South Panhandle, growing up in Tallahassee. Yet he would become one of the most forward-looking southern governors of this era, recognizing that he lived in a time of rapid change and that he (and his constituents) needed to reconcile themselves to a new reality. Collins resisted using the belligerent language and theatrics of some of his cohort in the mid- to late 1950s, and he has been credited by many historians with moderating the potentially explosive racial atmosphere of this era. Civil rights activists at the time recognized Collins's relatively moderate approach as well. Robert Saunders, Florida field secretary for the NAACP, wrote to the national office in 1957 that "Florida, when contrasted to the other states where there has been resistance to desegregation, stand [sic] . . . as a weather vane in the dead calm of what might be classed as the eye of 'Hurricane Freedom.' He added that Collins was trying to show "Florida's fitness to accommodate northern industrial giants . . . Still, his position is to maintain segregation for as long as he can."[14]

Collins was not an integrationist. In the spring of 1955, a special legislative session was held to develop a set of laws intended to delay or prevent implementation of *Brown,* but much of the debate continued to focus on the urgent need to address overcrowding.[15] By June, the legislators greeted "with relief" the *Brown II* ruling handed down in May; the reaction of legislators is indicative of the degree to which the United States Supreme Court had backed away from the implications of *Brown I.*[16]

In fact, the plan that Florida legislators enacted required several onerous steps for black students seeking admission to white schools. First, they needed to show that they had sought admission within a reasonable (although unspecified) time; secondly, that school boards had had sufficient time to overcome practical, logistical difficulties; third, that community committees were in place to deal with possible repercussions from integration; fourth, that studies would be done to measure whether integration would create a climate hostile to effective teaching and learning; and fifth, that the petitions of black students were made in "good faith and not out of capriciousness." Richard Kluger, who summarized this list in *Simple Justice,* described these requirements as "a horror chamber of legal restraints."[17]

At the start of the school year in the fall of 1955, no African American children were scheduled to attend an integrated school.[18] However, black parents in four counties (Hillsborough, Pinellas, Sarasota, and Broward) had filed petitions requesting the county school boards provide a plan for integration.[19] The school boards generally ignored these requests. Despite this slow start, NAACP activists continued to reassure their constituents that the association was at work, noting "our State (NAACP) Conference is very much in the picture."[20]

Shortly after the 1955–56 school year began, integration did occur in a somewhat unexpected manner. Eglin and Tyndall Air Force Bases, along the Gulf coast at the center of the Old South Panhandle, were federal military installations. The schools on the bases were staffed and run by the county but in 1954, the schools were taken over by the federal government.[21] And so, with little fanfare and no reported incidents, the schools were ordered integrated. Only two of the seventeen teachers affected requested a transfer because of opposition to teaching in an integrated setting.[22]

The most famous, and famously protracted, case regarding integration in Florida had been making slow progress through the courts for some time. The case involved the application, made in 1949, of an African American World War II veteran named Virgil Hawkins to be admitted to the University of Florida Law School. A number of federal and Supreme Court decisions by this time had ordered the admission of black students to graduate and professional schools throughout the country, including the South. The NAACP had taken Hawkins's case with a good deal of optimism, given the U.S. Supreme Court precedents of the late 1930s and 1940s addressing professional and graduate schools.[23] With the *Brown* decision, Hawkins and his lawyers felt even more confident of victory. But in an astonishing display of defiance, the Florida Supreme Court simply refused to recognize the *Brown* decision. Constance Baker Motley of the NAACP characterized the refusal of the Florida Supreme Court to order Hawkins's admission as a form of massive resistance.[24] While Governor Collins was willing to risk disapproval by the voters of his moderate policies, the Florida Supreme Court justices, who were elected officials, may have been more concerned about their political futures. The battle over Hawkins's admission to the University of Florida dragged on for nine years, and Hawkins never did attend the law school, although other African American applicants were admitted.

Aside from the integration of the schools on military bases, Florida's politicians managed to hold off integration elsewhere in the state. As in other states, Florida developed a set of "pupil-placement laws" that allowed local school boards to set the criteria for assigning students to particular schools. Despite the obvious possibilities the laws offered to circumvent or undermine any true attempt at integration, these laws stood the judicial test, because they did not list race as a consideration in placement, and became a popular means to evade *Brown*.[25]

In the summer of 1956, a group of black parents in Miami led by the Reverend Theodore Gibson, a local NAACP leader, filed suit on behalf of their children.[26] Although the case was initially thrown out for failing to prove a black child had actually applied to attend a white school, the NAACP immediately filed a request for an injunction to clarify the status of the plaintiffs' application.[27] Finally, in the fall of 1959, Miami became the first state-run school system to integrate when four black children were ordered admitted to the previously all-white Orchard Villa Elementary School. Yet even this decision was not as momentous as it seemed. The neighborhood around Orchard Villa was rapidly transforming from majority white to majority black, with nine hundred real estate transactions in the previous two years. White students who requested transfers to new schools received them and, as a result, only twelve students showed up on the first day of school, four of whom were African American. By October, Orchard Villa had four hundred black students and thirteen white.[28] As Shirley Zoloth, one of the Jewish activists in Miami interviewed by Ray Mohl, commented, as an experiment in integration, "Orchard Villa was doomed to failure before it started."[29]

Although white politicians in Florida seemed to be successful in the late 1950s in keeping schools segregated, other groups of whites were not content with that. White reaction against *Brown* and, particularly, against the NAACP, which had fought for and won *Brown,* intensified dramatically in the months and years after the ruling. White Citizens' Councils proliferated throughout the state; Ku Klux Klan rallies attracted large crowds in the Panhandle and the peninsula; and the Florida Legislature decided that it would see what it could do to undermine the effectiveness of the NAACP within the state.

Soon after the *Brown* decision was handed down, white Miami attorney Howard Dixon resigned as NAACP attorney for the local branch. Dixon said he had received a letter from the city editor of the *Miami Daily News,* who was preparing a story on the effort by the Miami NAACP to integrate Dade County schools. Dixon noted the increasing pressure being put on the NAACP and felt his left-wing ties would ultimately prove harmful to the association. In his statement, Dixon said, "It is obvious that attempts will be made to impugn and malign the motive and character of the Miami branch of the NAACP."[30] The editor was investigating alleged ties between the NAACP and the Communist Party.[31]

In 1956, the Florida Legislative Investigation Committee (FLIC) was formed by the Florida Legislature to study the "subversive activities" of the NAACP.[32] Similar committees were created in Texas, Alabama,

Mississippi, Louisiana, Virginia, and North Carolina; in Alabama, the NAACP was ordered to cease all operations within the state.[33] The effect was that as the NAACP undertook the arduous work of trying to get the *Brown* decision implemented, it also had to fend off attacks by southern legislatures. There can be little doubt that such attacks siphoned away precious legal resources from the NAACP.

One of the first targets of the FLIC was Virgil Hawkins. The committee counsel, Mark Hawes, grilled Hawkins at a February 1957 hearing about whether the NAACP was paying for his attorneys. In fact, Hawes was right that Hawkins's $4,000-a-year income from his work as director of public relations at Bethune–Cookman College was not sufficient to pay his legal costs, but it was the Florida State Teachers Association, an African American teachers group, that was covering those expenses, not the NAACP. The FSTA was so worried about potential threats to black teachers in its organization that it listed the Hawkins case simply as "Project X" in its budget.[34]

The FLIC also vigorously grilled William Fordham, the former president of the Florida State Conference of NAACP branches. The committee produced a document written by the national NAACP office advising local branches on how to seek desegregation within their school systems. The FLIC focused on the section that advised local branches to consult the national office as soon as possible when potential cases were identified, to avoid "compromising" a possible test case. The committee observed that this statement indicated the NAACP hoped to prevent local members from reaching any kind of compromise with local school boards but rather insisted on "full integration."[35]

The Reverend A. Joseph Reddick, a minister in Miami serving as State Conference president, was also grilled on this point. Reddick had sought to have his daughter admitted to a white school, and the FLIC insisted on knowing whether he had received a "national directive" from the national office, urging members to participate in integration petitions and lawsuits. Reddick replied that "the only directive we had was that the Supreme Court has passed a decision and that was the law of the land."[36]

The most sensational testimony in front of the committee came from Theodore Gibson. Gibson was not only the plaintiff in the first integration suit filed in Dade County, but he also served as president of the Miami branch of the NAACP. Gibson refused to hand over the membership list for the NAACP and refused to testify about the NAACP's alleged connections to Communism, citing the resolutions of the national NAACP office condemning Communism. When Gibson finally stormed out of the meeting, he was charged with contempt.[37] His case eventually went to the U.S. Supreme Court, where the contempt charge was dismissed.

The effect of the hearings was bad enough, but other forms of repression may have been even more frightening. Ruby Hurley, secretary for the southeastern office of the NAACP (which included Florida), wrote the national office in November 1957 to say that white supremacists "threatened to bomb the church and planted colored dolls with cut necks painted with nail polish on the church steps before the meeting to which I spoke Sunday in Jacksonville."[38] The White Citizens' Council undertook a letter-writing campaign to PTAs throughout the state, urging that parents be sure teachers did not permit interactions between black and white students.[39]

As Orchard Villa began enrolling black students, two other cases made their way through the court system. One was from West Palm Beach, where Dr. William Holland had sought to enroll his son in a white school. The *Holland* case had been filed at the same time as Gibson's, three years earlier, but had also made very little progress.[40] Hillsborough County, in which Tampa is located, also filed suit during the summer of 1959. African American parents in Pinellas (St. Petersburg) and Escambia (Pensacola) also sought to enroll their children in all-white schools.

And, not coincidentally, all these areas saw an increase in racial intimidation during that fall. In December 1959, the *Southern School News* listed a series of incidents, including the arrest in Dade County of three men armed with "dummy rifles" carved out of wood, from which hung signs with anti-integration messages. Individuals with similar "guns" had appeared in Tampa, West Palm Beach, and St. Petersburg. The signs read: "Death to all race mixers! Keep your schools white by massive armed force—Be a Paul Revere! Rally your neighbors to arms. Shoot the race-mixing invaders!"[41]

By 1960, there were suits and petitions being filed across the state. There was also a gubernatorial race underway. Governor Collins, while certainly less confrontational in his response to the *Brown* decision than Orval Faubus of Arkansas or any of the signers of the Southern Manifesto (which he declined to sign), nevertheless managed to forestall any movement toward meaningful integration during his administration. He did preserve the appearance of moderation, and there were no major outbreaks of violence while he was governor. His most-lasting speech was made in reference to the Tallahassee boycotts and sit-ins launched by Florida A&M students in 1960. In a televised address, Collins said that, in reference to the sit-ins at department stores in downtown Tallahassee, he thought it "unfair and morally wrong" to accept the patronage of African American customers in one section of the store and not another.[42] His speech received widespread acclaim by civil rights supporters and censure from segregationists. Collins typifies the attitude described by one reporter, who wrote, "A state divided, Florida sought a middle way between its Old South traditions and the point of view of its vast new population from areas outside the South."[43]

Despite Collins's pleas for moderation, the 1960 campaign resulted in the election of Farris Bryant, a segregationist Democrat of the "Old South" school. But Bryant also wanted to continue to attract business and industry to Florida. As a result, his rhetoric was not necessarily reflected in his behavior; in general, Bryant wanted to leave the issue of desegregation to the local school districts.[44] Bryant was caught in a difficult situation; his voting base expected him to maintain segregation but he was also committed to continue the modernization of Florida's economy. Florida's new image as part of the technologically cutting-edge Sunbelt was simply not consistent with its Old South commitment to white supremacy.

The first school district in northern Florida to implement a desegregation plan was Escambia County. Under pressure from the federal court, Escambia agreed not to fight an order requiring a desegregation plan be implemented in the fall of 1961.[45] Nevertheless, the plan still relied heavily on pupil-placement laws, with the mere promise that the laws would be applied without regard to race. Constance Baker Motley, the NAACP attorney, said such a plan was totally unacceptable.[46] In the fall of 1961, Volusia and Broward Counties, on the Atlantic coast, made steps toward token integration; along with Dade County, this brought the total number of Florida counties with any form of integration to three out of sixty-seven.[47] By October, Palm Beach County had been added to the list. The following month, in Hillsborough County, the NAACP State Conference president's son, Benjamin Lowry, was admitted to a white school for handicapped children, although he remained the only example of integration in Tampa.[48]

Tallahassee, the site of an active civil rights struggle since the mid-1950s, including the rise to prominence of Reverend C. K. Steele, one of the Southern Christian Leadership Conference leaders, was the second north Florida community to begin moving toward desegregation. The case coming out of Tallahassee ended up in federal judge Harrold Carswell's court; Glenda Rabby says, "It would be impossible to over-estimate the role of Judge Carswell in the desegregation suits" that were filed in the northern district of the federal court.[49] Although Carswell moved more slowly than the NAACP would have preferred, he did at least insist that some proof of implementation be provided by north Florida school boards.

By 1961, other demographic changes in Florida affected the process of school desegregation. The Cuban Revolution led to an exodus of wealthy, educated Cubans into south Florida. By December 1961, school administrators in Dade County reported that the influx of ten thousand Cuban children had eased the challenge of desegregation, as these children were accustomed to integrated schools in Cuba and were helping "regular" pupils with that change.[50]

By the fall of 1962, the pace of integration began to pick up. Federal district judges Emmett C. Choate and Bryan Simpson began passing down a series of decisions ruling that, as Judge Simpson said, "the Florida Pupil Assignment Law has been used to perpetuate segregation and not to accomplish good faith desegregation."[51] In Escambia County, Judge Carswell ruled that Pensacola must speed up desegregation; however, he noted that just because all students attending a given school are of one race did not necessarily mean their constitutional rights had been violated and that the law did not require "compulsory integration."[52] Carswell's interpretation, although gradualist enough to help win him a nomination from Richard Nixon to the U.S. Supreme Court (although his nomination was defeated), did require that Pensacola pick up the pace. He eventually used the "Escambia plan" in his rulings in the Talla-hassee case, ordering "grade-by-grade" integration beginning in the fall of 1963.[53]

Nineteen sixty-three and sixty-four resulted in additional pressure from the federal government on the integration process in Florida. The 1963 U.S. Commission on Civil Rights found that integration was proceeding too slowly and the Florida Advisory Group to the Commission noted that education for blacks was still "markedly inferior" to that offered whites.[54] But a much more powerful tool for integration was implemented in 1964, with the passage of the Civil Rights Act. Southern schools relied on the $200 million in federal aid and an additional federal education bill passed in 1965 offered the possibility of another $500 million in educational assistance. However, to receive these funds, President Johnson expected that southern schools would show greater progress toward desegregation.[55]

As the federal government gained new tools for forcing southern states to desegregate, African Americans in Florida sought to accelerate the process. In the spring of 1964, violence broke out in Jacksonville at New Stanton High School, when students stoned the cars of white reporters. At all-white Central High School, shots were fired, and at all-black James Weldon Johnson Middle School, students tried to set fire to the school building.[56] Tensions ran higher in the summer of 1964, when five members of the Ku Klux Klan were arrested on charges of conspiring to bomb the home of six-year-old Donald Godfrey, the only black student at Lackawanna Elementary School.[57] Civil rights demonstrations in St. Augustine, not far south of Jacksonville, throughout 1964 led to violent reprisals from white supremacists; these clashes received extensive media coverage and no doubt added to the volatility of the situation.

In early December 1964, the Southern Association of Colleges and Schools removed accreditation from fifteen high schools in Duval County (of which Jacksonville is the county seat), leaving the black population angry and frustrated. Led by the president of the Florida State Conference of NAACP Branches, Rutledge Pearson, who was also a teacher in the Duval County system, seventeen thousand black students began a three-day boycott of the schools. The boycott ended when school officials promised to do whatever was necessary to restore accreditation.[58] However, Pearson continued to be harassed by city officials and ultimately lost his job.

Governor Haydon Burns, elected in 1964, continued the policies of his predecessor, trying to avoid the extremist behavior of some southern governors while maintaining at least a rhetorical position in defense of segregation.[59] But the 1964 Civil Rights Act made this increasingly difficult, given that Florida received a total of $29 million in federal funding, which would be jeopardized by a failure on the part of the state to make acceptable progress toward desegregation.[60] So the news released in May 1965 that Florida was in compliance with Department of Health, Education and Welfare guidelines, with sixty of sixty-seven counties either desegregating or under Court ordered plans to do so, was welcomed by the State administration.[61]

However, the HEW guidelines proved to be a poor test of actual integration. Only 9.67 percent of Florida's public school students were in schools with any degree of integration.[62] In addition, a number of so-called segregation academies had opened across the state (and indeed, across the entire South) to ensure that white students did not attend school with blacks.

Somewhat unexpectedly, Florida elected its first Republican governor of the twentieth century, Claude Kirk, in 1966. Kirk's election is characteristic of changing dynamics within the two major parties in the South in the mid- to late 1960s. As the Democrats became increasingly identified with civil rights, the Republicans were well positioned to attract dissatisfied white voters who had been Democrats as well as snowbird Republicans migrating into the state. Kirk was elected on a strong pro-business platform but also wanted to slow down implementation of integration plans. Kirk declined to participate in a meeting of southern governors to devise a plan to resist federal intrusion into southern civil rights, organized by George Wallace and Lester Maddox, among others, but he shared some philosophical positions with them. As David Colburn has written, Kirk's position "reflected a growing perception among Floridians that because of demographic changes, the state should no longer be defined in just regional or southern terms."[63] Nevertheless, he strongly opposed the use of busing to achieve integration, writing in 1970 that "we have the task of continuing to wage war on forced busing wherever it rears its ugly head."[64]

In 1968, the United States Supreme Court struck down most pupil-placement and freedom-of-choice plans in *Green v. Board of Education of New Kent County, VA.* Freedom-of-choice laws permitted, at least ostensibly, students to request enrollment at whatever school they liked. Depending on various factors, such as the student's qualifications and space availability, students would be placed according to their requests. In reality, this mechanism enabled local school boards to develop coded language that allowed for continued segregation of students by race. After a number of challenges, the courts eventually concluded that these techniques were generally intended to forestall implementation of *Brown.*

At this point, desegregation plans moved forward more rapidly, although not without continued resistance by local officials. In Orange County (Orlando), substantive integration began in the fall of 1968. The names of all the teachers were placed in a fish bowl by race, and names were drawn to determine new assignments, with much "weeping and wailing."[65] One white principal called his new black teachers together to announce that they were not welcome in the school and that he could not guarantee their safety in the community so they were "excused" from any after school or extracurricular activities.[66] In 1968 in Pasco

County, a young black man, among the first to integrate the high school in that county, was detained after an incident on a school bus. As a result of this incident, his student draft deferment was revoked and he was declared eligible to be drafted to Vietnam.[67]

Despite these examples, reports by the Technical Assistance Program (TAP), which was a federal program created to assist states with desegregation as well as to monitor compliance with desegregation orders, seem to provide evidence of the growing commitment of many state officials to implement court orders. Whether this was due to a desire to maintain federal funding or to truly achieve racial integration is a fair question. Nevertheless, TAP staff found that in most parts of the state, there was a willingness to receive advice and direction and, in follow-up visits, to report progress.[68]

But the NAACP also kept up the pressure during this period. Although federal and state reports suggest the impetus for compliance came from within bureaucratic structures, it seems likely that efforts might have stalled without ongoing monitoring by African American groups. In January 1968, Kivie Kaplan, a longtime white supporter of the NAACP on the local and national level, led a protest in Clearwater against continuing segregation and inferior facilities at majority black schools. The protest led to the arrest of local branch president Talmadge Rutledge for obstructing traffic; his arrest, in turn, sparked additional protests by African American youths and NAACP supporters. Ultimately, Marvin Davies, NAACP field secretary for Florida, wrote in his 1968 Annual Report for the national office, Florida's desegregation process was "slow" because the so-called freedom-of-choice plans had "miserably failed."[69]

Kirk faced the most serious test of his position on integration in Manatee County, in the Florida Keys, in 1970. In late 1969, the Fifth Circuit Court of Appeals ordered Manatee County to cease operating a dual school system and achieve unitary (integrated) status. In order to implement this order, Judge Ben Krentzman instructed the school board to begin busing students. Kirk, who opposed the use of busing to achieve integration, released an executive order forbidding the Manatee County School Board from busing. When the school board chose to obey the judge and not the governor, Kirk took over control of the schools, calling the decision "immoral and illegal," and, after several days of unsuccessful negotiation, fired the school board.[70]

Kirk's decision was very controversial both within Florida and the nation, and he received a tremendous amount of correspondence. Most of the letters, from all over the country, indicate strong support for his position.[71] He was eventually found guilty of contempt and given a $10,000 a day fine for each day he kept the schools shut. Kirk relented and allowed busing to begin. David Colburn has noted that the Manatee County crisis was the "beginning of the end" of the debate over school integration in Florida; this might be an exaggeration considering the many expressions of support Kirk received, as well as the fact that some would argue that the debate is still underway in the twenty-first century.[72] Nevertheless, the crisis in Manatee did contribute to the election of Reuben Askew in 1970.

Askew was a moderate Democrat who promoted integration as both the law of the land and in the best interests of Florida's future. For the first time, integration of Florida's schools was strongly supported by the governor. Reapportionment of the legislature also occurred in the late 1960s and reflected the growing influence of the "new" Florida, which was more moderate and more supportive of *Brown*.[73] As Askew took office, the *New York Times* noted that he was part of a new wave of southern leaders, including Jimmy Carter of Georgia, who "rejected the racial politics" of their predecessors. Askew told his new constituents he wanted "improved economic opportunities and equal rights for all our people, rural as well as urban, black as well as white."[74]

The 1970s saw significant progress in integration within Florida, and indeed the rest of the South. However, the trend of the last quarter of the twentieth century shows that integration is not a goal that can be achieved with finality, but rather a process that requires ongoing monitoring. The Civil Rights Institute at Harvard University lists Florida as one of the states in which students of different ethnicities are increasingly less likely to be in school with one another.[75] In fact, the South still shows the greatest degree of integration in the nation, largely due to the continuation of court-supervised plans in the region. But in many respects, Florida and the rest of the South have become more like the rest of the country, that is, less segregated than in 1954 but more segregated than in 1980. Or perhaps, more accurately, the debate over whether Florida is, or was, really "southern" may have been made obsolete in more recent years as the entire country has become more like Florida, in terms of a rapidly diversifying population seeking to balance economic growth and equal opportunities.

African Americans continue to debate the legacy of the *Brown* decision in Florida as well as elsewhere in the country. At a conference on the civil rights movement in Florida held in June 2004, participants lauded the opportunities *Brown* brought them to attend schools with superior facilities, but many acknowledged the loss of community ties that are fostered through the operation of neighborhood schools. While none of the participants recommended a return to the pre-*Brown* era, several of them echoed sentiments heard in other forums throughout the country, wondering whether the focus on civil and political rights, under which education might reasonably be included, took too much attention away from other, equally important issues, especially in regard to economic justice.[76] Even if students are racially integrated, what difference does that really make when schools are still segregated by class? In Florida, as in other states, whites continue to disproportionately attend well-funded suburban schools while blacks and other minorities are far more likely to be relegated to impoverished urban schools. These questions remain unresolved at the beginning of the twenty-first century. Implementing *Brown* in Florida was hard, but finding consensus on its achievements and costs has proved just as challenging.

Promises of *Brown*

DESEGREGATING EDUCATION IN DELAWARE, 1950–1968

Bradley Skelcher

The long road to and from *Brown v. Board of Education* (1954) in Delaware began after Delaware State College's (now Delaware State University) loss of accreditation by the Middle States Association in 1948. State funding inequities between the University of Delaware and historically black Delaware State College meant that the latter could not offer a full complement of required courses and was unable to maintain library holdings suited for a four-year liberal arts college. This problem prompted a group of African American students from Delaware State College to file suit against the University of Delaware for admission. Vice Chancellor Collins J. Seitz heard the case in the Delaware Court of Chancery, titled *Parker v. The University of Delaware* (1950). Pointing out the inequities between the two schools, he ordered the immediate admission of the African American students to the University of Delaware, thereby making it the first public institution of higher education in the South to desegregate on the undergraduate level.[1]

Following this ruling, the state seriously considered closing Delaware State College and merging it with the University of Delaware. A strong lobby among alumni and faculty at Delaware State College, along with opposition from segregationists, convinced the state to keep it open. This debate revealed deep-seated opposition to desegregation at the time not only among segregationists, but also among African Americans who saw segregated black schools as nurturing environments. Many black teachers and administrators also feared losing their jobs, believing they could not compete equally with their white counterparts.

The *Parker* case also marked the beginning of a long collaboration between attorneys Louis L. Redding and Jack Greenberg. Redding was the first, and at the time, the only African American to have been barred in Delaware. His colleague, Greenberg, represented the NAACP Legal Defense and Education Fund; he was also the only white attorney in the LDF. The *Parker* case also proved to Thurgood Marshall, head of the LDF, and to his colleagues that they could directly test "Jim Crow" segregation laws by challenging "separate but equal" in public education.[2]

The following year, Redding and Greenberg represented Shirley Bulah from Hockessin and Ethel Louise Belton from Claymont in their suits for immediate admission into the all-white schools within their respective Delaware communities. In 1952, Seitz, now chancellor of the court of chancery in Delaware, heard *Bulah v. Gebhart* and *Belton v. Gebhart.* Following the testimony of social and behavioral scientists that provided evidence against state-sanctioned segregation, Seitz concluded that both black schools were inferior to their white counterparts and ordered the immediate integration of the latter. He did not, however, render a decision on the constitutionality of the state laws that had established the segregated educational system. Seitz thought only the U.S. Supreme Court held jurisdiction over such questions involving the constitutional doctrine of "separate-but-equal" established in *Plessy v. Ferguson* (1896).[3]

The supreme court of Delaware upheld the court of chancery decision, prompting the attorney general of the state to petition the U.S. Supreme Court for a *writ of certiorari,* which it granted in 1952. Two years later on May 17, the Court handed down its decision in *Brown v. Board of Education* (1954), declaring "separate but equal . . . is inherently unequal." It also upheld the Delaware Supreme Court's decision to immediately integrate the Hockessin and Claymont schools. The following year in *Brown II,* the Court determined integration of schools would proceed "with all deliberate speed." It also charged the Delaware Supreme Court with the responsibility to ensure the desegregation of education in the state.[4]

Between 1950 and 1968, Delaware struggled with desegregation as did the other southern states. To be sure, most of Delaware, at the time of the *Brown* decision, was southern in mind and tradition when it came to segregation, as historian Richard Kluger has correctly pointed out. It mirrored the South in its response to Reconstruction, refusing to ratify the Thirteenth, Fourteenth, and Fifteenth Amendments. Like other southern leaders during the rise of "Jim Crow" in the 1890s, Delaware legislators passed a segregationist state constitution in 1897, which created separate but equally funded schools systems. The state, however, did not achieve equal funding until the 1930s. Soon thereafter, the state slipped back to an increasingly disparately funded educational system favoring white schools. Delaware refused to equalize the separate educational systems for whites, African Americans, and Native Americans when challenged to do so—that is, before legal challenges beginning in the early 1950s. Following the *Brown* decision, Delaware claimed tradition in its justification for taking a deliberate approach to desegregation. Essentially, the state asserted that both white and black people preferred separation. Thus, Delaware insisted upon "gradual adjustments" toward desegregation of education, taking into account its traditional separation of the races.[5]

Between *Brown I* and *Brown II,* Delaware wrestled with two of five questions asked by the U.S. Supreme Court in 1953. These were key questions about "gradual adjustments" to desegregation. The Court asked if black children would be admitted to schools of their choice. The other question was a portent of what lay ahead for Delaware and the other southern states. Could the Court "permit effective gradual adjustment to be brought about from existing segregated systems to a system not based on color distinctions?"[6] At best, the state could only promise "gradual adjustment," taking into consideration the cultural and social attitudes of Delawareans who had accepted segregation as tradition.[7]

Civil rights activists, however, insisted upon immediate integration, allowing children to attend the school of their choice or that school boards assign them without regard to race. Still, to mount a successful challenge to segregation in Delaware, civil rights activists would have to rely as much on changes in social and cultural attitudes toward race as they would upon court pronouncements, such as the one in the *Brown* decision. The historian James Patterson correctly concludes that *Brown* and the civil rights revolution inspired "bureaucrats and judges" to ensure "these rulings would continue to make a difference."[8] Bureaucrats and judges throughout Delaware, however, would not be able to sustain desegregation efforts without the support of the citizenry, which would also require cultural and social transformation in attitudes toward race.

But was Delaware already undergoing a social and cultural transformation before *Brown,* making Court action unnecessary? Law professor Michael J. Klarman claims, in general, *Brown* was unnecessary, arguing that segregation was already withering on the vine. In brief, he argues that if left to their own devices, opponents of segregation would have achieved integration without court intervention. In Delaware, Klarman correctly points out that desegregation was already underway by the time of *Brown,* at least in the northern part of the state. In Wilmington, theaters, Catholic schools, and restaurants were desegregated before legal challenges to school segregation in Delaware. The National Guard had also begun to desegregate, partly in response to the desegregation of the military on the national level. Klarman explains that there was a growing acceptance of social science research, which showed no difference between white and black intellectual capacities. World War II had also exposed Americans to extreme racism and the racial policies that grew out of it in Nazi Germany. These experiences convinced white and black Americans to oppose state-sanctioned segregationist policies impeding progress toward achieving racial justice and equality. In all, Klarman contends, "the postwar momentum for racial reform could not be stopped."[9] He goes on to conclude, "the overall extralegal context was as favorably disposed as it had ever been toward advances in civil rights."[10] It is therefore clear to Klarman that *Brown* did not initiate desegregation. On the contrary, he argues that *Brown* led to massive resistance to desegregation and years of delay in achieving it.

Whether desegregation would have spread beyond Wilmington without court action is unclear. It, however, is evident that court action prompted resistance to desegregation, especially in the southern part of the state. In many respects, Delaware was a microcosm of the country in that southern Delaware mirrored reactions against court-ordered integration found within southern states, whereas northern Delaware experienced little opposition to desegregation. The middle part of the state took a slow and deliberate approach to desegregation with little massive resistance in comparison with southern Delaware.

Following *Brown,* to be sure, the road to desegregation in Delaware was a long one including massive resistance, "white backlash," and delay before there was any serious attempt to end segregation throughout the state. The most formidable obstacle to desegregation was the belief in white supremacy. Exploring the efforts to desegregate education in Delaware may lead to a broader understanding of similar efforts elsewhere in the country involving "gradual adjustments" to the *Brown* decision before massive litigation and federal congressional and judicial actions pressured the state to undertake immediate integration in the mid- to late 1960s.

Before the U.S. Supreme Court decision in 1954, desegregation went forward in Hockessin and Claymont as originally ordered by Chancellor Seitz in 1952. Arden schools near Wilmington also went ahead with desegregation before the 1954 decision, which technically violated the Delaware State Constitution. Desegregation occurred without serious resistance in these communities for the next two years, giving hope to many that this pattern would characterize the rest of the South. Psychotherapist Frederic Wertham confidently concluded, "The abolition of segregation [in Delaware] removes a handicap that interferes with the self-realization and social adjustment of the child. The much-predicted ill effects of such a step did not eventuate."[11] Altogether, Wertham proclaimed, "All human beings have conflicts; but this particular one [state-sanctioned segregation] is artificial and unnecessary and its relief evidently brings quick results."[12]

Northern liberals rejoiced following the initial and peaceful desegregation efforts in Delaware. In October 1954, William Peters published an article for *Red Book Magazine,* titled "The Schools That Broke the Color Line," in which he pronounced Delaware to be the model for others to follow in the desegregation of education. This optimism was, however, short lived.[13]

In the fall of 1954, violence broke out in opposition to the admission of black students to the all-white high school in the southern Delaware community of Milford. It was "The Town That Surrendered to Hate," as Selwyn James described Milford in 1955. Far less optimistic than William Peters, James described the quick turn of events in Delaware from the initial peaceful integration of northern Delaware schools to massive resistance in less than a year. As massive resistance gained strength, according to Klarman, a backlash against supporters of *Brown* followed, which indeed occurred in Delaware. The backlash also encouraged more massive resistance and delay, leading to years of legal challenges to desegregation in Delaware. In part, this can be explained as a southern response to desegregation similar to how Georgia and South Carolina responded to desegregation during this period. Southern Delaware shared a similar history as other parts of the South such as slavery and "Jim Crow," unlike the northern part of the state, which was more industrial and based upon a wage labor system.[14]

On September 8, 1954, eleven black students showed up for the first day of school at Milford High School. On September 10, the school board submitted its gradual desegregation plan to the state board of education for approval. During the summer of 1954, Dean Kimmel, president of the Milford School Board, had met with Reverend Randolph Fisher, head of the Milford branch of the NAACP, and Louis Redding to develop a gradual integration plan for the all-white Lake Avenue High School. This followed an injunction served on the Milford School Board by Redding and Fisher to integrate the all-white high school. Following negotiations during the summer, they agreed to begin with the tenth grade in the fall 1954 school year, culminating with full integration of the high school by 1957. At the time, black students attended the newly opened William C. Jason High School (1950) in Georgetown or the William Henry High School (1952) in Dover.[15]

There were factors that led Redding and the Delaware NAACP to choose Milford as the place to begin desegregation in the state. The NAACP had an active organization that included the African American clergy under the leadership of Fisher, who was also a minister in the Methodist Church in Milford. The African American community appeared tight-knit and united in the effort to desegregate the schools. Geographically, the Milford School District transcended southern Kent County and northern Sussex County, which was significant to future efforts further south. Additionally, there seemed to have been good relations between the white and black residents of Milford and the surrounding area. To comply with the *Brown* decision, it simply "made sense" to both the white and black communities in Milford.[16]

The decision to adopt a desegregation plan by the Milford School Board was congruent with the Delaware attorney general's position on integration, explained earlier that summer. Attorney General H. Albert Young determined that integration could legally proceed and had informed the state board of education that Wilmington could begin gradual integration of its schools. He also urged other school districts to follow suit. Furthermore, he did not require state board of education approval before implementing desegregation plans.[17]

Desegregation in Milford ran smoothly for the first few weeks, until rumors circulated that a black male student had asked a white female student to a school dance. Parents heard the rumor and organized a meeting at the local American Legion Hall, resulting in about twelve hundred people petitioning the school board to rescind its integration orders. Segregationists threatened school board members and also members of the black community. Fearing for the safety of the students, the school board decided to close the school. It eventually reopened with state police escorting ten of the black students to Milford High School.[18]

Milford served as a magnet, attracting segregationists and segregationist organizations from around the region. Among them was Bryant Bowles, head of the National Association for the Advancement of White People (NAAWP). Bowles played upon the fears and anger among the white opposition in Milford. Pointing to Communist plots to destroy America, he charged integration would lead to miscegenation. Holding up his three-year-old daughter in front of a cheering crowd of boycotters, Bowles stated: "Do you think that my daughter will ever attend school with Negroes? Not while there's breath in my body and gunpowder will burn—and gunpowder *will* burn! If the Negroes go to your children's school, let your conscience be you guide . . . I know what I would do!"[19]

In addition to Bowles, Allan Alderson Zoll leafleted and mass mailed anti-Semitic and anti-Communist literature throughout the state. Zoll carpeted Delaware with copies of *Common Sense*, an anti-Communist newspaper. He identified Jewish and Communist conspiracies to integrate the schools of Delaware. Ultimately, he predicted this action would lead to the downfall of the country, weakening it for an eventual Soviet takeover.[20]

Milford also attracted the attention of the Eisenhower administration in an outward display of what law professor Derrick Bell describes as "interest convergence." During a political campaign visit to Delaware in October 1954, Vice President Richard M. Nixon highlighted the convergence of U.S. foreign policy interests and the interests of the NAACP in Delaware when he pleaded for the end of the boycott in Milford. He informed the people of Milford that nonwhite people around the world "hold the balance of power" between the Soviet Union and the United States.[21] He stressed: "One of the factors that would be tremendously helpful is for us here in the United States to show by example, by word and deed that the dream of equality—equality of opportunity, of education and of employment and the like—is coming true."[22] It was clear to Nixon and others that massive resistance held serious consequences in the prosecution of the Cold War against the Soviet Union. Specifically, massive resistance projected the wrong image of America to the non-white populations abroad and "furnishes grist for the Communist propaganda mills."[23] In turn, according to law professor Charles J. Ogletree Jr., the government acted within the context of the Cold War at a time when the interests of U.S. foreign policymakers converged with those of the civil rights movement. Nonetheless, the segregationists of Milford seemed more interested in the immediate issue of desegregation of the high school and not concerned about broader foreign policy issues facing the country in its Cold War efforts.[24]

During the following weeks, it appeared that the interests of the state of Delaware converged more with the segregationists' interests than with those of the NAACP and U.S. foreign policymakers. The NAACP and the Milford School Board met with Delaware governor J. Caleb Boggs and the Delaware Board of Education. Fearing armed insurrection in southern Delaware, Boggs offered no support for the Milford School Board and urged it to expel the black students. The Delaware Board of Education came to the same conclusion, citing its policy adopted on August 19, 1954, in which it requested, "all schools . . . present a tentative plan for desegregation . . . before October 1, 1954." The board of education concluded that the Milford School Board had not received approval of its desegregation plan, contradicting H. Albert Young's pronouncement earlier that summer. Therefore it could not admit the black students.[24]

Feeling betrayed by Governor Boggs and the state board of education, Milford board members immediately resigned. Governor Boggs then appointed a new school board and a new president, Edmund F. Steiner, all of which supported segregation. The new school board then expelled the black children, stating that the action was for their safety.[26]

Louis L. Redding immediately appealed to the Delaware Court of Chancery. William Marvel, vice chancellor, responded by enjoining the Milford board from removing the black children. He then decided that the black students had a right to attend Milford High School, stating "that their right to a personal and present high school education having vested their admission . . . need not wait for decrees decided by the United States Supreme Court in May [1954] as prerequisite to their readmission [and] are entitled to an order protecting their status as students at Milford High School."[27]

The Milford School Board appealed the chancery court decision to the Delaware Supreme Court. In February 1955, the Delaware Supreme

Court upheld the Milford School Board's action. In an extraordinary decision, the Delaware Supreme Court concluded that the previous Milford board had "exceeded their powers under the law," thereby confirming the state board of education's power to set educational policy rather than the attorney general. The court went on to concede that the U.S. Supreme Court had ruled state segregation laws unconstitutional, but it "does not require immediate desegregation of the public schools."[28] Even before *Brown II*, the Delaware Supreme Court set the course for desegregation of education, "with all deliberate speed," which would stand for the next twelve years.

Many supporters of the effort to desegregate education blamed weak leadership in Delaware for encouraging massive resistance, by allowing it to go unchallenged. NAACP field reports portrayed local and state police authorities in Milford as being lax, with "no enforcement of laws against riot inciting or threatened safety of students by mob."[29] Kenneth Clark observed the Milford boycott firsthand and concluded that ineffective political leadership, by not confronting massive resistance, emboldened segregationists to resist desegregation more intensely. Specifically, Clark attacked Governor Boggs for his hesitation and indecisiveness in the face of "lawlessness."[30] Clark explained: "It is now clearly understood by social scientists who have studied these problems that this type of lawlessness can be victorious only under conditions of weak, indecisive or conspiratorial political leadership. Prolonged and intense opposition is more likely to occur when the attempts at school desegregation are apologetic, gradual and piecemeal."[31]

Clark added: "The handling of the Milford situation by state authorities created the conditions which made it possible for Bryant W. Bowles to step in a week after the trouble started and further incite the mob."[32] He then concluded, "It has been found that opposition to desegregation decreases when those in authority insist upon compliance with the law in the face of initial opposition."[33]

Clearly, fear of an armed insurrection in southern Delaware directed Boggs to take his position. White people throughout Kent and Sussex Counties protested desegregation and organized boycotts, leading to a widespread belief that an insurrection was truly at hand. From Milford, the boycott first spread to nearby Lincoln. Several other towns in Sussex County held informal votes on school integration in late fall 1954, in which all overwhelmingly voted against it. In Milton, 934 voted against integration of schools, while 6 favored it. Milford residents voted 2,332 against integration, while 25 voted in favor of integration. Likewise in Harrington, 1,106 opposed integration, while 11 favored it. Similarly, Millsboro, Frederica, Ellendale, and Lincoln voted against integration. With the exception of Dover, where gradual desegregation of the high school went smoothly, the other schools in Kent County delayed desegregation. [34]

Massive resistance thereby gained momentum throughout southern Delaware, leading to a backlash against any suspected supporters of desegregation. Segregationists organized boycotts against Jewish businesspeople who owned canning and poultry businesses in Sussex County. There was a widespread belief, fueled by anti-Semitic and anti-Communist literature, that there was a Jewish conspiracy to take over America by weakening the "white race" through miscegenation. Massive resistance also led to a backlash against elected officials who supported any form of desegregation.[35]

Attorney General H. Albert Young, who had argued against *Brown* before the U.S. Supreme Court in 1954, now struggled to enforce the Court mandate. Failing to do so, Young chose not to stand for reelection in 1954. Other Republicans who supported desegregation lost in the 1954 elections, all of which can be attributed to a white voter "backlash." Voters replaced them with pro-segregation or gradual desegregationist Democrats. The significance of this voter "backlash" became immediately apparent. The newly elected attorney general, Democrat Joseph D. Craven, was a gradualist who argued this position before the U.S. Supreme Court in *Brown II* (1955).

Craven tackled the question, posed by the Court, of whether integration should be immediate or gradual. He pleaded for time and freedom to integrate in Delaware's own way. Craven stressed, "We are a divided and troubled people in the face of the mandate of the court." He advocated for the Delaware Supreme Court to supervise desegregation, allowing the state board of education or local school boards to develop and implement plans on their own timetables. This argument was significantly different from his predecessor, who maintained that local school boards should: "exercise equitable discretion according to local conditions provided that a constructive transitional program is shown to be in progress and subject to the limitations that ultimate relief by way of admission on a non-segregation basis shall be affected no later than a date which this Court shall fix."[36] Believing his argument better reflected the sentiments of Delawareans, Craven opposed immediate desegregation of schools. The Eisenhower administration presented a similar argument to the Court, asking to "integrate as soon as feasible" without any fixed dates.[37]

The Court agreed with arguments that allowed for the consideration of local conditions, permitting a more deliberate or gradual approach to desegregation. In *Brown II*, the Court allowed desegregation "with all deliberate speed" or "with any perceptible movement," as the psychologist Kenneth Clark explained the Court's phrase. Local school authorities in Delaware used the Court decision to justify their deliberate or slow approach to school integration based upon local feasibility. Thus, school districts in southern Delaware proceeded slowly toward developing desegregation plans. For example, the Millsboro School Board pointed out that integration would "endanger the public welfare," citing that their school had "not recovered from the shock sustained" from a two-day boycott the previous year and continued "threats of violence."[38] It was clear to Irving Morris, who was deputy attorney general during *Brown II*, that Attorney General Craven "perpetuated the resistance to desegregation in Delaware" when he refused "to oppose publicly and unequivocally the segregation of the races in Delaware's public schools."[39] This stand resulted in massive resistance, which also provoked a white "backlash." To be sure, the U.S. Supreme Court was equally responsible for encouraging "massive resistance" in its *Brown II* decision. Nonetheless, it is also clear that when the NAACP attempted to force desegregation in Milford following *Brown I*, it resulted in massive resistance in the form of a white boycott leading to the replacement of the school board with ones in favor of segregation.[40]

The U.S. Supreme Court exposed the fundamental flaw in *Brown* with its 1955 guidelines for desegregation. Law professor Charles J. Ogletree Jr. maintains, "As an expression of moral rectitude, *Brown I* was the least the Court could have done, but the timidity expressed in *Brown II* nullified its import."[41] In effect, the Court acknowledged to the nation and the world that segregation was morally wrong. Yet, fearing "a massive rift between South and North and risk the legitimacy of the Court," the U.S. Supreme Court determined integration would proceed "with all deliberate speed," which strengthened massive resistance and encouraged delay. Taken together, Ogletree questions the Court's commitment to achieving an integrated and equal society, which could be said about the state government's commitment in Delaware.[42]

To be sure, massive resistance and the "backlash" intensified following *Brown II*. Even moderate politicians could no longer take a gradualist approach and remain in elected office. In essence, *Brown II* solidified southern Delaware and the South into a segregationist position. The immediate impact of *Brown II* could be seen in southern Delaware. One of the first to face the backlash was Mayor Edward R. Evans of Milford. After serving as mayor for fourteen years, Evans did not stand for reelection because of the integration crisis and his position favoring desegregation.[43]

Encouraged by *Brown II*, school districts throughout southern Delaware continued massive resistance against desegregation. In turn, massive resistance widened into a political "backlash" against supporters of desegregation. Milford PTA officials resigned in the face of segregationist opposition to them. Dr. Ramon C. Cobbs, superintendent of Milford Public Schools, was accused of striking and attempting to choke a boy. Even though the charges were dropped, Cobbs resigned and left the city, fearing more reprisals against him for his support of desegregation.[44]

The "backlash" spread into neighboring Sussex County communities. Howard T. West, chair of the Committee against the Proposed School Integration, called for the immediate resignation of the Milton School Board members who supported desegregation. He cried, "There won't be any Negro children in any school when it opens in September [1956]."[45] He claimed integration to be an "atheistic, hell-raising, communist plan for the immoral mixture of races."[46] In his opposition to desegregation, Nelson Abbott, an Ellendale electrician asked, "Did the [Ellendale] School Board do wrong or did they act in ignorance" when it decided to begin desegregation. He added, "Segregation is a tradition we will never sacrifice."[47] In all, where there was support for desegregation, the hesitancy among state officials to act immediately following *Brown I* led to an encouraged opposition and "backlash."

Several schools in southern Delaware broke athletic contracts with Dover High School, because it allowed black athletes to play on its teams. The Milford School Board fired Paul J. Malie, who was the advisor to the Student Council, claiming he had incited students to question its segregationist policies, leading to the cancellation of sporting events with Dover. Milford superintendent Chester Dickerson said, "You might say it is because of a difference in educational philosophy."[48] Several Milford schoolteachers applied for positions in Dover after this incident.

Even the venerable Louis L. Redding faced the "backlash" when he was hauled into court over charges of income tax evasion; the charges were dropped later.[49] Despite the adversity, Redding remained resolute in his struggle to achieve immediate integration. In 1956, Redding petitioned the state board of education to immediately integrate eight southern Delaware schools, which it rejected. In its rejection of this petition, the state board proved that it was equally unwavering in its determination to maintain a policy of gradual integration. The state board of education stated that "the fact that communities differ from one another in tradition and attitudes and, therefore, the desegregation process will require a longer period of time in some parts of the state than in others."[50]

Facing massive resistance, many advocates of immediate integration that were not as determined as Redding had also come to the conclusion that gradual desegregation was the only viable solution to implementing the *Brown* decision. By the end of the 1950s, seventeen leading social scientists who had provided research for the LDF in its efforts in *Brown*, including Isador Chein, Otto Klineberg, Albert Merton, Gordon Alport, and Alfred McClung Lee, had concluded that gradual desegregation was the most desirable approach.[51]

Consequently, it seems only the most committed remained firm in their conviction that immediate integration was the path to take. Louis L. Redding and Kenneth Clark remained convinced that immediate integration without delay could be achieved. They believed that a strong response to massive resistance by state officials was necessary despite threats of "backlash" and violence. Accordingly, they moved the desegregation struggle into a new phase of "massive litigation."[52]

In 1956, Redding initiated a new chapter in the desegregation of education in Delaware when he represented frustrated black parents in Clayton, located in central Delaware, in a suit against the Delaware Board of Education. They demanded the school district speed up the process of desegregation so their daughter, Brenda Evans, could attend an integrated school. The Clayton School Board had not submitted any desegregation plan and had no intention to do so. To pressure the Clayton School Board, Redding filed *Evans v. Buchanan* in the United States District Court in Wilmington, thus bypassing the state supreme court, which seemed as equally recalcitrant as the Delaware Board of Education in its deliberate approach to desegregation. Chief Judge Paul Leahy heard the case and ordered Clayton to submit a desegregation plan to the Delaware Board of Education. The state appealed to the U.S. Third Circuit Court, which refused to hear the case.[53]

Redding stepped up the pressure to hasten the desegregation process. In 1957, Redding consolidated six similar challenges to "deliberate speed" into the *Evans* case and returned to the U.S. District Court. Chief Judge Leahy ordered the state board of education and the superintendent of public instruction to submit a statewide plan for the 1957 fall term allowing "admittance, enrollment and education [of students] on a racially nondiscriminatory basis."[54] The state board of education and the superintendent of public instruction appealed the decision to the U.S. Third Circuit Court. Upholding Leahy's decision the following year, the U.S. Third Circuit Court remanded it back to the U.S. District Court with one modification. The circuit court did not set a time limit on desegregation of schools, which Leahy had required.[55]

By the time the Third Circuit Court sent *Evans* back to the district court, chief district judge Caleb R. Layton III had replaced Leahy as chief judge. Layton complied with the circuit court and ordered the state board of education to submit a desegregation plan. The state board of education complied and submitted a plan outlining grade-by-grade integration beginning with the first grade in the 1959 fall term. If accepted, it would take twelve years to complete. This "stair-step" approach affected only black children, since it only required them to register for the first grade, and not white children. The plan also did not allow students to choose the schools they wished to attend.[56]

In 1960, Redding challenged this "stair-step" plan by appealing to the U.S. Third Circuit Court in a case titled *Evans v. Ennis*. Agreeing with Redding, the circuit court rejected grade-by-grade integration and ordered full integration beginning in the fall of 1961. The court granted the state a continuance of the grade-by-grade integration plan until then.[57]

Back in the district court, Caleb M. Wright, the new chief judge, issued an order that allowed black students to attend any school of their choice, following freedom-of-choice plans found elsewhere in the South. However, in 1962, after a petition for the admission of nine black children from Millside School District into an integrated school in nearby Rose Hill Minquadale School District, the latter district's school board refused their entry. Attorney Leonard Williams joined Redding and Irving Morris in petitioning the district court for their admission. Judge Wright agreed, thereby reaffirming Delaware's freedom-of-choice policy to desegregate the schools in Delaware, although in practice only black students chose to attend white schools rather than the reverse. It was "one-way integration," as some have aptly described the procedure.[58]

Massive resistance to desegregation led many states to combine freedom of choice with "gradual adjustment," which appeared more deliberate than speedy. In a similar fashion, Delaware adopted desegregation plans that in theory allowed whites to choose to attend black schools and vice versa, with black students choosing white schools. In reality, virtually no white students chose to attend black schools even if they believed in desegregation, because of the prevailing belief that the black schools were inferior. Concomitantly, few black students chose to attend white schools, fearing harassment and retaliation against them and their parents by the white community. Legal challenges later showed that freedom-of-choice plans actually perpetuated dual education systems, which violated the *Brown* decision.[59]

By 1964, both Congress and the U.S. Supreme Court grew increasingly impatient with states that took "gradualist" approaches to desegregation. In *Griffin v. County School Board of Prince Edward County* (1964), the Court stated: "There has been entirely too much deliberation and not enough speed in enforcing the constitutional rights which we held in *Brown v. Board of Education* (1954)."[60] Equally annoyed, Congress passed and President Lyndon B. Johnson signed into law the U.S. Civil Rights Act of 1964, which addressed desegregation of education in Title IV and denial of federal assistance for a cause of racial discrimination under Title VI. This latter provision allowed the federal government to withhold funds from schools that resisted desegregation. The *Griffin* case, in combination with the passage of the U.S. Civil Rights Act of 1964, tolled the death knoll to segregated schools in Delaware.[61]

During this time, Richard P. Gousha served as the superintendent of public instruction in Delaware. Facing the potential loss of new and existing federal funds and the ever-increasing scrutiny of the federal courts, Gousha stepped up efforts to desegregate schools in Delaware in the mid-1960s. His efforts intensified with passage of the federal Elementary and Secondary Education Act in 1965. Under Title I of the act, the federal government addressed disadvantaged children, allowing grants to impoverished areas around the country to rectify the situation. After the passage of this legislation, Gousha charged Howard Row, assistant superintendent of public instruction, with the mission to supervise desegregation of schools in the state.[62]

Row's solution to desegregation was to consolidate schools, a policy the Delaware Board of Education adopted in February 1965. Row spearheaded the consolidation of black and white school districts while "phasing out certain schools." This process meant phasing out one- and two-room schools in black school districts. The state also abolished the all-black high schools in the three counties. Row went on to consolidate larger black school districts with their white counterparts. He accomplished this task by allowing school districts to voluntarily comply with the Delaware Board of Education resolution. If not, the state would withhold funds to noncompliant school districts. Additionally, Row had to guarantee teaching positions for the black teachers. Black teachers insisted upon maintaining their tenure rights to ensure their positions after consolidation.[63]

In 1967, Gousha and Row completed the task, having overseen the closing of the last black school in the state. Gousha claimed 100 percent of all black students in Delaware were attending desegregated schools at the time. Confirming this fact, the United States Civil Rights Commission certified Delaware as having completely desegregated its schools in 1967. This achievement came after thirteen years of struggle over how to implement *Brown I*. The euphoria was, however, short lived.[64]

In 1968, the U.S. Supreme Court launched full force into massive desegregation when it rejected a freedom-of-choice plan in *Green v. County School Board of New Kent County, Virginia* (1968).[65] In *Green*, the Court showed its impatience with the "deliberate speed" of New Kent County. The Court declared that time had run out. It also cited the U.S. Civil Rights Commission's impatience with freedom-of-choice schemes. The commission reported: "Freedom of choice plans, which have tended to perpetuate racially identifiable schools in the southern and border States, require affirmative action by both Negro and white parents and pupils."[66] This clearly had not happened thus far, according to both the Court and the Civil Rights Commission.

Soon after the *Green* decision, Delaware passed the Educational Advancement Act of 1968 (EAA), giving a year extension to school consolidation even though all had desegregated. The schools now facing further consolidation were already desegregated, but had small numbers of enrolled students. The legislators deemed it necessary to consolidate these small schools into larger districts out of a sense of efficiency. The act, however, exempted the city of Wilmington from consolidation because of its size. The legislation limited the size of the school districts included in the consolidation initially to 15,000 pupils. But when legislators discovered Wilmington had 12,000 pupils, they lowered the number to that size. The city of Wilmington also contained about half of the black school-age population in the state.[67]

Critics charged that the state passed the act solely in reaction to *Green*. Many believed it was an attempt to stop further desegregation plans for the largest black population in the state, which was located in Wilmington. Clearly, the aim of the *Green* decision was to "convert promptly to a system without a 'white' school and a 'Negro' school, but just schools." It appeared, however, that Wilmington schools would remain predominantly black since EAA exempted the city schools from consolidating with other predominantly white schools in neighboring school districts.[68]

By 1968, the percentage of black students attending city schools in Wilmington had increased to over 70 percent of the total student population. The African American population had risen to 44 percent of the total city population at the time. This was partly because of "white flight" to the surrounding suburbs, attributed to desegregation of schools and increasing violence within the city. White flight accelerated after the 1967 and 1968 riots, which were black responses to police harassment and the assassination of Martin Luther King Jr. Also, urban renewal and the construction of Interstate 95 through the heart of Wilmington led many white families to sell their homes and leave the city. Additionally, before the Civil Rights Act of 1968, housing discrimination against black potential homeowners locked them into housing in the city of Wilmington. The effect was the re-segregation of schools by 1968. Without the ability to consolidate with school districts outside the city limits, Wilmington and New Castle County would be locked into dual segregated educational systems not tolerated by the *Green* decision.[69]

It took another ten years before the U.S. Supreme Court upheld the U.S. Third Circuit Court's decision to desegregate schools in New Castle County, placing the responsibility to do so on the district court. The lower court replied by ordering the dissolution of all school districts in New Castle County, replacing them with one countywide school district beginning on July 1, 1978. The district court determined that the city of Wilmington "had been unconstitutionally excluded from other school districts by the state board of education, pursuant to a withholding of reorganization powers under the Delaware Educational Advancement Act of 1968."[70] The Third Circuit Court affirmed this action. In *Evans v. Buchanan* (1978), the U.S. Supreme Court affirmed the lower courts' actions and ordered the desegregation process to begin. Thus, after twenty-four years, Delaware began the process of complete desegregation of education throughout the state.[71]

To be sure, the LDF envisioned a speedier process in the desegregation of public education in Delaware when it began challenging Jim

Crow segregation in 1950. It took most of the following three decades to achieve desegregation moving through several phases. The first phase, beginning in 1950, happened without much opposition in northern Delaware. When faced with desegregation in southern Delaware following *Brown I,* white opponents reacted through massive efforts of resistance. Despite pleas from the NAACP to continue desegregation in the face of violent resistance, state officials hesitated and eventually succumbed to white opponents to integration. This official reaction from the state only energized massive resistance, culminating in a "backlash" against supporters of desegregation. Slowly, desegregation moved into a phase of "gradual adjustments" or deliberate delay, reinforced by *Brown II.*

Following *Brown II,* Leland Ware, historian and law professor, argues that the U.S. Supreme Court in fact encouraged a "gradualist approach" to desegregation of education in its decision to proceed with "all deliberate speed." Along with Ware, Robert J. Cottrol and Raymond T. Diamond, in *Brown v. Board of Education: Caste, Culture, and the Constitution,* argue: "Despite the conservatism of *Brown II* with its refusal to press for immediate desegregation . . . , supporters of segregation were furious." Essentially, to segregationists, it did not matter what the Court decided, whether deliberate desegregation or immediate integration; it was still an assault on segregation. Thus, opponents of integration intensified their massive resistance to it and convinced many, including some who supported integration, that a gradual approach to desegregation was the only choice.[72]

The judicial process led to further delays, characterized by the Delaware Board of Education plans that appeared to be more deliberate than speedy. This action gave way to court battles, resulting in a "gradualist" approach in the guise of stair-step desegregation, replaced by freedom-of-choice plans thereby pacifying segregationists and gradualists alike. What also seemed to have been a genuine attempt to consolidate small school districts into larger ones for efficiency and viability resulted in yet another block against desegregating the largest school district with the majority of black students in the state, Wilmington.

To be sure, the *Brown* decision provoked massive resistance, forcing states to take a deliberate or a gradual approach to desegregation and resulting in years of litigation and legal maneuvering to delay its implementation. It also forced the Delaware NAACP to seek relief in federal courts rather than state courts, thereby initiating a new phase in desegregation of education through a strategy of "massive litigation." It is clear that this strategy was successful and forced federal court intervention, which increasingly showed its impatience with delay tactics in developing desegregation plans and those guised to maintain a dual education system. Combined with congressional action, such as the Civil Rights Act of 1964, state education officials understood clearly that they had to speed up the process of desegregation, which was accomplished by 1967 in Delaware at least for most of the state, except Wilmington. Still advocates for desegregated schools persisted, which paid off, making Delaware's schools thoroughly desegregated by the end of the 1970s.

Clearly, *Brown* roused massive resistance to desegregation efforts in southern Delaware and in other parts of the country. Unlike northern Delaware, it is not clear that desegregation would have occurred without the *Brown* decision even though it provoked resistance once rendered. To be sure, the aftermath of attempting to implement *Brown I* did result in massive resistance beginning in Milford, Delaware. *Brown II* led to African American pressure to speed the deliberation process. Both did in fact lead to political office holders losing their elections if they supported desegregation in a "white backlash." This forced many who may not have been segregationists to take positions of either deliberate or slower approaches to desegregation or to oppose it altogether. Or in many cases, several just did nothing. In the end, however, the resultant massive litigation did result in breaking the legal log jam, which was the result of African American legal action. *Brown* and the subsequent events that followed most certainly also awakened both black and white ordinary citizens to what Jack Greenberg sees as the single most important factor in the slow progress toward desegregation, which was racism. Undoubtedly, the commitment to equality and justice among a dedicated group of white and black citizens in Delaware gave them the strength to prevail. After three decades of struggle, Delaware finally achieved the promises of *Brown*.[73]

Border State Ebb and Flow

School Desegregation in Missouri, 1954–1999

Peter William Moran

Missouri has long occupied a pivotal place in the history of race relations in the United States. As a border state, Missouri has historically been a crossroads of sorts for racially oriented issues. Indeed, at several different points in time, the entire nation was riveted by events that originated in the state of Missouri. Moreover, the outcome of those events occasionally carried sweeping implications upon which the future course of the country truly hinged. Among those events of national significance was the very admission of the state to the union. The issue of extending slavery beyond the Mississippi River was entangled in the statehood question and constituted the first of several national crises revolving around slavery. Ultimately, the Missouri Compromise of 1820 preserved the union, maintained the balance of power between free and slave states in the United States Senate, and resolved, for a time, the question of extending slavery in the Louisiana Purchase territory. Twenty-seven years later, the case of *Dred Scott v. Sandford* originated in Missouri and was argued in the state circuit court in St. Louis and at the state supreme court before being decided at the U.S. Supreme Court. The controversial split opinion laid bare the divide both within the Court and the nation as a whole regarding the legal status of slaves and the future extension of slavery into the territories. The Court's strained attempt to resolve the explosive issues presented in *Dred Scott* clearly underscored the polarization of the country, slave and free, and in part fueled the coming of the Civil War three years later.

In the realm of school desegregation, too, Missouri has been the battle-ground for a number of cases with profound implications for the nation. In fact, it is not unreasonable to argue that in some respects school desegregation started in Missouri, at least as far as the United States Supreme Court is concerned. The first of the graduate school admissions cases argued by the legal team of the National Association for the Advancement of Colored People before the Supreme Court originated in Missouri in the late 1930s. In *Missouri ex rel. Gaines v. Canada,* the Court ruled that the University of Missouri had violated the Fourteenth Amendment guarantee of equal protection of the law by refusing to admit Lloyd Gaines to graduate school solely on the basis of his race, and ordered that Gaines be admitted to the university's graduate pro-gram.[1] Beyond the *Gaines* precedent, to the extent that housing issues are frequently argued in school desegregation cases, St. Louis was the setting for the most important early housing segregation case, *Shelley v. Kraemer.* In its 1948 *Shelley* decision, the Court struck down restrictive covenants as legally binding instruments for maintaining the segregated all-white composition of residential areas.[2]

Just as one might argue that in some respect school desegregation got its start in Missouri, it is possible to conclude that the recent shift among the nation's judiciary toward dismantling school desegregation plans also originated in part from the Show-Me State. In particular, the Supreme Court's 1995 decision in *Missouri v. Jenkins* clearly signaled that the decades of judicial support for and defense of school desegrega-tion had come to an end. The 1995 decision in *Jenkins* severely curtailed the massive magnet schools desegregation plan operating in Kansas City and plainly implied that Court was anticipating the day when school dis-tricts operating under court-ordered desegregation plans would be declared unitary and returned to local control. This essay will explore developments in the state of Missouri from the period just prior to the Supreme Court's 1954 *Brown* decision through the most recent setbacks in Kansas City and St. Louis in the 1990s.

Missouri before *Brown v. Board of Education*

In 1950, fewer than 300,000 blacks resided in the state of Missouri, just 7.6 percent of the state's population. The African American population, however, was not evenly distributed across the state. About 154,000, or more than one-half of Missouri's African American population, lived in

St. Louis; while 56,600, or another roughly 20 percent of state's blacks lived in Kansas City. Beyond those two urban centers, other significant concentrations of African American residents were found in the southeast corner of the state—the so called Boot Heel region—and in those counties clustered along the Missouri River in the central part of the state.[3]

Prior to the 1954 *Brown v. Board of Education* decision, the state of Missouri was a de jure school segregation state. Separate-but-equal schools for white and African American students were mandated by both the state constitution and the state statutes.[4] Schools in Missouri adhered strictly to the mandate of segregation, but in that context Missouri was somewhat of a leader among states requiring segregated schools in providing African American students with equal educational opportunities. Whereas state funding for separate schools was grossly unequal in many states of the Deep South, at least until the Supreme Court's 1950 ruling in *Sweatt v. Painter,* the state funding formula used in Missouri financed schools for black and white students equally. With the exception of Delaware, Oklahoma, and Missouri, every state that required segregated schools by law funded its black and white schools unevenly. The average expenditure per white student in southern states ranged from $50 to $100 more than the expenditure per black student. In Mississippi, five times as much money was appropriated for each white student. Furthermore, most southern states had an uneven salary scale for teachers. On average, black teachers in the South earned about three-fifths that of their white counterparts. In Mississippi, the typical white teacher earned about three times as much as a black educator.[5]

In several important respects, the Missouri public school system was unlike that of other southern states. In Missouri generally a good-faith effort had been made to abide by the letter of the law and provide separate but substantively equal schools. State funds for education were appropriated without bias in Missouri. Each school district received the same amount of money per pupil, regardless of the student's race. In Kansas City and St. Louis, where the school districts had large pools of qualified applicants, the African American and white teaching staffs were equally qualified. Every teacher in the Kansas City and St. Louis School Districts, black and white, had a college degree, and all were paid according to the same salary scale. Indeed, the state threatened to withhold state aid from districts that did not pay African American teachers as much as whites.[6] Across the state, the school term was the same length for students at black and white schools, and in the larger urban districts, the curriculum was identical for students of both races. In St. Louis and Kansas City, black and white students used the same textbooks, selected by biracial committees of teachers, and studied the same curriculum, also developed by biracial committees. Although the committees that developed the curriculum and selected the textbooks were biracial, the faculties were segregated. Black schools had black faculties and principals while the white schools had white teachers and principals. At midcentury, there were no blacks in central administration posts in either the St. Louis or Kansas City School Districts.[7]

The *Brown* Decision and Missouri

On May 17, 1954, Chief Justice Earl Warren rose and read the Supreme Court's unanimous decision in *Brown v. Board of Education,* clearly one of the Court's most monumental rulings. By overturning the constitutionality of segregated schools, the Court had radically altered the foundation of school systems in at least twenty-seven states and the District of Columbia. At the time of the Supreme Court ruling, segregated schools were required by constitutional or statutory provision in seventeen states and Washington, D.C. Ten other states had permissive legislation allowing communities to operate a dual school system if they chose to do so. More than fifty-three million Americans lived in these twenty-seven states; thus about one-third of the nation's population would be affected by the Court's decision. Missouri was among those affected.[8]

Whereas the Court's 1954 decision and the 1955 implementation decree were bitterly criticized across the Deep South, the response in much of Missouri was markedly different. "In the midwestern states (Kansas and Missouri in particular) the decision was to a considerable extent *ex post facto,*" one observer wrote, "expressing in terms of law what was already for the most part the general social conviction." Missouri governor Phil M. Donnelly announced immediately after the 1954 decision that the state had every intention of complying with the ruling. Furthermore, Donnelly proclaimed he had no inclination to attend the conference of southern governors, scheduled for June 7 in Richmond, Virginia, which had been expressly called to discuss the southern response to the *Brown* decision. Hubert Wheeler, Missouri's commissioner of education, said that he "had been expecting the ruling for some time." Within one week of the first *Brown* decision, Wheeler was in consultation with the Missouri attorney general, John M. Dalton, determining the legal status of the state's school system and the possibility of moving toward integrated schools.[9]

While most Missouri school districts awaited word from the state attorney general regarding the impact of the *Brown* decision, Sam C. Blair, a distinguished Jefferson City circuit court judge, offered his assessment of the ruling. Blair believed "the Missouri constitutional and statutory provisions setting up segregation become a mere shambles under the decision of the high court."[10] State attorney general Dalton contemplated the legal ramifications of the Supreme Court decision for better than one month before arriving at the same conclusion. On June 30, Dalton dispatched a ten-page statement to each school district in the state documenting his assessment of the decision's implications. "It is the opinion of this office," Dalton wrote, "that provisions of the Missouri Constitution and Statutes relating to separate schools 'for white children and colored children' are superseded by the decision of the Supreme Court of the United States and are, therefore, unenforceable, and that school districts may at the present time permit 'white and colored children' to attend the same school."[11]

Most Missouri towns had small numbers of black students and therefore the decision did not involve any major realignment of the school system. In fact, for numerous Missouri towns the maintenance of a dual system had been a tremendous financial liability. Compliance with the state constitution had required separate facilities, separate teaching staffs, and duplication of instructional materials and resources. In small towns such expenses bordered on prohibitive, and for small communities with only a few black students, it had been unreasonable to maintain a separate school. In these circumstances, African American students had been transported to nearby cities which maintained black schools. For example, Grundy County, located in the north-central section of the state, provided daily taxi service for its lone black student to attend school some fifty miles away. The county's cost was approximately $1,225 per year. For such towns the *Brown* decision, considered strictly from a financial perspective, was probably greeted with a sigh of relief. In addition, as these towns generally had small black student populations, accommodating these students in the local schools did not incite mass anxiety throughout the community.[12]

By September 1955, the vast majority of Missouri communities had adopted plans to integrate their schools. The solutions were typically to redraw school attendance zones without racial bias or to adopt a plan which gave students the option to attend their school of choice. Within one year of the 1954 *Brown* decision, an observer wrote: "Integration in Missouri schools became an actuality with an attitude showing unanimity in thinking among school officials in accordance with the May 17 decision."[13] Another source reported that "integration in some form has begun on a voluntary basis in every section of the state,"[14] and in *Time Magazine*'s September 1955 "Report Card" on school desegregation, Missouri was the only state to receive a grade of "A."[15] Only in the southeast part of the state, the Boot Heel, did the practice of segregated schools persist as a rule. This rural section of the state bordered on Arkansas, Tennessee, and Kentucky, and was culturally much more akin to the old South than were other sections of Missouri. Thus, it is perhaps not surprising that this part of the state would resist desegregation.[16] Several school districts serving the counties of the southeastern section of the state maintained segregated schools well into the 1960s, and the last segregated black schools in the Boot Heel region were not closed until 1968.[17]

For some African Americans, particularly teachers, school desegregation came at a high price. As was true in several other states, school desegregation and the closure of segregated black schools in Missouri resulted in African American teachers losing their jobs. Although it is impossible to determine precisely how many black educators lost their teaching positions with the conversion to desegregated schools, in some districts every black teacher was thrown out of work. Such was the case in Moberly, where the school board determined that desegregation would allow the district to close its black school and cut the district's teaching force by fifteen positions. Among the fifteen teachers whose contracts were not renewed were all eleven of Moberly's black teachers. In the lawsuit that followed, the African American teachers and their legal counsel, Robert Carter of the NAACP's national office, argued that several of the dismissed black teachers had superior qualifications and experience in comparison to some of the white teachers whose contracts were renewed. Despite finding that the school board's actions were "unusual and somewhat startling," the Eighth Circuit Court of Appeals affirmed the district court's ruling that the school district's termination of its entire African American teaching corps had not violated the equal protection clause of the Fourteenth Amendment.[18] Similar cases of black teachers losing their jobs as a result of desegregation were reported in several school districts serving the southeastern section of the state during the 1960s.[19] Equally troubling to some observers was the fact that throughout the 1960s, few districts engaged in concerted efforts to recruit African American teachers, and districts that did employ black teachers tended to concentrate those teachers in schools with predominantly black student populations.[20]

Outside of St. Louis and Kansas City, other consequences of desegregation, both positive and negative, were perhaps more subtle. In a number of communities, desegregation resulted in a growing awareness of the needs and interests of African American students. Among other changes, the integration of athletic teams, cheerleading squads, clubs, and school organizations proceeded smoothly in numerous school districts across the state, and several districts added courses in black history and black literature to their high school curricula. Conversely, in some communities, particularly in the Boot Heel, black parents concluded that with desegregation their children had been victimized anew. African American parents in Hayti and New Madrid alleged that the high concentrations of black students placed in special education classrooms produced a new variety of segregation. They further claimed that black students were more likely to be suspended from school or receive corporal punishment than white students who disrupted classes or violated school policies.[21]

All told, desegregation brought some meaningful change to many Missouri school districts. The vast majority of the state's school districts adopted desegregation policies within two years of the initial *Brown* decision, and those communities that for a time resisted were desegregated during the 1960s. In school districts operating several schools, desegregation did not result in extensive racial mixing at the elementary level where attendance zones for schools were drawn around smaller neighborhoods, and frequently did not cross lines of residential segregation. Secondary schools, however, tended to be significantly more integrated because the attendance zones were larger geographically, encompassing larger numbers of students, and often crossed lines of residential segregation. The implementation of desegregation plans by school districts across Missouri is certainly significant, but it is important to note that developments elsewhere in the state were largely overshadowed by the course of desegregation in the state's two largest cities.

Implementing the *Brown* Decision in St. Louis and Kansas City

Clearly, the most important early steps toward school desegregation were taken in the cities of the Border States, including St. Louis and

Kansas City, which were hailed as "illuminating pilot operations for Southern cities."[22] Within months of the Court's 1954 *Brown* decision, Baltimore, Washington, D.C., and Wilmington, Delaware, had all unveiled plans to desegregate their public schools.[23] Similarly, the St. Louis Board of Education announced its desegregation plan on June 22, 1954. Since more than one-half of the state's black students were enrolled in the St. Louis district, the bold leadership demonstrated by St. Louis was essential to the success of desegregation in Missouri. The St. Louis plan was a graduated scheme to integrate the special schools in September 1954, the high schools in January 1955, and the elementary schools in September 1955. It also provided for integration of the staff to coincide with integration of the student population, wherein the racial composition of the staff was to reflect the racial composition of the student body at each integrated school. Furthermore, preliminary steps were taken to integrate gradually the administrative posts in the district. The prompt action in St. Louis was made possible by ten years of studying population trends and facility use in the district in preparation for an order to desegregate.[24] Within one month of the Supreme Court's 1954 ruling, Kansas City's school board had also announced plans to desegregate its public schools beginning in September 1955.[25]

The St. Louis and Kansas City plans largely mirrored each other. Both dissolved their former systems of using two sets of attendance zones around schools to maintain segregation. In such a system one set of school boundaries applied to African American students and assigned students to the nearest segregated black school, while the other set of lines applied to white students and segregated white schools. Both cities replaced their dual attendance zones with a single set of attendance zones based on a neighborhood schools concept, and all students— African American and white—were assigned to schools nearest their homes. Of course, due to the extensive residential segregation in both cities, neither plan produced widespread racial mixing in the neighborhood schools. Moreover, in some sections of both cities, the new attendance zone lines largely conformed to the existing lines of residential segregation and served to reinforce the separation of the races.[26] Thus, when Kansas City superintendent James Hazlett proudly announced in September 1955 that forty-four of the district's ninety-two schools were integrated he was including numerous instances of "token integration." Forty-three Kansas City schools remained 100 percent white and five others remained 100 percent black. For more than 70 percent of Kansas

City's African American student population, the shift to integrated schools had brought little change as they remained consigned to schools that were more than 90 percent black. Indeed, almost 30 percent of those students remained in schools that were exclusively African American.[27]

Kansas City's desegregation plan was projected to result in more racial mixing in the schools than actually occurred. The difference between the projected enrollments, based on counts of schoolchildren within each school's attendance zone area, and those that enrolled in their neighborhood schools in September is attributable to a section of the desegregation plan that provided for the continuation of a long-standing school district policy that liberally granted transfers between schools. The affect of the transfer policy is most apparent in the formerly segregated black schools and in schools located in or very near to African American residential areas. At these schools, thousands of white students who lived within the attendance zones enrolled in other public schools in September 1955. For instance, almost three hundred whites lived within the attendance zones served by the district's two formerly segregated secondary schools, Lincoln High School and Coles Junior High, but when school opened, just two whites enrolled at Lincoln and four at Coles.[28]

Initially, the St. Louis plan prohibited transfers between schools except in extraordinary circumstances. However, in 1963 the school district reinstituted a policy allowing for transfers to schools where there was space available. Although the policy was conceived as a means of providing some relief for crowding in schools, transfers were also utilized to elude integration, particularly in those schools having majority black student populations.[29]

The initial desegregation plans in St. Louis and Kansas City certainly complied with the Supreme Court's admonition to make a prompt and reasonable start toward admitting African American students to school on a nondiscriminatory basis. The two plans, however, produced rather limited integration. By shackling the desegregation plans to a neighborhood schools concept, both school districts assured that the impact of the plan would be confined almost entirely to those schools where the new attendance zone lines crossed the prevailing lines of residential segregation. Moreover, the continuation of the liberal transfer policy in Kansas City and the reintroduction of a transfer policy in St. Louis further mitigated the extent of racial mixing in the schools. The transfer policy provided an easily accessible vehicle for eluding desegregation, and it is clear that thousands of white families took advantage of transfers when their children were assigned to majority African American schools. Despite reams of data confirming that transfers were the preferred tool to avoid attending an integrated school, the Kansas City School Board did not reform the policy until 1974.

In short, the public schools in St. Louis and Kansas City remained largely segregated. It is important to remember, however, that throughout the 1950s and early 1960s the Supreme Court required nothing more than the dissolution of the former segregated system and nondiscriminatory placement of students in schools. When measured against that modest standard, both cities were in compliance with the law, and, by virtue of promptly implementing desegregation plans, were indeed in the vanguard of cities engaged in school integration.

Discrimination and Resegregation in the 1960s and 1970s

For the first twenty years of desegregated schooling in Missouri little changed after the implementation of the initial desegregation plans. The vast majority of Missouri's school districts were organized around neighborhood schools concepts and the extent of racial integration in the schools was largely determined by the residential patterns of the community. In smaller towns, such arrangements typically resulted in rather limited integration in the elementary schools, but generally produced considerably more racial mixing in the secondary schools, which enrolled more students and drew from larger geographic sections of the city. In Kansas City and St. Louis, this was not necessarily the case. In both cities, it was quite likely that a typical African American student would attend an elementary school that was virtually exclusively black and then move on to secondary schools that were equally imbalanced. Moreover, during the early 1960s, for thousands of black elementary students in St. Louis and Kansas City who were bused from the core African American residential areas to predominantly white schools, the bus ride did not result in their being placed in integrated classrooms.

During the early 1960s, both cities experienced severe crowding in the elementary schools serving the African American residential areas. Crowding was a byproduct of neighborhoods located on the fringes of the expanding black residential area turning over from largely white occupancy to virtually entirely black occupancy. As these neighborhoods resegregated, the age structure of the area changed dramatically. A large share of the new African American residents were young families with elementary-age children, and these families replaced fleeing whites, many of whom did not have elementary-age children. The process, then, inexorably led to crowding in the elementary schools, some of which operated at nearly twice their capacity. In order to relieve the crowding associated with neighborhood change, both the St. Louis and Kansas City School Districts implemented similar busing plans. In both cities, entire classrooms of black students and their teachers boarded buses at overcrowded schools destined for predominantly white schools that had vacant classrooms. Upon arrival, the black students and teachers were placed in vacant classrooms and mixed with the rest of the school's students and faculty only during lunch, recess, and other school-wide functions. Despite school district attempts to convince black parents otherwise, the intact classroom busing plans clearly did not advance integration, and for many patrons smacked of a return to "Jim Crow." Under pressure from the local branches of the NAACP and other civil rights organizations, both cities ended intact busing in the mid-1960s and began integrating black bus students at the receiving schools.[30] Nevertheless, the reasoning behind the intact busing program revealed one of the central concerns of school administrators in both cities.

During the 1960s, St. Louis and Kansas City began to experience massive white flight to the growing suburban rings, and school officials in both cities were gravely concerned about the impact that integration had in accelerating the white exodus. It had been the experience in both cities that when large numbers of African American students were introduced in a school, what chance there was for stable integration rapidly evaporated and those schools resegregated, often in as short a period as five years. This pattern of segregated white, brief (but highly unstable) integration, and resegregation had been repeated in dozens of neighborhood schools in St. Louis and Kansas City.

For example, in 1955, Kansas City's Horace Mann Elementary was located in an exclusively white residential area about one mile south of the leading edge of the large, core African American neighborhood. In 1955, the school was 100 percent white, but within two years, as the large black neighborhood expanded toward the south, the racial composition at Horace Mann and in the surrounding neighborhood began to undergo a dramatic transformation. In 1956, the first black students enrolled at Horace Mann, thirteen in all, and from that modest beginning the school completely resegregated over the next six years. By 1959, the school was 53 percent African American, and three years later was 97 percent black. The rapid resegregation of Horace Mann was no aberration. Dozens of schools in Kansas City and St. Louis underwent similar transitions as black residents moved into previously all-white residential areas. Moreover, at Horace Mann and elsewhere the process resulted in grossly overcrowded schools. In 1962, ten classrooms from Horace Mann boarded the buses bound for other schools having vacant rooms.[31]

The rapid resegregation of Horace Mann Elementary was characteristic of a number of schools in both cities during the 1960s and 1970s, and was a microcosm of larger demographic shifts occurring in the central cities and surrounding suburbs. During the 1960s, the African American population in St. Louis grew by almost 40,000, while the city's white population declined by more than 167,000. Over the same period, Kansas City's black population grew by 29,800, while the white population fell by nearly 50,000. Such massive demographic shifts carried profound implications for school management and the rapid resegregation of neighborhoods rendered the objective of stable, integrated schooling largely unattainable. Particularly troubling to school officials were the huge numbers of whites fleeing the cities, a demographic trend that continued throughout the 1970s. During the 1970s, St. Louis's white population fell by 122,000, while in Kansas City the white population declined by more than 86,000 and the city's public schools lost almost 25,000 white students.[32] At the same time, the suburban ring around each city experienced tremendous growth, the overwhelming majority of which was new white residents. Between 1950 and 1980, the suburbs around Kansas City added more than 500,000 new residents, while the suburban ring in metropolitan St. Louis grew by almost one million persons.[33]

Of course, the changing demographics of the cities were also apparent in the schools. In 1969, black students became the majority of Kansas City's public school enrollment, and the St. Louis schools were more than 60 percent African American.[34] One consequence of the growing concentration of black residents in the central cities and white flight to the suburbs was the increasingly precarious fiscal standing of both school districts. Although both cities received substantial sums of federal money under the Elementary and Secondary Education Act and other federal initiatives, both teetered on the verge of insolvency during the late 1960s and early 1970s. Whereas black students were a majority of the enrollment in both cities by the late 1960s, white residents continued to comprise the majority of the population in both districts, and white voters demonstrated little inclination to approve of fiscal measures which would benefit a majority African American school district. In Kansas City, for example, nineteen consecutive building bond issues and proposals to increase the tax levy were defeated by the city's voters between 1969 and 1984.[35] Consequently, new schools to address the problem of overcrowding could not be built, maintenance at all schools suffered, new programs were never launched, pupil-teacher ratios rose, and the schools in both cities became less pleasant environments for education with each passing year. Still other disruptions brought on by fiscal difficulties created turmoil in both districts. Kansas City and St. Louis suffered through teacher strikes in the 1970s and 1980s in the wake of school district policy decisions to cut hundreds of staff and teaching positions and freeze teachers' salaries. Moreover, the declining quality of the public schools in both cities fueled middle-class and white flight from the city. Thousands of families that possessed the means abandoned the cities for the growing suburban rings, further compounding the problem of racial isolation in the inner-city schools.

Increases in the African American student population coupled with declining numbers of white students typically translated into a growing number of de facto segregated schools. In 1967, for instance, 76 of St. Louis's 182 schools were more than 90 percent black, and six years later that number had risen to 105. A similar pattern characterized Kansas City on a smaller scale. Of Kansas City's 96 schools, 26 were more than 90 percent black in 1967. Six years later there were 37 such schools.[36] Racial isolation for a significant part of the black student population had been evident in both cities since integrated schooling had begun in the mid-1950s. By the early 1970s, however, the breadth of de facto segregation in the schools had reached unprecedented proportions, and neither city remained in compliance with the most recent legal decisions regarding desegregation.

During the 1960s and early 1970s, the nation's courts handed down a steady number of orders requiring school districts to eliminate "root and branch" the vestiges of segregation and promote more racial mixing in the nation's schools.[37] The St. Louis and Kansas City School Districts had accomplished neither of those objectives. Vestiges of the segregated system persisted in both cities, where schools that had been black prior to the *Brown* decision remained entirely African American twenty years later having never enrolled a single white student. Moreover, the steadily rising number of virtually all black schools in both districts plainly violated the standards announced by the Supreme Court in *Swann v. Charlotte-Mecklenberg*. In *Swann*, the justices acknowledged that eliminating all of the one-race schools might not be possible in all cities, but reiterated that the continuation of a number of racially isolated schools must be justifiable and the number of such schools kept to a minimum. The sheer number of virtually all-black schools in St. Louis and Kansas City violated the Court's standards, and opened both districts to litigation in the early 1970s.

In Kansas City, the school district's legal problems stemmed from the findings of an eighteen-month investigation launched by the United States Department of Health, Education and Welfare in 1973. The HEW probe found that due to the patterns of residential segregation in the city, the manner in which attendance zones were drawn, and the impact of the transfer policy, Kansas City's public schools remained highly segregated and that the majority of the district's schools were racially identifiable by virtue of the composition of their student enrollments and teaching staffs. When negotiations with Kansas City school officials failed to produce meaningful reforms in the district's integration policies, HEW initiated proceedings to terminate the school district's federal funding, which at the time accounted for more than 10 percent of the district's operating budget.[38] Over the course of two years and under pressure from HEW, the school district finally ended the transfer policy, forcibly reassigned more than five hundred teachers to balance the faculties at schools, and in 1977 adopted Plan 6-C, a district-wide busing plan to promote additional integration. Although Plan 6-C succeeded in producing meaningful integration in the largely white schools located on the fringes of the city, it promised little change for more than seventeen thousand African American students who continued to attend the twenty-five schools that remained more than 90 percent black.[39] By neglecting to deal aggressively with the extensive racial isolation in the schools serving the black residential corridor, Plan 6-C failed to address the obvious vestiges of segregation that lingered in the district, and thereby laid the foundation for the litigation that would dominate school district affairs in the 1980s and 1990s.

Looking toward the Suburbs

Given their substantial problems with de facto segregation and declining white student populations in the late 1960s, school administrators in both Kansas City and St. Louis began to look toward the suburbs as a lasting solution for stable school integration. Arguing that school integration was crucial to the "social health of the total community," Kansas City superintendent James Hazlett offered a number of proposals designed to facilitate increased racial integration in the metropolitan area's public schools. Among several other options, Hazlett's 1968 pamphlet, "Concepts for Changing Times," proposed pairing and clustering schools across district lines, voluntary exchanges of students and faculty between the city and suburbs, and the creation of a single school district encompassing the metropolitan area. Although Hazlett's proposals were endorsed by a broad cross-section of the city's religious, civic, and business leaders, his report met with what one commentator characterized as "deafening silence" in the suburbs.[40]

One year later, a special committee appointed by the state legislature to study school district consolidation across the state again raised the prospect of metropolitan desegregation. In its 1969 report, "Equal Treatment to Equals," the Spainhower commission concluded that the population in the state's metropolitan areas was divided "into distinct groups, the poor and the affluent, the well-educated and the poorly-educated, black and white." In order to address the fiscal disparities existing between city and suburb, and to fulfill the promise of the *Brown* decision to provide equal educational opportunities for all children, the commission recommended the creation of metropolitan-wide school districts.[41] In a manner similar to the frosty reception that Hazlett's proposals for metropolitan school desegregation met with in the suburbs, the Spainhower commission's recommendations never garnered much support outside of the two major cities. No bill proposing the creation of metropolitan school districts for St. Louis and Kansas City was ever drafted in the state legislature, and the idea quietly withered in Jefferson City. Unable to make any headway toward the creation of metropolitan school districts either through legislative action or the voluntary cooperation of the suburbs, both the Kansas City and St. Louis School Districts turned toward the judiciary. The initial course of both lawsuits was painfully slow in the 1970s, but each ultimately resulted in profound changes to both school districts in the 1980s and 1990s.

Kansas City: The *Jenkins* Litigation

By the mid-1970s, the general consensus among Kansas City school administrators was that meaningful, stable integration confined solely to the city was impossible. Throughout the 1970s, the Kansas City schools witnessed a remarkable exodus of white students. On average, the white enrollment in the district fell by about two thousand students each year. In some years, the declines were much sharper, such as following the 1973 teachers' strike when the white enrollment plummeted by nearly six thousand students. By 1978, the school district was two-thirds black, and the white enrollment had fallen from more than fifty thousand students in the mid-1960s to fewer than thirteen thousand.[42]

Searching for causes of the substantial declines in the white student enrollment, Kansas City school administrators placed blame squarely on the suburbs, and in 1977 filed a lawsuit seeking the creation of a metropolitan-wide school desegregation plan by judicial order. Kansas City's case was unique in some respects. First, the lawsuit marked the first time that a school desegregation case was conceptualized as crossing state lines. Among the numerous defendants named in Kansas City's complaint were the governor of the state of Kansas, the Kansas State Board of Education and its executive officers, five suburban school districts across the state line in Kansas, the governor of Missouri, the Missouri State Board of Education and its officers, thirteen suburban school districts in Missouri, and the federal departments of Transportation, Housing and Urban Development, and Health, Education and Welfare. The suit was also unusual in that the Kansas City School District served as the plaintiff in the case and essentially argued that the city's schools were segregated but that the school district was not responsible.

At the district court, the case was assigned to Judge Russell Clark. Although his experience with school desegregation cases was extremely limited, Clark was in for a long tutorial; he would preside over the case for the next two decades. The judge's first order, announced in 1978, fundamentally changed the nature of the entire lawsuit. He dismissed the Kansas defendants from the litigation and realigned the case by adding the Kansas City School District to the defendant group.[43] After numerous delays and motions to dismiss the case, the suit resumed in 1983 with a new plaintiff group comprised of African American students and their parents, represented by local attorney Arthur Benson and attorneys from the NAACP's national offices. Although the 1983 case, *Jenkins v. Missouri,* did not result in the creation of a metropolitan school desegregation plan, it did radically remake the entire school district.

In *Jenkins,* Judge Clark reasoned that the suburban school districts and the federal agencies named in the suit bore no responsibility for the vestiges of segregation that persisted in the Kansas City schools. Clark did, however, find both the school district and the state of Missouri liable and proceeded over the course of the next several years to craft by judicial order a unique and wildly expensive plan to refashion the school district and restore the victims of segregation to a position of equal educational opportunities. Among the remedial measures ordered by Judge Clark was a sweeping array of educational enhancements, so called "*Milliken II* programs," in order to raise achievement levels among African American students. He also ordered the conversion of fifty-six schools to magnet schools such that African American students would be provided with educational opportunities comparable to those available in suburban districts, and in hopes of drawing additional white students to the Kansas City schools. Clark further reasoned that implementing the magnet themes, improving the "desegregative attractiveness" of the Kansas City schools, and rendering the district's facilities comparable to those in the suburbs demanded a massive program of capital improvements. Under the capital improvement orders, seventeen new schools were built and fifty-five others were extensively renovated.[44]

The expense of the plan was staggering, more than $1.5 billion in the first ten years, with roughly 75 percent of the costs falling to the state and the school district responsible for the remainder. Even though its fiscal burden was considerably lighter, within two years the school district could not meet its share of the expenses. In order to ensure that the remedy was fully funded, Judge Clark exercised what he termed the court's "broad, equitable powers" and doubled property taxes in Kansas City in 1987.[45] In subsequent orders, Clark also ordered salary increases for every employee of the school district, extensions of the educational enhancements, and substantial increases in additional expenses related to desegregation, such as student transportation.

In short, most of the remedy in Kansas City revolved around three interrelated objectives, all of which, Clark reasoned, addressed the dual goals of improving educational opportunities for the city's African American students and making the school system and its innovative curricular programs attractive to potential white transfer students from the suburbs. Clark suggested that the progress of the remedial plan might be measured in two ways—by analyzing growth among African American students on standardized achievement tests, and by monitoring the number of white transfer students drawn into Kansas City's magnet system. Although Clark's logic may have been convincing for some observers, others pointed to Kansas City as a glaring example of judicial excess and argued that numerous elements of the remedy were thoroughly unrelated to the constitutional violations.

On three occasions Clark's orders in *Jenkins* were appealed to the nation's highest court, and in 1995, the Supreme Court dealt the magnet schools desegregation plan a mortal blow.[46] Writing for the majority, Chief Justice William Rehnquist undermined the district court's rationale for the magnet system and Clark's orders requiring the state to continue funding salary increases and *Milliken II* programs in Kansas City. Rehnquist found that Clark had overreached his authority in ordering those provisions in the remedy which were designed to attract white students from the suburbs. Without having found constitutional violations that were interdistrict in nature and that implicated the suburbs, the majority determined that Clark had no basis for ordering a remedy that was interdistrict in scope. Furthermore, Rehnquist's majority opinion chided Clark for utilizing test scores as the standard by which the progress of the remedy's educational components was measured. Essentially, the Court's majority found that full implementation of the educational components was a valid objective, but rejected Clark's reasoning that the state's funding of the *Milliken II* programs should continue until the district's standardized test scores improved significantly.

In essence, the Court's 1995 *Jenkins* decision undermined the entire foundation of the desegregation plan. The majority opinion clearly indicated growing reluctance on the part of the Court to uphold the continuing judicial oversight of school desegregation cases. After four decades of defending school desegregation, the Court signaled its intention to return Kansas City and other school districts that had been operating under court orders for years, to local control. The significance of the 1995 *Jenkins* decision was not lost on the some two hundred school districts operating under court-ordered desegregation plans. Within months of the ruling, scores of school districts had returned to court seeking to be relieved of judicial oversight.[47]

Indeed, within two months of the *Jenkins* decision, the state of Missouri and attorneys for the plaintiff schoolchildren and the school district were engaged in negotiations to produce a settlement for Kansas City. The process dragged on for four years before an agreement was finally struck in 1999 that provided for the state's massive infusions of money into the Kansas City schools to gradually be reduced over a five-year period.[48]

St. Louis: The *Liddell* Litigation

The legal odyssey in St. Louis began in February 1972 with a class-action filed against the school district by a small organization of African Americans called Concerned Parents for North St. Louis. The parents group argued that the school district had maintained segregated schools on St. Louis's northside through a combination of attendance zone adjustments, intact busing, the use of portable classrooms to keep students attending overcrowded schools in their neighborhood schools, and the construction of ten new schools in north St. Louis during the mid-1960s to keep black students in virtually all black schools. The lawsuit did not, however, result in a court order. After nearly three years of hearings and litigation, the plaintiff parents and the school district entered into a modest consent decree to resolve the issues presented in the case. The decree called upon the school district to do the following: promote staff integration by initiating a plan of voluntary and, if necessary, mandatory, teacher reassignments; study ways in which the feeder patterns and attendance lines could be modified to promote racial integration in the city's academic high schools; and establish magnet school programs that would draw integrated enrollments from across the city.[49] For a time, the agreement reached in the consent decree was widely hailed as a workable alternative to forced busing and court-ordered desegregation. The initial euphoria, however, was short lived and litigation resumed in 1977.

In 1977, the NAACP joined the suit as plaintiffs and successfully petitioned the district court to have the state of Missouri, the state board of education, and the state commissioner for education join the school district in the defendant group. In the trial that followed, district court judge James Meredith ruled that the St. Louis schools were not unconstitutionally segregated. Ignoring all of the legal precedents established in the late 1960s and early 1970s that mandated school districts promote greater integration, Meredith found that the neighborhood schools plan, which St. Louis had adhered to with few modifications since 1954, continued to satisfy the legal standards for desegregation. On appeal, the Eighth Circuit Court overturned Meredith's decision, finding numerous vestiges of the segregated system that remained in St. Louis, most notably that of the twenty-eight segregated black schools that the district operated in 1954, twenty-six remained virtually all black in 1980.

The case was remanded to the district court with instructions to order a mandatory desegregation plan for St. Louis.[50]

Over the course of the next three years, the details of the St. Louis desegregation plan were settled in the district court and at the Eighth Circuit. Due to massive white flight from the city in the 1960s and 1970s, the St. Louis public schools were more than two-thirds African American in 1980 and any plan confined strictly to the city school district was certain to result in little integration. Furthermore, given that the suburban school districts surrounding St. Louis had not been named in the 1977 suit, and thus had not been found liable for the segregation that remained in the inner city, the courts were prohibited by the U.S. Supreme Court's 1974 *Milliken v. Bradley* decision from ordering the suburbs to participate in the desegregation of the St. Louis schools. Faced with this Hobson's choice, the task of overseeing the crafting of a desegregation plan fell to district court judge William Hungate, who was named to preside over the suit following the death of Judge Meredith. Judge Hungate proved to be equal to the task, relying on a creative approach to persuade the school district, the state, and the suburbs to craft a settlement agreement. On one hand, Hungate announced that he was prepared to begin hearing an NAACP suit alleging that the twenty-three suburbs in St. Louis County had committed constitutional violations that had the effect of exacerbating segregation in the St. Louis schools. The judge further stipulated that, should the NAACP suit reveal constitutional violations by the suburbs, he was prepared to order the creation of a single metropolitan school district encompassing St. Louis and the surrounding county. On the other hand, Hungate offered the suburbs a more attractive alternative. He assured that any suburban districts which voluntarily participated in the St. Louis desegregation plan would be dropped from the NAACP's metropolitan lawsuit.[51] Hungate's carrot-and-stick approach produced the desired result—all twenty-three suburban school districts and the state of Missouri agreed to participate in a voluntary desegregation plan for St. Louis.

Essentially, the settlement agreement included four major components. First, it required each suburban district to increase the number of African American students by 15 percent by accepting transfer students from St. Louis. Second, the plan called for the establishment of magnet school programs in St. Louis in order to attract voluntary white transfer students to the urban schools. Third, the plan required the state to pay all transportation costs and to pay both the home district and the host

district of each transfer student the per-pupil cost of educat
within those districts. Fourth, the agreement provided fo
improvements and educational enhancements for the more
thousand African American students who would remain in the in
schools.[52]

The basic parameters of the settlement agreement in St. Louis
remained in place for fifteen years and did result in significant integration, particularly in the suburban districts. By 1988, about twelve thousand African American transfer students from the inner city were
attending classes in the suburban school districts. White transfer students to the city's magnet programs were slower to materialize and
much smaller in number. After a decade of very slow growth, the number of white transfers in the city's magnets climbed above one thousand
and peaked at just under fifteen hundred in 1997. Of course, the expense
of the plan was considerable, and the state of Missouri continually
assailed the rising costs. In 1993, transportation costs alone ran as high
as $3,500 per year for a single suburban student driven daily by taxi to
the inner-city magnets. All told, the cost of the ambitious plan over its
first fifteen years was more than $1.5 billion.[53]

As was true following the Supreme Court decision in Kansas City's
Jenkins case, by the late 1990s the state was actively pursuing a settlement defining the gradual termination of the state's obligations to finance
the desegregation plan in St. Louis. Armed with the recently won *Jenkins*
decision and its admonition to end the decades of judicial oversight in
school desegregation and return school districts to local control, the
state had considerably greater leverage in the negotiations that ensued
in St. Louis. A settlement in St. Louis's *Liddell* litigation was finalized in
1999 with the state's obligations to the voluntary student transfer desegregation plan gradually diminishing over a ten-year period. As the new
millennium approached, Jay Nixon, the attorney general for the state of
Missouri, had in hand two settlement agreements that clarified the gradual reduction in the disproportionate sums of state revenue that the two
urban desegregation plans consumed and defined the end of the state's
role in both school desegregation cases.

Conclusion

Developments in the state of Missouri present an interesting case study
of the course of school desegregation in the United States. On one hand,

school districts across Missouri were among the first in the country to implement desegregation plans following the *Brown* decisions and were properly recognized for their initiative. Most significant were the plans adopted by St. Louis and Kansas City, and both cities were rightly applauded for being among the vanguard in school desegregation. Although, in retrospect, the decision to adopt neighborhood schools plans for desegregation may seem shortsighted, it is important to recognize that the law required nothing more until the mid-1960s. Given the extent of residential segregation in both cities, the neighborhood schools plans had severe limitations, but they do mark an important starting point.

More troubling is the benign neglect practiced by school administrators in both cities for the next twenty years. Until the mid-1970s, school officials in Kansas City and St. Louis consistently bowed to the interests of white patrons with respect to school integration and consciously implemented policies that underscored the separation of the races in the public schools. In both cities, school district leaders clung doggedly to the sanctity of the neighborhood schools concept long after it was clear that such a plan could not produce integration. It is telling that in Kansas City, school administrators resisted reforming the transfer policy and adopting a busing plan until the district was threatened with the termination of its federal funds in the mid-1970s. Meanwhile, in St. Louis, ten new schools were built in the 1960s to ensure that African American students living on the all-black north side would remain in northside schools. Moreover, school officials consistently rejected other alternatives that promised to promote more racial mixing in the schools. For instance, in 1963 both school districts rejected plans presented by civil rights organizations to integrate additional schools in each district. In fact, the original consent decree forged in St. Louis in 1975 is largely based upon the recommendations made by the Citizens' Advisory Committee twelve years earlier.[54]

The consequences of inaction were profound for both districts. By the mid-1970s, both school districts had fallen out of compliance with the prevailing legal standards and both were embroiled in school desegregation lawsuits. In 1980, the Eighth Circuit Court, noting that the schools of north St. Louis were virtually all-black in 1954 and remained so twenty-six years later, while south St. Louis remained virtually all-white, concluded that "the Board of Education has simply never dealt with this overwhelming reality."[55] The *Liddell* case ultimately compelled school officials in metropolitan St. Louis to address the racial isolation of African American students just as the *Jenkins* suit would finally bring substantial changes to Kansas City.

The *Liddell* and *Jenkins* cases are noteworthy for the manner in which both lawsuits illustrate shifts in school desegregation law and desegregation remedies over time. By the mid-1980s, the backlash against forced busing for integration had compelled school districts operating under court orders to consider less coercive approaches to desegregation. The notion that desegregation should be voluntary figures prominently in the remedies for both cities. On one hand, the nation's most expansive and expensive magnet schools system was created in Kansas City with the dual goals of remedying the effects of past segregation for African American students while also drawing in white students for purposes of integration. While on the other hand, the remedy for St. Louis established magnet schools to attract white students while also providing African American students the opportunity to voluntarily transfer to the surrounding suburban districts. Both approaches were to a degree successful, but both were inadequate in addressing the reality of urban demographics. Both plans implicitly recognized that voluntary integration would leave tens of thousands of African American students relegated to racially isolated schools in the inner city. Although these schools would be the beneficiaries of considerable spending for educational enhancements, the considerable segregation which remained in the city was testament to the racial polarization of both metropolitan areas. For thousands of students in St. Louis and Kansas City, the decades of judicial oversight and the implementation of ambitious desegregation plans brought little change to their daily circumstances.

Finally, Missouri is illustrative of the judiciary's retreat from school desegregation and the dismantling of school desegregation plans that has occurred since 1995. The Supreme Court's *Jenkins* decision in 1995, coupled with previous decisions in *Board of Education of Oklahoma City v. Dowell* in 1991 and *Freeman v. Pitts* in 1992, revealed the shifting posture of the Court's majority in school desegregation cases.[56] By the mid-1990s, a majority of the Supreme Court had essentially concluded that forty years of school desegregation had sufficiently remedied the injustice of past segregation. In *Jenkins*, the majority opinion lays bare the determination to curb the role of the nation's courts in desegregation cases, while emphasizing that judicial oversight should only be temporary and that local districts should reassume responsibility for their affairs. Indeed, in the wake of *Jenkins,* school desegregation has come full circle. Scores of cities across the country have been relieved of court supervision, and many have returned to neighborhood schools. When coupled with the patterns of residential segregation in the city and the massive white flight that numerous cities have experienced, the return to neighborhood schools has generally resulted in a degree of racial mixing comparable to what was achieved across Missouri in 1955.

The Complexity of School Desegregation in the Borderland

THE CASE OF INDIANA

Jayne R. Beilke

In his autobiographical novel *The Learning Tree,* celebrated photographer, writer and composer Gordon Parks described the rural town inhabited by the Wingers, a poor black family during the 1920s: "Like all other Kansas towns, Cherokee Flats wallowed in the social complexities of a borderline state. Here, for the black man, freedom loosed one hand while custom restrained the other."[1] Parks went on to explain that while the law books stood for equal rights, the law itself (often represented by an illiterate white law officer) never bothered to enforce it. Principles that had been codified de jure were overridden by de facto practices in all spheres of society, including education. In Cherokee Flats, blacks attended separate schools until they were allowed to enroll in the town's only high school during the freshman year. Parks's narrative is representative of the pervasive racial ambiguity in regards to education that manifested itself in border and northern states in general.[2] This chapter examines the uneven (if not contradictory) progress toward school desegregation in Indiana, a midwestern border state, during the post-1954 period.

Despite its geographical position north of the Mason-Dixon line and its political status as a free (non-slaveholding) state, southerners who settled Indiana imported the discriminatory educational and social policies and practices of the South toward African Americans. Although some white schools admitted blacks, especially before 1820, most northern states either excluded them altogether or established separate schools. By the 1830s, statute or custom placed black children in separate schools in nearly every northern community.[3] During the period 1824 to 1869, the only educational opportunities officially open to blacks in Indiana were private schools maintained by the African American community, philanthropic societies, or religious groups such as the Religious Society of Friends (Quakers) and Baptists. Although the 1837 Indiana School Law restricted common schools to white students, the School Law of 1852 explicitly *excluded* black children.[4] In 1855, the School Law stated that black and mulatto children were not to be included in the enumeration for school purposes, nor were taxes to be collected from blacks and mulattos for the support of schools. In 1869, the legislature authorized separate schools for black children with the same rights and privileges as schools for whites. If there was an insufficient number of black children to form a separate school, school trustees were to use the proportion of local funds dedicated for the schooling of black children to provide other means of education.[5]

The 1877 School Law opened the door to school integration by granting local school authorities the freedom to provide schools for blacks. When no separate school was available, black children could attend white schools. Additionally, if black children tested for a higher grade than was taught in the school, they could attend appropriate white schools.[6] There are documented instances of blacks attending schools with whites when the community condoned it, particularly in cases where a small number of blacks lived in or near white settlements. Although both whites and blacks criticized the 1877 School Law during the 1880s, the Indiana Supreme Court upheld it. It would not be until 1949 that segregation would be successfully challenged in Indiana. During the interim, Indiana became the northern stronghold of the Ku Klux Klan and white supremacy, as evidenced by pervasive anti-immigrant, anti-black, anti-Catholic, and anti-foreigner attitudes.[7]

Adherence to and interpretation of the 1877 School Law underscored the racial topography of the borderland: in the southern half of Indiana and many cities throughout the state, schools were usually segregated de facto or de jure. In Evansville, which had the largest black population in the area, the elementary schools were officially segregated.

Some of the rooms in the Clark Elementary School served as the black high school until Lincoln High School was constructed. The cities of Bloomington and Terre Haute maintained separate elementary schools, and the few blacks that attended high school went to the same school as whites. In the state capitol of Indianapolis, home to nearly half of the state's black population, elementary schools were segregated with few exceptions. School systems in cities and towns north of Indianapolis were seldom segregated de jure, but residential segregation meant that there was often a black elementary school, usually taught by an African American teacher. The company town of Gary, Indiana, which was built to support the steel industry at the turn of the nineteenth century, developed its own peculiar system of segregation: that is, black and white children sometimes occupied the same building but were taught in separate classes.[8]

In Jeffersonville, a small town on the Ohio River, African Americans and the local branch of the National Association for the Advancement of Colored People had campaigned for the improvement of the black high school. Built in 1891, the school lacked both plumbing and a gymnasium. When the school board announced plans for a new vocational training school open only to whites, the simmering resentment in the black community boiled over. In 1941, George Martin, a black student, filed a suit in federal district court for admission to the all-white Jefferson High School, in order to enroll in courses that were not offered at the black school. After the school board refused to admit him, he filed a suit for damages and an injunction. The NAACP hired a Louisville lawyer, Prentice Thomas, who in turn sought advice from Thurgood Marshall, the head of the NAACP Legal Defense Fund. Although details of the litigation are incomplete, the suit was dismissed, perhaps on a technicality—Thomas had not been admitted to the Indiana bar.[9] The desegregation effort in Jeffersonville had little impact on the southern counties of the state. Instead, attention turned to the northern part of the state during World War II.

Racial tensions and fear of race riots in northern Indiana, particularly in Gary, led to efforts by the Gary Chamber of Commerce and members of the white establishment to take steps to eliminate discriminatory policies. As part of these efforts, the Gary School Board issued a policy in August 1946 that students should not be discriminated against because of race, color, or religion in the district in which they lived or in the schools they attended. The school board took this action after a prolonged strike at Froebel High School. In September 1945, white students walked out of Froebel, demanding the removal of all black students and the replacement of the Froebel principal. Receiving national publicity, the strike revealed the deep division in Gary between the black community and the white immigrant working-class community, which encouraged its children to strike and offered them support. The students finally returned to classes after the school board promised to investigate, but racial tensions did not subside. Nevertheless, community leaders and organizations, including the Urban League, the League of Women Voters, the YWCA, and the Gary Council of Churches sponsored human relations workshops and worked behind the scenes to persuade the school board to move toward integration of all public schools. The board finally issued the statement in August 1946, but implementation did not begin until September 1947.[10] Although the *principle* of integration had been established, most Gary schools remained predominantly white or black because of residential patterns. Only 116 African Americans enrolled in previously all-white schools, including thirty-eight who were assigned to Emerson High School. In response, about 80 percent of the white students at Emerson boycotted classes for ten days. White students and other demonstrators gathered every day to jeer and threaten black students who dared to attend. However, the school board refused to negotiate with the truants, and the boycott ended.[11]

Nearby East Chicago, Indiana, had no separate schools for African Americans, but for twenty-five years school authorities had followed a policy of excluding them from extracurricular activities and social events. In 1947 a coalition of citizens from a variety of organizations began to push for ending these practices. James Hunter, a longtime member of the state legislature, joined the president of the chamber of commerce and the president of the League of Women Voters to form a committee to carry out this objective. At their urging, the city council passed a resolution demanding that the school board end discriminatory policies.[12] The actions in Gary and other cities in the northern part of the state in 1946 and 1947 left Indianapolis and Evansville as the only large American cities outside the South with de jure segregated school systems.

In the capitol city of Indianapolis, organizations urging desegregation concentrated their efforts on the General Assembly. Early in 1947, two Republicans from Marion County—William Fortune, a white representative, and Wilbur Grant, a black—introduced a bill to abolish segregation in all public schools, including state colleges and universities. Under the measure, which was in large part the work of the Race Relations Committee of the Indianapolis Church Federation, desegregation was to take place gradually over a period of years. At a public hearing, representatives from groups supporting the bill pointed out that Indianapolis was the only large city in the North with a segregated school system. In addition, they called the segregated system "expensive, unfair, undemocratic, unreasonable, and immoral."[13] Opponents countered that in a city where separation of the races was the norm in employment and in social relations, desegregation would lead to racial problems. In a test case in 1947, Henry J. Richardson Jr. and Roselyn Comer Richardson tried to enroll their eldest son, Henry III, in the neighborhood school near their home. He was refused admission and sent back to the black school, which was several miles away.[14] After this, the Indianapolis branch of the NAACP began to consider court action. In 1948, Richardson (an attorney and former Indiana legislator) presented a plan to the school board for ending segregation in the Indianapolis schools within three years and threatened to appeal to the courts if the board rejected his proposal. Members of the Indianapolis NAACP were already requesting financial support from the national office and consulting with Thurgood Marshall about legal strategies to end school segregation.[15]

State and local NAACP officers concentrated their efforts on the passage of a law abolishing segregation at the 1949 session of the General Assembly. Richardson, Willard Ransom, Robert Lee Brokenburr, and other Indianapolis lawyers authored a bill that called for desegregation in public education and provided a schedule for implementation. As finally enacted by the legislature, the law declared that it was the public policy of the state to prohibit segregation and discrimination "in the public kindergartens, common schools, colleges, and universities of the state."[16] The implementation, however, was based upon the principle of gradualism—that is, slow, evolutionary change. No new segregated schools were to be built or established, and beginning in September 1949 pupils entering kindergarten and the first year of elementary school were to attend the kindergarten or school in the district in which they lived. Desegregation of elementary and high schools was to be completed within five years, by 1954. In regards to the high schools, blacks were assigned to Crispus Attucks regardless of where they lived, while whites could attend any of the other high schools. In addition, the law guaranteed that no public school, college, or university should "discriminate in hiring, upgrading tenure or placement of any teacher on the basis of race, creed or color."[17] Not surprisingly, Indianapolis would become the focal point of school desegregation in Indiana.

The conditions in Evansville, the only other large Indiana city where schools were officially segregated, remained largely unchanged. At the beginning of the school year in 1950, the Indiana Parents Association, a white group, opposed any steps leading toward desegregation. In 1954 tentative compliance began when Hayward Elementary School admitted thirty African American pupils whose parents demanded that their children attend the school in the district in which the parents paid taxes, instead of being bused to black schools. White parents responded by picketing the schools, and about 40 percent of the white pupils were absent. But when the protests produced no effect, picketing ceased and white pupils returned to the school.[18]

By 1957 about half the elementary schools in Evansville had racially mixed enrollments and all high schools had been officially desegregated. The NAACP continued to protest the all-black enrollment at Lincoln School and the fact that other elementary schools remained entirely black in spite of claims that desegregation had been completed. In December 1957, *Wayne Martin et al. v. Evansville-Vanderburgh School Corporation* was filed in the federal district court presided over by Judge S. (Samuel) Hugh Dillin, who would later hear the Indianapolis school desegregation suit. The lawsuit petitioned the court to close Lincoln and eliminate all black elementary schools. In 1970 Dillin accepted a plan that closed two black elementary schools and transferred their pupils to predominantly white schools. Meanwhile, the school board had also adopted a plan for further desegregation of the high schools. The plans finally adopted for desegregating the city's elementary and high schools involved busing some two thousand pupils "two ways"—that is, black students would be bused to predominantly white schools and white students to predominantly black schools. This number represented a small fraction of the total number of pupils who regularly rode buses in the school district, which included all of Vanderburgh County as well as the city of Evansville. Over the objections of both black and white parents, the court-approved plan remained in force.[19]

During the 1960s, black parents in other cities would sue their school districts over the broken promise of 1949. The first was *Bell v. School City of Gary*. In March 1962, in the absence of the Gary School

Board president and its only black member, three white members approved the recommendation of the superintendent that a new high school be built in the center of the black community. Citizens argued that another site would foster racial integration. The board rescinded its vote, but no compromise followed. The Gary branch of the NAACP provided counsel for Odessa Khaton Bell and other parents who sued the Gary schools. In January 1963, the federal district court ruled against the plaintiffs, stating the problem was one of segregated housing. According to the court, there was no evidence to prove that the school board intentionally desired to further segregated schools even when those decisions resulted in greater segregation. Holding that neighborhood schools were a goal of school zoning, the court rejected the plaintiffs' contention that the school board had an affirmative duty to bring about racial balance in schools. Despite school segregation, whites began to leave Gary schools in droves. By 1970, the Gary schools were more than 60 percent black. And by the end of the 1980s, the schools were nearly 100 percent black.[20] In the meantime, the focus shifted back to Indianapolis, which would become the site of Indiana's most high-profile and longest continuous school desegregation lawsuit.

By the mid-1960s, all of the Indianapolis Public School (IPS) high schools were desegregated except for Crispus Attucks, which remained all black. However, out of a total of 106 elementary schools, two-thirds were nearly racially homogeneous. At that time, approximately 30 percent of the IPS enrollment was black. Although the high schools had integrated teaching staffs, only 24 elementary schools had done so. The school board failed to take any significant action to further integration. Despite the minimal integration of IPS schools, white flight was rising precipitously. In 1967, Andrew Ramsey, president of the State Conference of the NAACP, wrote to John Gardner, secretary of the Department of Health, Education, and Welfare, requesting a federal investigation of discrimination in the assignment of teachers. A few weeks later, the assistant attorney general for civil rights of the U.S. Justice Department charged the Indianapolis school system with "overt racial discrimination in the assignment of students and faculty members."[21]

This action was based on a section of the Civil Rights Act of 1964 that authorized the attorney general to act upon receipt of a complaint in writing by parents or a group of parents that their children, as members of a class, were being deprived by school authorities of equal protection of the laws. If the complaint was found to have merit, and if school authorities did not correct the alleged conditions within a reasonable time, the Justice Department was authorized to institute a civil action in the district court in the name of the United States. In 1968, the United States Justice Department filed suit against the IPS Board of Schools commissioners of the city of Indianapolis and the superintendent of schools in order to force school desegregation.

Hoping to avert the suit, the school board made the disastrous mistake of announcing the closure of the two most identifiably black high schools, Crispus Attucks and Shortridge. Crispus Attucks High School not only symbolized the African American community, but was also a "cultural haven."[22] Originally, blacks had opposed the creation of the all-black high school in the early 1920s. At the time, nearly eight hundred blacks were enrolled in three black schools (Arsenal Technical, Emmerich Manual, and Shortridge), but athletics and other extracurricular activities were largely segregated. Whites who wanted to prevent blacks from moving to the city's Northside residential area were among the supporters of the creation of a black high school. Originally named Thomas Jefferson High School, a petition drive resulted in the school being named for Crispus Attucks, a black man who was the first American to die in the Revolutionary War. When Crispus Attucks opened in 1927 with black teachers and a black principal, the resentment on the part of blacks changed to one of community pride.[23] It also, however, set a precedent for other cities to establish segregated high schools, such as Roosevelt (located in Gary, Indiana) and Evansville (Indiana) Lincoln High School.

The schools' respective champions rallied to their support and undermined any efforts to close them, publicly exposing the board's inability to manage the desegregation of IPS and making court intervention all but inevitable. Moreover, by the time the Justice Department initiated the suit, experts in the field of education had become convinced that resegregation would continue as long as more African Americans settled in northern cities and residential patterns remained unchanged. The only realistic method of continued, progressive desegregation would be two-way busing, as was used in the Evansville case. Black children would be sent to predominantly white schools and white children to black schools. In an earlier precedent, busing had been utilized as a means to improve the quality of rural and suburban education by transporting students to consolidated schools. But the use of busing as a method of promoting "racial mixing" of students was immediately denounced by segregationists.

The trial got underway in late summer, 1971. The judge in the case was none other than S. Hugh Dillin, who had presided over the Evansville desegregation case. At the trial, Justice Department lawyers presented a report detailing the charges of de jure segregation by IPS and asked the court to order measures that would eliminate segregation "root and branch."[24] For their part, lawyers for IPS denied the charges and insisted that racially identified schools were entirely the result of residential patterns and not due to policies of the school board. On August 18, Judge Dillin handed down his decision, which found IPS guilty of de jure segregation since the date of *Brown* in 1954 through the time of the trial. In reaching his decision, he followed closely the guidelines written by Chief Justice Warren Burger in the case of *Swann v Charlotte-Mecklenburg County Board of Education,* which had been decided unanimously by the United States Supreme Court in April 1971. In that decision, which upheld busing as an appropriate remedy to bring about the dismantling of the segregated school system, Burger pointed out a number of practices that might be used to maintain a dual system—including choosing locations for new schools and drawing school attendance boundaries, to reinforce current patterns—and thus perpetuate unlawful segregation.[25]

In his opinion, Dillin cited the IPS redistricting for intentionally and blatantly perpetuating segregation. Since 1954, more than 90 percent of the school boundary changes had promoted segregation. The use of "feeder" elementary school districts had prevented the assignment of white pupils to Crispus Attucks. In response to the growing school population, the school board had built additions to existing black schools instead of transferring black children to white schools whose buildings were underutilized. Sites for new high schools were positioned on the edges of the city in order to minimize black enrollment. Dillin ordered the board to take the following steps: (1) reassign personnel to ensure that no school was racially identifiable from the composition of faculty and staff; (2) desegregate and geographically relocate Crispus Attucks; (3) review transfer policies; and (4) negotiate with suburban school corporations for possible transfer of minority students.[26] Dillin anticipated that IPS would become a one-race district unless an interdistrict plan could be implemented. In order to avoid that situation, Dillin took the bold step of joining all Marion County school districts and those bordering Marion County in surrounding counties to the lawsuit.

In this action, Dillin took advantage of the UniGov law, a consolidation of city-county government that was introduced to Indianapolis by Mayor Richard Lugar in 1969. Indianapolis was the first northern city to adopt a unified government and the first to do so without a public referendum since the 1897 consolidation of New York City.[27] Over the years, UniGov has been criticized by opponents for contributing to an erosion of black voting power in Indianapolis in favor of the white, suburban (and largely Republican) vote.[28] The UniGov law consolidated some offices and powers of the city government of Indianapolis and Marion County, but it expressly provided that school corporations were not to be affected. In Marion County, outside the boundaries of IPS, there were eight township school corporations and two more in the incorporated towns of Beech Grove and Speedway. Blacks made up only 2.62 percent of school enrollments in the outlying school systems, and only fifteen out of more than three thousand teachers were African American.[29] Questions regarding the state's responsibility for perpetuating segregation by passage of the UniGov law and other actions led Dillin to order that the state of Indiana be made a defendant in the desegregation case and that school corporations outside the boundaries of IPS also be made defendants.

Dillin urged the General Assembly to create a metropolitan school system for the whole of Marion County or be faced with a desegregation plan thrust upon it by the court. Since there were virtually no black students in the suburbs, Dillin held that suburban school corporations had not been guilty of perpetuating de jure segregation. But he also concluded that a permanent remedy to segregation in IPS was impossible without the inclusions of the suburban schools. To Dillin, this meant the one-way busing of African American students from IPS to designated suburban township schools. Residents of the suburbs adamantly opposed what they considered to be "forced" busing, even though most white children within their districts were bused to township schools. Claiming that he could not transfer children into IPS as long as the township school districts remained separate entities, Dillin did not order township children into IPS. He also exempted two townships with already sufficiently integrated schools (Pike and Washington) from the order.[30]

According to Richard B. Pierce, "Indianapolis fought school desegregation with a ferocity rarely matched by any other northern city."[31] The bitter opposition from both whites and blacks resulted in years of litigation. In 1973, the Seventh Circuit Court of Appeals upheld Dillin's decision that IPS was guilty of de jure segregation, finding "a purposeful pattern of racial discrimination based on the aggregate of many decisions of the board and its agents."[32] But in upholding Dillin's decision, the Court sent back to the district court the question of determining the responsibility of the state of Indiana and the issue of whether or not the suburban school corporations should be included in the remedy for segregation in IPS.

The second trial before the district court was evidence that the political winds had shifted. After 1974, the U.S. Supreme Court's decision in *Milliken v. Bradley* prevented the implementation of an interdistrict plan unless outlying districts committed acts causing segregation within the segregated district or civil boundary lines deliberately supported racial segregation in public schools.[33] Reflecting the Richard M. Nixon administration's opposition to busing as a remedy for school segregation, the Justice Department sought a city-only plan for Indianapolis. Because of the ruling in *Milliken v. Bradley,* the Seventh Circuit reversed Judge Dillin's order requiring an interdistrict remedy outside of UniGov, thereby releasing those school districts outside of Marion County from the court case. The district court had to decide whether the establishment of the UniGov boundaries, without a similar establishment of IPS boundaries, warranted an interdistrict remedy in accordance with *Milliken.*

In April 1978, Dillin rejected a city-only school desegregation plan for all grade levels as well as additional evidentiary hearings on the issue of whether or not there was cause to involve the eight Marion County school systems in the desegregation remedy. In so doing, he also reiterated his opinion that that there was sufficient evidence of de jure segregation to send the case back to the Seventh Circuit Court of Appeals. In bolstering his decision, he drew upon residential housing patterns. If housing projects had not been confined to IPS, the black pupils in those projects and in surrounding neighborhoods would have attended suburban school systems.[34] In May, he ordered a hearing to consider the merits of the proposed city-only school desegregation plan. Dillin ruled on the question of the city-only desegregation plan on June 2, allowing certain aspects to be implemented but finding that a city-only remedy would be impractical in light of the suburban issue yet to be resolved. This time, Dillin cited the Indiana Transfer Act as authorization for the reassignment of students to the suburbs. The Transfer Act had been passed by the Indiana Legislature in order to alleviate Indianapolis of a portion of the financial burden for busing students encumbered under the original ruling. The act provided formulae for paying costs of transportation and tuition and for distributing state funds.

Amidst continued protests by blacks and integrationist whites, the court of appeals ordered that an Indianapolis-only plan for desegregation be put into effect. Implementation meant drawing new school districts and closing some neighborhood schools. Compliance also required extensive busing within the IPS area. Some busing for desegregation had begun in 1973, but the numbers of students to be involved were now much larger. Over protests from neighborhood groups and threats of defiance, large-scale two-way busing of blacks and whites within IPS boundaries began in September 1980. In October 1980, the U.S. Supreme Court again refused to grant a review of the Indianapolis case, as it had consistently done on previous appeal and both IPS and state and township officials bowed to the inevitable. Buses began to transport IPS students to suburban schools at the beginning of the 1981–82 school year.[35]

After the plan's implementation, the township schools' enrollments were 10 to 20 percent black. A proposed IPS plan with two-way busing might well have increased white flight from the county. In fact, statistics showed that white students in IPS dropped by half after initiation of the desegregation lawsuit. Contrary to federal law, the plan clearly placed an unequal burden for desegregation on blacks. Many Indianapolis blacks resented being discriminatorily burdened with correcting a wrong they did not cause. However, massive resistance by suburban whites was probably avoided by not ordering their children into IPS schools.[36]

Since 1981, the courts have approved two major changes to the interdistrict plan that controlled school integration within IPS. Overcrowding in elementary schools coupled with excess capacity in high schools was the rationale used to convert two high schools, Crispus Attucks and John Marshall, into junior high schools and four junior high schools into elementary schools during the 1986–87 school year. Affected citizens, however, saw it as a political move. Supporters of John Marshall, the newest IPS high school and one perceived as white, felt that their school had been chosen for conversion as an appeasement to blacks. In 1993, the IPS interdistrict plan was modified to permit execution of a school-choice plan. Under the plan, each school must maintain a racial balance within 15 percent of the system's overall 50:50 racial balance. Judge Dillin approved the plan because about one-third of the IPS schools were not within the desegregation guidelines of the 1981 and 1986 plans. Finally, in 1998, Judge Dillin lifted the desegregation and busing order imposed on IPS.[37]

The Justice Department suit against the IPS was more prolonged than any other litigation over school desegregation in Indiana, and the only one that imposed one-way interdistrict busing as a remedy. Filed in 1968, it was also the longest-running northern desegregation suit.[38] But numerous other desegregation suits were settled by court rulings or consent decrees. In Kokomo, United States district judge Cale Holder ordered the closing of two predominantly black elementary schools in 1967 as part of a settlement of a suit brought by the local NAACP. In Terre Haute, where black students constituted approximately 6 percent of the school population, the director of the Indiana Civil Rights Commission brought a complaint in 1973 that led to a consent agreement to bring about racial balance in each school for both pupils and faculty members through redistricting.[39]

In larger cities in the northern part of the state where there had been no official segregation (Fort Wayne and South Bend), the practice of redlining (deliberately segregated housing) contributed to predominantly black schools. In 1968 the Office of Civil Rights of the U.S. Department of Health, Education and Welfare (the same agency that had begun the investigation of Indianapolis schools) began to investigate possible violations of the Civil Rights Act of 1964 in Fort Wayne. There was evidence of the gerrymandering of existing school districts and other violations related to the location of sites chosen for new schools. More than 73 percent of minority pupils (black and Hispanic) were concentrated in schools with predominantly minority enrollments. There was also evidence of discrimination in teacher assignments. After the initial inquiry the Justice Department began a full investigation and black parents produced evidence of discrimination. However, lawyers for the Justice Department decided that the evidence was insufficient to initiate a lawsuit.[40]

The Indiana Civil Rights Commission later charged the Fort Wayne school system with discrimination in hiring and promotion of teachers. As a result, school authorities undertook a reorganization plan that included closing six elementary schools with predominantly black enrollments and negotiated an agreement about minority teacher assignments. Just as in the case of Indianapolis parents, African American parents complained that the plan, which involved busing black pupils to predominantly white schools, placed the entire burden of desegregation on the black community, and their complaints continued after implementation.[41]

In South Bend, where by the 1970s about one-fifth of public school pupils were African American, a civil suit was brought against the South Bend Community Schools in 1966. The case was settled the following year by a five-year reorganization plan involving new construction to replace some existing buildings, including Central High School, and new attendance zones to bring about racial balance. This plan led to busing about nineteen hundred pupils. However, complaints over racial imbalance continued and an expanded busing plan was launched at the beginning of the 1981 school year.[42]

School districts and their constituents continued to seek redress through the courts. The case of Muncie, Indiana, demonstrated that desegregation alone would not remedy a pattern of discrimination. Prior to 1949, Muncie schools had not been segregated de jure, although de facto residential segregation accomplished the same result. In the late 1960s, just over 11 percent of Muncie's public schoolchildren were black. Most of Muncie's black citizens resided in two historically black neighborhoods whose elementary schools were more than 80 percent black by the 1969–70 school year. There was available classroom space, but white children passed these elementary schools to attend predominantly white schools.[43] Although the Muncie elementary system was considerably more segregated, it was an outbreak of racial problems at the secondary school level that provoked desegregation litigation.

In the late 1960s, Muncie high school students attended one of two schools that were both about 13 percent black. A third high school (Northside) scheduled to open in 1970 was located in northwest Muncie, an overwhelmingly white, middle-class area. African Americans feared that the new high school would adversely affect the racial balance of Muncie high schools. In addition, Muncie provided no transportation to high school students, and it was anticipated that lower socioeconomic class blacks would find it difficult to attend Northside. In addition to these issues, there had been a history of racial tension at Southside High School. Located on the south side of Muncie, the student population was made up of blacks and whites that lived in "Shedtown," historically an enclave of whites who had migrated to Muncie from Appalachia (particularly Tennessee and Kentucky). Opened in 1962, Southside High School quickly imported a nineteenth-century southern United States cultural theme that was a constant reminder to African Americans of the legacy of slavery. For example, the Southside "Rebels" athletic teams played under the banner of the Confederate flag, while student fans mimicked the legendary yell of Confederate soldiers as they went into battle. The "Southern Belle and Her Court" reigned over homecoming. The lockers of the black students were located in an area called "The Congo." No blacks had been chosen to be honor society members (although some were qualified), cheerleaders, or members of the "Southern Aires" choral group. In 1968, only 2 custodians, of the school's 103 full-time employees, were black.[44]

In 1969, Mrs. Rosemary Banks filed a suit in the U.S. District Court on behalf of her son, David Banks, against the Muncie Community Schools. The Muncie chapter of the NAACP also joined the suit. The court was asked to resolve the following three issues: (1) whether or not the Muncie schools should be allowed to construct or redistrict if that action would "substantially contribute to and enhance school segregation"; (2) whether or not it is proper to "adopt known anti-Negro symbols of dissent as official school symbols"; and (3) whether or not a school system "may maintain busing at public expense which contributes to school segregation."[45]

The suit against the Muncie Community School authorities was inconclusive, with the federal district court ruling that a pattern of discrimination could not be proven against the Muncie schools. However, after the suit was filed the school board announced plans to construct a new Muncie Central High School near one of the historically black communities.[46] Moreover, the Indiana State Advisory Committee's report to the U.S. Commission on Civil Rights recommended that the Southside High School administration take immediate action to eliminate the Confederate titles and symbols; to assign black teachers, counselors, and clerical personnel to the school; to restrict local administrators' autonomy particularly in disciplinary matters; and to ensure that all extracurricular activities were open to all students. However, the district court found that the admittedly offensive symbols did not deny black students access to school facilities. The court concluded, "the adoption of symbols by the majority of students is merely the exercise of their First Amendment right of free speech and the state has not insinuated itself into private acts of discrimination."[47] The racial tension at Muncie Southside High School highlighted how physical desegregation alone failed to produce racial integration.

As Indiana historian Emma Lou Thornbrough points out, blacks that came to Indiana from southern states often learned that segregation and discrimination had followed them to the borderland.[48] In the area of education, the black struggle for access and equality in education would consume the better part of two centuries. All in all, a total of eight Indiana school districts—Evansville-Vanderburgh, Fort Wayne, Gary, Hammond, Indianapolis, Kokomo, Muncie, and South Bend—

were sued by African Americans in Indiana's federal district courts to enforce the 1949 state law and, subsequently, the decision in *Brown v. Board of Education.* Of those districts, the schools of Fort Wayne, Hammond, Muncie, and South Bend were segregated de facto rather than de jure. Desegregation consent agreements in two districts—Vigo County (Terre Haute) and Marion (Grant County)—avoided litigation in those districts. The Greater Clark County Schools (Jeffersonville) adopted an affirmative employment policy after a district court ordered the federal government to begin court proceedings to withhold federal funds from the district.[49]

It is nearly impossible to form generalizations about the process of desegregation in Indiana. With the exception of Judge Dillin's unique interdistrict desegregation order for the Indianapolis Public Schools, the process of desegregating Indiana's public schools often mirrored that of southern states. It is perhaps telling that in his attempt to fashion a workable solution for IPS, Dillin drew upon precedents set by both a northern and a southern school system: that is, the school systems of Detroit, Michigan (*Milliken v. Bradley*), and Charlotte, North Carolina (*Swann v. Charlotte-Mecklenburg County Board of Education).*

What is certain, however, is that the context of the development of schooling itself in Indiana has historically followed more of a southern pattern. According to the historian Carl F. Kaestle, regional differences existed in the development of the common-school system: "Thus, in the northern tier of the Midwest, settled predominantly by northeasterners, the states adopted common-school systems early despite the difficulties of frontier life. In the southern part of the region—Ohio, Illinois, and Indiana—the population included migrants from the South, and the development of common-school systems was slower and more controversial."[50] The consequences of that slow growth included less enthusiasm for local common schooling and more successful resistance to the creation of state systems. In other words, a stronger tradition of local control on the part of white property owners took hold.

Nevertheless, blacks used their own resources to create and maintain a strong sense of community and to develop successful strategies to resist de jure segregation. Adopting the strategies utilized by the NAACP and the NAACP Legal Defense Fund, black parents challenged school desegregation and discriminatory employment practices throughout the state. In the meantime, they built notable institutions such as Crispus Attucks High School, a meeting place for business, community and professional groups and a source of pride when the Crispus Attucks Tigers became Indiana's first all-black high school basketball team to win the state championship in 1955. Attucks and similar institutions throughout Indiana bore witness to the exclusionary policies of the borderland as well as the unqualified belief in the power of education held by African Americans. In the continuing debate over the legacy of the *Brown* decision, the history of Indiana contributes a literal as well as figurative representation of the ideological and political borderland that constituted school desegregation in the post-1954 period.

Northern Desegregation and the Racial Politics of Magnet Schools in Milwaukee, Wisconsin

Jack Dougherty

Conventional histories of *Brown v. Board of Education* typically do not address the experience of northern school desegregation. Richard Kluger's *Simple Justice,* for example, paints a richly detailed portrait of the southern struggle and the U.S. Supreme Court, but merely sketches an outline of northern desegregation in eight paragraphs at the conclusion of his eight-hundred-page volume.[1] But the North deserves greater attention because it can teach us important lessons about the dynamics of civil rights and white privilege, as well as the shifting meaning of *Brown* over time. This chapter demonstrates how northern school desegregation evolved from individual state cases in the nineteenth century to a broader movement sponsored by the National Association for the Advancement of Colored People in the mid-twentieth century. Then the study focuses on the mixed experience of desegregation in the northern industrial city of Milwaukee, Wisconsin. In the early 1960s, black Milwaukeeans gradually rallied behind the struggle for integrated schools, following an attorney-activist who directly challenged white power. After a prolonged court battle, school officials promoted a desegregation plan featuring voluntary participation through magnet schools in the late 1970s. Yet in practice, the plan favored white interests over black, leading a subsequent generation of activists to question its efficacy. Thus the local

Milwaukee story connects to broader national concerns, both North and South, about the racial politics of implementing school desegregation, and whether or not it fulfills the original promise of *Brown.*

The Northern Road to *Brown*

Long before 1954, civil rights activists challenged segregated schooling in northern states. Several accounts point to the 1849 case of *Roberts v. City of Boston* as the earliest example. Benjamin Roberts, an African American father, sued for the right to send his daughter to a white school that was closer to their home than the black-designated schools. Despite their principled argument that racial discrimination violated constitutional guarantees of equality, the Massachusetts Supreme Judicial Court ruled against the plaintiffs, yet white abolitionists subsequently influenced the Massachusetts state legislature to outlaw school segregation in 1855. Most northern states followed suit and passed similar bans against segregated schools after the Civil War: Rhode Island (in 1866), Connecticut (1868), Michigan (1867), New York (1873), and so on. The last holdout was Indiana, where the state legislature abolished all officially sanctioned segregation in 1949.[2]

Despite these unambiguous northern state laws, many local school districts openly violated them by operating racially designated schools in the early twentieth century, in some cases as late as the 1950s. Northern states where school segregation was most deeply contested stretched across the Mason-Dixon line: New Jersey, Pennsylvania, Ohio, Indiana, and Illinois. For example, Cleveland and Columbus, Ohio, which had racially integrated schools in the late nineteenth century, both reversed themselves in the 1910s and 1920s, by intentionally assigning most black students to schools by race, gerrymandering attendance boundaries, and refusing to permit black teachers in white schools. Several activists sued for the proper enforcement of state anti-segregation laws, and national NAACP legal director Thurgood Marshall attempted to organize a northern campaign in the 1940s. But the success of these localized efforts varied widely. On one hand, Marshall found support in states like New Jersey, where black voters were organizing and gaining sufficient political clout to demand a halt to segregated schooling. On the other hand, in Pennsylvania, he failed to locate either a black plaintiff or a black lawyer who was willing to risk helping him file a case in the local courts. Marshall became frustrated. As a result, the national

NAACP refocused its attention on the mounting challenges to legalized segregation in southern states, and these individual northern efforts remained largely disconnected.[3]

The *Brown* victory soon changed the political climate of the nation, and of the North in particular. Even though the U.S. Supreme Court outlawed segregated schooling only in southern and border states, where it was codified by law, the justices' broader claim that "separate educational facilities are inherently unequal" energized activists in the North. In New York City, where Marshall's expert witness, Dr. Kenneth Clark, had spoken out against segregated schools a few months before the May 1954 decision, *Brown* emboldened local NAACP organizers like Milton Galamison to challenge city officials and demand desegregated schools. *Brown* also reignited the smoldering school segregation protests that had been taken up in earlier years by NAACP branches in Philadelphia, Detroit, and Chicago. The stance of the Chicago NAACP's hard-hitting 1957 report, "De Facto Segregation in the Chicago Public Schools," marked a historic shift. Activists demanded not only the elimination of discriminatory policies, but began to challenge the existence of predominantly black schools, regardless of the cause. Although the law remained unclear on this point, activists in key northern cities began to raise school integration as a moral issue.[4]

Pockets of northern school integrationists coalesced into a broader and coherent movement. They drew inspiration from the *Taylor v. New Rochelle* decision, regarding a suburb of New York City in 1961. Federal district judge Irving Kaufman looked beyond de facto residential patterns and ruled that New Rochelle's school board actions (and inactions) had reinforced and intensified racial segregation. He wrote that "compliance with the [*Brown* decision] was not to be less forthright in the north than in the south" and required that New Rochelle submit a school desegregation plan to the court, the first ever mandated for a northern district. Later that year at the NAACP's national convention in Philadelphia, executive secretary Roy Wilkins announced that the association would renew its demand for "desegregation of schools in northern cities as well as the South."[5]

NAACP general counsel Robert Carter, who previously served with Thurgood Marshall on the *Brown* case, and June Shagaloff, who stepped into the newly created position of NAACP special assistant for education, traveled extensively to help coordinate a unified school integration movement in fifteen northern and western states. Shagaloff assisted local branches on launching investigations on segregation, preparing recommendations for school boards to reform, and filing legal protests or leading mass demonstrations if necessary. Together, they successfully pressured school boards to close segregated buildings and begin open enrollment policies in several northern New Jersey cities. Organizing efforts also took root in several Long Island communities, and pressure on the New York state commissioner of education led him to publicly declare that segregated schools were undesirable and to call for their elimination by local authorities. In other areas where school boards were unresponsive, such as Philadelphia and Chicago, local NAACP branches filed school desegregation lawsuits and mobilized protests. By the close of 1962, the national NAACP counted political and legal actions against school segregation in sixty-nine cities across the North and West. Carter described the northern legal campaign as a "crucial and critical legal battleground," as important as the southern struggle.[6]

The Struggle to Integrate Milwaukee's Schools

When a young black civil rights attorney named Lloyd Barbee moved to Milwaukee, Wisconsin, in 1962, there was no movement for school integration. No one in this city of three-quarters of a million people—black or white—had ever consistently voiced their concern that students might be segregated. This fact puzzled Barbee, a rising activist from the state capital of Madison, where he had served as the president of the local NAACP, then the State Conference of NAACP branches. A year earlier, Barbee led a thirteen-day sit-in on the floor of the state capitol in an unsuccessful attempt to pressure the legislature to pass a fair housing bill. Through his NAACP and legal connections, he saw how activists in other northern cities (such as Chicago, Detroit, and New York) were extending the struggle to challenge public school segregation. But why, Barbee asked, was there no comparable movement for integrated education in Milwaukee?[7]

Prior to World War II, Milwaukee's black population had been relatively small (fewer than 10,000) in comparison to other midwestern cities. Although housing was blatantly segregated and over 90 percent of black Milwaukeeans lived in the city's near Northside, the neighborhood still had significant numbers of ethnic white residents. Compared to the South, Milwaukee schools in this neighborhood appeared to be racially mixed and supplied with better resources. Furthermore, black community leaders had defined jobs as Milwaukee's top civil rights issue during the Depression. As late as 1939, not a single black teacher was permanently employed by the Milwaukee Public School system. In the eyes of Barbee's predecessors, the goal was to gain jobs for black teachers in the white-controlled school district, not student integration.[8]

But postwar southern black migration into Milwaukee set important changes into motion. The 1950s manufacturing boom attracted thousands of black working-class migrants from Mississippi, Arkansas, and Alabama, and from northern regions as well. Milwaukee's black population rose 187 percent (from 21,772 to 62,458) during the 1950s, the highest rate of increase for any major U.S. city during that decade. Local historians have dubbed it the "Late Great Migration," since comparable cities like Chicago and Detroit experienced peak years of black population growth—and racial tensions—in the 1910s and 1920s. Within predominantly rural Wisconsin, the city made up approximately three-quarters of the state's entire black population. White Milwaukee public officials and mass media sensationalized individual criminal events involving black migrants during the 1950s, typically blaming the race as a whole and portraying racial change as an impending sign of urban chaos and disorder. North Division High School shifted from a white-majority to a black-majority institution in 1957, the first secondary school to do so in the entire city. Using school transfers or moving vans, white families pulled further away from the neighborhood that would soon be labeled as the "Inner Core" by city officials. Black families, even those headed by middle-class professionals, were actively discouraged from moving into outlying white neighborhoods. As a result, residential segregation intensified and inner-city schools became increasingly black and overcrowded by the 1960s.[9]

In July 1963, Barbee dragged Milwaukee into the northern school integration movement by publicly declaring that the city's public education system was racially segregated. "If the *Brown* decision means anything," he announced at a meeting of the city's white attorneys, "it means that school segregation is unconstitutional wherever it exists, north or south." Barbee pointed to the rising number of predominantly black schools as proof of his allegation. His words clearly provoked leading members of the school board, who defended Milwaukee's neighborhood school policy as a "normal, natural procedure," distancing themselves from segregated housing over which they claimed to have no control. Barbee's statement also rallied a small but growing number of integration advocates, both black and white, who had previously organized a direct-action protest against the racist behavior of a public official. But the city's established black leadership, particularly members of the Milwaukee NAACP, did not flock to support him. Most held fast to their generation's vision of a jobs-oriented civil rights agenda and the quiet though effective tactics of diplomacy in winning black teachers' jobs. Barbee was still a relative newcomer to the city, whose NAACP status was tied to the state and the regional organizations, not the local branch.[10]

Barbee's first tactic was to take his case against segregated schools to state officials. In 1963, the Wisconsin NAACP formally requested the intervention of the state superintendent of public instruction to order the Milwaukee School Board to desegregate, similar to actions taken by other top school officials in New York, New Jersey, and California. But Wisconsin state officials refused to intervene. Black Milwaukeeans had relatively little political clout in the predominantly white state. In addition to being a numerical minority, the vast majority of Wisconsin's black population at that time resided in one city—Milwaukee—not in communities across the state where broader coalitions might be formed. In contrast to most of the South, Milwaukee school segregation was perceived to be a localized dispute, not a statewide policy issue.[11]

Instead, Barbee and his supporters pursued their cause through public awareness campaigns designed to arouse a complacent population. Allies in the black press captured readers' attention with visual images of "intact busing," the school district's controversial practice of dealing with overcrowded inner-city schools without altering attendance zones (or the racial boundaries they reinforced). Each morning, classrooms of black children and their teachers would load onto buses at their black neighborhood school, then travel several blocks to an underutilized white school, where they would unload and remain "intact" as a separate classroom for the day. Despite being in the same building, regular white students and "intact" black students usually had separate bathroom, lunch, and recess times. In the most extreme cases, black students were bused back at the noon hour to their home school to walk home for lunch, then reconvene and travel back again to the receiving school, and home again in the afternoon, for a total of two round-trips per day. The national NAACP sent Shagaloff, its northern school integration organizer, who denounced intact busing as a blatant example of "segregation, Milwaukee-style." She was joined by Derrick Bell Jr., the young black NAACP Legal Defense Fund attorney, who declared to audiences that "Direct action can work in Memphis, Miami and Montgomery—and it can work in Milwaukee, too."[12]

By 1964, Barbee's supporters took on a new name—the Milwaukee United School Integration Committee (MUSIC)—to build a coalition of supporters drawn together from disparate organizations, including direct-action protesters from the Milwaukee Congress of Racial Equality as well as more diplomatic black leaders from the Milwaukee NAACP and Urban League. Under Barbee's leadership, MUSIC developed a three-prong strategy of mass protests, federal pressure, and legal proceedings. On the community action front, MUSIC began with three hundred citizens picketing the school administration building, the city's largest civil rights march of this size in over two decades. Teams of nonviolent direct-action protesters (many of them women) formed human chains to surround "intact buses." On the tenth anniversary of the *Brown* decision, nearly eleven thousand black and white children boycotted the city's schools, with many joining hands at MUSIC's alternative Freedom schools to raise their voices for integrated education. Barbee's repeated clashes with racist opponents elevated the movement's status as a defiant black challenge to the white power structure. But the nonviolent direct action did little to change the conservative stance of the school board majority against school integration.[13]

On the second front, MUSIC attempted to pressure federal administrators to investigate "Milwaukee-style segregation" and leverage the district to desegregate. In 1965, Barbee (now a state assemblyman) wrote a letter of complaint to the Department of Health, Education, and Welfare in President Lyndon B. Johnson's administration. "Because of the school board's conduct," Barbee declared, "you are hereby requested to withhold federal funds, grants, and aid from [the board] until they cease practicing discrimination." Milwaukee school administrators were eagerly awaiting over $2 million in Title I grants that they were eligible to receive under the new Elementary and Secondary Education Act. Barbee recognized how southern activists were using federal dollars to force desegregation compliance and attempted the same strategy in the North. At first, federal authorities announced that they would probably send investigators to Milwaukee and other northern cities where they had received similar requests. But the threat of federal intervention collapsed due to events in Chicago in fall 1965. Mayor Richard J. Daley responded to an ambiguous HEW letter (which lacked hard data proving

Chicago's intention to segregate) by mobilizing his powerful Democratic machine and personally persuading Johnson to call off the federal investigation. HEW also dropped its case against Milwaukee.[14]

Given the limitations of mass protest and federal politics, MUSIC poured its remaining energy into a courtroom challenge. After working for several months under the supervision of national NAACP attorney Robert Carter, Barbee finally filed a school desegregation lawsuit in federal court in 1965. The suit alleged that Milwaukee officials maintained school segregation through its attendance zone boundaries, construction site decisions, transfer policies, intact busing, and teacher assignments. The case, initially known as *Amos v. Board,* was named after Craig Amos, from the alphabetical listing of forty-one black and white schoolchildren whose families had signed on as plaintiffs, reportedly the first integrated group for a legal action of this kind in the nation.[15]

Yet the legal proceedings moved much more slowly than expected. Lloyd Barbee and Marilyn Morheuser, the lead researcher, systematically built their school segregation case while facing tremendous obstacles. Milwaukee school officials slowed down the pace of the investigation by releasing only the exact documents requested rather than allowing researchers to browse through decades of files stored at the three-story central office building. Also, defense lawyers attempted to block access to personnel records on transfers and promotions, and only relented after receiving a court order to cooperate. Finally, when Barbee and Morheuser had prepared several legal exhibits and were ready for trial in 1970, defense attorneys stalled the proceedings for several months by arguing that they had no way of verifying the accuracy of items that had been compiled from their clients' own records.[16]

Even Barbee's allies sometimes ran up against him. The national NAACP had spent over $60,000 on the *Amos* case, mostly to support the work of its own attorney, Joan Franklin Mosley. But in New York City, a heated conflict arose between NAACP general counsel Robert Carter and the board of directors over control of their legal and political strategy, prompting Carter to resign in late 1968. Barbee's primary supporter at the national NAACP was gone. Meanwhile, as legal expenses continued to pile up in Milwaukee, national NAACP executive director Roy Wilkins complained that "the *Amos* case has become a Frankenstein monster . . . The people have not been rallied to its support." Although the national NAACP had originally inspired Barbee to join its northern school integration campaign in the early 1960s, Wilkins withdrew financial support from the Milwaukee case in 1969 and privately recommended that Barbee drop the entire lawsuit. Also, some plaintiffs later questioned the value of integration and dropped their names (including the Amos family), and the lawsuit was eventually renamed *Armstrong v. O'Connell*. Finally, on the eve of the trial in September 1973, the other two members of Barbee's legal team—Marilyn Morheuser and Joan Franklin Mosley—abruptly resigned over a bitter dispute regarding courtroom strategy. Barbee continued onward, though with a much smaller circle of supporters than in the mid-1960s.[17]

The long delay in starting Milwaukee's courtroom trial—over eight years after the lawsuit had originally been filed—brought important changes in the national climate. Barbee now faced stiffer resistance from federal officials in the early 1970s. In President Richard M. Nixon's executive branch, the "southern strategy" to bring white voters to the Republican Party derailed much of the remaining federal activity in school desegregation litigation and enforcement. Wisconsin's two Democratic U.S. senators split their votes on a racially charged bill against "forced busing" in 1972. Yet at the U.S. Supreme Court, the long delay brought two favorable changes for Barbee. First, in the 1973 *Keyes v. Denver* decision, the Court ruled that the Denver School Board had intentionally confined black residents by its policy actions on student transfers, attendance boundaries, and school facilities. The Court's first major school desegregation decision involving a northern or western state, where there had been no law (or de jure segregation) requiring the separation of race, was a tremendous boost for Barbee's case. The second favorable result from the delay was the reassignment of the courtroom trial to U.S. district judge John Reynolds, a former Democratic governor and attorney general of Wisconsin who was perceived as liberal on racial issues.[18]

The trial inched along through mountains of statistical data and hundreds of exhibits, with closing arguments in February 1974. Then Judge Reynolds waited nearly two more years before issuing his ruling, perhaps to give school board members an opportunity to change their ways voluntarily. Apparently, they had not done enough. Judge Reynolds issued his first ruling in favor of the plaintiffs in January 1976. "I have concluded that segregation exists in the Milwaukee public schools," he wrote, "and that this segregation was intentionally created and maintained by the defendants." Reynolds instituted a three-year school desegregation plan to be overseen by the court's special master, John Gronouski, a former Wisconsin state politician and U.S. ambassador to Poland, in an effort to win favor with the city's Polish-American working-class South-side. In a subsequent ruling, Reynolds also issued numerical goals: black student enrollments in one-third of Milwaukee schools needed to fall between 25 to 45 percent in 1976–77, with the remaining two-thirds of the schools meeting that goal over the next two years. Continuing their legal defense of neighborhood schools, the Milwaukee School Board appealed the decision to the U.S. Supreme Court, which later vacated the decision and sent it back to lower court for further consideration in 1977. Based on the *Dayton v. Brinkman* decision, where the Court narrowed the scope of desegregation remedies on the grounds that systemwide solutions were appropriate only when the original violations had systemwide effects, the Milwaukee case was remanded back to Judge Reynolds's courtroom to determine more precisely whether local school officials had deliberately intended to segregate all schools or if their actions had simply led to segregation in some areas. Barbee was forced to go back to trial and meet a higher standard, requiring more delay. Reynolds issued a second decision in Barbee's favor in 1978, with stronger language against the defendants. The law firmly ruled that Milwaukee would desegregate—the only question remaining was how.[19]

The Racial Politics of Magnet Schools

A year before Judge Reynolds issued his first ruling in 1976, the Milwaukee School Board hired a new superintendent, Lee McMurrin, who designed the city's grand compromise on race and public education: the magnet school plan. In the wake of racial violence over mandatory busing in Boston and Louisville, the superintendent crafted rhetoric that would appeal to both sides of this heated issue. McMurrin vowed to anti-desegregation forces that he would not permit mandatory busing in the city, yet he promised desegregation supporters that he could integrate the schools through voluntary means. One of his trial proposals, prior to the court's ruling, was to reorganize the city's fifteen high schools into citywide magnet schools, each with its own specialized curricular offering, to encourage student enrollment from outside traditional neighborhood boundaries. In theory, the stronger the attraction of special offerings at each magnet school, the greater the likelihood that black and white students would voluntarily cross neighborhood boundaries and obtain a high quality education at a racially integrated school. Furthermore, McMurrin knew how to obtain federal Emergency School Assistance Act funding to make it possible.[20]

But magnet schools also opened a new set of questions and controversies. First, as the sociologist Mary Haywood Metz has argued, they openly contradicted the myth of equal educational opportunity in American public schooling. For magnet schools to attract students, they needed to offer something more than what students typically received in their traditional neighborhood schools. School desegregation supporters had long demanded equality for all students, but the magnet school remedy sought to resolve the issue by designating some schools as superior in resources or reputation. McMurrin's initial plan to transform *all* high schools into magnets theoretically addressed these concerns about inequality, but if all high schools were equally good, why would anyone move? Second, McMurrin's administration faced difficult pragmatic questions about magnet school location and enrollment. Would white families send their children to a magnet school in the middle of an inner-city black neighborhood? Would they come if the percentage of black students was guaranteed not to rise above a certain level? And would sufficient numbers of whites participate in the voluntary integration plan? McMurrin and his assistants brushed aside these questions and pushed ahead on Milwaukee's "speciality school" magnet plan, expressing confidence that it would eliminate "some of the negative imagery of desegregation" in the minds of many white Milwaukeeans. The old slogan of "forced busing" into black neighborhoods had been replaced by the seductive rhetoric of voluntary "choice."[21]

But in reality, Milwaukee's so-called voluntary magnet desegregation plan entailed some mandatory busing for black students. After Judge Reynolds's initial ruling in 1976, twenty-four magnet schools opened up. But about thirty-three hundred black students were reassigned to white neighborhood schools due to overcrowding or the closure of their former black neighborhood schools. Another thirteen hundred black students (but only two hundred whites) were reassigned when their neighborhood schools were converted into magnets. At the opening of the 1976 school year, Superintendent McMurrin proudly announced that Milwaukee had surpassed the court's first-year desegregation goals. But the burden of desegregating Milwaukee's schools fell disproportionately onto black shoulders, a policy issue that was rapidly attracting attention. A community organization named "Blacks for Two-Way Integration" demanded that the burdens of desegregation be distributed evenly, by halting the disproportionate closings of black schools and busing of black students. But their demands fell on deaf ears. McMurrin questioned whether blacks were complaining about privileges that they had won after years of civil rights struggles. "Years ago, [black] people were jumping at the chance to ride the bus across the town to a better school," he said. "Now all of a sudden it's a 'burden.' Is it truly a burden to close down a few overcrowded, deteriorating schools and replace them with the most modern and better facilitated schools in the system?"[22]

As the Milwaukee school system moved into the third year of Judge Reynolds's desegregation order, pressure to meet the racial balancing goals increased. Black neighborhood schools became even more vulnerable to closings and magnet conversions, particularly as overall district enrollments fell and fuel costs for older inner-city buildings rose. During the spring 1978 magnet school lottery, nearly all of the "losers" who did not receive their top three choices had been black; being white sharply increased one's chances of gaining entry to one of the "better" schools, even if it was located in your neighborhood. Over 90 percent of the students "voluntarily" bused for desegregation were black.[23]

The racial politics of desegregation quickly centered on the all-black inner-city North Division High School. Longtime black community supporters had successfully lobbied for the construction of a new facility to replace the original 1907 structure. But the brand-new facility attracted only thirty-six white students (amid fourteen hundred black students) when it opened in 1978, signaling that the district would fail the court's order for all schools to be racially balanced in the plan's third year. Barbee and the defendants reached a settlement in 1979 that allowed a small number of the city's schools to remain nearly all black. But in a controversial vote, black and white members of the Milwaukee School Board decided to close North Division as a traditional neighborhood school and reopen it as a magnet. To change the new North's reputation, all students currently in the feeder pattern would be assigned elsewhere, and the number of incoming black students would be limited to the equivalent number of whites. Therefore, the newly "cleansed" North Division would displace most of the black students who had traditionally attended their neighborhood school. "Integration is going to be painful," acknowledged Superintendent McMurrin, "but it's for the good of all parents, students, and the community."[24]

"Enough is enough," chanted hundreds of marchers, waving banners in protest against the black burden of desegregation. "Save North

Division," they shouted, seeking to reverse the school board's plan from closing the all-black neighborhood school and converting it into a magnet. The leader of this new generation of protesters was not Barbee, but Howard Fuller, a North Division alumnus and community organizer whose rhetoric appealed to supporters both of fair integration and black self-determination. "The *Brown* decisions were not in themselves based on racist tenets," Fuller later wrote, ". . . [but] the manner in which desegregation has been carried out in many cities through America is racist." Prevailing methods of desegregation implied that black students must be assimilated into white schools, and that traditionally black schools had nothing positive to offer.[25]

Milwaukee's local struggle tapped into an emerging national movement of black dissent regarding the politics of desegregation. Its most notable speakers were former NAACP attorneys Derrick Bell Jr. and Robert Carter, who had directly assisted Lloyd Barbee during Milwaukee's early school integration campaign. In 1978, Carter reflected on twenty-five years of litigation since *Brown* and recalled that the NAACP's major challenge in 1954 was to destroy the "separate but equal" doctrine of the 1896 *Plessy* decision. To do so, Carter and his colleagues "fashioned *Brown* on the theory that equal education and integrated education were one and the same." But after their initial legal victory in 1954, the real target of their attack—racism—had changed over time, adapting itself to privilege white interests in school desegregation arrangements in several locations. While Carter personally continued to support integration, he eventually came to understand that "the goal was not integration but equal educational opportunity," thereby distinguishing between the two concepts he had fused together since the 1950s. Now that these two concepts had been separated, it became possible for Carter and others to question whether desegregation was fulfilling the promise of equal educational opportunity.[26]

The struggle over North Division widened the gulf between Milwaukee's two diverging black communities. Those who embraced Howard Fuller's vision successfully reclaimed North Division as a neighborhood school, yet faced an uphill battle to improve the day-to-day quality of education within this racially isolated neighborhood. Those who pursued Lloyd Barbee's dream continued to demand integration with whites, even as they fled the city limits for distant suburbs. These two opposing camps even drew different conclusions from the same statistics about Milwaukee's experience with desegregation. Both sides agreed that in 1979, about two thousand black students who had previously attended schools in the North Division vicinity were now enrolled out-side of that attendance area. But how this transformation had occurred was a subject of intense debate. Barbee's supporters described these stu-dents as having "chosen" to attend either magnet schools or desegre-gated schools in white neighborhoods. But Fuller's supporters referred to the same students as being "sent out" of the North Division area against their will, an expression of the unfair burden of desegregation. Yet neither interpretation of the data was entirely correct. Judging from the existing studies of school application forms and black parent sur-veys, it appears that some inner-city black residents clearly welcomed the opportunity to leave their neighborhood schools, while some others fought very hard to stay. Opposing views on the racial politics of deseg-regation led both sides to generalize about the data in ways that fit their particular visions for black education reform.[27]

Milwaukee's story reveals an important lesson about the evolution of school desegregation struggles. The protests of Lloyd Barbee's genera-tion shifted during Howard Fuller's generation due to the changing nature of racism, the underlying antagonist in this narrative. In the early 1960s, when Barbee demanded that black students deserved an inte-grated education, powerful whites resisted his movement as long as pos-sible, using "intact busing" and legal tactics that delayed the trial for eight years. After 1976, when Judge Reynolds's ruling made it impos-sible to put off desegregation any longer, school officials continued to defend white interests, but shifted their tactics. Rather than oppose desegregation, they embraced it, by adopting a so-called voluntary mag-net school plan whose implementation offered more choices to families living in white neighborhoods than to those living in black ones. Fuller's 1979 coalition is best understood as a diverse coalition of black commu-nity members who publicly questioned whether desegregation, as prac-ticed in their city, fulfilled the promise of the 1954 decision.

The meaning of *Brown* is not frozen in time. Rather, its definition is fluid, dependent upon the historical context. Our understanding of school desegregation is contingent upon whether we examine Topeka in 1954, or New Rochelle in 1961, or Milwaukee in 1979. Across all of these settings, one question remains constant: who benefited from how desegregation was implemented? But the answers will vary across time and place, teaching us a great deal about the shifting dynamics of race, reform, and power.

Brown, Integration, and Nevada

Michael S. Green

Since Nevada became a state in 1864, its economy has been tied to gambling—first, gambling that ore waited underground, then on gambling itself and the attractions that go with it. Politically, it has been the creature of its dominant industry, whether mining or gaming. Socially, it often reflects national trends because many residents moved here from other states and brought their attitudes with them. It consistently ranks among the fastest-growing states, with a population of 2.4 million, 1.8 million of them in Las Vegas, in 2005, the year the young city celebrated its centennial.[1]

That reflects another trend in Nevada: not only is it a newer area, but one part of it dominates the rest. In the nineteenth century, the Comstock Lode made Virginia City the seat of political and economic power. A turn-of-the-century mining boom shifted power to central Nevada, but as the boom went bust, its leaders moved to Reno. But World War II changed Nevada. Federal projects and the growth of gaming in southern Nevada drew large numbers of residents. After the war, the nascent gaming industry, especially in Las Vegas, benefited from such postwar trends as the growth of interstate highways, the introduction of jet airplanes, and the expansion of leisure time—especially in Las Vegas with its ample land, agreeable weather, and lack of an established elite that might frown on innovation and the presence of organized crime figures.[2]

In 1954, when the Supreme Court handed down *Brown,* Nevada's population had topped 200,000 and Las Vegas was becoming the state's biggest city, with about 40,000 residents. While Nevada's population grew by 78 percent during the 1950s, and Las Vegas's by more than 160 percent, the African American population expanded even faster. The 664 blacks in Nevada in 1940 reached 4,302 in 1950 and 13,484 in 1960. Most of Nevada's African Americans lived in Las Vegas, with perhaps 2,000 in Reno and a smattering of others around the state. The city to which blacks moved in the greatest numbers, Las Vegas, became known as "the Mississippi of the West"—or, as National Association for the Advancement of Colored People attorney Franklin Williams said in 1954, it was "a non-southern city with the pattern of the deep south." Thus, while civil rights leaders there worked with their Reno counterparts on political and legislative issues, Las Vegas was the driving force in the movement and must be the main focus of any study of school integration in Nevada. While *Brown* did little to change Nevada's schools for more than a decade, it contributed to a civil rights movement that radically changed Nevada and Las Vegas.[3]

On May 17 and 18, 1954, Nevadans learned of what one editor called "A Momentous Supreme Court Decision." The *Las Vegas Evening Review-Journal*'s eight-column banner said, "SEGREGATION BANNED." The next day readers learned that Chief Justice Earl Warren had improved his chances of succeeding President Dwight Eisenhower—and that "Dixieites Plan Battle" and it "May Be Years before Ban Effective." Editorial comments were few: most Nevada newspapers were weeklies focused on local news or small dailies full of national wire service stories and local press releases. Reno's Republican *Evening Gazette* and Democratic *Nevada State Journal* agreed the time for desegregation had come. The *Gazette* hoped *Brown* "may be the point at which the South will accept—and not without loud protest—the standards of the nation at large as the legal basis for its relationship with the Negroes." The *Journal* said, "The decision will create considerable discussion in some southern states, but in course of time will be accepted." In conservative Elko, the *Daily Free Press* took a more liberal stand: "We have favored this move for some time, recognizing that America has relied upon its Negro citizenry as well as its whites to protect our Democratic principles. We have called upon the Negroes of our country to fight shoulder to shoulder with our own sons upon the battlefields of the world. They have acquitted themselves with honor. They have earned the right to equal treatment in our schools."[4]

Ironically, in *Brown*'s wake, Nevada significantly changed its system of public education in ways unrelated to the decision, yet they affected how the state responded to the issues *Brown* created and addressed. While the population shot up, school enrollments rose even faster, thanks to the postwar baby boom. Nevada was ill prepared for it. In 1951, a federally funded study showed that one-third of the state's students attended classes in buildings that failed to provide the proper educational atmosphere—and most of the other two-thirds were in buildings that were overcrowded or on double sessions. Republican governor Charles Russell and most legislators paid little attention to the problem, despite a groundswell of complaints from parents, teachers, and such legislators as Maude Frazier, who had run Las Vegas's school district for twenty years. Finally, Russell named a survey committee that imported a group from the George Peabody College for Teachers, which suggested overturning the existent structure. Instead of two hundred school districts serving everything from cities to hamlets, each of the seventeen counties should have one coordinated school district. In 1955, Russell and the legislature agreed, and citizen groups pushed through new taxes to finance them. While desegregation and integration played no role in their actions, eliminating multiple districts would both help and hinder those causes by reducing the number of administrators and jurisdictions involved.[5]

Long before the *Brown* decision, Nevada's schools had been desegregated, at least technically. While Nevada's constitution, drafted in 1864, was silent, the first state legislature in 1865 passed a law requiring "Negroes, Mongolians, and Indians" to attend separate schools. But in 1870, 357 African Americans lived in Nevada, and only three black children had gone to school the previous year—and they lived in different counties. Accordingly, Nelson Stoutmeyer, a black laborer in Carson City, sued the three local school district trustees for denying his request to enroll his seven-year-old son David in the white public school. Attorney T. W. W. Davies's arguments would recur in *Brown* and other cases, including references to the Fourteenth Amendment and contending that segregating children "tends to create a feeling of degradation in the blacks." In 1872, the Nevada Supreme Court held, 2–1, that the state constitution allowed racial segregation in schools, but only if "the same advantages of education are given to all." Nevada had to build new schools or admit black children to existing ones. Given the limits of budgets and population, de jure school segregation effectively ended in Nevada. When minorities went to segregated schools, it would be for other reasons, legal and de facto.[6]

As Nevada's population grew during the twentieth century and more African Americans moved to the state, they faced segregation that was more de facto than de jure, with education affected by the process. In Reno and Las Vegas, in particular, public and private officials redlined residents into one section of town. In Las Vegas, this area was west of the railroad tracks and the townsite auctioned by the Union Pacific and Senator William Clark of Montana, builders of the railroad that created the town. At first, blacks could live in the railroad's townsite, but as their numbers grew, railroad and city leaders limited their ability to obtain loans, housing, or business licenses, forcing them into an older townsite without paved streets, power lines, or running water. While Reno blacks set up an NAACP chapter in 1919, only a decade after the national organization's birth, their Las Vegas counterparts initially were less successful, taking a decade to marshal their forces and stepping up their efforts when the Ku Klux Klan's national revival during the 1920s included a Las Vegas Klavern whose members marched down the town's main street. Another contributor to black activism was the Boulder Dam project: Six Companies, the builder, originally refused to hire blacks, prompting the creation of the Colored Citizens' Labor and Protective Association of Las Vegas in November 1931 with 247 members, more than 100 more African Americans than were living in the community in the previous year's census.[7]

World War II proved even more important to the growth of Las Vegas's black community and its NAACP. A wave of black migrants came to Las Vegas from Arkansas and Louisiana, leaving depressed cotton mill towns for the prospect of work at the Basic Magnesium plant southeast of Las Vegas. Some of them proved unable to obtain jobs and found work in the expanding downtown and Strip casino districts, mostly as porters and maids. Segregation meant a corresponding expansion of West Las Vegas, which developed its own sense of community and business districts and greater political influence. New blood infused the NAACP, reestablished in Las Vegas and Reno in 1945 after a lull of several years: Woodrow Wilson, who worked for the chemical companies that took over the Basic plant and helped start the Westside Federal Credit Union, the segregated area's first lending institution; businesswoman Lubertha Johnson; and teacher Mabel Hoggard and her husband, David, who worked in various municipal services. In 1953, they joined such white progressives as attorney George Rudiak to push unsuccessfully for state and city civil rights laws. But the African American population faced a problem: its members could exercise the right to vote without the limitations they encountered in the Deep South, but Las Vegas African Americans lacked the numbers and the leadership strength to use their votes to wield much influence.[8]

With this growth in numbers and activism came another wave of new residents who contributed greatly to the local NAACP's power and the civil rights movement in general. The efforts of earlier arrivals sometimes received less attention amid the work of 1950s newcomers Charles West, the city's first black doctor; James McMillan, the first local black dentist; William "Bob" Bailey, Las Vegas's first black television host and an entertainer at the Moulin Rouge, its first integrated local hotel-casino; Charles Kellar, a longtime New York attorney who came west to practice in Nevada; and the Reverend Donald Clark, who shared Wilson's Republican affiliation and enhanced the black community's ties to both major parties. While they formed a more powerful professional class, with greater abilities at organization and negotiation, the growth of Las Vegas also attracted more blue-collar and, especially, service workers, including welfare rights advocate Ruby Duncan and others who gave that movement body and depth.[9]

Their efforts produced major advances in civil rights throughout Nevada in the decade and a half after *Brown*. Reno and Las Vegas blacks began community newspapers and organizations for political activism. Black support helped elect liberal Democrat Grant Sawyer governor in 1958 and, despite strong opposition from political and business leaders, he pushed through an Equal Rights Commission and, in response to the U.S. Civil Rights Act of 1964, a similar Nevada measure in 1965. In 1960, with support from Mayor Oran Gragson and *Las Vegas Sun* publisher Hank Greenspun, McMillan's threat of a boycott helped inspire Las Vegas casino owners to agree to the Moulin Rouge Agreement, which let blacks patronize their establishments. In 1963, by threatening to march during coverage of a boxing match in Las Vegas, the NAACP induced gaming executives to start hiring more blacks. In 1964, black votes helped decide a close U.S. Senate race in favor of incumbent Howard Cannon, who cast a key vote to help passage of the Civil Rights Act. In 1966, federally mandated reapportionment of Nevada's legislature led to the election of its first black member, Wilson.[10]

Despite progress, Nevada's African Americans were as impatient as their counterparts across the nation. While ameliorating some of the most-searing effects of racism and poverty, Lyndon Johnson's Great

Society also prompted a backlash inside and outside the civil rights movement. Conservatives decried Johnson's programs and the civil rights movement itself—the political activism of its leaders and the increasingly violent protests—nationally and in Nevada. The movement became more divided between youth and age, liberalism and radicalism —just as it did to some extent in Nevada. McMillan's forceful actions and style apparently bothered the local NAACP executive board, which apparently preferred a more collegial—some said conservative— approach. Divisions between Democratic and Republican members some-times caused disagreements, and some lower-income blacks felt that professional and middle-class members of the state movement some-times paid short shrift to them.[11]

In Nevada, this helped inspire what might be called a second civil rights movement in the late 1960s and especially the early 1970s. Work-ing across the political aisle with Democratic governor Mike O'Callaghan, a southern Nevadan who had strongly supported civil rights, Republican assemblyman Woodrow Wilson and civil rights advocates pushed through a fair housing law in 1971. For the first time in the twentieth century, Nevada's African Americans would have a reasonable chance of buying a home wherever they could afford it, rather than an area into which government and business had red-lined them. At the same time, state welfare department efforts to reduce benefits and impose limita-tions prompted Las Vegas welfare mothers, with considerable help from northern Nevada activist and philanthropist Maya Miller and Las Vegas attorney B. Mahlon Brown III, to take to the courts and the streets in pursuit of more equitable treatment.[12]

Another shift in the civil rights movement had a rippling effect in Nevada. As the movement evolved nationally, unrest took new forms. The student movement grew as teenagers and college students rebelled against what they considered an excessively smug society, especially as they faced the prospect of going to war in Vietnam. Johnson promised a "War on Poverty," but some of those it was designed to help questioned whether the war was winnable or even being fought. Upset with their plight and sensing that the effects of civil rights legislation might not trickle down to them, they turned to protests and violence. Smoke rose from cities from Los Angeles to Baltimore. In Nevada but especially in Las Vegas, with its larger black populace, civil rights leaders began push-ing harder for change, and some of their followers turned to violence.[13]

African Americans in Nevada began demanding greater, quicker progress in two key areas: hotel-casino employment and education. In both of these areas, Charles Kellar proved to be a crucial and controversial figure as president of the Las Vegas NAACP chapter and the attorney who filed the main lawsuits that led to action—and inaction. Born in Barbados in 1909, Kellar grew up in Brooklyn, earned his law degree at St. John's, and became president of the NAACP's Brooklyn chapter. There he met Thurgood Marshall, who headed the NAACP's Legal Defense Fund and urged attorneys like Kellar to move to states that lacked black lawyers. Nevada fit that category when Kellar arrived in 1959—and stayed in that category longer than expected. Kellar passed the bar exam in 1960, but the Nevada Bar Association refused to admit him, questioning the outcome: his score was so high, the examiners reasoned that he must have cheated. As one white civil rights advocate remembered, "he had some difficulties because he was considered too abrasive." Not until 1965 did he win his case before the Nevada Supreme Court to be admitted to the bar, and by then other African American attorneys were arriving.[14]

While Kellar's admission to the bar was controversial, it was only the beginning. Despite a 1963 agreement to hire black employees, casinos still refused to employ them as dealers. In 1967, Kellar announced that the NAACP would consider "a march in front of Strip hotels to protest unequal employment of Negroes." He attacked the Culinary Union and its leader, Al Bramlet, for not supporting black hirings and vowed to "cut the union down to size." He met with union and hotel officials to demand promotions, better jobs for black employees, and that black waiters and waitresses working in hotel coffee shops have the chance to work in showrooms, where the tips were greater. Eventually, he filed suit with the National Labor Relations Board in San Francisco against the hotels and the unions to force action, declaring that "negotiations with union officials have been absolutely futile. They were so secure in their bailiwick they felt nothing could touch them. They'll soon learn otherwise." For his troubles, someone fired shots through his windows and blew an eight-inch hole in his office door. Ultimately, the U.S. Justice Department filed a complaint alleging civil rights violations under Title VII of the Civil Rights Act of 1964, and the Nevada Resort Association, representing the casinos, agreed to hire and promote more black employees. While the consent decree went largely unenforced, Kellar had started the ball rolling.[15]

Kellar took other action. When North Las Vegas police shot and killed a seventeen-year-old black in 1969, he demanded an investigation. "There are many people in the community who view Kellar as a troublemaker, which I feel certain will not deter the West Las Vegas lawyer from pursuing what he considers to be a rightful course of action. As president of the NAACP, he has a job to perform and there is little use in questioning his dedication or sincerity. He will relentlessly continue on his quest," Greenspun wrote about his fellow St. John's law graduate. "And if anyone—be he a lawyer, judge, public official or ordinary citizen—underrates Mr. Kellar, he is a fool." Eventually, local police departments and government agencies created review boards for such circumstances.[16]

Other challenges to the status quo involved law enforcement and violence. Reports spread of discrimination, including police holding a black minister in downtown Las Vegas against his car, calling him a "nigger," and telling him he was "not supposed to be on this side of town." In 1968, the Nevada League of Women Voters issued a report on progress made since the state's civil rights act took effect three years before. Finding that "non-whites are beginning to be employed in stores and other consumer services, but most non-white employment remains in menial labor," the group sought open housing and school integration. Despite prodding from Republicans Gragson and Governor Paul Laxalt to back off, Kellar and the local NAACP responded by organizing marches at local hotels during a regional NAACP convention.[17]

Eventually, Las Vegas followed in the footsteps of other cities. Racial unrest prompted altercations at high schools. On January 23, 1969, North Las Vegas police quickly ended a confrontation at Rancho High School, but on the next Monday at Las Vegas High, several whites threw a black student through a trophy case; school district officials blamed the presence of several reporters for causing the disturbance. Two days later, a student sit-in at a newer high school, Clark, culminated with nearly one thousand students in a melee and the closure of high schools for the week. Clark County School District superintendent James Mason responded by banning the public and media from campuses, temporarily closing some schools, blaming Clark High's Afro-American Club for contributing to the unrest, banning sit-ins, and declaring that any more incidents "would be put down by force and students would be expelled." But Mason also tried to be, as the historian Eugene Moehring wrote, "somewhat conciliatory." He set up meetings involving black and white student leaders and offered amnesty to everyone involved in the rioting. When schools reopened, the violence had subsided. But on October 6, gang violence broke out in the traditionally

segregated Westside, with dozens injured, curfews imposed, police seal-
ing off the area, and looting. And the violence grew worse: ten arrests,
six injuries, and the closing of Western High School in November; several incidents at Las Vegas High; and a fight at Rancho the next May
involving three hundred students and the use of pipes and fire hoses.[18]

These high schools were integrated, but not for reasons related to
Brown. Until Rancho opened in North Las Vegas in 1955, Las Vegas
High had been the urban area's only high school, except for Basic in
nearby Henderson and Boulder City High. Black and white students
attended classes together. Nor were elementary schools formally segregated. Westside Elementary had opened in 1922, before a large enough
black population lived in the area to claim that it was a segregated
school; whites living in West Las Vegas attended the school, and blacks
went there not because of any school district policy, but because city
officials forced them to live in the area. By the time the population
mushroomed in the 1950s, according to a U.S. Civil Rights Commission
report, "additional elementary schools were constructed on the west side
to match the growing black student population, [but] no secondary
schools were constructed. This was at the behest of black community
leaders, who took the position that the construction of new units would
extend segregation to the secondary schools." For their part, local
school trustees and administrators argued that segregation was a product of neighborhoods, not education, and therefore they had no responsibility for what had happened or for doing anything about it.[19]

What local schools and districts did struck civil rights advocates as
piecemeal. Some schools and districts held in-service training programs
to, as the Clark County plan put it, enhance "the sensitivities of a mixed
input of teachers and administrators in terms of knowledge, understand-
ings, and skills concerning the problems of minority group students"
while "improving programs and staff relations regarding integration."
Some administrators set up planning groups and sought federal aid for
integrated school projects.[20] The Clark County School District created
an Advisory Council on Integration, with a cross-section of about forty-
five African American leaders, including McMillan, West, Wilson,
Bailey, Kellar, attorneys Robert Mullen and Robert Reid, and ministers
Marion Bennett and Prentiss Walker. Once Mason became school superintendent in 1966, he and the school board issued a statement on integration. "The Clark County Board of School Trustees is opposed to the
segregation of children for reasons of race, religion, economic handicap,

or any other difference, and is willing to assume *shared responsibility* to help alleviate such segregation. The Board recognizes that de facto segregation is a situation that the schools inherit but do not create. The Board has initiated a great number of activities and programs designed to implement and encourage desegregation. The Board's stated policy has been, and always will be, to provide the best educational services to all children of all citizens brought together in schools and in classrooms for the optimum fulfillment of each individual child. Every reasonable and constructive measure that can be afforded will be taken toward the ultimate elimination of de facto segregation in our schools." How much federal laws and guidelines influenced this statement and how much was due to local pressure is uncertain. Revising the policy in December 1966, the district made plans to encourage integration in the next decade and a half by relying on the Head Start program, improved staffing and training, new attendance zones, multicultural learning, and community programs, and by examining the possibility of "prestige schools" to attract whites to West Las Vegas.[21]

Nationally, NAACP officials had wearied of delaying tactics, half-measures, and neglect. NAACP attorneys and other civil rights advocates began pushing harder for the courts to go beyond desegregation and seek integration—not only to assure that African American children had access to the same education that white children received, but also to strike at social segregation by bringing children together in the same schools. Kellar agreed. After meeting with NAACP officials at the July 1967 convention, he returned to Las Vegas and, the following May, filed suit in U.S. District Court to demand the integration of Clark County schools. Nor did it seem likely to hurt Kellar's cause when that month, in *Green v. County School Board of New Kent County, et al.*, the U.S. Supreme Court ruled that a Virginia county's attempt to desegregate by setting up freedom-of-choice schools, much like the "prestige schools" in West Las Vegas, was unacceptable.[22]

Just as the NAACP had been lucky that Earl Warren was chief justice, Kellar was likely to receive a sympathetic hearing from one of Nevada's three U.S. district judges. Two were the judiciary's only father-son combination: senior judge Roger T. Foley and Roger D. Foley, who had encouraged civil rights advocates when he was state attorney general from 1959 to 1962 before succeeding his father. But the Foleys were longtime Las Vegans with possible conflicts of interest, so the case went before Bruce Thompson, who came down from Reno to hear the case.

A John F. Kennedy appointee, like the younger Foley, Thompson was the son of a longtime professor at the University of Nevada in Reno, the brother of a state supreme court justice, a former assistant U.S. attorney and university regent, and a Democrat with a liberal cast of mind.[23]

Thompson's ruling, issued in 1968, was to the point. Deeming Clark County's high schools integrated and elementary schools segregated, he ordered the school board to come up with an integration plan that assured African American student enrollment would be no more than 60 percent in any elementary school grade level. He demanded an integration plan to "accomplish integration and not just talk about it," arguing that "if we wait another three, four, or five years, it may be more difficult to solve and more critical than it is right now." Giving all sides the benefit of the doubt, Thompson wrote, "I can't help but believe that the portions of the program that have been in effect for approximately two years are really temporizing measures. They have been adopted with the hope, I presume, of placating the Negro community and perhaps solving or salving the conscience of the white community. And I know that there are people who entertain very real and governing racial prejudices and bigotry. But I don't think the situation is going to be any different in 1970 or 1975 than it is right now with respect to the attitude of the people of Clark County."[24]

While the district worked on an integration plan, local citizens became involved. The Las Vegas League of Women Voters joined the case as an intervenor pursuing integration, while several parents formed Parents Who Care to oppose busing. School officials set up a task force comprised of blacks and whites, school trustees and administrators, and interested citizens. The members admitted that their "assignment has been a challenging, frustrating, and yet satisfying experience." They "unanimously agreed that children of all colors and creeds in the same educational setting is an important measurement of a quality education. We also believe that school racial integration has some positive factors," including "reduction of ethnocentrism," the "improvement of human relations," and the ability to "help children learn how to create democratic order out of diversity." But they produced a voluntary plan: black students could choose to take a bus to mostly white schools. As for West Las Vegas elementary schools, Madison would be turned into a vocational center; C. V. T. Gilbert would become a prestige school; Kit Carson would include a pre-school, a reading clinic, and a talented-student center; Matt Kelly would add a pre-school, a placement center, and a community adult-education program; and Jo Mackey and Highland would combine with two low-income white schools into "an educational park program." The district also proposed to add a middle school nearby to concentrate on vocational education.[25]

Joined by several West Las Vegas leaders and the League of Women Voters, Kellar objected to the proposal. According to Kellar, "the plan's commitment to the concept of voluntary reassignment of students shifts the burden of integration to the black community and offers no guaranty of successful integration; the Plan effectively abolishes the neighborhood school in the Westside while preserving this 'institution' in the white community; the Plan denounces the use of forced and cross bussing but utilizes these procedures in transporting negro students." Kellar and the intervenors called for a general plan that would include expanded attendance zones as of September 1970, giving the district more than a full school year to acclimate itself, parents, and children to the changes, and "a program of preparation . . . in which the community is educated as to the positive benefits of integration, parents are informed of the educational advantages of integration, administrators and teachers are instructed in those areas where problems might arise when the integration plan is implemented, and the students are exposed to integrated situations." Kellar pointed out that while the school board adopted what sounded like a strong commitment to integration, "it has taken a court order to prompt the school board into taking any type of action to integrate the elementary school system and even then the action taken was feeble at best." Likening the plan to the freedom-of-choice plans that southern school districts used to avoid integrating, Kellar reminded Thompson of his earlier decision when he noted, "It could truly be stated that the Plan does not accomplish integration but merely talks about it." For its part, an *amicus* brief from the League of Women Voters added that "the Plan's most likely effect will be to perpetuate the segregated conditions that now exist. If this Plan is accepted in its present form, segregation in the Clark County elementary school system will not only be perpetuated, but such segregation will have judicial sanction." It called the district's plan "conceptually preoccupied with the Westside schools to the exclusion of a community solution." But, in June 1969, Thompson decided to let the school district try its plan, reasoning that it "has possibilities of successfully solving the problem and should be approved until proven unworkable" and three hundred black children entered the program.[26]

Whether or not the program was successful depended upon who analyzed it. In March 1970, the school district reported that forty-eight of the fifty local elementary schools now enrolled black students. The number of black students attending traditionally white schools tripled, so that nearly half of them were going to school outside of their segregated neighborhood schools. The prestige school and academic enrichment programs were expanding. A district report proposed continuing voluntary busing for another year and concluded, "It would be extremely advantageous to the whole nation if the people of Clark County took this opportunity to prove that Americans can take steps to eliminate social injustice without being forced to do so." But the League of Women Voters and its attorney, Frank Schreck, disagreed. They countered that black enrollment remained at about 99 percent at five Westside elementary schools. While more blacks attended traditionally white schools, at only two schools had black enrollment topped 20 percent; twenty-eight of the forty-four schools reported white enrollment of 95 percent or more. Nor were the district's special programs "in fact Integration and cannot be considered as such." Schreck also attached to his brief a *Las Vegas Sun* editorial making another key point: "For the most part black and white youngsters are introduced to one another in the Las Vegas school system at the sixth grade level and, to put it plainly, in far too many instances that's too late. The youngsters have already formed hard and fast attitudes on racial questions at that age and far too often, those attitudes are wrong."[27]

Judge Thompson found the league's interpretation more accurate than the school district's. "The neighborhood school concept must be abandoned to accomplish integration in a racially segregated area. Because of the demonstrated reluctance of white parents to volunteer their children for education in the Westside schools, the burden of accepting busing to accomplish elementary school integration has been placed on the black parents," he wrote in December 1970. "While the latter have evinced an increasing acceptance of such busing for their children, it cannot be inferred from the evidence before the Court that the present plan will ever eliminate an almost one hundred percent population of black students in the Westside elementary schools so long as such schools are maintained and operated." He demanded a plan to ensure that black enrollment in West Las Vegas "shall not exceed fifty percent of the total student enrollment." While the district appealed his ruling to the Ninth Circuit Court of Appeals, Thompson granted its request to hold another hearing in light of the U.S. Supreme Court's holdings in the school integration cases in Charlotte, Denver, and other cities. The district argued that the high Court limited integration to areas in which segregation had been de jure, which had not been the case in Las Vegas, while Kellar and the NAACP countered that segregation was impermissible wherever it existed.[28]

Meanwhile, the district worked on a new plan. It sought input from local citizens during a six-week study period. Finally, in April 1971, school trustees agreed to sixth-grade centers and busing. West Las Vegas's six elementary schools—and one, Quannah McCall, in a predominantly black section of North Las Vegas—would become sixth-grade centers, and buses would transport white students there. Black students would take the bus to mostly white schools for the first through fifth grades. Kindergarten students would be exempt because they attended school for only half a day and were just starting school. As the U.S. Commission on Civil Rights pointed out, "under the Sixth Grade Center Plan the burden of busing falls almost entirely upon the black student population. Under the plan, white children are bused during only one of their six elementary school years, while black children are transported five of six years." As McMillan later complained, "they came up with what they called 'sixth grade centers' to try to pacify us, get rid of the suit." Operation Bus Out, an organization formed by white parents to oppose busing, found even that unacceptable, mounting a one-day school boycott that resulted in seven thousand students missing classes. Their obvious effort to influence Judge Thompson proved futile. He accepted the plan, albeit under unusual circumstances: the school board that submitted the proposal already had decided to appeal his earlier ruling, which the Ninth Circuit Court of Appeals upheld in February 1972.[29]

But the fight was far from over. In June 1972, Congress passed the Higher Education Act, including the Broomfield Amendment, which banned federal funding of busing and held in abeyance any school desegregation plan still working its way through the judicial system. When the League of Women Voters sued, contending that Clark County schools had failed to comply, school district attorneys countered that the Broomfield provision and the appeals process freed them from having to take action. Thompson read the law differently. He ruled for the league's position, holding that nothing about the amendment was retroactive: the district had agreed to a plan before Congress passed the Broomfield

Amendment, and would have to abide by its earlier promises. Indeed, a district official wrote privately, "We have no plans whatsoever to drop integration entirely if the courts hold us blameless for segregated neighborhood schools. We believe simply that a voluntary plan is the most effective because people who make a decision to change take with them a commitment to help make the program work."[30]

In turn, Operation Bus Out stepped up its efforts. The parents who formed it, and their attorney, argued that sixth-grade centers would have too great a financial impact by reducing the value of their homes: neighborhood schools enhanced property values, which would suffer if children had to leave home to attend schools. They also claimed that the busing plan violated the Nevada Constitution's requirement of "a uniform system of common schools." A Nevada district court judge agreed and issued an injunction that September to stop the busing and close all local elementary schools. This put the Clark County School District in the anomalous position of defending a program it had tried to block. The district appealed the ruling to the Nevada Supreme Court, arguing that the state courts had no business interfering in a federal case, and continued the sixth-grade center plan while awaiting a decision. After issuing a stay order until it could hear arguments on the injunction, the justices agreed that a state court had no power to interfere with a federal court order and vacated the state district court's order.[31]

Meanwhile, the school district had prepared for the inevitable the previous year. It sent letters to parents to explain the change and held orientation sessions and workshops for parents and teachers to discuss the law and psychology of desegregation. The district transferred all sixth-grade teachers to one of the seven schools in predominantly black areas and, trying to integrate the workforce, juggled staffers to make sure no more than 20 percent of those working in the schools were African American. The district also expanded its fleet of school buses and instituted a more complete and demanding training program than the one the state required for other bus drivers. In all, a federal report estimated, desegregating elementary schools ultimately cost the Clark County district a little more than $1.5 million, a third of which went toward buying new buses that probably were needed anyway.[32]

Introducing busing to Clark County schools brought out the best and worst in all involved. State legislators tried to introduce a bill to outlaw busing for integration in Clark County, but others defeated the bill. Neither black nor white parents were thrilled with sending their students anywhere on school buses, much less early in the morning and late in the afternoon, but only the white parents mounted any significant protest, with Operation Bus Out calling the plan "unfair" and at one point joining Parents for Neighborhood Schools to gather more than thirty thousand signatures on an anti-busing petition. But Kenny Guinn, who succeeded Mason as school superintendent, estimated that 85 percent of Las Vegans agreed that "the court order was the law and it should be obeyed," while a black community leader declared, "The sixth grade plan is now the law of the land and all citizens should obey it and make it function during the following year. If it is not pleasing to us during that period we should work together to develop a new plan. People have screamed for law and order for five years. Now we have a law so let's have order too." As for the most important group affected, the children, teachers and administrators reported "minimal" racial fights or disagreements, and that they accepted and sometimes even liked busing—or, as one school administrator said, "The problem has never been with the children. The problem comes with the parents' preconceived ideas. The children get along beautifully. They always have. There are conflicts no matter what color they are, but that's true in any school." They also benefited from the district's expansion of a high school ethnic studies program to the lower grades, and a social enrichment program to enhance the "commonality and universality of experience" by scheduling joint field trips and intercultural activities for black and white children.[33]

Today, the Clark County School District is the nation's fifth-largest, serving more than 300,000 students—twice as many as a decade ago. About one-eighth is African American; today, the largest ethnic minority in local schools is Latinos, at about 38 percent. In 1977, Thompson ended his jurisdiction, finding the school district had complied with his requirements, and the sixth-grade center system continued until 1994. Today, sixth graders go to middle school with seventh and eighth graders—some at West Las Vegas schools built during McMillan's tenure from 1993 to 1997 on the school board. As McMillan said, "Most black children go to those six schools that were in the segregated area. . . . The black community agreed to that situation as an alternative to busing everybody out. We're also now using five magnet schools in the black community to help desegregate the system," including a performing arts magnet school at the old Las Vegas High School downtown—once the heart of the white residential district, but now, like many urban downtowns, home to more lower-income and minority residents. West Las

Vegas also is the home of A-Tech, a vocational and technical high school, and the elementary school named for Mabel Hoggard is the magnet for students interested in computers. "It's a plan," McMillan said. "I don't think it really does the thing that we need it to do, but at least it does integrate the school systems to that extent."[34]

West Las Vegas remains home to ethnic minorities—but, as the district's enrollment figures suggest, it is no longer entirely African American. Since the state passed its open housing law in 1971, segregation has become far more economic than racial in nature. The influx of Latinos has literally changed the complexion of the once-predominantly black Westside and of what once were mostly white middle-class and lower-middle-class neighborhoods in the eastern portions of Las Vegas. Indeed, the community has changed in other, significant ways. African Americans now live throughout the valley—to their benefit and detriment. As McMillan observed shortly before his death, "You can have all the civil rights you want, you know. You can get a job sweeping the floor downtown in a hotel or be a cocktail waitress, but if you don't have capital in your community . . . I hate to say this, but in Las Vegas, through the success of the civil rights movement and our NAACP actions, we actually hurt the black population. When blacks were confined to the Westside, that's where their money stayed. . . . I'm saying that black businesses went under when we got our civil rights. When desegregation finally came, and blacks began taking their money elsewhere, white businesses on the Westside were hurt too." But more African Americans hold office in the legislature and local governing bodies. The Clark County School District has employed an African American superintendent, and several African Americans have sat on the school board. And when he died in 2002 at age ninety-three, Charles Kellar was remembered not as an agitator who upset race relations, but as a fighter for what was right. Clark County students can learn information about the local civil rights movement at schools named for William H. "Bob" Bailey, the first local African American television host and a veteran of the movement; Dorothy Eisenberg of the League of Women Voters; H. P. Fitzgerald, the first local black principal; Oran Gragson; Theron and Naomi Goynes, longtime school district educators; Addeliar Guy, one of the first local black attorneys and judges; Edythe and Lloyd Katz, whites who fought for civil rights; James McMillan; Joe Neal, the first black state senator, who spent thirty-two years in the legislature; Eva Simmons, a longtime school district administrator; and there are middle schools named for Charles

West; Hank Greenspun and his wife, Barbara; and civil rights advocates and governors Grant Sawyer and Mike O'Callaghan. In Nevada, the struggle to overcome racism and segregation continues, but *Brown* and its aftermath paved the way for significant change.[35]

Notes

Introduction

1. James T. Patterson, *Brown v. Board of Education: A Civil Rights Milestone and Its Troubled Legacy* (New York: Oxford University Press, 2001), and Michael J. Klarman, *From Jim Crow to Civil Rights: The Supreme Court and the Struggle for Racial Equality* (New York: Oxford University Press, 2004), both offer excellent discussions of the *Brown* decision and its implementation, though both offer largely a top-down, national perspective.

2. Notable exceptions include David S. Cecelski, *Along Freedom Road: Hyde County, North Carolina, and the Fate of Black Schools in the South* (Chapel Hill: University of North Carolina Press, 1994); Davison M. Douglas, *Reading, Writing and Race: The Desegregation of the Charlotte Schools* (Chapel Hill: University of North Carolina Press, 1995); and many of the essays in Peter F. Lau, ed., *From the Grassroots to the Supreme Court: Brown v. Board of Education and American Democracy* (Durham: Duke University Press, 2004).

3. Patterson, *Brown v. Board of Education,* ch. 3.

4. Our limited understanding of the NAACP's implementation efforts should come as no surprise. The larger history of the association is also not well known, particularly in the post-*Brown* years. Though scholars have produced monographs detailing the activities of most other leading civil rights organizations, the history of the NAACP remains somewhat unknown. This fact is surprising, considering the importance of the association. As the historian Adam Fairclough explains, "The NAACP is, paradoxically, the most important but also the least studied of the civil rights organizations." See Adam Fairclough, *Race and Democracy: The Civil Rights Struggle in Louisiana, 1915–1972* (Athens: University of Georgia Press, 1995), xiv. Charles Eagles concurs: "the larger stories of the NAACP as well as its Legal Defense and Educational Fund, especially after the school desegregation cases, have not been told." See Charles W. Eagles, "Toward New Histories of the Civil Rights Era," *Journal of Southern History* 66 (November 2000): 833.

5. Douglas, *Reading, Writing and Race;* Cecelski, *Along Freedom Road.*

6. "Remarks of Thurgood Marshall at Press Conference, June 30, 1954," Supplement to Part 1 (1951–55), reel 10, in John Bracey and August Meier, eds. *Papers of the NAACP* (microfilm) (Bethesda, MD: University Publications of America, 1982). Also see Robert L. Carter and John Hope Franklin, *A Matter of Law: A Memoir of Struggle in the Cause of Equal Rights* (New York: New Press, 2005).

7. Quoted in Richard Kluger, *Simple Justice: The History of Brown v. Board of Education and Black America's Struggle for Equality* (New York: Random House, 1975), 747.

8. Patterson, *Brown v. Board of Education,* ch. 6; Charles C. Bolton, *The Hardest Deal of All: The Battle over School Integration in Mississippi, 1870–1980* (Jackson: University Press of Mississippi, 2005), ch. 5.

9. Patterson, *Brown v. Board of Education,* ch. 8–9.

Implementing *Brown* in Arkansas

1. Arkansas Advisory Committee to United States Commission on Civil Rights, *Report on Arkansas,* September 1963.

2. A good overview of the situation in Arkansas can be found in A. Stephen Stephan, "Integration and Segregation in Arkansas—One Year Afterward," *Journal of Negro Education* 23, no. 3 (Summer 1955): 172–87; "The Status of Integration and Segregation in Arkansas," *Journal of Negro Education* 25, no. 3 (Summer 1956): 212–20.

3. John A. Kirk, *Redefining the Color Line: Black Activism in Little Rock, Arkansas, 1940–1970* (Gainesville: University Press of Florida, 2002), 19; Robert L. Carter to Mr. Marshall, Mr. White, Mr. Wilkins, Mr. Current, September 3, 1954; Mr. Current to Mr. Marshall, October 26, 1954, NAACP Papers, Part II, box 226, Desegregation Schools—Branch Action, Arkansas, 1954–1955, NAACP Papers, Library of Congress, Washington, DC.

4. Data provided by C. Fred Williams, Ph.D. For instance, after World War II eighteen Japanese Americans (who formerly had been incarcerated at the War Relocation Centers in Jerome and Rohwer) remained in Arkansas. Most of the families settled at Scott doing tenant farming. However, all of the families but Sam Yada left Arkansas by the early 1950s. Yada opened a nursery landscape business in North Little Rock (Sherwood) where both of his sons attended public schools. In addition, some Asian exchange students attended Central during the desegregation crisis.

Native Americans most certainly have populated Arkansas since before statehood in 1836. However, until the Great Society programs and the American Indian Movement by the 1970s, little incentive (and many disincentives) existed for individuals to desire to be identified as Native American. The funding formulas for small business and the Red Power movement of the sixties resulted in some Indians identifying themselves in the U.S. Census. The 1970 census reported just over twelve thousand Native Americans living in approximately a dozen Arkansas counties.

As for Hispanics, the U.S. Government and Mexico had a labor agreement (the Bracerro Program) from 1948 to 1964 that allowed thousands of Mexicans to come to Arkansas as farm workers. Local school districts did admit some of the children, but due to their migratory nature, accurate data on numbers of Hispanic students in any particular district at any govern time do not exist.

5. Seth Blomeley, "Changes Hit Some Schools in Wallet; Many Districts See State Funds Shrink," *Arkansas Democrat-Gazette*, Sunday, April 17, 2005, A1, A16–17.

6. Information provided by C. Fred Williams; *Report on Arkansas, 5.*

7. Fon Louise Gordon, "The Black Experience in Arkansas, 1880–1920" (Ph.D. dissertation, University of Arkansas), 95.

8. Mattie Ware Davis, Interview by Doramae Ricks, February 20, 1995, transcript, National Dunbar History Project, Archives and Special Collections, University of Arkansas at Little Rock.

9. James D. Anderson, *The Education of Blacks in the South, 1860–1935* (Chapel Hill: University of North Carolina Press, 1988), 206.

10. Jim Lester, *The People's College: Little Rock Junior College and Little Rock University, 1927–1969* (Little Rock, AR: August House, 1987), 39.

11. National Register of Historic Places Inventory-Nomination Form for Dunbar Junior and Senior High School and Junior College. Courtesy of Arkansas Historic Preservation Program.

12. Kirk, *Redefining the Color Line,* 86–87; Cherry quote from *Southern School News,* September 1954, 2.

13. Dale Bumpers, *The Best Lawyer in a One-Lawyer Town* (New York: Random House, 2003), 138. Bumpers was born in Charleston, Franklin County, Arkansas, August 12, 1925. He served in the United States Marine Corps from 1943 to 1946 and graduated from Northwestern University Law School in 1951. After being admitted to the Arkansas bar in 1952, Bumpers practiced in Charleston and embarked on a political career which included stints as the Charleston city attorney, 1952–1970; governor of Arkansas, 1970–1974; and four terms as Democrat in the United States Senate, 1975–1999.

14. Ibid.

15. Minutes of School Board meeting, Fayetteville School District No. 1, May 21, 1954; and *Southern School News,* September 3, 1954, 2; Bumpers, *The Best Lawyer in a One-Lawyer Town,* 140. Nine black students enrolled in the Fayetteville High School in September 1954.

16. Harlan D. Unrau, "Historical Significance of School Desegregation in Charleston, Arkansas: August 23, 1954," Unpublished report for the National Park Service, February 25, 1998, 5; Bumpers, *The Best Lawyer in a One-Lawyer Town,* 139–40. Bumpers notes that the superintendent's speech to the Charleston Commercial Club was mentioned in the local newspaper. He also gives the number of black students entering the formerly white public schools as thirteen.

17. Bumpers, *The Best Lawyer in a One-Lawyer Town,* and *Arkansas Gazette,* September 14, 1954; Kirk, *Redefining the Color Line,* 88.

18. Unrau, "Historical Significance of School Desegregation in Charleston, Arkansas," 5; *Southern School News,* December 1956; Kirk, *Redefining the Color Line,* 87.

19. *Southern School News,* September 3, 1954, 2; Kirk, *Redefining the Color Line,* 87–88.

20. *Southern School News,* May 4, 1955; Kirk, *Redefining the Color Line,* 94.

21. *Southern School News,* September 1954, 2.

22. *Southern School News,* October 1954, 3, November 1954, 2; Kirk, *Redefining the Color Line,* 88.

23. Charles J. Russo, J. John Harris III, and Rosetta F. Sandidge, "*Brown v. Board of Education* at 40: A Legal History of Equal Educational Opportunities in American Public Education," *Journal of Negro Education* 63: 3 (Summer 1994): 300.

24. Kirk, *Redefining the Color Line,* 94–95.

25. Ibid., 96.

26. *Southern School News,* July 1955, 3; August 1955, 15, September 1955, 10, 11.

27. *Southern School News,* August 1955, 15. The best overview of the Hoxie situation is Jerry J. Vervack, "The Hoxie Imbroglio," *Arkansas Historical Quarterly* 48 (Spring 1989): 17–33.

28. "A 'Morally Right' Decision," *Life* 39 (July 25, 1955): 31. The *Southern School News,* August 1955, page 15, lists the number of black students as twenty, while *Life* and Vervack use the number twenty-one.

29. *Southern School News,* August 1955, 15.

30. *Southern School News,* September 1955, 10.

31. Vervack, "The Hoxie Imbroglio," 27; *Southern School News,* October 1955, 9.

32. *Southern School News,* October 1955, 9; *Southern School News,* November 1955, 3; *Southern School News,* February 1956, 11. The school board asked the judge to declare: (1) That the board has the right and duty to refuse to obey Arkansas laws which contradict the laws of the United States by requiring segregation. (2) That the board is authorized and required by the

Fourteenth Amendment to desegregate without regard to whether the Arkansas law is repealed. (3) That the plaintiffs would be subject to civil and criminal liability if they restored segregation at Hoxie. On January 9, 1956, Judge Albert L. Reeves ruled for the Hoxie school board, holding that the Supreme Court has in effect nullified Arkansas's segregation laws and that the directors of a school district are required to end racial segregation as soon as all administrative obstacles are removed.

33. Vervack, "The Hoxie Imbroglio," 33.

34. The Hoxie incident may have caused the Biggers-Reyno school district in northeast Arkansas to abandon its June 30, 1955, plan to send two black students to its junior and senior high schools (while the twelve black elementary students continued to be bused to the segregated school at Pocahantas) on October 14, only ten days before the fall school term began. *Southern School News*, August 1955, 15, November 1955, 3.

35. *Southern School News*, November 1955, 3; February 1956, 11; April 1956, 8. In October 1955 Judge Miller made a similar ruling in an earlier case filed against the Bearden School District in 1952, *Alvin J. Matthews et al. v. Bearden School District No. 53 of Ouachita County, et al.*, when he ordered the school board to meet periodically to discuss future integration. The Bearden school district had six hundred white students and three hundred black students.

36. *Southern School News*, December 1955, 9, December 1956, 8.

37. *Southern School News*, January 1957, 8–9, August 1957, 7.

38. *Southern School News*, May 1956, 10.

39. *Arkansas Gazette*, August 21, 1960.

40. *Southern School News*, June 1956, 10, September 1956, 15; *Arkansas Gazette*, August 21, 1960.

41. Tony Allen Freyer, *The Little Rock Crisis: A Constitutional Interpretation* (Westport, CT: Greenwood Press, 1984), 16–17.

42. Robert Raymond Brown, *Bigger Than Little Rock* (Greenwich, CT: Seabury Press, 1958), 54.

43. *Southern School News*, February 1956, 11.

44. *Southern School News*, March 1956, 4, April 1956, 9; *Arkansas State Press*, January 27, 1956.

45. *Southern School News*, September 1956, 15.

46. *Southern School News*, March 1957, 13, April 1957, 15, May 1957, 2.

47. *Southern School News*, October 1956, 13.

48. *Southern School News*, February 1957, 3. Watkins and Parham told Dove they had not planned to integrate in the 1956–57 academic year.

49. *Southern School News*, March 1957, 13; June 1957, 8; August 1957, 7.

50. *Southern School News*, August 1957, 9.

51. *Southern School News*, July 1957, 10; Tony Allen Freyer, "Politics and

the Law in the Little Rock Crisis, 1954–1954," *Arkansas Historical Quarterly* 40, no. 3 (Autumn 1981): 31 and 205. The doctrine of interposition had held no legal basis in constitutional law since the end of the Civil War. The idea, however, appealed to white southerners seeking to delay integration.

52. Pete Daniel, "Bayonets and Bibles: The 1957 Little Rock Crisis," Unpublished paper presented at the Southern Historical Association's annual meeting, October 31, 1996, Little Rock, Arkansas, 3.

53. *Arkansas Gazette,* August 28, 30, and 31, 1957.

54. *Arkansas Democrat,* September 3, 1957.

55. Roy Reed, *Faubus: The Life and Times of an American Prodigal* (Fayetteville: University of Arkansas Press, 1997), 207–8. Later in his life, Faubus acknowledged that the initial report of increased weapons sales was false, but insisted that sales did increase several weeks later after the crisis events developed. Faubus's televised speech and the turmoil in Little Rock affected desegregation elsewhere in Arkansas: in Ozark, three black students enrolled in Ozark High School on September 2 only to withdraw two days later because of harassment; and North Little Rock delayed the start of its desegregation plan until the courts ruled on the state's four segregation laws. *Southern School News,* October 1957, 1, 5.

56. *Arkansas Gazette,* September 5, 1957.

57. Telegram from Governor Orval E. Faubus to President Dwight D. Eisenhower, September 5, 1957, Dwight D. Eisenhower Library.

58. *Arkansas Gazette,* September 4, 5, and 21, 1957.

59. Henry M. Alexander, *The Little Rock Recall Election* (New York: McGraw-Hill, 1960), 4–12.

60. *Arkansas Gazette,* June 15, and September 3, 1960.

61. Ibid., March 3 and May 3, 1961.

62. Ibid., April 23, 1965.

63. Robert L. Brown, "The Second Crisis in Little Rock: A Report on Desegregation within the Little Rock Public Schools," Unpublished report sponsored by the Winthrop Rockefeller Foundation, 1988, 7.

64. *Arkansas Gazette,* September 30, 1962.

65. Ibid.

66. Ibid., September 29, 1963.

67. *Arkansas Gazette,* November 1 and 11, 1960, November 15, 1961, and July 27, 1963.

68. Ibid., September 5, 1963.

69. Ibid., January 12, 1960. The district had only two schools, all-white Dollarway and all-black Townsend Park School. Both schools enrolled grades 1–12. Total district enrollment was evenly divided between white and black students with about thirteen hundred each. *Southern School News,* March 1959, 2.

70. *Arkansas Gazette*, January 23, 1960, and September 8, 1960.

71. Ibid., September 8, 1960.

72. Ibid., March 15, 1960.

73. Ibid., January 23 and 31, 1963. The other black student was second-grader Samuel Wayne Cato, who was in his second year at Dollarway School. Two white students, Cathy and Earline Hudman, also stayed home during this time because they reportedly were threatened by white students for attempting to help Sarah Howard.

74. Ibid., March 13, 1966.

75. Ibid., September 28, 1964.

76. Ibid., March 7 and April 30, 1965.

77. Ibid., September 13, 1963, August 20, 1964, October 16, 1964, October 29, 1965, and February 8, 1966.

78. Ibid., January 7, 1966.

79. Ibid., March 24, 1966.

80. Ibid., December 6, 1966.

81. Statewide statistics of desegregation by year, district, and school do not exist for Arkansas. When asked about the success and legacy of *Brown v. Board* Little Rock 9 member Minnijean Brown Trickey replied that it was futile to discuss the decision's success when it was never fully embraced or properly implemented initially.

The Cost of Opportunity: School Desegregation's Complicated Calculus in North Carolina

1. Works that highlight African American losses because of poor choices made during the desegregation process include Russell W. Irvine and Jacqueline J. Irvine, "The Impact of the Desegregation Process on the Education of Black Students: Key Variables," *Journal of Negro Education* 52 (1983): 410–22; David S. Cecelski, *Along Freedom Road: Hyde County, North Carolina, and the Fate of Black Schools in the South* (Chapel Hill: University of North Carolina Press, 1994); Vanessa Siddle-Walker, *Their Highest Potential: Caswell County Training School* (Chapel Hill: University of North Carolina Press, 1996); Virginia Hill, "Local Histories/Local Memories of Desegregation: Extending Critical Theory to Improve Understanding of Continuing Problems" (Ph.D. dissertation, University of North Carolina, 1997); Van Dempsey and George Noblit, "Cultural Ignorance and School Desegregation: A Community Narrative," and Patricia A. Edwards, "Before and after School Desegregation: African American Parents' Involvement in Schools," in *Beyond Desegregation: The Politics of Quality in African American Schooling*, Mwalimu J. Shujaa, ed. (Thousand Oaks, CA: Corwin Press, 1996), 115–61. Barbara Shircliffe has suggested that scholars treat

critically the rosy memories many older African Americans have of segregated schools but also that nostalgia may serve as an "artful critique" of current school problems. See Shircliffe, "'We Got the Best of That World': A Case for the Study of Nostalgia in the Oral History of School Segregation," *Oral History Review* 28 (2001): 59–84; and similar points in Jack Dougherty, "From Anecdote to Analysis: Oral Interviews and New Scholarship in Educational History," *Journal of American History* 86 (1999): 712–23.

2. For evidence of the achievement gaps between white and various minority group students nationally, see the results of the National Assessment of Educational Progress online at <http://nces.ed.gov/nationsreportcard>. See also Richard Herrnstein and Charles Murray, *The Bell Curve: Intelligence and Class Structure in American Life* (New York: Free Press, 1994); and responses in Russell Jacoby and Naomi Glauberman, eds., *The Bell Curve Debate: History, Documents, Opinions* (New York: Times Books, 1995); Steven Fraser, ed., *The Bell Curve Wars: Race, Intelligence, and the Future of America* (New York: Basic Books, 1995); John U. Ogbu, "Racial Stratification and Education in the United States: Why Inequality Persists," *Teachers College Record* 96 (1994): 264–98; Christopher Jencks and Meredith Phillips, eds., *The Black-White Test Score Gap* (Washington, DC: Brookings Institution Press, 1998); "Why There Has Been No Progress in Closing the Black-White SAT Scoring Gap," *Journal of Blacks in Higher Education* 22 (Winter 1998–99): 6–10, 12; and Eric A. Hanushek, "Black-White Achievement Differences and Governmental Interventions," *American Economic Review* 91 (2001): 24–28.

3. See Gary Orfield, "Schools More Separate: Consequences of a Decade of Resegregation" (Cambridge, MA: The Civil Rights Project at Harvard University, July 2001). Available online at <http://www.civilrightsproject.harvard.edu/research/deseg/Schools_More_Separate.pdf>.

4. The lost cause school includes harsh assessments of the effects of desegregation remedies such as busing in Raymond Wolters, *The Burden of Brown: Thirty Years of School Desegregation* (Knoxville: University of Tennessee Press, 1984); and David Armor, *Forced Justice: School Desegregation and the Law* (New York: Oxford University Press, 1995).

5. This article is based on research presented more fully in J. Michael McElreath, "The Cost of Opportunity: School Desegregation and Changing Race Relations in the Triangle" (Ph.D. dissertation, University of Pennsylvania, 2002).

6. Many African Americans supported school desegregation mainly as a way to gain access to equal resources. Still, the hope that desegregation would eventually affect white minds as well as pocketbooks was fairly general.

7. Statistics on state and local expenditures for public education are published biennially by the state's Department of Public Instruction (DPI).

8. My views on the Pearsall Plan are close to those of Davison Douglas, who has noted, "the Pearsall Plan promised far more than it actually delivered" to North Carolina's die-hard segregationists. See Douglas, *Reading, Writing, and Race: The Desegregation of the Charlotte Schools* (Chapel Hill: University of North Carolina Press, 1995), 33. Many of the records of the Pearsall Committee that produced the Pearsall Plan are available in the papers of Thomas J. Pearsall at UNC-CH. The Southern Oral History Program (SOHP) at UNC-CH also has a transcript of conversations among the authors of the plan and certain political leaders describing their intent a few years after the plan went into effect. It is titled, "Transcription Session on History of the Integration Situation in North Carolina, Saturday, September 3, 1960, Governor's Office, State Capitol, Raleigh."

9. For an assessment of Luther Hodges's moderate leadership and response to desegregation, see Numan V. Bartley, *The New South, 1945–1980* (Baton Rouge: Louisiana State University Press, 1995), 212–22. Also see Hodges's memoir, *Businessman in the Statehouse: Six Years as Governor of North Carolina* (Chapel Hill: University of North Carolina Press, 1962).

10. The Pearsall Plan was ruled unconstitutional in *Hawkins v. North Carolina State Board of Education, Race Relations Law Reporter* (RRLR) 11 (1966): 746, 747. The statewide figure is an estimate provided by *School Desegregation in the Southern and Border States* (*SDSBS*, a successor publication to the *Southern School News*), February 1967. The state stopped collecting data on students by race in 1965. In 1964–65, 23 percent of Chapel Hill's black students attended majority-white schools, but almost no whites attended or worked in majority black schools. The corresponding percentages in Durham and Raleigh were 6 and 1. None of the county districts (Wake, Durham, and Orange) had as much as 1 percent of blacks enrolled with whites. Sources: For Chapel Hill, *Southern School News,* February 1965, 5; for Durham City, *Southern School News,* December 1964, 9; Raleigh City Board of Education Minutes, April 23, 1965; Durham County Board of Education Minutes, April 21, 1965; Wake County Board of Education Minutes, May 3, 1965; Orange County Board of Education Minutes, April 16, 1965.

11. See Jean Bradley Anderson, *Durham County: A History of Durham County, North Carolina* (Durham, NC: Duke University Press, 1990), 367.

12. See *McKissick v. Durham City Board of Education,* 176 F. Supp. 3 (1958). Under duress, the Durham City Board of Education approved the transfers of eight black students to white schools a few days before the *McKissick* case was resolved in September 1959. It seems very unlikely that the transfer approvals would have come at that time, however, had *McKissick* not put pressure on the board to act.

13. Joseph and Elwyna Holt took on the Raleigh administration and

school board, seeking a cross-racial assignment for their son Joe starting in 1956. The district stymied their efforts using bureaucratic maneuvers, and Mr. Holt lost his job. See *Holt v. Raleigh City Board of Education,* 164 F. Supp. 853 (1958). Holt's story is told in the documentary *Exhausted Remedies: Joe Holt's Story,* produced by Holt's daughter, Deborah L. Holt (M.A. thesis, University of Maryland, 1995).

14. The case was *Vickers v. Chapel Hill City Board of Education,* 196 F. Supp. 97 (1961).

15. There was a brief spate of desegregation activity in southern Orange County in 1960, but it ended in 1961 when the district closed a small elementary school used for whites only in the community of White Cross. In that instance, the county preserved segregation by the expedient of forcing all of White Cross's residents to attend schools in Hillsborough, located in the center of the county.

16. Wake County Board of Education Minutes, July 1, 1963; *News and Observer,* July 2, 1963, 26, and July 3, 1963, 12; *Southern School News,* August 1963, 19.

17. Consent Order in *Thompson v. Durham County Board of Education,* March 31, 1964, 10 RRLR 174; Durham County Board of Education Minutes, July 2 and August 3, 1964.

18. T. W. Bruton to Charles F. Carroll, *Race Relations Law Reporter* 10 (January 21, 1965): 454.

19. Chapel Hill-Carrboro Board of Education Minutes, April 23, July 8, 22, and 26, August 30, 1965. Chapel Hill-Carrboro was the only district in the Triangle to assign any students on the basis of geography, regardless of race. The desegregating effects of these assignments were largely undone by a provision allowing white students assigned to black schools to transfer to predominantly white schools. In practice, no more than a handful of white students ever attended Chapel Hill's two black elementary schools before 1966–67.

20. Raleigh City Board of Education Minutes, April 23, 1965; Francis Keppel to Jesse O. Sanderson, May 15, 1965, "Raleigh City" folder, box 87-B.9, DPI archives, Old Records Center (ORC), Raleigh, MARS ID 104.320. (MARS = Manuscript and Archives Reference System, North Carolina State Archives, Raleigh.) Wake County Board of Education Minutes, May 3, July 26, September 3, 1965; Francis Keppel to Superintendent Fred A. Smith, September 2, 1965, "Wake County" folder, box 87-B.9, DPI archives, ORC, Raleigh, MARS ID 104.320. Orange County Board of Education Minutes, April 16, May 26, June 28, July 6, 8 and 26, August 2, and September 7 and 13, 1965; Francis Keppel to G. Paul Carr, September 13, 1965, "Orange County" folder, box 87-B.7, DPI archives, ORC, Raleigh, MARS ID 104.320.

21. David S. Seeley to Charles F. Carroll, September 1, 1965, "Durham County" folder, box 87-B.3, DPI archives, ORC, Raleigh, MARS ID 104.320.

22. Durham City Board of Education Minutes, June 9, 1965; "Consent Order Approving 1965–66 Plan," July 16, 1965, 11 RRLR 192; Francis Keppel to Lew W. Hannen, September 20, 1965, "Durham City" folder, box 87-B.3, DPI archives, ORC, Raleigh, MARS ID 104.320; "Plan for Desegregation of the Durham City Schools," October 15, 1965, 11 RRLR 197; David S. Seeley to Lew W. Hannen, November 10, 1965; *Wheeler v. Durham*, 249 F. Supp. 145 (1966), 154.

23. 45 C.F.R. 181.54, United States Office of Education, Department of Health, Education and Welfare, *Revised Statement of Policies for School Desegregation Plans under Title VI of the Civil Rights Act of 1964* (Washington, DC: U.S. Government Printing Office, 1966).

24. *Briggs v. Elliott*, 132 F. Supp. 776 (1955), 777.

25. *SDSBS*, September, 1965, NC4–5.

26. Harold B. Williams to Swiers, May 31, 1967, "Chapel Hill" folder, box 87-B.7, DPI archives, ORC, Raleigh, MARS ID 104.320.

27. Wake County Board of Education Minutes, August 29, 1966.

28. Fred A. Smith to John Hope II, August 31, 1966, "Wake County" folder, box 87-B.9, DPI archives, ORC, Raleigh, MARS ID 104.320.

29. *SDSBS*, August 1966, NC3–4.

30. Ibid., NC4; Wake County Board of Education Minutes, September 19 and October 3, 1966; *SDSBS*, October, 1966, NC5.

31. Orange County Board of Education Minutes, April 24 and June 4, 1968; G. Paul Carr to Charles F. Carroll, July 2, 1968; Eloise Severinson to G. Paul Carr, November 4, 1969, "Orange County" folder, box 87-B.7, DPI archives, ORC, Raleigh, MARS ID 104.320. Wake County Board of Education Minutes, February 7, 13, 14, 26, and 28, March 4, April 1, and May 6, 1968; *SDSBS*, February 1968, NC3.

32. Judge John D. Larkins Jr., "Findings of Fact, Conclusions of Law, and Judgment," in *Smith v. Raleigh City Board of Education* (E.D.N.C., August 7, 1971), 3, in "Raleigh City" folder, box 87-B.9, DPI archives, ORC, Raleigh, MARS ID 104.320. Larkins's order relied on both *Green v. County School Board of New Kent County*, 391 U.S. 430 (1968), and *Swann v. Charlotte-Mecklenburg Board of Education*, 402 U.S. 1 (1971).

33. *Alexander v. Holmes County Board of Education*, 396 U.S. 19 (1969), 20.

34. Durham County Board of Education Minutes, January 13 and May 26, 1969; *Thompson v. Durham County Board of Education*, consolidated with and reported under *Nesbit v. Statesville City Board of Education*, 418 F. 2d 1040 (4th Cir. 1969).

35. Telephone interview with Robert L. Farmer, Raleigh, December 7, 2000. On the history of school desegregation and white flight, see, for example, Robert A. Pratt, *The Color of Their Skin: Education and Race in Richmond Virginia, 1954–89* (Charlottesville: University Press of Virginia,

1992); Ronald H. Bayor, *Race and the Shaping of Twentieth Century Atlanta* (Chapel Hill: University of North Carolina, 1996), 221–51; Eleanor P. Wolf, *Trial and Error: The Detroit School Segregation Case* (Detroit: Wayne State University Press, 1981); and R. David Riddle, "Race and Reaction in Warren, Michigan, 1971–1974: *Bradley v. Milliken* and the Cross-District Busing Controversy," *Michigan Historical Review* 26 (2000): 1–49.

36. Raleigh assistant superintendent D. Stuart Thompson explained that state teachers were allocated based on the number of students. "If you have fewer teachers the state automatically gives you less money for everything. The county commissioners also allocate current operating funds on a per-pupil basis." "City's School Woes Nudge County," *News and Observer,* April 14, 1975; Wake County Board of Education Minutes, December 6, 1967; Raleigh City County Board of Education Minutes, January 5, 1968.

37. "League Study Outlines Pros, Cons of Merger," "School Board Chairmen Debate Pros, Cons of Merged System Here," *News and Observer,* January 18 and February 2, 1975.

38. Telephone interview with A. Roy Tilley, Fuquay Varina, April 29, 2002.

39. Ibid.

40. County board member Mary Gentry, representing Garner, declared, "They want to merge because of the increase in black students. It will only intensify the problem for everybody else. I see no educational advantage to merger. I see it hauling the children out of the county into the city." "City's School Woes Nudge County," *Raleigh News and Observer,* April 14, 1975, 21.

41. Telephone interview with Robert L. Farmer, Raleigh, December 7, 2000; "Legislators: Hands Off Merger," "Merger Bill Tied to Board Request," "Wake School Chairman Calls for Merger Talks," *News and Observer,* February 21, March 28, and April 9, 1975.

42. Wake County Board of Education Minutes, April 14 and May 5, 1975; Tilley interview. Tilley says, "I don't know if I would have called Ranzino if Painter hadn't called me. Painter was killed in a car crash not long after."

43. The General Assembly ratified the Wake schools merger bill on June 25, 1975. Tilley interview; Farmer interview; telephone interviews with Al Adams, Raleigh, November 17, 2000; interviews with Walter Brown, Raleigh, December 11, 2000; Casper Holroyd, Raleigh, December 12, 2000; Vernon Malone, Raleigh, April 10, 1999; Claude Sitton, Oxford, Georgia, February 20, 1999; Raleigh City Board of Education Minutes, June 23, July 28, 1975; Wake County Board of Education Minutes, July 7, 1975; *News and Observer,* September 3–5, 1975.

44. Interview with Edwin Caldwell Jr., Chapel Hill, February 15, 2000; tape recording in possession of the author. Telephone interview with R. D. Smith, Chapel Hill, May 20, 2002; Bob Gilgor, "Lincoln High School: Mighty

Tigers" (unpub. manuscript); *Hillife* (Chapel Hill High School Yearbook), 1967, Chapel Hill High School Library; Don Fuller and Skip Via, Letter to the Editor, *Chapel Hill Weekly,* June 1, 1969, 3. An African American community leader discovered the trophies in a trash can and rescued at least some of them. There is much disagreement about whether the school colors were changed to Lincoln's. The closure of Lincoln and its consolidation with CHHS is the subject of a series of oral history interviews done by Bob Gilgor for an exhibit at the CH Museum in 2001. More interviews on CH school desegregation were conducted by a group of graduate and undergraduate students at UNC in an oral history course in spring 2001. The latter series of interviews is now part of the SOHP at UNC.

45. Caldwell interview; interview with Steven Scroggs, Chapel Hill, January 25, 2001; tape recording in possession of the author. See also Caldwell interviewed in Chapel Hill Bicentennial Commission, *Chapel Hill 200 Years: Close to Magic* (Chapel Hill: Sheer Associates, 1994), 72–73.

46. Minutes of the Chapel Hill-Carrboro City Board of Education, May 19, 1969; *Chapel Hill Weekly,* May 21, 1969.

47. Telephone interview with Steven Piantadosi, Baltimore, Maryland, March 14, 2001; Minutes of the Chapel Hill-Carrboro City Board of Education, May 19, 1969.

48. Ibid.; "School Board Abolishes Marshals; Member Ed Tenney Quits in Lather," *Chapel Hill Weekly,* May 21, 1969.

49. "High School Confrontation," *Chapel Hill Weekly,* May 21, 1969, 2.

50. "High School Calm, Parents Angry Now," *Chapel Hill Weekly,* May 25, 1969.

51. Ibid.; "School Board Sticks to Stand on Marshals," *Chapel Hill Weekly,* June 1, 1969. Guthrie was right in one way: Wake County's school board had to deal with the issue of ensuring racially diverse graduation marshals three years later. A divided board voted to allow principals to choose ushers so that good black students could be honored even if all the marshal slots (determined by grade point average) were filled by whites. Wake County Board of Education Minutes, May 9, 1972.

52. Interview with Wayne Bare, Garner, June 2, 2000; tape recording in possession of the author.

53. Ibid. Bare decided, with some input from his staff, that at least two students of each race would have places on the cheerleading squad. The student body at Garner Senior High School was about 20 percent African American in 1968–69.

54. Telephone interview with Beth Levine, Raleigh, April 24, 2002.

55. On positive spillover effects from school desegregation on community race relations, see Cecelski, *Along Freedom Road,* 165–66; Douglas, *Reading Writing and Race,* 250–52; and Amy Stuart Wells and Robert L. Crain,

"Perpetuation Theory and the Long-Term Effects of School Desegregation," *Review of Educational Research* 64 (Winter 1994): 531–55.

56. Tim Simmons, "Taking Different Roads," *Raleigh News and Observer,* February 20, 2001, A1; Rebecca E. Eden, "Dropping Diversity in Schools," *Durham Herald-Sun,* August 22, 2001, A1.

57. Elizabeth Wade Hall, "Durham Students Express Strong Feelings on Redistricting," and "9 of 10 in N.C. Back Integration," *Durham Herald-Sun,* February 25 and May 5, 1994, A2, C1.

58. Simmons, "Taking Different Roads."

"Keep on Keeping On": African Americans and the Implementation of *Brown v. Board of Education* in Virginia

1. As historian Charles Eagles writes in the November 2000 issue of the *Journal of Southern History,* "the larger stories of the NAACP as well as its Legal Defense and Educational Fund, especially after the school desegregation cases, have not been told." Charles W. Eagles, "Toward New Histories of the Civil Rights Era," *Journal of Southern History,* 66, no. 4 (November 2000). The historian Adam Fairclough agrees: "The NAACP is, paradoxically, the most important but also the least studied of the civil rights organizations." Adam Fairclough, *Race and Democracy: The Civil Rights Struggle in Louisiana, 1915–1972* (Athens: University of Georgia Press, 1995), xiv. See also Matthew Lassiter and Andrew Lewis, editors, *The Moderates' Dilemma: Massive Resistance to School Desegregation in Virginia* (Charlottesville: University Press of Virginia, 1998), 5. On new scholarship put out near the fiftieth anniversary of *Brown,* see, for example, "*Brown v. Board of Education:* The Contested Legacy of a Landmark Decision," The Chronicle Review, *The Chronicle of Higher Education,* April 2, 2004 (Washington, DC); Cheryl Brown Henderson, "*Brown v. Board of Education* at Fifty: A Personal Perspective," *College Board Review* 200 (Fall 2003), *Brown v. Board of Education* issue (New York: College Board Publications).

2. This essay is part of a larger work-in-progress on African Americans and the implementation of *Brown v. Board of Education* in Virginia. Regarding the lack of scholarship on implementing *Brown* in Virginia, Lassiter and Lewis note, "Many important aspects of African-American history during the civil rights era in Virginia remain unexplored by scholars, including the activities of state and local branches of the NAACP" (*The Moderates' Dilemma,* 206). The historian Robert Pratt, a native Virginian, mused in 1996: "One of the questions that students ask most often is, 'While civil rights battles were being fought in the streets of Birmingham and Selma, what was going on in Virginia?' Unfortunately, I can never provide an answer that satisfies either them or me." Robert A. Pratt, "New Directions in

Virginia's Civil Rights History," *Virginia Magazine of History and Biography* 104, no. 1 (Winter 1996): 151.

3. On Virginia's earliest NAACP branches, see James H. Hershman Jr., "A Rumbling in the Museum: The Opponents of Virginia's Massive Resistance" (Ph.D. dissertation, University of Virginia, 1978), 17; J. Douglas Smith, *Managing White Supremacy: Race, Politics, and Citizenship in Jim Crow Virginia* (Chapel Hill: University of North Carolina Press, 2002), 243. The term "State Conference" refers to both the collective membership of the state's NAACP branches—that is, the Virginia State Conference had 25,000 members—as well as to the state headquarters of the NAACP, including its staff (based in Richmond, Virginia, in this case). Here the phrase is placed in quotation marks for definition purposes. Andrew Buni, *The Negro in Virginia Politics, 1902–1965* (Charlottesville: University Press of Virginia, 1967), 177; Oliver White Hill and Jonathan K. Stubbs (editor), *The Big Bang: Brown v. Board of Education and Beyond, The Autobiography of Oliver W. Hill, Sr.* (Winter Park, FL: Four-G Publishers, Inc., 2000), 179; Larissa M. Smith, "A Civil Rights Vanguard: Black Attorneys and the NAACP in Virginia," in *From the Grassroots to the Supreme Court*, ed. Peter Lau (Durham: Duke University Press, 2004), 133; Warren St. James, *The National Association for the Advancement of Colored People: A Case Study in Pressure Groups* (Smithtown, NY: Exposition Press, 1958), 75. The NAACP hierarchy will be explained further below.

4. On the Virginia State Conference being the largest in the South, see Buni, *The Negro in Virginia Politics*, 177; Hill, *The Big Bang*, 186. In 1941, with thirty-nine branches, the Virginia NAACP had been the largest in the nation; see Larissa Smith, "Vanguard," 141. For Virginia NAACP membership figures, see Letter from Lucille Black to William Abbot, November 5, 1954, Part II, box C212, Papers of the National Association for the Advancement of Colored People, Manuscripts Division, Library of Congress, Washington, DC (hereafter cited as NAACP Papers); Buni, *The Negro in Virginia Politics*, 177; Hill, *The Big Bang*, 179, 186; Benjamin Muse, *Virginia's Massive Resistance* (Bloomington: Indiana University Press, 1961), 47. Although the NAACP was the largest black civil rights organization in the state, its membership was limited to only a small percentage of the state's black population—in the mid-1950s, Virginia's black population numbered roughly 750,000; Buni, *The Negro in Virginia Politics*, 194; Hershman, "A Rumbling in the Museum," 10. The relatively small number of NAACP members was due to an annual membership fee as well as the NAACP's stipulation that branches contain at least fifty dues-paying members. For national NAACP membership policies, see Letter from Lucille Black to John Henderson, December 8, 1941, Part 26a, reel 23, frame 643, in John Bracey, and August Meier, eds., *Papers of the NAACP* (microfilm) (Bethesda, MD:

University Publications of America, 1982) (hereafter cited as NAACP Papers microfilm). Reflecting a southwide trend, the largest NAACP branches in Virginia were located in urban areas, but the association's urban focus did not reflect the racial demographics of the state. Instead, most African Americans resided in rural areas, particularly in southern and eastern Virginia, in regions known as "Southside" and "Tidewater," respectively. These two regions, encompassing roughly thirty-five contiguous counties, represented Virginia's section of the Black Belt and the state's leading agricultural area. As a whole, it was the slowest region of the state to desegregate. For more on the Black Belt, see Davison M. Douglas, *Reading, Writing, and Race: The Desegregation of the Charlotte Schools* (Chapel Hill: University of North Carolina Press, 1995), 9; Robbins L. Gates, *The Making of Massive Resistance: Virginia's Politics of Public School Desegregation, 1954–1956* (Chapel Hill: University of North Carolina Press, 1962), 27; Muse, *Virginia's Massive Resistance,* 2.

5. Governor J. Lindsay Almond Jr. explained the Byrd Organization this way: "It's like a club except it has no bylaws, constitutions, or dues. It's a loosely knit association, you might say, between men who share the philosophy of Senator Byrd." Quoted in J. Douglas Smith, "When Reason Collides with Prejudice," in *Moderates Dilemma,* 22. For more on the Byrd Organization, see Muse, *Virginia's Massive Resistance,* 25–26; J. Harvie Wilkinson III, *Harry Byrd and the Changing Face of VA Politics, 1945–1966* (Charlottesville: University Press of Virginia, 1968); Ronald L. Heinemann, *Harry Byrd of Virginia* (Charlottesville: University Press of VA, 1996).

6. Quotes are from Richard Kluger, *Simple Justice: The History of Brown v. Board of Education and Black America's Struggle for Equality* (New York: Random House, 1975), 85. The previous constitution, known as the Underwood Constitution, had been adopted during Reconstruction and had allowed Virginia to end military rule in exchange for protecting black civil rights. The new constitution also mandated black voter disenfranchisement via a poll tax and literacy test; see J. Douglas Smith, *Managing,* 20–26; Hill, *The Big Bang,* xvii–xviii; Kluger, *Simple Justice,* 457–58; Buni, *The Negro in Virginia Politics,* 23–24.

7. Statistic is from J. Douglas Smith, *Managing,* 135; see also 234–35. For more on separate but not equal education in Virginia, see Hill, *The Big Bang,* 136; Kluger, *Simple Justice,* 472; "Special Release, October 31, 1947, by the Press Service of the NAACP," Part II, box C211, NAACP Papers.

8. Letter from L. P. Whitten to William Pickens, August 14, 1940, Part II, box C203, NAACP Papers. The *Courier* was one of America's foremost black newspapers. The same inequities held true for higher education in Virginia, see "Special Release, October 31, 1947 by the Press Service of the NAACP," Part II, box C211, NAACP Papers.

9. By the late 1940s, Virginia NAACP staff even handled equalization

cases for the National NAACP outside of Virginia; see "Plans Complete for NAACP Meet," *Norfolk Journal and Guide,* October 22, 1949, in Part II, box C211, NAACP Papers; Kluger, *Simple Justice,* 19. For the litigation in Virginia, see "Special Release, October 31, 1947 by the Press Service of the NAACP," Part II, box C211, NAACP Papers; "Delegates to the Twelfth Annual Convention of State NAACP Branches," *Norfolk Journal and Guide* (November 15, 1947), in Part II, box C211, NAACP Papers. The *Washington Post* estimated that the NAACP's equalization lawsuits forced Virginia to spend over $50 million equalizing black and white schools; see Benjamin Muse, "Negro Crusaders Should Relax Awhile," Virginia Affairs Column, June 6, 1954, in Part II, box A228, NAACP Papers; also Kluger, *Simple Justice,* 474. Still, as late as 1950, Virginia spent less than two-thirds as much money on black schoolchildren as it did on whites; Kluger, *Simple Justice,* 481.

10. Larissa Smith, "Vanguard," 129–53; J. Douglas Smith, *Managing,* 256–58; "Plans Complete for NAACP Meet," *Norfolk Journal and Guide,* October 22, 1949, in Part II, box C211, NAACP Papers. For an analysis of Hill and Robinson's role in the national NAACP's equalization campaign, see Kluger, *Simple Justice,* 471–73.

11. Marshall and Hill graduated first and second, respectively, in the Class of 1933 at Howard Law School; Kluger, *Simple Justice,* 179–80, 471. Hill explains that the two became "close friends" at Howard (*The Big Bang,* 62 and 79–81). Spottswood Robinson easily blended into this mix. Also trained at Howard under Charles Hamilton Houston, "Spot" graduated with the highest GPA ever from Howard Law and later served as its dean; see Kluger, *Simple Justice,* 197, 253, 324, 472. By the late 1940s Robinson worked for the NAACP's Legal Defense Fund; Muse, *Virginia's Massive Resistance,* 48.

12. For the impact of World War II on the campaign for civil rights in Virginia, see Hershman, "A Rumbling in the Museum," 19; J. Douglas Smith, *Managing,* 63; Hill, *The Big Bang,* 219; Buni, *The Negro in Virginia Politics,* 151; "The Home Front," February 1944, Part 26a, reel 23, frame 668, NAACP Papers microfilm. On returning veterans, see Fairclough, *Race and Democracy,* 105; Kluger, *Simple Justice,* 227; Kenneth Robert Janken, *White: The Biography of Walter White, Mr. NAACP* (New York: New Press, 2003), 303–7. This era witnessed the massive growth of the national NAACP as well; wartime membership grew from 70,000–500,000; see Ayers, Gould et al., *American Passages,* vol. 2 (New York: Harcourt Brace, 2000), 913.

13. For more on Griffin, see Kluger, *Simple Justice,* 463, 476–79. For more on the school boycott, see Hershman, "A Rumbling in the Museum," 20–28; Hill, *The Big Bang,* 149–51. Similar strikes occurred elsewhere at this time; see James T. Patterson, *Brown v. Board of Education: A Civil Rights Milestone and Its Troubled Legacy* (Oxford: Oxford University Press, 2001), 4; August

Meier and Elliott Rudwick, *Along the Color Line: Explorations in the Black Experience* (Urbana: University of Illinois Press, 1976), 360–62. Talking about the NAACP's abandonment of equalization and its attack on the constitutionality of segregation, NAACP labor secretary Herbert Hill later recalled: "'There was lots of resistance in the branches because real progress toward equalization was now beginning to be made in schools and other facilities like parks, libraries, and swimming pools'"; see Kluger, *Simple Justice*, 291. Hill says the national office position was: "'the black community ought to settle for nothing less than integrated facilities only. It was a big lurch'" (*The Big Bang*, 291). The NAACP's case was handled primarily by Hill and Spottswood Robinson.

14. Quote is from Muse, *Virginia's Massive Resistance*, 5. On Virginia's defense of segregation, see Hershman, "A Rumbling in the Museum," 28; Kluger, *Simple Justice*, 480–507.

15. For Governor Stanley's initial response to *Brown*, see *Richmond Times-Dispatch*, May 18, 1954. Future governor J. Lindsay Almond, explaining Senator Byrd's reaction to Governor Stanley's initial, conciliatory statement, said, "I heard . . . that the top blew off the U.S. Capitol"; Alexander Leidholdt, *Standing before the Shouting Mob: Lenoir Chambers and Virginia's Massive Resistance to Public-school Integration* (Tuscaloosa: University of Alabama Press, 1997), 66. A number of historians have suggested that Byrd's opposition to *Brown* was political—maintaining segregation in the commonwealth's schools would solidify the organization's political preeminence within the state; see Buni, *The Negro in Virginia Politics*, 175–76; Gates, *The Making of Massive Resistance*, 204; Lassiter and Lewis, *The Moderates' Dilemma*, 14–15; Hershman, "A Rumbling in the Museum," 45. It is also worth noting that the Court's ruling surprised many of Virginia's public officials; see Hershman, "A Rumbling in the Museum," 32–39. This may help account for the moderate nature of some of the initial responses to *Brown*. The fact that Byrd was out of the country may also help explain the divergent responses to the decision; see Hill, *The Big Bang*, 168.

16. Quote is from Gates, *The Making of Massive Resistance*, 28. Clearly, *Brown* was needed to propel Virginia into the modern age.

17. Gates, *The Making of Massive Resistance*, 34–35; Kluger, *Simple Justice*, 729–30; "Statement on Behalf of the Virginia State Conference, NAACP Branches at Public Hearing before the Commission to Study Public Education at the Mosque on November 15, 1954," by Oliver W. Hill, Part II, box A228, NAACP Papers; *Fredericksburg Lance-Star*, May 16, 2004, A8.

18. Quote is from Gates, *The Making of Massive Resistance*, 36. Southside Virginia represented a strongly segregationist portion of the state and wielded disproportionate political power as well. See Ben Beagle and Ozzie Osborne, *J. Lindsay Almond: Virginia's Reluctant Rebel* (Roanoke, VA: Full Court

Press, 1984), 94–96; Gates, *The Making of Massive Resistance,* 36–38; Muse, *Virginia's Massive Resistance,* 2; Hershman, "A Rumbling in the Museum," 48.

19. Gates, *The Making of Massive Resistance,* 30–31.

20. Quote is Muse, *Virginia's Massive Resistance,* 159; see also 172. As Sarah Patton Boyle put it, Virginia "was the backbone of the South, which was the backbone of the nation, which was the backbone of the world." Sarah Patton Boyle, *The Desegregated Heart: A Virginian's Stand in Time of Transition* (Charlottesville: University Press of Virginia, 1962), 5. In 1956, with massive resistance on the rise throughout the South, Senator Byrd offered another justification for Virginia's leadership: "If Virginia surrenders, if Virginia's line is broken, the rest of the South will go down, too." *Richmond Times-Dispatch,* August 26, 1956; see also Gates, *The Making of Massive Resistance,* 173; Muse, *Virginia's Massive Resistance,* 29. Many in the region felt that the first post-*Brown* battles would be fought in the Upper South, and that states like Virginia would be the initial battlefields. The year following *Brown* witnessed growing defiance within the Commonwealth. While many of its neighbors initiated school desegregation plans, Virginia mandated contin-ued segregation for the 1954–55 term; see Gates, *The Making of Massive Resistance,* 43. Other leaders spoke of eliminating the state's guarantee of free public education, a move that would require altering the state constitution; Gates, *The Making of Massive Resistance,* 31. As James Hershman explains, "during the entire year between the two rulings black Virginians could find no sign in the state government's actions which indicated any alteration in school segregation or racial relations was contemplated. All indications pointed in the other direction"; Hershman, "A Rumbling in the Museum," 103. Virginia's response clearly differed from that of its southern neighbor, whose political leaders favored token desegregation over defiance, see Davison Douglas, *Reading, Writing, and Race,* 28.

21. "Centrality," or hierarchical control, was a key concept for the national NAACP. See Scope and Content Note, Guide to Part I, 1909–1950, NAACP Papers microfilm; Christopher Robert Reed, *The Chicago NAACP and the Rise of Black Professional Leadership, 1910–1966* (Bloomington, IN: Indiana University Press, 1997); Aldon Morris *The Civil Rights Movement in America* (New York: McGraw-Hill, 2001), 155–56; Fairclough, *Race and Democracy,* 48; Hill, *The Big Bang,* 186. Minnie Finch, in *The NAACP: Its Fight for Justice* (Metchen, NJ: Scarecrow Press, 1981), 20, notes: "From the very beginning, the national office maintained control and supervised the work of all the branches."

22. The executive secretary for the two decades following *Brown* was Roy Wilkins, who succeeded Walter White in 1955. Wilkins worked closely with the NAACP Board of Directors, which was increasingly active in formulating policy; see Warren St. James, *NAACP: Triumphs of a Pressure Group,*

1909–1980 (Smithtown, NY: Exposition Press, 1980), 253–56. An examination of board members in the mid-1940s reveals a strong northern bias, an interesting consideration for the implementation of *Brown v. Board* in the South; see Letter from Ella Baker to Walter White, July 3, 1946, Part 26a, reel 23, frame 515, NAACP Papers microfilm. St. James notes that the chairman of the board was perhaps the most powerful individual within the NAACP; Channing Tobias held the position from 1952 to 1960; *A Case Study,* 54, 60, 94–97; *Triumphs,* 112–13.

23. For more on the NAACP's Legal Defense Fund, see Warren St. James, *Triumphs,* 206, which notes that the two organizations had overlapping board and staff members. See also August Meier and John H. Bracey Jr., "The NAACP as a Reform Movement, 1909–1965: 'To reach the conscience of America,'" *Journal of Southern History* 59, no. 1 (February 1993): 3–30; Finch, *The NAACP,* 20; Aldon Morris, *The Origins of the Civil Rights Movement* (New York: Free Press, 1984), 13; Janken, *White,* 73–77; Muse, *Virginia's Massive Resistance,* 50.

24. Morris (in *The Origins of the Civil Rights Movement* 33) notes, "Decision-making within the NAACP was highly centralized. Most plans of action had to be cleared through the hierarchy in New York." For more on the hierarchical nature of the NAACP, see note 21 above. The NAACP hierarchy also included a Regional Office system that was developed in the late 1940s to provide additional support for branches, but the regional offices were understaffed and struggling in the mid-1950s; see Finch, *The NAACP,* 122; Warren St. James, *A Case Study,* 98; Memorandum from Mr. Current to Mr. Wilkins, October 8, 1946, Part 17, reel 14, NAACP Papers microfilm; Western Union telegram from Roy Wilkins to Franklin Williams, December 19, 1957, and an identical telegram the same day from Wilkins to Ruby Hurley, both in Supplement to Part 1 (1956–60), reel 2, NAACP Papers microfilm.

25. Realizing that a favorable decision would initiate the most important project in its history, the National Office began formulating an implementation program earlier in the spring of 1954. This would ensure the national office maintained control of this important process. See Report of the Executive Secretary for the Month of March, 1954, Part 16b, reel 21, NAACP Papers microfilm; Board of Directors Meeting Minutes, June 30, 1954, Supplement to Part One (1951–1955), reel 1, NAACP Papers microfilm; "Suggested Program for Southern Branches, 1954–1955," Supplement to Part One (1951–55), reel 11, NAACP Papers microfilm.

26. "Press Release for May 23, 1954," Part 3, series C, reel 17, NAACP Papers microfilm; also "Motions and/or Recommendations Adopted by the Atlanta Conference," May 22–23, 1954, Part V, box V2595, NAACP Papers.

27. Italics added by author. Untitled letter from Channing Tobias and

Walter White to "Dear Branch Officer," May 25, 1954, Part 3, series C, reel 5, NAACP Papers microfilm.

28. NAACP Press Release, "Dixie NAACP Leaders Map Plans to Implement Court's Ruling," May 23, 1954, Part V, box V2595, NAACP Papers. The signatures, to be collected on NAACP-developed petitions, could later be used in court if necessary. Thurgood Marshall noted that each petition would be accompanied by a request for a meeting with the local school board to help develop school desegregation plans; the threat of litigation was played down by the national NAACP. Channing H. Tobias, chairman of NAACP Board of Directors, "called for a 'spirit of give and take' in the discussions. 'Let it not be said of us that we took advantage of a sweeping victory to drive a hard bargain or impose unnecessary hardships upon those responsible for working out the details of adjustment.'" Recognizing Tobias's authority within the NAACP, it is not surprising that the NAACP's initial implementation plan was somewhat conciliatory. The NAACP also initially focused on negotiations because of its lack of legal authority before *Brown II*.

29. "Atlanta Declaration," Part 3, series C, reel 13, NAACP Papers microfilm. See also, National NAACP Press Release, "Dixie NAACP Leaders Map Plans to Implement Court's Ruling," May 23, 1954, Part V, box V2595, NAACP Papers. It is also worth noting that the NAACP vowed to protect black teachers that might be affected in any way by school desegregation. Teachers, who had been strong supporters of the equalization campaign, were in danger of losing their jobs as a result of school integration.

30. Though NAACP annual conventions offered branches and delegates an opportunity to influence national NAACP policy, generally the conventions reinforced decisions made by national NAACP staff and the board of directors. For more on the role of the annual convention in the formulation of NAACP policy, see Warren St. James, *A Case Study*, 68, 119; Guide to Supplement to Part One (1951–1955), xii, NAACP Papers microfilm; Article IX of National NAACP Constitution (Blue Book).

31. "Developing Community Action Program to Speed Up Integration," Part 3, series C, reel 5, NAACP Papers microfilm; "Resolutions Adopted, Education [1954 Annual Convention]," Supplement to Part 1 (1951–55), reel 10, NAACP Papers microfilm.

32. "Resolutions Adopted, Education," Supplement to Part 1 (1951–55), reel 10, NAACP Papers microfilm; Davison Douglas, *Reading, Writing, and Race*, 62. Roy Wilkins later explained: "popular opinion to the contrary, the NAACP would prefer using legal action as a last resort in the many situations which will arise in hundreds of communities"; Roy Wilkins, "The Role of the NAACP in the Desegregation Process," *Social Problems* (Official Journal of the Society for the Study of Social Problems), April 1955, Volume 2, No. 4 (New York: Johnson Reprint Corp.), 201. It is interesting to note that the

NAACP initially accepted what would later be called token desegregation, meaning the integration of small numbers of black students into white schools, as opposed to full-scale integration. See Letter from Roy Wilkins to Dr. E. B. Henderson, October 25, 1955, Part II, box A228, NAACP Papers. The national office also spent a good deal of time at the annual convention working with the southern State Conference leaders. Meetings and workshops made sure the state units of the NAACP understood and followed the national implementation program. NAACP special counsel Thurgood Marshall noted the importance of this after the convention, "the state level is the implementation level of national policy"; "Remarks of Thurgood Marshall at Press Conference, June 30, 1954," Supplement to Part 1 (1951–55), reel 10, NAACP Papers microfilm; see also "Developing Community Action Program to Speed Up Integration," Part 3, series C, reel 5, NAACP Papers microfilm. It is worth highlighting that different circumstances in each state affected the NAACP's implementation efforts. Keeping in close contact with its State Conferences, the NAACP discerned where to direct more, or less, attention— allowing it to respond to state legislatures and other events more effectively. This emphasis on the state level as the level of implementation continued throughout the desegregation process, and is one reason for the state level format for this book. See Kluger, *Simple Justice,* 746.

33. Joseph Thorndike, "The Sometimes Sordid Level of Race and Segregation," in *Moderates Dilemma,* 62, quotes Thurgood Marshall: "'I'm afraid we assumed that after a short period of time of one to five years the states would give in.'" See also Kluger, *Simple Justice,* 714; Fairclough, *Race and Democracy,* 167; Janken, *White,* 366. See also Christina Greene, "The New Negro Ain't Scared No More!" in Lau, *Grassroots,* 255. Patterson (*Brown v. Board of Education,* xxix) quotes Dr. Ken Clark, one of the NAACP's expert witnesses in the *Brown* litigation, in 1993: "'I look back and shudder at how naïve we all were in our belief in the steady progress racial minorities would make through programs of litigation and education.'"

34. Quote is from Kluger, *Simple Justice,* 639.

35. Quote is from Hill, *The Big Bang,* 73. See also page 147, in which Hill notes, "Looking back, I guess that I should have known better and not been surprised."

36. "Report of the Committee on Offenses against the Administration of Justice," Appendix 10, Part 20, reel 12, NAACP Papers microfilm. It is worth noting that the Virginia State Conference carefully followed the directives of the national office when working to implement *Brown*. In between the Atlanta Conference and the annual convention, the State Conferences were asked to call together their branches and "instruct them on procedure to implement the [Atlanta] Declaration"; Address by Thurgood Marshall to 1954 Convention, Supplement to Part One (1951–55), reel 10, NAACP Papers microfilm. See

also "Follow-Up RE Atlanta Conference," undated (May or June 1954), Part V, box V2595, NAACP Papers, which lays out a course of action for southern State Conferences to follow, allowing one to see similarities between national policy and State Conference actions in 1954. See also Hershman, "A Rumbling in the Museum," 41.

37. "Report of the Committee on Offenses against the Administration of Justice," Appendix 11, Part 20, reel 12, frame 1018, NAACP Papers microfilm. For more on the meeting, see "Press Releases, Virginia State Conference, June 7, 1954," Part II, box A228, NAACP Papers.

38. Hershman, "A Rumbling in the Museum," 42; Gates, *The Making of Massive Resistance,* 29–30; Hill, *The Big Bang,* 170.

39. Quote is from "Statement on Behalf of the Virginia State Conference, NAACP Branches at Public Hearing before the Commission to Study Public Education At the Mosque on November 15, 1954," by Oliver W. Hill, Part II, box A228, NAACP Papers. See also *Richmond Times-Dispatch,* November 17, 1954; Hershman, "A Rumbling in the Museum," 53–54, 106; Gates, *The Making of Massive Resistance,* 40. Hill and Thompson's remarks echoed national NAACP requests urging Virginia to prepare for school desegregation by September 1955. At its 1954 annual convention, the national office had decided that September 1955 was to be the target date for desegregation in the South; see "Association Press Release, July 4, 1954," Supplement to Part 1 (1951–55), reel 10, NAACP Papers microfilm. In April 1955, during arguments on implementation, NAACP attorneys asked the Supreme Court to adopt this date as well; Madison Jones, "The Impact and Consequences of the U.S. Supreme Court Decision of May 17, 1954," Part 3, series C, reel 17, NAACP Papers microfilm; Kluger, *Simple Justice,* 726–30.

40. Boyle, *The Desegregated Heart,* 194–96.

41. Quoted in Hershman, "A Rumbling in the Museum," 52.

42. Beagle and Osborne, *J. Lindsay Almond,* 96; Hershman, "A Rumbling in the Museum," 48–49; Gates, *The Making of Massive Resistance,* 36–38, 161–62. On segregationists in Virginia being less likely to resort to physical violence than segregationists elsewhere, see J. Douglas Smith, *Managing,* 3–4; Buni, *The Negro in Virginia Politics,* 214; Hershman, "A Rumbling in the Museum," 10–11.

43. Muse, *Virginia's Massive Resistance,* 8; Hershman, "A Rumbling in the Museum," 103; Gates, *The Making of Massive Resistance,* xix. Patterson notes that in 1942 only 2 percent of southern whites believed black and white students should go to the same schools; by 1956 the numbers had risen to 15 percent (*Brown v. Board of Education,* 7).

44. Initially, a number of liberals supported the efforts of the NAACP either individually or via religious organizations; see Hershman, "A Rumbling in the Museum," 49; Gates, *The Making of Massive Resistance,* 50–52; Muse,

Virginia's Massive Resistance, 38. A leading white liberal organization, the Virginia Council on Human Relations, worked with African Americans but sought to minimize publicity surrounding their support for civil rights; see Part 20, reel 13, frame 20, NAACP Papers microfilm. Whites who openly supported desegregation faced significant repercussions; see Boyle, *The Desegregated Heart,* 245, 264–65; Hershman, "A Rumbling in the Museum," 187, 249; "NAACP Press Release, June 7, 1956," Part 3, series D, reel 9, frame 52, NAACP Papers microfilm.

45. Hershman, "A Rumbling in the Museum," 70; Gates, *The Making of Massive Resistance,* xix. Moderates did not support racial equality or the mixing of the races. They also angrily opposed the NAACP; see Hershman, "A Rumbling in the Museum," 95; Muse, *Virginia's Massive Resistance,* 48. In *Managing White Supremacy,* J. Douglas Smith discusses Louis Jaffe, the Pulitzer-Prize–winning editor of the *Norfolk Virginian-Pilot.* Jaffe, who "did more than any white opinion-shaper in the Old Dominion to prod whites to recognize their moral responsibility to provide better services, improve health-related conditions, and end the stain of lynching" was nonetheless a supporter of segregation; see 238. See also J. Douglas Smith in *The Moderates Dilemma,* 40, on Armistead Boothe. In this essay, I use the phrases "white liberals" and "white moderates" with some trepidation; the lines between were often blurry and subject to change. They are employed here because of space limitations.

46. The moderate position, because it reluctantly accepted desegregation, was considered anathema to many white Virginians, so long as other options existed. The relationship between the NAACP and Virginia's white liberals, moderates, and diehard segregationists fluctuated over time, and will be covered in more detail in my larger work-in-progress on the implementation of *Brown* in Virginia. It is worth noting that even white liberals periodically asked the NAACP to slow down its implementation efforts, see "Negro Crusaders Should Relax Awhile," Virginia Affairs Column (in the *Washington Post*), Benjamin Muse, June 6, 1954, and Letter from Roy Wilkins to Dr. E. B. Henderson, December 9, 1954, both in Part II, box A228, NAACP Papers.

47. The original ruling declared school segregation unconstitutional but provided no guidelines for enforcement. *Brown v. Board of Education, Topeka, KS,* 347 U.S. 483 (1954). The follow-up decision is *Brown v. Board of Education, Topeka, KS,* 349 U.S. 294 (1955). For more on *Brown II,* see Kluger, *Simple Justice,* 744–47.

48. Italics added by author. "Memorandum to Emergency Regional Conference, from Roy Wilkins and Thurgood Marshall, June 4, 1955," Part 3, series C, reel 14, NAACP Papers microfilm; see also "Resolutions," Supplement to Part One (1951–55), reel 12, NAACP Papers microfilm. Marshall initially believed *Brown II* was a "damned good decision," which helps explain why the national office stuck with its initial implementation program; Kluger, *Simple Justice,* 746.

49. "NAACP Press Release, June 26, 1955," Part 3, series C, reel 12, NAACP Papers microfilm.

50. "Report of the Committee on Offenses against the Administration of Justice," Appendix 12, Part 20, reel 12, frame 1019, NAACP Papers microfilm. Again the Virginia State Conference was clearly following the dictates of the national office; see Letter from Roy Wilkins to Lester Banks, June 9, 1955, Part II, box C212, NAACP Papers; "State NAACP to Sue in Some Areas Soon," *Richmond Times-Dispatch*, October 10, 1955.

51. *NAACP Annual Report, 1955* (New York: National Association for the Advancement of Colored People, 1955). "Report of the Commission on Law Reform and Racial Activities," Part 20, reel 12, NAACP Papers microfilm; Hershman, "A Rumbling in the Museum," 110–11; Anna Holden, *The Bus Stops Here: A Study of Desegregation in Three Cities* (New York: Agathon Press, 1974), 22; "State NAACP to Sue In Some Areas Soon," *Richmond Times-Dispatch*, October 10, 1955; Buni, *The Negro in Virginia Politics*, 177.

52. Fairclough, *Race and Democracy*, 187; Patterson, *Brown v. Board of Education*, 80–82; Kluger, *Simple Justice*, 754; Robert Burk, *Dwight D. Eisenhower: Hero and Politician* (Boston: Twayne Publishers, 1986), 159–60; Stephen Ambrose, *Eisenhower*, vol. 2 (New York: Simon and Schuster, 1983), 414–20. See Kluger, *Simple Justice*, 650, for more on Eisenhower's southern political aspirations.

53. Quote is from Harvard Sitkoff, *The Struggle for Black Equality, 1954–1992* (New York: Hill and Wang, 1993), 36. Over time, Eisenhower's refusal to endorse *Brown* and his cultivation of southern political support undermined his support among African Americans. For other evidence of the National NAACP's growing frustration with President Eisenhower, see Report of the Executive Secretary for the Month of April, 1956, Supplement to Part One (1956–1960), reel 1, NAACP Papers microfilm; Finch, *The NAACP*, 196. For Oliver Hill's perspective on Eisenhower, see Hill, *The Big Bang*, 247. Eisenhower later referred to his appointment of Earl Warren—the chief architect of the *Brown* decision—to the Supreme Court as "the biggest damnfool mistake I ever made." Sitkoff, *The Struggle for Black Equality*, 24–25; Irons, *Jim Crow's Children*, 201. Warren, for his part, was extremely upset by Eisenhower's lack of public support for the ruling. See J. Harvie Wilkinson III, *From Brown to Bakke: The Supreme Court and School Integration: 1954–1978* (Oxford: Oxford University Press, 1979), 24.

54. On the Southern Manifesto and Senator Byrd, see Lassiter and Lewis, *The Moderates' Dilemma*, 7; Gates, *The Making of Massive Resistance*, 118; Kluger, *Simple Justice*, 752. On Congress, see Martin Luther King Jr. in Peter Houck and Leslie Camm, *African American Anthology* (unpublished manuscript in the author's possession), 245–57; Board of Directors Meeting Minutes, November 8, 1954, Supplement to Part One (1951–1955), reel 1, NAACP Papers microfilm.

55. Commenting on the importance of these cases before they were decided, Thurgood Marshall and assistant special counsel Robert Carter wrote, "Certainly the hearings in these cases will be of major significance because these courts may be the first to give definite and specific content to 'a prompt and reasonable start' and 'good faith compliance at the earliest practicable date'"; see Carter and Marshall, "Meaning and Significance," 400–401; see also Kluger, *Simple Justice,* 747. The cases were *Briggs v. Elliott,* 132 F. Supp. 776 (1955); *Davis v. County School Board, Prince Edward County, Virginia,* 142 F. Supp. 616 (1956). Wilkins hoped that the decrees were "not necessarily 'typical of what will happen throughout the South.'" "NAACP Press Release, July 22, 1955," Part 3, series C, reel 17, NAACP Papers microfilm.

56. On Emmett Till's death, see Roy Wilkins in "NAACP Chief Assails Foes of Integration," *Richmond Times-Dispatch,* October 8, 1955; also *Dallas Morning News,* January 9, 1956, in Part 3, series D, reel 9, frame 4, NAACP Papers microfilm. On the growing intimidation of NAACP officials in the Deep South, see Letter from Ruby Hurley to Gloster Current, September 10, 1954, Part 25a, reel 4, frame 445, NAACP Papers microfilm.

57. Some NAACP attorneys had predicted this earlier; see Marshall and Carter, "Meaning and Significance," 402. Meetings with southern NAACP attorneys in the fall of 1955 encouraged the shift toward litigation; see "Board of Directors Meeting Minutes," October 10, 1955, Supplement to Part One (1951–55), reel 1, NAACP Papers microfilm. Growing frustration was also evident within the Virginia NAACP. Hershman explains: "For those blacks and whites strongly committed to the ideal of racial integration, 1955 was a year of frustration and delay with every indication that compliance with *Brown* would be a slow and difficult process" ("A Rumbling in the Museum," 101). The national office recognized the lack of progress in the commonwealth as well; see Letter from Roy Wilkins to Dr. E. B. Henderson, October 25, 1955, Part II, box A228, NAACP Papers.

58. "NAACP Press Release, January 3, 1956," Supplement to Part One (1956–60), reel 2, NAACP Papers microfilm; "Special Report to the *New York Times,* February 20, 1956," Part 3, series D, reel 3, NAACP Papers microfilm. It is worth noting that a small number of school desegregation lawsuits had been filed in late 1955 by the NAACP. See "NAACP Press Release, January 3, 1956"; Brian J. Daugherity, "'With All Deliberate Speed': The NAACP and the Implementation of *Brown v. Board of Education* at the Local Level, Little Rock, Arkansas, 1954–1957" (unpublished M.A. thesis, University of Montana, 1997). This press release also notes that 1955 was financially the best year in the history of the NAACP; an important consideration for the expansion of litigation.

59. "Report of the Executive Secretary for the Month of February, 1956,"

Supplement to Part One (1956–1960), reel 1, NAACP Papers microfilm; "Keynote Address by Thurgood Marshall to 47th Annual NAACP Convention," Supplement to Part One (1956–1960), reel 4, NAACP Papers microfilm. Lester Banks, Oliver Hill, and Spottswood Robinson attended the Atlanta Conference; see "New NAACP School Suits Planned in State by June," *Richmond Times-Dispatch,* February 20, 1956. For more on the Atlanta Conference and the process of deciding where to file suits, see Letter from Thurgood Marshall to State Conference Presidents, January 20, 1956, Part V, box V2595, NAACP Papers. For more on the NAACP's litigation protocol at this time, see Letter from Thurgood Marshall, August 15, 1955, Part 3, series C, reel 4, NAACP Papers microfilm.

60. The NAACP's determination to treat the southern states individually, based on the actions of their state governments and the status of desegregation in each state, represents one of the reasons for the state-based approach of this book. The eight states were Alabama, Florida, Georgia, Louisiana, Mississippi, North Carolina, South Carolina, and Virginia. Branches in other southern states were strongly encouraged to continue avoiding litigation; "Resolutions Adopted, 1956 Annual Convention," Supplement to Part One (1956–1960), reel 4, NAACP Papers microfilm; "Special Report to *New York Times,*" February 20, 1956, Part 3, series D, reel 3, NAACP Papers microfilm. For more on these 1956 lawsuits, see Minutes of the Board of Directors Meeting, May 14, 1956; Minutes of the Board of Directors Meeting, June 11, 1956, both in Supplement to Part One (1956–1960), reel 1, NAACP Papers microfilm.

61. Virginia NAACP attorneys had discussed this shift in strategy with national office staff at the state NAACP's twentieth annual meeting in October 1955. Wilkins, Marshall, Hill, and others closely involved in the implementation of *Brown* attended. Afterward, Spottswood Robinson approached representatives of the Arlington NAACP and informed them that the State Conference was ready to prepare to file suit in that community. See "Report of the Commission on Law Reform and Racial Activities," Part 20, reel 12, NAACP Papers microfilm; Gates, *The Making of Massive Resistance,* 56; "State NAACP to Sue in Some Areas Soon," *Richmond Times-Dispatch,* October 10, 1955. The NAACP Legal Defense Fund helped the state NAACP with its lawsuits. For more on the litigation, see Hershman, "A Rumbling in the Museum," 220–26; Gates, *The Making of Massive Resistance,* 125–27; Robert A. Pratt, *The Color of Their Skin: Education and Race in Richmond, Virginia, 1954–89* (Charlottesville: University Press of Virginia, 1992), 7.

62. Quote is from "State NAACP to Sue in Some Areas Soon," *Richmond Times-Dispatch,* October 10, 1955.

63. Hershman, "A Rumbling in the Museum," 253; Muse, *Virginia's Massive Resistance,* 31; Boyle, *The Desegregated Heart,* 245, 264–65. For

more on how white moderates and liberals responded to the NAACP suits, see Hershman, "A Rumbling in the Museum," 215–17.

64. Quote is from Muse, *Virginia's Massive Resistance*, 48. See also Gates, *The Making of Massive Resistance*, 59; Pratt, *The Color of Their Skin*, 7.

65. Buni, *The Negro in Virginia Politics*, notes: "What provoked action from white Virginian leadership, however, was that Negroes continued to press for school integration through the federal courts" (177; see also 184). Gates notes that future governor J. Lindsey Almond urged Governor Stanley to call 1956 special session after the NAACP filed its suits (*The Making of Massive Resistance*, 128).

66. On the State Department of Education decision, see Hershman, "A Rumbling in the Museum," 111. On the Gray Commission report, see Gates, *The Making of Massive Resistance*, 63–69. On Virginia's Resolution of Interposition, see Gates, *The Making of Massive Resistance*, 114; Beagle and Osborne, *J. Lindsay Almond*, 100. Muse notes that the resolution was forwarded to each member of the U.S. Congress and the Supreme Court (*Virginia's Massive Resistance*, 21–22, 27).

67. Describing the Southern Manifesto, Harry Byrd said the document was part of "the plan of massive resistance we've been working on." See Beagle and Osborne, *J. Lindsay Almond*, 93–101.

68. Quote is from Joseph Thorndike, "The Sometimes Sordid Level of Race and Segregation," in *Moderates Dilemma*, 54. Thorndike also notes the NAACP's belated recognition of Kilpatrick's influence on southern desegregation; see 62–63 for quotes from Thurgood Marshall. Senator Byrd was a strong public supporter of Kilpatrick; see Muse, *Virginia's Massive Resistance*, 21.

69. For more on the special session and its legislation, see Gates, *The Making of Massive Resistance*, 169–90; Beagle and Osborne, *J. Lindsay Almond*, 102–3; Hershman, "A Rumbling in the Museum," 187–89. Many in Virginia believed the General Assembly's actions encouraged Massive Resistance further South; see Hill, *The Big Bang*, 247.

70. Quote is from Hershman, "A Rumbling in the Museum," 208. Thomson was a brother-in-law of Harry Byrd Sr. For more on the state's anti-NAACP laws, see Hershman, "A Rumbling in the Museum," 209; Gates, *The Making of Massive Resistance*, 184; "Acts of Special Session of General Assembly of Virginia (Passed September 29, 1956), anti-NAACP legislation," Part 20, reel 12, NAACP Papers microfilm. Fairclough notes that Louisiana adopted similar anti-NAACP measures (*Race and Democracy*, 225). Most other southern states did the same. Sitkoff notes: "By 1958 the NAACP had lost 246 branches in the South, and the South's percentage of the NAACP's total membership had dropped from nearly 50 percent to just about 25 percent" (*The Struggle for Black Equality*, 28). See also Fairclough, *Race and Democracy*, 207–16. The anti-NAACP climate may have affected the National

NAACP in other ways; in 1956 the IRS forced the NAACP and its Legal Defense Fund to formally separate; see Tomiko Brown-Nagin, "The Impact of Lawyer-Client Disengagement on the NAACP's Campaign to Implement *Brown v. Board of Education* in Atlanta," 236, in *Grassroots*.

71. The committees subpoenaed and questioned NAACP leaders, demanded financial and membership records, and interviewed plaintiffs involved in the school desegregation cases. Such requests continued into the 1960s. Hill, *The Big Bang*, 179–80; Hershman, "A Rumbling in the Museum," 210–14; "Report of the Committee on Law Reform and Racial Activities" and "Report of the Committee on Offenses against the Administration of Justice," both in Part 20, reel 12, NAACP Papers microfilm.

72. On the public stance, see Buni, *The Negro in Virginia Politics*, 187. For more on the negative effects of the anti-NAACP laws, see Muse, *Virginia's Massive Resistance*, 49, 52–53; Hershman, "A Rumbling in the Museum," 214, 253. State Conference leaders faced some of the most severe harassment; Oliver White Hill, interview with the author, Richmond, Virginia, December 3, 1999. For the financial impact on the Virginia NAACP, see "Income Received from Branches in the State of Virginia, Jan. 1, thru Aug. 31, for 1955, 1956, 1957," Part 20, reel 12, NAACP Papers microfilm. Black teachers were also pressured to disassociate themselves from the NAACP; see "NAACP Keynotes Gives Plan to Make Integration Reality," *Richmond Times-Dispatch*, October 6, 1956; also Letter from Clarissa Wimbush Carey to Roy Wilkins, February 5, 1963, Part 3, box C155, NAACP Papers. For the Virginia NAACP's legal attacks on the state's anti-NAACP laws, see Part 20, reel 12, frame 999, NAACP Papers microfilm.

73. "Letter from E. B. Henderson to Dear ———:, February 28, 1957," Part 20, reel 12, NAACP Papers microfilm.

74. "Letter from Lester Banks to Roy Wilkins, March 14, 1957," Part 20, reel 12, NAACP Papers microfilm.

75. "Confidential letter from Lester Banks to 'Dear Co-Worker,'" misdated February 14, 1956 (actual date is 1957), Part 20, reel 12, NAACP Papers microfilm.

76. Charlottesville was to begin in the fall of 1956, and Arlington in January 1957. Gates, *The Making of Massive Resistance*, 191; Hershman, "A Rumbling in the Museum," 227–31. The role of Virginia's federal judges in forcing the state to comply with *Brown* should be noted; Hill, *The Big Bang*, 176.

77. For more on the litigation surrounding pupil placement, see Hershman, "A Rumbling in the Museum," 227–31; Gates, *The Making of Massive Resistance*, 191; *Ruth Pendleton James v. J. Lindsay Almond, Jr.*, civil action number 2843, Part V, box V2836, NAACP Papers. Renewed orders were for Charlottesville and Arlington; that summer, orders were handed down for Norfolk and Warren County.

78. Almond did so using components of the state's new massive resistance legislation. The closed schools were white schools that black plaintiffs were admitted to by the courts; local black schools remained open. A former Virginia attorney general, Almond was elected governor on a massive resistance platform in November 1957.

79. Quote is from Pratt, *The Color of Their Skin,* 10; see also 9. Hershman, "A Rumbling in the Museum," 304; Gates, *The Making of Massive Resistance,* 210; Boyle, *The Desegregated Heart,* xvii. The largest white moderate organization was the Virginia Committee for Public Schools, organized in late 1958. The NAACP suit was abandoned in October in lieu of a separate lawsuit filed against the school-closing law, and private funding scheme, by a moderate white organization from Norfolk—the second suit represented all the affected students, not just the black plaintiffs. See Hershman, "A Rumbling in the Museum," 114–15.

80. Hershman, "A Rumbling in the Museum," 115; Gates, *The Making of Massive Resistance,* 210–11. Almond, an attorney by profession, was undoubtedly influenced by the events that had unfolded in Little Rock, Arkansas, in the fall of 1957.

81. Hershman, "A Rumbling in the Museum," 348; Gates, *The Making of Massive Resistance,* 211, Pratt, *The Color of Their Skin,* 11; Oliver Hill, interview with the author, Richmond, December 3, 1999.

82. On the pupil placement law, see J. Douglas Smith, "When Reason Collides with Prejudice," in *The Moderates' Dilemma,* 46–47; Lassiter and Lewis, *The Moderates' Dilemma,* 8. On the new tuition grant law, see Andrew Lewis, "Emergency Mothers," in *The Moderates' Dilemma,* 98; "Sanctuaries for Tradition: Virginia's New Private Schools," Special Report, Southern Regional Council, February 8, 1961, Part 3 series D, reel 13, frame 882, NAACP Papers microfilm. The NAACP fought the state's tuition grant legislation in court for most of the 1960s; see "Eight Schools May Still Get State Grants," *Richmond Times-Dispatch,* October 7, 1965.

83. Quote is from Lassiter and Lewis, *The Moderates' Dilemma,* 4; see also 18–19. As the editor of *The News,* of Lynchburg, explained on April 19, 1963: "We are opposed to integration in the public schools. We strongly support law and order. We will go along with only such integration as we feel is necessary to comply with the law as interpreted by the Federal courts." Prince Edward County, Virginia, took more dramatic action. Facing desegregation in the fall of 1959, county officials discontinued funding for the public schools, closing them for the indefinite future. The schools remained closed until 1964, when state and federal courts ordered them reopened. See Edward H. Peeples, "A Perspective on the Prince Edward County School Issue" (M.A. thesis, University of Pennsylvania, 1963), unpublished manuscript available at the Virginia Historical Society, Richmond, Virginia.

84. The pupil placement system had been revived by the Virginia state

government in 1959. For factors used by the state PPB to deny black applicants in the early 1960s, see "Negro Transfer Discussion Held," *The News,*
June 28, 1961. Having the state PPB force desegregation on districts throughout the state must have seemed ironic considering its previous commitment to
maintaining segregation statewide. It changed in part because of growing pressure from the NAACP and federal courts; see "New State Policy on Pupil
Shifts Disclosed Here," *Richmond Times-Dispatch,* May 15, 1963.

85. Part 3d, reel 13, frames 918–19, NAACP Papers microfilm, discusses
pupil placement in Arlington County, Virginia. In 1963, Arlington also
became the first district in Virginia to allow black teachers to work with students of both races; see "Negro Teachers for Whites Seen," *Richmond Times-
Dispatch,* April 5, 1963.

86. On the high court's acceptance of tokenism, see Sitkoff, *The Struggle
for Black Equality,* 27; Kluger, *Simple Justice,* 752; Fairclough, *Race and
Democracy,* 239. On its growing impatience, see "High Court Warns States on
Schools," *Richmond Times-Dispatch,* May 28, 1963. The number of black
students in desegregated schools in Virginia grew from 30 in the spring of
1959, to 103 in February 1960, to 547 in September 1961, to 1,100 in June
1963; see Muse, *Virginia's Massive Resistance,* 159; Gates, *The Making of
Massive Resistance,* 211; "1,200 Negroes Hope to Enter White Schools,"
Richmond Times-Dispatch, May 3, 1963; see also Eugene Piedmont,
"Changing Racial Attitudes at a Southern University: 1947–1964," *Journal of
Negro Education* 36, no. 1 (Winter 1967): 33–34.

87. Kluger, *Simple Justice,* 759; "School Desegregation Plans Submitted by
470 Districts," *Richmond Times-Dispatch,* April 11, 1965.

88. The Virginia State Department of Education now strongly urged compliance and monitored the compliance process. It was influenced by the $64.2
million dollars in federal aid for education that Virginia was scheduled to
receive in the fiscal year starting July 1; see "Mixed Schools Are Required by
Fall, 1967," April 30, 1965, "Middlesex Plan Is Sent to HEW," June 4, 1965,
both in *Richmond Times-Dispatch.* Several Virginia localities initially planned
to forfeit their federal funds; Amelia County was one of the last to submit
compliance paperwork to HEW. Had it refused, the county would have forfeited about $240,000 of a school budget of $575,000; see "Public School
Desegregation in Amelia Seen," *Richmond Times-Dispatch,* May 11, 1965.
For more information on this process throughout Virginia, see "Sussex Says
Deadline No Factor," June 16, 1965; "78 Pledges On Schools Are Received,"
March 4, 1965; "Signed Form Not to Assure School Funds," April 22, 1965,
all in the *Richmond Times-Dispatch.* For HEW's guidelines, see Title VI of the
Civil Rights Act of 1964 and 78 Stat. 246, 42 U.S.C. 2000c-d, 45 CFR
80.1–80.13, 181.1–181.76 (1967). Freedom of choice was initially accepted
partly due to continued resistance in the Deep South.

89. Statistic is from "Nottoway, Lunenburg, Bland Ordered to Integrate

Schools," *Richmond Times-Dispatch,* July 14, 1965. African Americans, how-ever, were not usually accepted as equals during token desegregation. In the Fredericksburg area in 1961, the first black students were brought to the white schools on segregated buses; *Fredericksburg Lance-Star,* May 16, 2004, A8. In other cases, black students were asked to give up extracurricular activi-ties, or such activities were simply eliminated; *Fredericksburg Lance-Star,* May 16, 2004, A8. At the same time, segregated black schools continued to suffer from white indifference or racism. When educators in King George County asked for science equipment in 1962, new equipment was purchased for the white high school and its old equipment was given to the black school; *Fredericksburg Lance-Star,* May 16, 2004, A8. During tokenism, it was gener-ally white schools that were desegregated by black students; black schools often remained segregated.

90. HEW's guidelines decreed that school districts applying for federal aid "must be totally integrated by the fall of 1967" and that "all grades of a school system must be put on a non-discriminatory basis by the fall of 1967"; quotes are from "Mixed Schools Are Required by Fall, 1967," *Richmond Times-Dispatch,* April 30, 1965. It is important to point out, however, that this simply meant that freedom-of-choice plans had to be in effect for all grades by 1967; it is doubtful that this would have brought about significant school integration. In March 1966, the U.S. Office of Education established new criteria for compliance, including faculty desegregation and the elimina-tion of unequal facilities and programs; see Davison Douglas in *Grassroots,* 365.

91. In 1965 the Supreme Court let stand a Tenth Circuit Court of Appeals ruling which held that the Constitution prohibited the segregation of students by race, but did not require the integration of the races in the public schools. See "School Segregation Ruling Is Upheld," *Richmond Times-Dispatch,* March 2, 1965; see also "Court Won't Rule on New York Plan for School Balance," *Richmond Times-Dispatch,* October 12, 1965. The historian J. Harvie Wilkinson writes, "Where during this time, one might ask, was the United States Supreme Court? And the answer, not much exaggerated, is that from 1955 to 1968, the Court abandoned the field of public school desegrega-tion" (Wilkinson, *From Brown to Bakke,* 61).

92. Statistic is from "Grant Decision Opposed," *Richmond Times-Dispatch,* March 15, 1965, and Francis M. Wilhoit, *The Politics of Massive Resistance* (New York: George Braziller, 1973), 289. Southwide in 1964, only 2 percent of southern black students went to school with white students; Wilkinson, *From Brown to Bakke,* 46. For information on non-southern school segregation, see Patterson, *Brown v. Board of Education,* 5; Kluger, *Simple Justice,* 758.

93. Quote is from "NAACP Official Urges More Desegregation," *Richmond Times-Dispatch,* May 16, 1965; see also "About 120 Negroes

Apply at Nottoway White Schools," *Richmond Times-Dispatch,* May 27, 1965; Hershman, "A Rumbling in the Museum," 363. By May 1965, nine virtually identical suits had been filed in federal courts in Virginia; see "Goochland Now Facing School Integration Suit," *Richmond Times-Dispatch,* May 21, 1965; "Grant Decision Opposed," *Richmond Times-Dispatch,* March 15, 1965.

94. "City School Integration Ordered," *The News,* November 15, 1961; "NAACP Hits School Plan in Roanoke," April 12, 1963; "Midlothian Entry Asked by Negroes," April 13, 1963; "2 Desegregation Suits Filed in Federal Court," May 3, 1963, all in the *Richmond Times-Dispatch;* Part 3d, reel 13, frame 912, NAACP Papers microfilm.

95. One NAACP-suggested replacement for freedom-of-choice plans was geographic zoning plans not based on race. See "About 120 Negroes Apply at Nottoway White Schools," *Richmond Times-Dispatch,* May 27, 1965.

96. My research on this lawsuit and Supreme Court decision—*Green v. New Kent County, Virginia*—is part of a larger work-in-progress about the story behind the lawsuit, the high court's decision, and its implications on school desegregation throughout the nation.

97. Court precedents supported the NAACP's losses. "Federal Court Upholds Frederick School Plan," *Richmond Times-Dispatch,* September 16, 1965; "NAACP Appeals Two School Cases," *Richmond Times-Dispatch,* August 4, 1965; *Gilliam v. School Board of City of Hopewell,* number 9625–26, Part V, box V2836, NAACP Papers.

98. Henry L. Marsh III, interview with the author and Jody Allen, November 25, 2002. Marsh went on to explain the decision-making process whereby *Green* was chosen over other, similar cases. See "Grant Decision Opposed," *Richmond Times-Dispatch,* March 15, 1965, for a list of similar cases.

99. "School Segregation Ruling Is Upheld," *Richmond Times-Dispatch,* March 2, 1965.

100. *United States v. Jefferson County Board of Education,* 380 F. 2d 385, 387 (5th Cir. 1967) as cited in Davison Douglas, "*Brown v. Board of Education* and Its Impact on Black Education in America," *Grassroots,* 365. See also *United States v. Jefferson County,* 372 F. 2d 836 (5th Cir. 1966).

101. *Griffin et al. v. County School Board of Prince Edward County, Virginia,* 317 U.S. 218 (1964). Perhaps the court system was shaken, as were many Americans, by the outbreak of race riots in the United States in 1964. Over the next half decade, urban unrest challenged the idea of racial progress and laid bare the second-class status of minorities. The U.S. Supreme Court was also increasingly liberal because of new appointments, including that of Thurgood Marshall in 1967; see Kluger, *Simple Justice,* 760.

102. *Charles C. Green v. County School Board of New Kent County, Virginia,* 391 U.S. 430 (1968).

103. Ibid.; Waldo Martin, Vicki Ruiz, Susan Salvatore, Patricia Sullivan, and Harvard Sitkoff, *Racial Desegregation in Public Education in the U.S. Theme Study* (Washington, DC: National Park Service, 2000), 91; Kluger, *Simple Justice,* 766.

104. *Charles C. Green v. County School Board of New Kent County, Virginia,* 391 U.S. 430 (1968). The high court also ordered the U.S. District Court to maintain oversight of the case.

105. Justice William H. Rehnquist in *Keyes v. School District No. 1, Denver, Colorado,* 413 U.S. 189 (1972). This was somewhat ironic considering that in the original arguments on *Brown,* Thurgood Marshall emphasized: "'The only thing that we ask for is that the state-imposed racial segregation be taken off, and to leave the county school board, the county people, the district people, to work out their own solution of the problem to assign children on any reasonable basis they want to assign them on.'" Quoted in Kluger, *Simple Justice,* 572.

106. Federal courts used *Green,* as well as subsequent Supreme Court decisions, to order integration in northern cities. This included the use of busing. See Charles J. Ogletree Jr., *All Deliberate Speed: Reflections on the First Half Century of Brown v. Board of Education* (New York: W. W. Norton, 2004), 59; Peter Irons, *Jim Crow's Children: The Broken Promise of the Brown Decision* (New York: Viking, 2002), 199–206, 209.

107. Henry L. Marsh III, interview with the author and Jody Allen, November 25, 2002; Cynthia Kay Bechter, "How the Goochland County Public Schools Desegregated," *Goochland County Historical Society Magazine* 27 (1995): 38–41; *Fredericksburg Lance-Star,* May 16, 2004, A8. HEW refashioned its integration requirements and again helped enforce compliance; see Fairclough, *Race and Democracy,* 440.

108. Robert R. Merhige Jr., interview with the author and Jody Allen; Richmond, Virginia, November 6, 2003; Henry L. Marsh III, interview with the author and Jody Allen, November 25, 2002.

109. *Alexander v. Holmes County Board of Education,* 396 U.S. 1218 (1969). Busing was accepted by the high court in *Swann v. Charlotte-Mecklenburg Bd. of Ed.,* 402 U.S. 1 (1971). Fairclough discusses unsuccessful southern efforts to thwart the Supreme Court by turning to the Nixon administration (*Race and Democracy,* 441–45).

110. Martin, Ruiz, Salvatore, Sullivan, and Sitkoff, *Racial Desegregation in Public Education,* 91. The study also refers to *Green* as the "most important [Supreme Court] decision regarding school desegregation since *Brown*" (91).

111. Davison Douglas, "*Brown v. Board of Education* and Its Impact on Black Education in America," in *Grassroots,* 365. *The Encyclopedia of Civil*

Rights in America argues that *Green* "did more to advance school integration than any other Supreme Court decision since *Brown v. Board of Education."* David Bradley and Shelley F. Fishkin, eds., *The Encyclopedia of Civil Rights in America* (Armonk, NY: Sharpe Reference, 1998), 2: 411. Former Virginia State Conference attorney Henry Marsh concurs: "That's when we had real meaningful desegregation—all over in 1968. Before we had the [*Green*] decision, desegregation was stymied because you only had desegregation where you had black applicants willing to run the gauntlet in white schools. After *Green v. New Kent* as long as 'freedom of choice' was not working, it was unlawful. So HEW took that decision and implemented desegregation on a wide basis—before that decision it didn't happen, so that was a crucial case." Henry L. Marsh III, interview with the author and Jody Allen, Richmond, Virginia, November 25, 2002.

112. In Fredericksburg, one longtime educator later recalled, "Many African-American administrators were demoted." *Fredericksburg Lance-Star,* May 16, 2004, A8. This article contains other examples of how integration negatively impacted African American educators. See also "Desegregation Curtailing Activities at Negro High School in Staunton," September 19, 1965; "Negro Teacher Job Survey Begun in State, " September 28, 1965; "Negro Teacher's Rehiring Urged," September 28, 1965, all in the *Richmond Times-Dispatch.* David Cecelski, *Along Freedom Road: Hyde County, North Carolina, and the Fate of Black Schools in the South* (Chapel Hill: University of North Carolina Press, 1994), discusses this subject in more detail in a story centered around eastern North Carolina.

The Palmetto Revolution: School Desegregation in South Carolina

1. Orville Vernon Burton, "Dining with Harvey Gantt: Myth and Realities of 'Integration with Dignity,'" in *Matthew J. Perry: The Man, His Times, and His Legacy,* ed. W. Lewis Burke and Belinda Gergel (Columbia: University of South Carolina Press, 2004), 183–220; Dan T. Carter, *The Politics of Rage: George Wallace, the Origins of the New Conservatism, and the Transformation of American Politics* (New York: Simon and Schuster, 1995); William H. Chafe, *Civilities and Civil Rights: Greensboro, North Carolina, and the Black Struggle for Freedom* (New York: Oxford University Press, 1980); John Dittmer, *Local People: The Struggle for Civil Rights in Mississippi* (Urbana: University of Illinois Press, 1994); Glenn Eskew, *But for Birmingham: The Local and National Movements in the Civil Rights Struggle* (Chapel Hill: University of North Carolina Press, 1997); Adam Fairclough, *Race and Democracy: The Civil Rights Struggle in Louisiana, 1915–1972* (Athens: University of Georgia Press, 1995); Charles M. Payne, *I've Got the Light of Freedom: The Organizing Tradition and the Mississippi Freedom*

Struggle (Berkeley: University of California Press, 1995); Stephen G. N. Tuck, *Beyond Atlanta: The Struggle for Racial Equality in Georgia, 1940–1980* (Athens: University of Georgia Press, 2001); Charles W. Eagles, "Toward New Histories of the Civil Rights Era," *Journal of Southern History* 66 (2000): 815–48.

2. Peter Wood, *Black Majority: Negroes in Colonial South Carolina from 1670 through the Stono Rebellion* (New York: Knopf, 1974); Rachel Klein, *Unification of a Slave State: The Rise of the Planter Class in South Carolina, 1760–1808* (Chapel Hill: University of North Carolina Press, 1990); Robert Olwell, *Masters, Slaves, and Subjects: The Culture of Power in the South Carolina Low Country, 1740–1790* (Ithaca, NY: Cornell University Press, 1998); Stephen W. Channing, *Crisis of Fear: Secession in South Carolina* (New York: Norton, 1970); William W. Freehling, *Prelude to Civil War: The Nullification Controversy in South Carolina, 1816–1836* (New York: Harper and Row, 1966); Lacy K. Ford Jr., *The Origins of Southern Radicalism: The South Carolina Upcountry, 1800–1860* (New York: Oxford University Press, 1988); Orville Vernon Burton, *In My Father's House Are Many Mansions: Family and Community in Edgefield, South Carolina* (Chapel Hill: University of North Carolina Press, 1985); Thomas Holt, *Black Over White: Negro Political Leadership in South Carolina during Reconstruction* (Urbana: University of Illinois Press, 1977); Peggy Lamson, *The Glorious Failure: Black Congressman Robert Brown Elliott and the Reconstruction in South Carolina* (New York: Norton, 1973); Joel Williamson, *After Slavery: The Negro in South Carolina During Reconstruction, 1861–1877* (Chapel Hill: University of North Carolina Press, 1965); William J. Cooper Jr., *The Conservative Regime: South Carolina, 1877–1890* (Baltimore: John Hopkins University Press, 1968); Francis B. Simkins, *Pitchfork Ben Tillman, South Carolinian* (Baton Rouge: Louisiana State University Press, 1944); Steven Kantrowitz, *Ben Tillman and the Reconstruction of White Supremacy* (Chapel Hill: University of North Carolina Press, 2000); J. Morgan Kousser, *The Shaping of Southern Politics: Suffrage Restriction and the One–Party South, 1880–1910* (New Haven, CT: Yale University Press, 1974); Michael Perman, *Struggle for Mastery: Disfranchisement in the South, 1888–1908* (Chapel Hill: University of North Carolina Press, 2001); George B. Tindall, *South Carolina Negroes, 1877–1900* (Chapel Hill: University of North Carolina Press, 1952); Charles A. Lofgren, *The Plessy Case: A Legal-Historical Interpretation* (New York: Oxford University Press, 1987), 201–4; Linda M. Matthews, "Keeping Down Jim Crow: The Railroads and the Separate Coach Bills in South Carolina," *South Atlantic Quarterly* 73 (1974): 117–29.

3. Orville Vernon Burton, "'The Black Squint of the Law': Racism in

South Carolina," in *The Meaning of South Carolina History: Essays in Honor of George C. Rogers, Jr.*, ed. David R. Chesnutt and Clyde N. Wilson (Columbia: University of South Carolina Press, 1991), 161–85; Bryant Simon, *A Fabric of Defeat: The Politics of South Carolina Millhands, 1910–1948* (Chapel Hill: University of North Carolina Press, 1998), 9–78, 205–6, 230–33; Bryant Simon, "The Appeal of Cole Blease of South Carolina: Race, Class, and Sex in the New South," *Journal of Southern History* 62 (1996): 57–86; Bryant Simon, "The Devaluation of the Vote: Legislative Apportionment and Inequality in South Carolina, 1890–1962," *South Carolina Historical Magazine*, 97 (1996), 227–45.

4. James Byrnes quoted in Burton, "Black Squint of the Law," 170–71; Gunnar Myrdal, *An American Dilemma: The Negro Problem and Modern Democracy* (New York: Harper and Brothers, 1944), 488n; V. O. Key, with assistance of Alexander Heard, *Southern Politics in State and Nation* (New York: Knopf, 1949), 130–55.

5. Jack Bass and Walter DeVries, *The Transformation of Southern Politics: Social Change and Political Consequence since 1945* (New York: Basic Books, 1976). When Bass and DeVries deliberately updated Key, they called their South Carolina chapter "The Changing Politics of Color."

6. William Watts Ball to Albert Watkins, May 11, 1914, William Watts Ball Papers, Duke University; Louis R. Harlan, *Separate and Unequal: Public School Campaigns and Racism in the Southern Seaboard States, 1901–1915* (Chapel Hill: University of North Carolina Press, 1958), 170–209, see especially 185, Ball editorial; Simon, *A Fabric of Defeat*, 9–78, 205–6, 230–33; Simon, "The Appeal of Cole Blease of South Carolina," 57–86; Simon, "The Devaluation of the Vote," 227–45; Leon F. Litwack, *Trouble in Mind: Black Southerners in the Age of Jim Crow* (New York: Vintage Books, 1999), 53, 63, 84, 103–4, 107; Orville Vernon Burton, "Black Squint of the Law," 161–85.

7. I. A. Newby, *Black Carolinians: A History of Blacks in South Carolina from 1895 to 1968* (Columbia: University of South Carolina Press, 1973), 308.

8. Simon, *A Fabric of Defeat*, 79–232; J. I. Haynes, *South Carolina and the New Deal* (Columbia: University of South Carolina Press, 2001); Mary L. Gehrig, "'Cotton Ed' Smith: The South Carolina Farmer in the United States Senate," in *The Oratory of Southern Demagogues*, ed. Cal M. Logue and Howard Dorgan (Baton Rouge: Louisiana State University Press, 1981), 131–48; Daniel W. Hollis, "'Cotton Ed Smith': Showman or Statesman?" *South Carolina Historical Magazine* 71 (1970): 235–56; Winfred B. Moore Jr., "'Soul of the South': James F. Byrnes and the Racial Issue in American Politics, 1911–1941," *Proceedings of the South Carolina Historical Association* (1978):

42–52; *Journal of the House of Representatives of the Second Session of the 85th General Assembly of the State of South Carolina* (Columbia: State Printers, 1944), 569–70.

9. John H. McCray to J. A. Mason, May 15, 1944, J. Bates Gerald to John H. McCray, October 29, 1948, John H. McCray to Joseph A. Rainey, June 24, 1944, Oscar R. Ewing to John McCray, July 7, 1944, A. J. Clement to John McCray, August 11, 1944, John H. McCray to Progressive Democratic Party, September 21, 1944, John H. McCray to Progressive Democratic Party, October 2, 1944, John H. McCray Papers, South Caroliniana Library, University of South Carolina (hereinafter cited as McCray Papers); Patricia Sullivan, *Days of Hope: Race and Democracy in the New Deal Era* (Chapel Hill: University of North Carolina Press, 1996), 170–71, 189–90; Kari Frederickson, *The Dixiecrat Revolt and the End of the Solid South, 1932–1968* (Chapel Hill: University of North Carolina Press, 1998), 124–28; Miles S. Richards, "The Progressive Democrats in Chicago, July 1944," *South Carolina Historical Magazine* 102 (2001): 219–37; Robert H. Ferrell, *Choosing Truman: The Democratic Convention of 1944* (Columbia: University of Missouri Press, 1994); Brenda L. Heaster, "Who's on Second: The 1944 Democratic Vice-Presidential Nomination," *Missouri Historical Review* 80 (1986): 156–75.

10. Tindall, *South Carolina Negroes,* 86; Frederic Ogden, *The Poll Tax in the South* (University: University of Alabama Press, 1958), 42, 123, 188; *Smith v. Allwright* 321 U.S. 649 (1944); V. O. Key Jr., *Southern Politics in State and Nation* (New York: Knopf, 1949), 627–32; *Rules Adopted by State Convention, May 15, 1946* (Columbia: Democratic Party of South Carolina, 1946), 2; Tinsley E. Yarbrough, *A Passion for Justice: J. Waties Waring and Civil Rights* (New York: Oxford University Press, 1987), 65–66; *Elmore v. Rice,* 72 F. Supp. 516, 527 (E. D. S. C. 1947); *aff'd sub nom Rice v. Elmore,* 165 F. 2d 387 (4th Cir. 1947), *cert. denied* 333 U. S. 875 (1948); *Brown v. Baskin,* 78 F. Supp. 933 (E. D. S. C. 1948,) 80 F. Supp. 1017 (E. D. S. C. 1948), *aff'd* 174 F. 2d 391 (4th Cir. 1949); Walter J. Fraser, *Charleston! Charleston!: The History of a Southern City* (Columbia: University of South Carolina Press, 1989), 398–99; *S. C. Acts* (1950), No. 858; *Charleston News and Courier,* February 9, 12, 24, March 15, April 14, 1950; Donald G. Nieman, *Promises to Keep: African Americans and the Constitutional Order, 1776 to the Present* (New York: Oxford University Press, 1991), 144.

11. J. A. DeLaine to J. M. Hinton, March 5, 1948, Joseph A. DeLaine Papers, South Caroliniana Library (hereinafter cited as DeLaine Papers; Francis W. White to Harold C. Booker Jr., August 3, 1940, Sam Latimer Papers, South Caroliniana Library; Arnold Derfner, "Racial Discrimination

and the Right to Vote," *Vanderbilt Law Review* 26 (1973): 523–84; I. A. Newby, *Black Carolinians: A History of Blacks in South Carolina from 1895 to 1968* (Columbia: University of South Carolina Press, 1973), 291. Newby puts registration at three thousand (0.8 percent of voting-age African Americans in South Carolina); *The Constitution of the State of South Carolina* (Columbia: R. L. Bryan, 1909), 55.

12. Yarbrough, *A Passion for Justice;* Egerton, *Speak Now against the Day;* Newby, *Black Carolinians;* Minutes for the Richland County Board of Education, July–November 1944, SC State Archives. *Duvall v. School Board,* C.A. No. 1082 (E.D.S.C.); R. Scott Baker, "Ambiguous Legacies: The NAACP's Legal Campaign against Segregation in Charleston, South Carolina, 1935–1975" (Ph.D. dissertation, Columbia University, 1993), 69, 80–93; Millicent Ellison Brown, "Civil Rights Activism in Charleston, South Carolina, 1940–1970" (Ph.D. dissertation, Florida State University, 1997), 38.

13. For a fuller discussion of this meeting and the efforts to persuade Delaine to lead the protest, see Richard Kluger, *Simple Justice: The History of Brown v. Board of Education and Black America's Struggle for Equality* (New York: Knopf, 1976), 19–21. Petition of Harry Briggs, et al., to the Board of Trustees for School District No. 22, November 11, 1949; available online at <www.palmettohistory.org/exhibits/briggs>.

14. The Byrnes statement on "gerrymandering of districts" from the 1950 radio address is in a file pertaining to the 1950 gubernatorial campaign, in the Papers of James F. Byrnes, Cooper Memorial Library, Clemson University. Interview with Dr. Marcia Synott, March 3, 2001; Deposition of Dr. Marcia Synott, *U.S. Plaintiffs, Richard Ganaway, et al., Plaintiffs-Intervenors v. Charleston County School District and State of South Carolina;* "Plaintiffs' Proposed Post-Trial Findings of Fact," in *U.S. Plaintiffs, Richard Ganaway, et al., Plaintiffs-Intervenors v. Charleston County School District and State of South Carolina,* C.A. No. 81–50–8, 24–36; Baker, "Ambiguous Legacies," 176, 265–66.

15. "Building Program," *Southern School News,* September 3, 1954, 12; "Finance Commission Allocates $408,568," *Southern School News,* March 1962, 2; Andrew H. Myers, *Black, White, and Olive Drab: Military-Social Relations during the Civil Rights Movement at Fort Jackson, South Carolina* (Charlottesville: University Press of Virginia, forthcoming) uses the *Southern School News* effectively to trace many of these developments in a revision of his dissertation being published by the University Press of Virginia. Mark V. Tushnet, *The NAACP's Legal Strategy against Segregated Education, 1925–1950* (Chapel Hill: University of North Carolina Press, 1987); Nieman, *Promises to Keep,* 150–53; James T. Patterson, *Brown v. Board of Education:*

A Civil Rights Milestone and Its Troubled Legacy (New York: Oxford University Press, 2001), 11–45; Kluger, *Simple Justice,* 126–314; Burton, "Black Squint of the Law," 177; Newby, *Black Carolinians,* 274–313; John G. Sproat, "Firm Flexibility: Perspectives on Desegregation in South Carolina," in *New Perspectives on Race and Slavery in America: Essays in Honor of Kenneth M. Stampp,* ed. Robert H. Abzug and Stephen E. Maizlish (Lexington: University of Kentucky Press, 1986), 164, 166–69; *Charleston Evening Post,* May 17, 1954; *Charleston News and Courier,* May 18, 1954; Michael J. Zwolanek, "'Right and Wise': James F. Byrnes and South Carolina's Educational Revolution" (Unpublished M.A. thesis, Clemson University, 1997); Jeremy Richards, "The Story of South Carolina's Gressette Committee," unpublished paper delivered at the Citadel Conference on the Civil Rights Movement in South Carolina on March 7, 2003, available online at <http://citadel.edu/citadel/otherserv/hist/civilrights/papers/richards.pdf>; Thomas S. Morgan, "James F. Byrnes and the Politics of Segregation," *Historian* 56 (Summer 1994): 645–54.

16. Transcript of Proceedings, Public Meeting held at Manning, South Carolina, May 22, 1964, pages 4–116, in South Carolina State Advisory Committee, U.S. Commission on Civil Rights Papers, South Caroliniana Library, University of South Carolina; Memorandum of Joseph DeLaine dated circa November 11–December 4, 1949, Summary of Meeting in Sumerton, South Carolina, June 8, 1949, J. A. DeLaine note on Harold Boulware letter dated March 8, 1949, J. A. DeLaine note on circular dated December 13, 1949, warning dated October 7, 1955, that suggested DeLaine had ten days to live if he did not leave Lake City, South Carolina, DeLaine Papers; Kluger, *Simple Justice,* 3–26, 315–66; Yarbrough, *A Passion for Justice,* 113, 181, 187, 189; *Briggs v. Elliott,* U.S. District Court Opinion, 98 F. Supp. 529, available online at <http://brownvboard.org/research/opinions/briggs1.htm>.

17. *Brown v. Board of Education of Topeka* 347 U.S. 483 (1954), 349 U.S. 294 (1955), available online at <http://laws.findlaw.com/us/347/483.html> and <http://laws.findlaw.com/us/349/294.html> respectively; Nieman, *Promises to Keep,* 151–55; Patterson, *Brown v. Board of Education,* 46–85; Kluger, *Simple Justice,* 543–747; for an excellent discussion of the difficult position that the lower federal courts found themselves in, see Jack Bass, *Unlikely Heroes: The Dramatic Story of the Southern Judges of the Fifth Circuit Who Translated the Supreme Court's Brown Decision into a Revolution for Equality* (New York: Simon and Schuster, 1981); a different view that presents a simplistic view of southern politics in the period and faults the Warren Court for being too aggressive can be found in Michael J. Klarman, "How *Brown* Changed Race Relations: The Backlash Thesis," *Journal of American History* 81 (1994): 81–118, and developed more fully in *From Jim Crow to Civil Rights: The Supreme Court and the Struggle for*

Racial Equality (New York: Oxford University Press, 2004); Timmerman quoted in "Governor's Viewpoint," *Southern School News,* March 1955, 14; South Carolina attorney general T. C. Callison, quoted in "What They Said," *Southern School News,* June 1955, 6.

18. *Briggs v. Elliot,* 132 F. Supp. 776 (E.D.S.C. 1955); Myers, *Black, White, and Olive Drab.*

19. Ralph E. Cousins, Joseph R. Horn, Larry A. Jackson, John S. Lyles, and John B. Morris, compilers, *South Carolinians Speak: A Moderate Approach to Race Relations* (Dillon, SC: South Carolinians Speak [?], 1957), 10, 25, 37; Howard H. Quint, *Profile in Black and White: A Frank Portrait of South Carolina* (Washington, DC: Public Affairs Press, 1958), 21–37; William D. Smyth, "Segregation in Charleston in the 1950s: A Decade of Transition," *South Carolina Historical Magazine* 92 (1991): 99–123; Stephen O'Neill, "To Endure, but Not Accept: *The News and Courier* and School Desegregation," *Proceedings of the South Carolina Historical Association* (1990): 87–94; Numan Bartley, *The Rise of Massive Resistance: Southern Politics in the 1950s* (Baton Rouge: Louisiana State University Press, 1969).

20. H. R. E. Hampton to J. Heyward Gibbes, January 13, 1955, James F. Byrnes to J. Heyward Gibbes, June 16, 1954, J. Heyward Gibbes Papers, South Caroliniana Library, University of South Carolina (hereinafter cited as Gibbes Papers); Edgar A. Brown to Irvine F. Belser, May 27, 1954, Irvine F. Belser Papers, South Caroliniana Library, University of South Carolina.

21. This view of Gibbes is based on a close reading of his correspondence; Heyward Gibbes to Jack, October 27, 1955, J. Waties Waring to J. Heyward Gibbes, June 12, 1945, James F. Byrnes to J. Heyward Gibbes, June 16, 1954, Gibbes Papers.

22. J. Heyward Gibbes to James F. Byrnes, June 7, 1954, Gibbes Papers.

23. Segregation Note of J. Heyward Gibbes, July 9, 1955, Segregation Note of J. Heyward Gibbes, August 8, 1955, Resolution adopted by South Carolina Association of School Boards, August 6, 1955, Gibbes Papers; E. E. Richburg to J. A. DeLaine, October 15, 1956, DeLaine Papers; Baker, "Ambiguous Legacies," 168–96; Brown, "Civil Rights Activism," 64–109; Stephen O'Neill, "From the Shadow of Slavery: The Civil Rights Years in Charleston" (Unpublished Ph.D. dissertation, University of Virginia, 1994), 144–97; "South Carolina," *Southern School News,* September 1954, 12; "Legislative Action," *Southern School News,* February 1956, 16; "Legislative Action," *Southern School News,* April 1956, 12; Quint, *Profile in Black and White,* 15–17; Walter Edgar, *South Carolina: A History* (Columbia: University of South Carolina Press, 1998), 523.

24. E. E. Richburg to J. A. DeLaine, October 15, 1956, John H. McCray to Joseph A. DeLaine, DeLaine Papers; J. Heyward Gibbes note, August 12, 1955, Jake D. Hill to J. Heyward Gibbes, March 21, 1956, Gibbes Papers;

Deposition of Charles M. Gibson, December 16, 1986, pp. 68–69, *U.S. v. Richard Ganaway, et al.,* CA No. 81–50–8; *Columbia Record,* October 11, 1955; Quint, *Profile in Black and White,* 86; Septima Poinsette Clark, *Echo in My Soul* (New York: Dutton, 1962); Sproat, "Firm Flexibility," 170–71, 183; Burton, "Black Squint of the Law," 175; "Attacks NAACP," *Southern School News,* November 1955, 11; McCray Papers.

25. S. L. Blomgren to Marcus Bloom, December 15, 1922, S. L. Blomgren to Marcus Bloom, December 12, 1922, S. L. Blomgren to Marcus Bloom, December 14, 1922, John D. E. Meyer Papers, South Carolina Historical Society; Cole L. Blease to Ralph W. Blakely, June 27, 1930, L. W. C. Blalock to George D. Shore, July 12, 1930, Ralph R. Blakeley to Yandell Blakeley, August 25, 1930, Ralph Blakeley Papers, Duke University (hereinafter cited as Blakeley Papers); Tom Henderson Wells, "The Phoenix Election Riot," *Phylon* 31 (1970): 58–69; Willard B. Gatewood, "Theodore Roosevelt and Southern Republicans: The Case of South Carolina, 1901–1904," *South Carolina Historical Magazine* 70 (1969): 251–66; *Before the Republican National Committee: Tolbert, et al. vs. Hambright et al., Contest from the State at Large and Six Congressional Districts* (1936); *The Republican Party of South Carolina: Organized October 28, 1930* (1930); Richard B. Sherman, *The Republican Party and Black America: From McKinley to Hoover, 1896–1933* (Charlottesville: University Press of America, 1973); Donald J. Lisio, *Hoover, Blacks, and Lily-Whites: A Study in Southern Strategies* (Chapel Hill: University of North Carolina Press, 1985); Hanes Walton, *Black Republicans: The Politics of the Black and Tans* (Metuchen, NJ: Scarecrow Press, 1975); Neil R. McMillen, "Perry W. Howard, Boss of Black-and-Tan Republicanism in Mississippi, 1924–1960," *Journal of Southern History* 48 (1982): 205–24; David J. Ginzl, "Lily-Whites Versus Black-and-Tan Republicanism in Mississippi during the Hoover Administration," *Journal of Mississippi History* 42 (1980), 194–211.

26. J. Y. Blakeley to Ralph R. Blakeley, April 10, 1952, Yandell Blakeley to Ralph Blakeley, April 28, 1952, Yandell Blakeley to Ralph Blakeley, August 14, 1952, Yandell Blakeley to Ralph Blakeley, December 2, 1952, Yandell Blakeley to Ralph Blakeley, March 16, 1953, Yandell Blakeley to Ralph Blakeley, March 30, 1956, Blakeley Papers; Quint, *Profile in Black and White,* 131–43; Theodore H. White, *The Making of the President, 1960* (New York: Atheneum, 1961); Guy Paul Land, "Mississippi Republicanism and the 1960 Presidential Election," *Journal of Mississippi History* 40 (1978): 33–48; Guy Paul Land, "John F. Kennedy's Southern Strategy, 1956–1960," *North Carolina Historical Review* 56 (1979): 41–63; Jeffrey R. Young, "Eisenhower's Federal Judges and Civil Rights Policy: A Republican 'Southern Strategy' for the 1950s," *Georgia Historical Quarterly* 78 (1994): 536–65; Michael S. Mayer, "With Much Deliberation and Some Speed: Eisenhower

and the *Brown* Decision," *Journal of Southern History* 52 (1986): 43–76;
Robert F. Burk, *The Eisenhower Administration and Black Civil Rights*
(Knoxville: University of Tennessee Press, 1989); Michal R. Belknap, *Federal
Law and Southern Order: Racial Violence and Constitutional Conflict in the
Post-Brown South* (Athens: University of Georgia Press, 1987), 27–72; Carl
M. Brauer, *John F. Kennedy and the Second Reconstruction* (New York:
Columbia University Press, 1977); Bruce Kalk, *The Origins of the Southern
Strategy: Two-Party Competition in South Carolina, 1950–1972* (Lanham,
MD: Lexington Books, 2001); David Robertson, *Sly and Able: A Political
Biography of James F. Byrnes* (New York: Norton, 1994); also see James F.
Byrnes, *All in One Lifetime* (New York: Harper and Brothers, 1958).

27. For more on the transition of South Carolina from a predominantly
Democratic state to a Republican state see, for example, Russell Merritt,
"The Senatorial Election of 1962 and the Rise of Two-Party Politics in South
Carolina," *South Carolina Historical Magazine* 98 (1997): 281–301.

28. Maxie M. Cox, "1963—The Year of Decision: Desegregation in South
Carolina" (Unpublished Ph.D. dissertation, University of South Carolina,
1996), 352, 404–21; O'Neill, "From the Shadow of Slavery," 198, 218,
225–38; Brown, "Civil Rights Activism," 81, 166, 170–216; Baker,
"Ambiguous Legacies," 198–201, 213–18; Edgar, *South Carolina*, 540; Alada
Shinault-Small, "Several Rungs Up the Ladder: The Struggle for Civil Rights
in Charleston, Summer 1963," *Avery Review* 2 (1999): 8–29.

29. John H. McCray to William L. Dawson, May 9, 1961, John H.
McCray to James M. Hinton and Eugene A. Montgomery, May 10, 1961,
John H. McCray to Louis E. Martin, April 12, 1962, John H. McCray to
Colonel A. T. Walden, June 1,1962, John H. McCray to Lester Bates, May 30,
1963, John H. McCray to Lester L. Bates and City Council of Columbia, June
10, 1963, John H. McCray to Joseph T. Taylor, August 14, 1963, John H.
McCray to E. P. Riley, January 26, 1964.

30. Burton, "Dining with Harvey Gantt," 183–220; Interview with
Harvey Gantt and Matthew Perry, July 14, 2002; Interview with Matthew
Perry, June 21, 2003; Interview with Harvey Gantt, July 14, 2003; Cox,
"1963—The Year of Decision," 352; O'Neill, "From the Shadow of Slavery,"
198; Brown, "Civil Rights Activism," 166; Baker, "Ambiguous Legacies,"
198–201; *Charleston News and Courier,* July 10, December 22, 1962, January
23, 1963; H. Lewis Suggs, "Harvey Gantt and the Desegregation of Clemson
University, 1960–1963," in *Integration with Dignity: A Celebration of Harvey
Gantt's Admission to Clemson,* ed. Skip Eisiminger (Clemson: Clemson
University Digital Press, 2003), 19–30; The *State,* July 10, December 22,
1962, January 23, 1963, Gregory K. Bast, "'As Different as Heaven and Hell':
The Desegregation of Clemson College," *Proceedings of the South Carolina
Historical Association* (1994): 38–39; *New York Times,* July 10, 1962;

Newby, *Black Carolinians,* 343–45; "Leaders Urge Calm as Suits Near Decision," *Southern School News,* January 1963, 1, 15; "Clemson College Admits Negro in State's First Desegregation," *Southern School News,* February 1963, 1, 8; "Compliance Plan Has Opposition," *Southern School News,* February 1963, 8. "Rapid Legal Maneuvers Cleared Way for Gantt," *Southern School News,* February 1963, 9; "Six Negro Students Attending Public Schools with Whites," *Southern School News,* November 1963, 16. Daniels was appointed to the U.S. Senate by Governor James F. Byrnes in 1954 to fill the unexpired term of the late Burnet R. Maybank.

31. "New Clarendon Suit Filed Challenging Segregation," *Southern School News,* May 1960, 3; Wyche quoted in "Lull in Legal Action Ends; 2 Suits Filed," *Southern School News,* June 1962, 1; "Court Overturns State Contention," *Southern School News,* January 1963, 15; "Class Actions Banned in Bill Passed by House," *Southern School News,* May 1963, 14.

32. *Brown v. Charleston District Twenty School Board,* 226 F. Supp. 819 (E. D. S. C. 1963); Brown, "Civil Rights Activism," 96, 98, 102; Cox, "1963—The Year of Decision," 168–69, 186, 217–30, 235–37, 240–43.

33. "Proposed Tuition-Grants Plan Arouses Heavy Debate," *Southern School News,* May 1963, 14; Lowe, "*Brown* on Trial," 33–55; Cox, "1963—The Year of Decision," 161, 230–31, 243–44; O'Neill, "From the Shadow of Slavery," 239–40; Baker, "Ambiguous Legacies," 225; Brown, "Civil Rights Activism," 90, 93.

34. *Charleston News and Courier,* April 29, 1965; Gary Orfield, *Public School Desegregation in the U.S.* (Washington, DC: Joint Center for Policy Studies, 1983), 23. The best account of events at Orangeburg is still Jack Nelson and Jack Bass, *The Orangeburg Massacre,* orig publ. 1970 (Macon, GA: Mercer University Press, 1984), for quotation, 197. See also William C. Hine, "Civil Rights and Campus Wrongs: South Carolina State College Students Protest, 1955–1968," *South Carolina Historical Magazine* 97 (1996): 310–31; Cleveland Sellers (with Robert Terrell), *The River of No Return: The Autobiography of a Black Militant and the Life and Death of SNCC* (New York: William Morrow, 1973), 206–26; I. A. Newby, *Black Carolinians: A History of Blacks in South Carolina from 1895 to 1968* (Columbia: University of South Carolina Press, 1973), 345–60; *New York Times,* March 4, 1970, 1, March 5, 1970, 1.

35. *South Carolina v. Katzenbach,* 383 U.S. 301 (1966). South Carolina filed the original complaint. At the Court's invitation, Alabama, Georgia, Louisiana, Mississippi, and Virginia filed briefs as *amicus curiae* supporting South Carolina's claim that certain provisions of the Voting Rights Act were unconstitutional. Numerous other states filed briefs supporting the constitutionality of the act. 383 U.S. 301, 308–9, 310n, 329–30 (1966); Belknap,

Federal Law and Southern Order, 72–127; Nieman, *Promises to Keep,* 162–88; Charles W. Whalen, *The Longest Debate: A Legislative History of the 1964 Civil Rights Act* (Cabin John, MD: Seven Locks Press, 1985); David J. Garrow, *Bearing the Cross: Martin Luther King Jr. and the Southern Christian Leadership Conference* (New York: William Morrow, 1986); Hugh Davis Graham, *The Civil Rights Era: Origins and Development of National Policy, 1960–1972* (New York: Oxford University Press, 1990).

36. *Manning Times* quoted in Wolters, *The Burden of Brown,* 164. T. W. Anderson to Parents, August 28, 1965, Minutes of South Carolina Advisory Committee Meeting on December 16, 1965, South Carolina Advisory Committee Papers; Hugh Davis Graham, "Richard Nixon and Civil Rights: Explaining an Enigma," *Presidential Studies Quarterly* 26 (1996): 93–106; Dean Kotlowski, "Nixon's Southern Strategy Revisited," *Journal of Policy History* 10 (1998): 207–38; Bruce Kalk, "Wormley's Hotel Revisited: Richard Nixon's Southern Strategy and the End of the Second Reconstruction," *North Carolina Historical Review* 71 (1994): 85–105; Billy Hathorn, "The Changing Politics of Race: Congressmen Albert William Watson and the S. C. Republican Party, 1965–1970," *South Carolina Historical Magazine* 89 (1988): 227–41; Orville Vernon Burton, "Race Relations in the Rural South since 1945," in *The Rural South since 1945,* ed. R. Douglas Hurt (Baton Rouge: Louisiana State University Press, 1998), 28–58; Dean J. Kotlowski, *Nixon's Civil Rights: Politics, Principle, and Policy* (Cambridge, MA: Harvard University Press, 2001), 1–44; Nieman, *Promises to Keep,* 191–200; Stephen L. Wasby, Anthony A. D'Amato, and Rosemary Metrailer, *Desegregation from Brown to Alexander: An Exploration of Supreme Court Strategies* (Carbondale: Southern Illinois University Press, 1977), 376–428; Harry S. Dent, *The Prodigal South Returns to Power* (New York: Wiley, 1978); Leon Panetta and Peter Gall, *Bring Us Together: The Nixon Team and the Civil Rights Retreat* (Philadelphia: Lippincott, 1971); Edgar, *South Carolina,* 543–45.

37. Act 844 (R294, H1931), "An Act to make Additional Provisions . . . ," March 22, 1952, 2085–87, and Act 379 (R256, H1150), 546–661, both in *Statutes at Large of South Carolina;* Article 4, *1960 Cumulative Supplement,* 53, 185; Act 890 (R1103, H2252) "An Act to Amend Section 21–1631 of the Code of Laws of South Carolina, 1952, Relating to the Election or Appointment of Trustees of School Districts in Charleston County, So as to Make Further Provision For the appointment of the Trustees of St. John's School District No. 9 and St. Paul's School District No. 23, in the County, 19 April 1956," *Statutes at Large of South Carolina: General and Permanent Laws, 1956,* 2144; Article 4, Charleston County, ch. 27, S.C. Code 1962, 1975 Cumulative Supplement, 211–12, 371–74; Act 1037 (R1272, S838), "An Act to Amend Section 21–1631 of the 1962 Code, Relating to the Elective or Appointment of Trustees of School Districts in Charleston

County, So As to Make Further Provision for the Appointment of the Trustees of St. James Santee School District No. 1, 24 April 1964, *Statutes at Large of South Carolina: General and Permanent Laws—1964*, 2368; Act No. 340 (R472, S20), "An Act to Abolish the School District of Charleston County and to Abolish the County Board of Education of Charleston County," *Statutes at Large of South Carolina: General and Permanent Laws, 1967*, June 8, 1967, 470–76; Act No. 936 (R983, S612) "An Act to Amend Act No. 340 of 1967 . . . , 13 March 1970, *Statutes at Large: General and Permanent Laws, 1970*, 2032–34; Act No. 397 (R644, H1870) "An Act to Amend Section 21–1631 . . . So as to Provide that All Trustees Shall Be Elected," *Statutes at Large: General and Permanent Laws, 1973*, 692–93; Act No. 914 (R945, H2556), "An Act to Amend Section 21–1631, As Amended . . . To Delete References to Appointments of the Trustees of School District No. 20 of Charleston County . . . ," *Statutes at Large: General and Permanent Laws, 1974*, 1978–79; "Editorial: Break with the Past," "School Bill Clears Senate," *Charleston News and Courier*, February 19, March 24, and June 8, 1967.

38. Baker, "Ambiguous Legacies," 270.

39. Orville Vernon Burton, Terence R. Finnegan, Peyton McCrary, and James W. Loewen, "South Carolina," in *Quiet Revolution in the South: The Impact of the Voting Rights Act in the South, 1965–1990*, ed. Chandler Davidson and Bernard Grofman (Princeton, NJ: Princeton University Press, 1994), 202–3.

40. Edgar, *South Carolina*, 545; Steve Morrison, "Our Covenant with South Carolina's Children: Plaintiffs attorney Steve Morrison indicts South Carolina's systematic neglect of poor, rural school districts, 50 years after *Brown v. Board*," in *Emphasis: The South Carolina Education Association* 24, no. 4 (December 2004–January 2005): 12–13; Raymond Wolters, *The Burden of Brown: Thirty Years of School Desegregation* (Knoxville: University of Tennessee Press, 1984), 129–74; "Long Road to Justice: Civil Rights in South Carolina," (Columbia) *The State*, March 6, 2003, A7; "South Carolina Education Accountability Act of 1998" available online from <http:www.scstatehouse.net/sess112_1997–1998/bills/850.htm>.

41. Morrison, "South Carolina's Children," 10–14; information about this lawsuit is available online at <http:www.scschoolcase.com>.

42. *New York Times*, April 21, 1991; Peter Irons, *Jim Crow's Children: The Broken Promise of the Brown Decision* (New York: Viking Penguin, 2002), 332–37.

43. See also Wolters, *The Burden of Brown*, 129–74; Jeff Miller, "What Tomorrow Can Bring," *Southern Exposure* 22 (Summer 1994): 16–23.

Defiance, Protest, and Compromise: The Struggle to Implement *Brown* in Georgia, 1950–1973

1. In the chapter the terms "Blacks" and "Whites" are used to identify Americans of African descent and of European descent, respectively. *Missouri ex rel. Gaines v. Canada,* 305 U.S. 337 (1938); *Alston v. School Board of City of Norfolk,* 112 F. 2d. 992 (1940); *Sipuel v. Oklahoma State Board of Regents,* 332 U.S. 631 (1948); *McLaurin v. Oklahoma State Board of Regents for Higher Education,* 339 U.S. 637 (1950); *Sweatt v. Painter,* 339 U.S. 629 (1950).

2. Thomas V. O'Brien, "The Dog That Didn't Bark: *Aaron v. Cook* and the NAACP Strategy in Georgia before *Brown,*" *Journal of Negro Education* (Winter 1999): 79–88; *Statesman,* September 28, 1950; *New York Times,* September 24, 1950.

3. Thomas V. O'Brien, *The Politics of Race and Schooling: Public Education in Georgia, 1900–1961* (Lanham, MD: Lexington, 1999), 86.

4. Ernest W. Swanson and John A. Griffin, *Public Education in the South Today: A Statistical Survey* (Chapel Hill: University of North Carolina Press, 1955).

5. O'Brien, "The Dog That Didn't Bark," 80.

6. Harold H. Martin, *William Berry Hartsfield: Mayor of Atlanta* (Athens: University of Georgia Press, 1978), 50, 68, 100–101; David N. Plank and Marcia Turner, "Changing Patterns in Black School Politics: Atlanta, 1872–1973," *American Journal of Education* 95 (August 1987): 596; Virginia H. Hein, "The Image of a City 'Too Busy to Hate': Atlanta in the 1960s," *Phylon* 33 (Fall 1972): 211.

7. John P. Wesberry, "Georgia Politicos Are Desperate," *Christian Century,* February 14, 1951, 195; O'Brien, *Politics,* 104.

8. *Georgia Laws,* 1953, 24, quoted in O'Brien, *Politics,* 131–32.

9. Jane Hammer, *The Georgia Voter* 24, no. 6 (February 1954), 1–6; *Atlanta Daily World,* October 5, 1954; *Atlanta Constitution,* October 28, 1954; *Atlanta Journal,* October 28, 1954.

10. *Atlanta Constitution,* November 3, 1954; *Southern School News,* December 1, 1954.

11. Diane Ravitch, *The Troubled Crusade* (New York: Basic Books, 1983), 115; *Atlanta Journal,* May 18, 1954; *New York Times,* June 30, 1954, September 5, 1954.

12. *Georgia Laws,* 1956, 6, 9–15; *Atlanta Constitution,* November 3, 1954; *Southern School News,* December 1, 1954; *Atlanta Journal,* February 6, 1956; Edward D. Ball, *A Statistical Summary, State by State of Segregation-Desegregation Activity Affecting Southern Schools from 1954 to Present Together with Pertinent Data on Enrollment, Teacher Pay, Etc.* (Nashville:

Southern Education Reporting Service, 1958), 9; Numan Bartley, *The Rise of Massive Resistance: Race and Politics in the South during the 1950s* (Baton Rouge: Louisiana State University Press, 1969), 75.

13. *Augusta Courier,* September 9, 1949, September 29, 1949; William Anderson, *Wild Man from Sugar Creek: The Political Career of Eugene Talmadge* (Baton Rouge: Louisiana State University Press, 1975), 216; Numan V. Bartley, *From Thurmond to Wallace: Political Tendencies in Georgia, 1948–1968* (Baltimore: Johns Hopkins University Press, 1970), 21.

14. *Hunt v. Arnold* (1956), *Holmes v. University of Georgia* (1960), in Reed Sarratt, *A Statistical Summary, State by State of Segregation-Desegregation Activity Affecting Southern Schools from 1954 to Present Together with Pertinent Data on Enrollment, Teachers, Colleges, Litigation, and Legislation* (Nashville: Southern Education Reporting Service, 1964); *Calhoun v. Latimer* 377 U.S. 263 (1964); Mark H. Huie Sr. "Factors Influencing the Desegregation Process in the Atlanta School System, 1954–1967" (Ph.D. dissertation, University of Georgia, 1967), 28; Calvin Trillin, *An Education in Georgia* (New York: Viking, 1964).

15. Charles Pyles, "S. Ernest Vandiver and the Politics of Change," in *Georgia Governors in an Age of Change: From Ellis Arnall to George Busbee,* ed. Harold P. Henderson and Gary L. Roberts (Athens: University of Georgia Press, 1988), 148–56.

16. Trillin, *An Education in Georgia.*

17. For various interpretations of this controversy, see Sue Bailes, "Eugene Talmadge and the Board of Regents Controversy," *Georgia Historical Quarterly* 53 (Fall 1969): 409–523; James F. Cook, "Talmadge-Cocking Controversy"; Allen Lumpkin Henson, *Red Galluses: A Story of Georgia Politics* (Boston: House of Edinboro, 1945), 221–43; Anderson, *Wild Man from Sugar Creek,* 195–204; Harold Paulk Henderson, *The Politics of Change: A Political Biography of Ellis Arnall* (Athens: University of Georgia Press, 1991), 33–50; Calvin McLeod Logue, *Eugene Talmadge: Rhetoric and Response* (New York: Greenwood, 1989), 173–212.

18. *Atlanta Constitution,* January 10, 1961; *Southern School News,* February 1961; Trillin, *An Education in Georgia;* Charlayne Hunter-Gault, *In My Place* (New York: Farrar, Straus, Giroux, 1992).

19. *Southern School News,* July 1959, January 1960; *New York Times,* November 25, 1959, December 1, 1959.

20. *Southern School News,* January 1960; *New York Times,* December 13, 1959; *New York Times,* December 31, 1959.

21. O'Brien, *Politics,* 53; Paul E. Mertz, "'Mind Changing Time All Over Georgia' HOPE, Inc. and School Desegregation," *Georgia Historical Quarterly* 77 (Spring 1993): 41–61.

22. For more on Pauley, see *Everybody's Grandma and Nobody's Fool:*

Frances Freeborn Pauley and the Struggle for Social Justice (Ithaca, NY: Cornell University Press, 2000).

23. John A. Sibley, *The General Assembly Committee on Schools, Majority and Minority Reports: Report to the General Assembly,* Atlanta, GA, April 28, 1960; James A. MacKay, "Will Georgia's Public Schools Close?" in Fort (ed.), *Emory Alumnus,* December 1960, 4–7, 39; *New York Times,* April 29, 1960; *New York Times,* May 8, 1960.

24. *Southern School News,* June 1960; O'Brien, *Politics,* 182.

25. *Southern School News,* November 1960; *New York Times,* May 8, 10, 1960; Alton Hornsby Jr., "A City That Was Too Busy to Hate," in *Southern Businessmen and Desegregation,* ed. E. Jacoway and D. Colburn (Baton Rouge: Louisiana State University Press), 121–36; Helen H. Miller, "Private Business and Public Education in the South," *Harvard Business Review* 38(4) (1960): 75–88.

26. *New York Times,* December 11, 1960; Mertz, "'Mind Changing Time," 43–46.

27. Mertz, "Mind Changing Time," 44–47; Donald L. Grant, *The Way It Was in the South: The Black Experience in Georgia* (New York: Birch Lane Press, 1993), 396; O'Brien, *Politics,* 158.

28. O'Brien suggests that the relative lack of support for the SRCG was due to the county unit system in Georgia which enhanced the power of local and state government leaders, and rendered the council superfluous. O'Brien, *Politics,* 126. Also see Neil R. McMillen, *The Citizens' Council: Organized Resistance to the Second Reconstruction, 1954–1964* (Urbana: University of Illinois Press), ch. 5.

29. *Southern School News,* January 1955, Reed Sarratt, *The Ordeal of Desegregation: The First Decade* (New York: Harper and Row), 302–3.

30. Walter F. Murphy, "The South Counterattacks: The Anti-NAACP Laws," *Western Political Quarterly* 12 (Summer 1959): 374–78.

31. Melvin W. Ecke, *From Ivy Street to Kennedy Center: Centennial History of the Atlanta Public School System* (Atlanta: Atlanta Board of Education, 1972), 364–68; *Southern School News,* June 1961; *New York Times,* May 2, 1961, May 3, 1961, June 15, 1961.

32. *Southern School News,* July 1962, September 1962; *New York Times,* July 2, 1961, August 8, 1961.

33. *Atlanta Constitution,* November 23, 1961; *Southern School News,* August 1961, November 1961; *New York Times,* October 17, 1962; *Atlanta Journal Constitution,* September 15, 1993.

34. "An Appeal for Human Rights," reprinted in David Garrow, *Atlanta, Georgia, 1960–1961* (Brooklyn: Carlson, 1989), 187; Harvard Sitkoff, *The Struggle for Black Equality, 1954–1992* (New York: Hill and Wang, 1993), 69–73.

35. *Southern School News*, March 1961, April 1961; *New York Times*, February 19, 1961, March 8, 1961, March 11, 1961.

36. *Atlanta Constitution*, August 30, 1961; *Southern School News*, September 1961, October 1961; *New York Times*, August 31, 1961, September 1, 1961.

37. Constance Baker Motley, *Equal Justice under the Law* (New York: Farrar, Straus, Giroux, 1999), 142–44.

38. *New York Times*, June 15, 1962, July 6, 1962, July 21, 1962, August 1, 1962.

39. Taylor Branch, *Parting the Waters: America in the King Years, 1954–1963* (New York: Simon and Schuster, 1988), 600–632.

40. *Southern School News*, September 1962; *New York Times*, August 15, 1962, September 4, 1962, September 5, 1962, July 14, 1963, August 29, 1963.

41. *Southern School News*, January 1965, June 1965; Grant, *The Way It Was*, 523.

42. *Southern School News*, September 1964; *New York Times*, April 7, 1964, September 4, 9, 1964.

43. *Atlanta Daily World*, April 11, 1969; *New York Times*, December 14, 1968, February 22, 1969, February 23, 1969. Title IV originally had targeted at de jure and de facto racial segregation nationwide, but against Southern protests, it was scaled back to address only those states where segregation was required or permitted by law.

44. *New York Times*, September 1, 1963, September 2, 1963, June 15, 1963, July 4, 1963, October 3, 1963.

45. *Stell v. Savannah Board of Education* (1963) in Reed Sarratt, *A Statistical Summary, State by State of Segregation-Desegregation Activity Affecting Southern Schools From 1954 to Present Together with Pertinent Data on Enrollment, Teachers, Colleges, Litigation, and Legislation* (Nashville: Southern Education Reporting Service, 1964); *New York Times*, May 11, May 14, 1963, May 25, 1963, August 28, 1963; *Southern School News*, August 1963; Andrew Winston, "Science in the Service of the Far Right: Henry E. Garrett, the IAAEE, and the Liberty Lobby—International Association for the Advancement of Ethnology—Experts in the Service of Social Reform: SPSSI, Psychology, and Society, 1936–1996," *Journal of Social Issues* (Spring 1998): 3.

46. *Southern School News*, September 1963, October 1963; *New York Times*, August 28, 1963, September 13, 1963.

47. *Southern School News*, April 1964, June 1964; *New York Times*, March 7, 1964, April 1, 2, 12, 14, 1964.

48. *Southern School News*, July 1964; *New York Times*, June 19, 1964, October 1, 1964, December 8, 1964.

49. *New York Times,* February 6, 1964; *Southern School News,* March 1965, March 1964; *New York Times,* February 17, 18, 1964; *Southern School News,* March 1965; *New York Times,* February 23, 1964.

50. *Southern School News,* October 1964; *New York Times,* September 4, 1964, September 8, 10, 12, 1964, December 20, 1964, April 2, 1966.

51. Newspapers reported this amounted to 200 to 300 students. *Atlanta Daily World,* October 1, 1965, October 9, 1965; *New York Times,* October 12, 1964, October 13, 1964.

52. *New York Times,* October 12, 1964, October 13, 1964, October 29, 1964.

53. *Atlanta Daily World,* October 28, 1965; *New York Times,* October 29, 1964, January 13, 1966; *Georgia Descriptions in Data, 1987* (Atlanta: Office of Planning and Budget), 15-17.

54. *Atlanta Daily World,* April 11, 1969; *New York Times,* July 10, 1969; *Atlanta Constitution,* August 2, 1969.

55. Quote from David J. Armor, *Forced Justice: School Desegregation and the Law* (New York: Oxford, 1995), 26; *Atlanta Journal,* March 8, 1966.

56. *U.S. v. Jefferson County School Board of Education* 372 F. 2d. 836 (1966); *Green v. County School Board of New Kent County* 391 U.S. 430 (1968); Patterson, *Brown v. Board of Education,* 146: Jack Greenberg, *Crusaders in the Courts* (New York: Basic, 1994), 383.

57. *Alexander v. Holmes Count Board of Education* 396 U.S. 19, 20 (1969).

58. *Southern School News,* February 1965; *New York Times,* February 17, 1964; *Atlanta Journal Constitution,* December 12, 1994.

59. For a general treatment of this topic, see Margaret R. Gladney, "I'll Take My Stand: The Southern Segregation Academy Movement" (Ph.D. dissertation, University of New Mexico, 1974).

60. *Atlanta Journal,* October 30, 1970; *Atlanta Inquirer,* July 18, 1970; *Atlanta Constitution,* July 1, 1970.

61. Grant, *The Way It Was,* 525–26.

62. *Southern School News,* December 1964; *Atlanta Daily World,* September 4, 1965; *New York Times,* April 16, 1966, July 3, 1966; James Patterson, *Brown v. Board of Education: A Civil Rights Milestone and Its Troubled Legacy* (New York: Oxford University Press), 185; Joseph W. Newman, *America's Teachers,* 4th ed. (Boston: Allyn and Bacon, 2002), 282.

63. "Former Georgia Gov. Maddox Dies." CNN.com, June 25, 2005; James F. Cook, *The Governors of Georgia, 1754–1995* (Macon, GA: Mercer University Press, 1995), 283–90.

64. *New York Times,* April 9, 1967; *Atlanta Journal,* April 19, 1967, *New York Times,* August 28, 1967, September 1, 1967, March 2, 1967, September 1, 1967.

65. *New York Times,* December 12, 1968, February 15, 16, 1968, February 17, 1968.

66. *New York Times,* December 14, 1968, February 22, 23, 1969.

67. Vanessa Siddle Walker, *Their Highest Potential* (Chapel Hill: University of North Carolina Press, 1996); *Atlanta Inquirer,* February 18, 1978; Grant, *The Way It Was,* 531.

68. *New York Times,* June 11, 1971, April 21, 1971, September 4, 1971.

69. *New York Times,* February 9, 12, 15, 16, 17, 1972, September 2, 7, 1972.

70. *New York Times,* February 17, 29, 1972, March 18, 1972; Harold Henderson and Gary Roberts, *Georgia Governors in an Age of Change* (Athens: University of Georgia Press, 1988), 239–45; Cook, *The Governors of Georgia,* 295.

71. *Atlanta Constitution,* January 5, 1969; *New York Times,* January 10, 1970.

72. *Atlanta Constitution,* January 12, 1970, January 25, 1970; *New York Times,* January 11, 1970.

73. *Atlanta Constitution,* January 5, 1969, October 30, 1969; *Atlanta Daily World,* February 6, 1970; *Atlanta Constitution,* March 10, 1970.

74. *New York Times,* February 24, 1970; *Atlanta Constitution,* March 12, 1970; *Atlanta Daily World,* April 2, 1970; *Atlanta Constitution,* April 7, 1970.

75. *Atlanta Constitution,* January 5, 1970, January 12, 1970; *Atlanta Daily World,* February 6, 1970.

76. *Atlanta Constitution,* January 12, 1970; *New York Times,* March 22, 1970; *Atlanta Constitution,* March 10, 1970; *Atlanta Daily World,* March 1, 1970.

77. *New York Times,* June 8, 1972, June 9, 1972.

78. Hein, "The Image of a City 'Too Busy to Hate,'" 44.

79. Ecke, *From Ivy Street to Kennedy Center,* 418; Benjamin E. Mays, *Born to Rebel* (Athens: University of Georgia Press, 1971).

80. I am referring to Effective Schools Research (ESR), which began at Harvard University in the late 1960s in response to the highly influential federally commissioned report, *Equality of Educational Opportunity* (1966), also known as the Coleman Report. For a brief history of ESR, see L. W. Lezotte, "School Effectiveness: Reflections and Future Directions," Conference paper presented at the American Educational Research Association Annual Meeting, San Francisco, California, 1986.

81. *New York Times,* February 23, 1970, February 25, 1973; Numan V. Bartley, *The New South, 1945–1980* (Baton Rouge: Louisiana State University Press, 1995), 422.

82. Ronald H. Bayor, *Race and the Shaping of Twentieth-Century Atlanta* (Chapel Hill: University of North Carolina Press, 1996), 247.

83. Benjamin E. Mays, "Why an Atlanta School Suit?" *New South* 5 (September/October 1950): 1–2.

84. Bayor, *Race and the Shaping of Twentieth-Century Atlanta*, 249.

85. *Atlanta Constitution,* January 10, 1970, January 12, 1970, February 20, 1970; *New York Times,* February 25, 1970; *Atlanta Constitution,* March 21, 1970.

86. Bayor, *Race and the Shaping of Twentieth-Century Atlanta*, 249.

87. Baker Motley, *Equal Justice under the Law,* 197.

88. Bayor, *Race and the Shaping of Twentieth-Century Atlanta*, 251; Catherine Freeman, David L. Sjoquist and Benjamin Scafidi, "Racial Segregation in Georgia Public Schools, 1994–2001: Trends, Causes, and Impact on Teacher Quality," Conference paper presented at *The Resegregation of Southern Schools? A Crucial Moment in the History (and the Future) of Public Schooling in America.* Chapel Hill: North Carolina, August 30, 2002.

89. *Atlanta Journal Constitution,* December 11, 1994, May 16, 2004, July 4, 2004; Gary Orfield and Carol Ashkinaze, *The Closing Door: Conservative Policy and Black Opportunity* (Chicago: University of Chicago Press, 1991); Jonathan Kozol, *Savage Inequalities* (New York: HarperCollins, 1991); Jeannie Oakes, *Keeping Track: How Schools Structure Inequality* (New Haven, CT: Yale University Press, 1984); Matthew Landner and Christopher Hammons, "Special but Unequal: Race and Special Education," in *Rethinking Special Education for a New Century,* ed. C. E. Finn Jr., A. J. Rotherham, and C. R. Hokanson Jr. (Washington, DC: Progressive Policy Institute-Thomas B. Fordham Foundation, 2001), 85–110.

The Last Holdout: Mississippi and the *Brown* Decision

1. Charles C. Bolton, *The Hardest Deal of All: The Battle over School Integration in Mississippi, 1870–1980* (Jackson: University Press of Mississippi, 2005), ch. 1; James D. Anderson, *The Education of Blacks in the South, 1860–1935* (Chapel Hill: University of North Carolina Press, 1988).

2. "Public School Enrollment and Expenditures in Six Southern States," September 21, 1944, General Education Board Papers, Early Southern Program: Mississippi, reel 78; Number and Average Salaries of Classroom Teachers, n.d., 1960s?, Volume 378, Records of the Legislature, Record Group 47, Mississippi Department of Archives and History, Jackson (MDAH); and memo from Mr. Dudley to Mr. Current, March 29, 1948, II-B-144, NAACP Papers, National Archives, Washington, DC. While in Vicksburg, Dudley had found that two hundred black children were turned away from the black junior high because of a lack of space, and he heard rumors that as many as two hundred thousand black kids statewide failed to attend classes for the same reason. A complete discussion of the inadequacies of black

education in Mississippi during the first half of the twentieth century can be found in Neil R. McMillen, *Dark Journey: Black Mississippians in the Age of Jim Crow* (Urbana: University of Illinois Press, 1989), ch. 3, and Bolton, *The Hardest Deal of All*, ch. 1 and 2.

3. Charles C. Bolton, "A Mississippi's School Equalization Program, 1945–1954: 'Last Gasp to Try to Maintain a Segregated Educational System,'" *Journal of Southern History* 66 (November 2000): 781–814.

4. Southern Regional Council, *Wanted: An Educated South* (Atlanta: Southern Regional Council, 1947), 20.

5. Catherine M. Jannik, "Gladys Noel Bates: Educator and Activist" (M.A. thesis, University of Southern Mississippi, 1999); A. H. Ramsey to Walter Sillers, March 25, 1953, box 137, Walter Sillers Papers; Bolton, *The Hardest Deal of All*, ch. 2.

6. John Dittmer, *Local People: The Struggle for Civil Rights in Mississippi* (Urbana: University of Illinois Press, 1994), 45–46; Bolton, *The Hardest Deal of All*, 66–67.

7. Bolton, *The Hardest Deal of All*, 66–67, 73–75; Jack E. Davis, *Race against Time: Culture and Separation in Natchez since 1930* (Baton Rouge: Louisiana State University Press, 2001), 158–60; J. P. Coleman, interview by Connie Lynnette Cartledge, October 30, 1981, box 1, J. P. Coleman Collection, Mitchell Memorial Library, Mississippi State University, Starkville.

8. Neil R. McMillen, *The Citizens' Council: Organized Resistance to the Second Reconstruction, 1954–64* (Urbana: University of Illinois Press, 1994); Yasuhiro Katagiri, *The Mississippi State Sovereignty Commission: Civil Rights and States' Rights* (Jackson: University Press of Mississippi, 2001).

9. Bolton, *The Hardest Deal of All*, 61–72; *Southern School News*, November 4, 1954; Friends of Public Schools press release, November 1, 1954, G. W. Owens Papers, MDAH.

10. Kenneth Toler, "Millions Spent to Bring Negro Schools Up to Date," *Memphis Commercial Appeal*, September 11, 1960.

11. Erle Johnston Jr., "The Practical Way to Maintain a Separate School System in Mississippi," box 58, Paul B. Johnson Jr. Papers, McCain Library and Archives, University of Southern Mississippi, Hattiesburg.

12. Bolton, *The Hardest Deal of All*, ch. 3; Entry of July 21, 1959, Jackson Public School Board minutes, MDAH.

13. Gilbert R. Mason with James Patterson Smith, *Beaches, Blood, and Ballots: A Black Doctor's Civil Rights Struggle* (Jackson: University Press of Mississippi, 2000); Winson Hudson and Constance Curry, *Mississippi Harmony: Memoirs of a Freedom Fighter* (New York: Palgrave Macmillan, 2002); "Courts to Be Asked to Open P.S. Here," *Mississippi Free Press*, March 2, 1963.

14. Bolton, *The Hardest Deal of All*, 96–101, 113–15, 150.

15. Gary Orfield, *The Reconstruction of Southern Education: The Schools and the 1964 Civil Rights Act* (New York: Wiley-Interscience, 1969).

16. Orfield, *The Reconstruction of Southern Education;* Statement to Mr. Francis Keppel by Special Committee of Mississippi Association of School Administrators, April 6, 1965, series 29, box 5, John C. Stennis Papers, Congressional and Political Research Center, Mississippi State University, Starkville; Bolton, *The Hardest Deal of All,* ch. 5.

17. Mary Blackmon, interviewed by M. G. Trend, March 16, 1982, transcript, Oral History Collection, Madison County-Canton Public Library, Canton, Mississippi.

18. Kenneth L. Dean, "An Evaulation of School Desegregation in Mississippi," [1966?], NAACP Legal Defense and Educational Fund General Office Files, Southern Civil Rights Litigation Records (SCRLR), reel 161; Dora J. Adams, interviewed by Clarence M. Simmons, March 14, 1970, transcript, Oral History Collection, Mary Holmes College, West Point, Mississippi; FDP WATS Report, September 1, 1965, Mississippi Freedom Democratic Papers, The King Center, Atlanta, Georgia; Marion S. Barry Jr. and Betty Garman, ASNCC: "Special Report on Southern School Desegregation," [1965?], SNCC Papers, 1959–1972, reel 58.

19. Bolton, *The Hardest Deal of All,* ch. 5–6.

20. Armand Derfner to Jerry J. Berman, December 4, 1969, Lawyers Constitutional Defense Committee, SCRLR, reel 79.

21. Bolton, *The Hardest Deal of All,* ch. 6; Memo from Ursula to Mariam, Iris, and Paul, May 9, 1967, *Dian Hudson v. Leake County School Board,* NAACP Legal Defense and Educational Fund, Litigation Files, SCRLR, reel 148.

22. James T. Patterson, *Brown v. Board of Education: A Civil Rights Milestone and Its Troubled Legacy* (New York: Oxford University Press, 2001), 141–55.

23. Mrs. Lana Booker to Mr. Stennis, August 9, 1969, Mr. and Mrs. Rudolph Harrison to Senator Stennis, August 18, 1969, and Mrs. Lavon Wade to Senator Stennis, July 23, 1969, all in series 53, box 2, John C. Stennis Papers.

24. John Stennis to President Nixon, August 11, 1969, box 34, White House Special Files, Staff Members and Office Files: Ehrlichman, Nixon Project, National Archives, Washington, DC; Jack Rosenthal, "Stennis Linked to Desegregation Delay," *New York Times,* September 19, 1969.

25. Luther Munford, "White Flight from Desegregation in Mississippi," *Integrated Education* 11 (May–June 1973): 12–26; Quarterly Report, December 1971, Greater Jackson Area Committee of Mississippi Committee of Public Education, Mississippians for Creative Public Education Records, Tougaloo College Archives, Jackson, Mississippi.

26. Bolton, *The Hardest Deal of All*, ch. 7–8.

27. Ibid.

A State Divided: Implementation of the *Brown* Decision in Florida, 1954–1970

1. See Wali Rashash Kharif, "The Refinement of Racial Segregation in Florida after the Civil War" (Ph.D. dissertation, Florida State University, 1983).

2. See Caroline Emmons, "Not a Single Battle but Rather a Real War: The NAACP and the Fight to Equalize Teachers' Pay in Florida," *Florida Historical Quarterly* 81, no. 4 (Spring 2003): 418–39.

3. Raymond A. Mohl, *South of the South: Jewish Activists and the Civil Rights Movement in Florida, 1945–1960* (Gainesville: University Press of Florida, 2004), 20.

4. See Caroline Emmons, *Flame of Resistance: The NAACP in Florida, 1910–1960* (Ph.D. dissertation, Florida State University, 1998).

5. *Pittsburgh Courier,* January 12, 1952, 1.

6. Mohl, *South of the South,* 77.

7. David Colburn, "Florida's Governors Confront the *Brown* Decision: A Case Study of the Constitutional Politics of School Desegregation, 1954–1970," in *An Uncertain Tradition: Constitutionalism and the History of the South,* ed. Kermit Hall and James Ely Jr. (Athens: University of Georgia Press, 1989), 328.

8. James Button, *Blacks and Social Change: Impact of Civil Rights Movements in Southern Communities* (Princeton, NJ: Princeton University Press, 1989), 69.

9. *Southern School News,* September 3, 1954, 5.

10. Ibid.

11. *The Crisis,* May 1955, 242.

12. Emmons, *Flame of Resistance,* 215.

13. *Southern School News,* October 1, 1954, 6; Colburn, "Florida's Governors Confront the *Brown* Decision," 330.

14. R. Saunders, *1957 Annual Report for the Florida NAACP, Papers of the NAACP,* Part 29, series A, reel 3, ed. John Bracey and August Meier (Bethesda, MD: University Microfilms of America, 1993). Hereafter referred to as NAACP Papers-Edited.

15. *Southern School News,* March 3, 1955, 6.

16. *Southern School News,* June 8, 1955, 3.

17. Richard Kluger, *Simple Justice: The History of Brown v. Board of Education and Black America's Struggle for Equality* (New York: Vintage, 1975), 725.

18. Colburn, "Florida's Governors Confront the *Brown* Decision," 328. According to Colburn, Florida was only one of four states with no integration of any kind in 1954.

19. *Southern School News*, September 1955, 13.

20. *1954 Annual Report from the Southeastern Regional Office of the NAACP. Part II: C224, Papers of the NAACP* (Washington, DC: Library of Congress).

21. Button, *Blacks and Social Change*, 31.

22. *Southern School News*, October 1955, 15.

23. See Mark Tushnet, *The NAACP's Legal Strategy against Segregated Education, 1925–1950* (Chapel Hill: University of North Carolina Press, 1987).

24. Lawrence Dubin, "Virgil Hawkins: A One-Man Civil Rights Movement," *Florida Law Review* 51, 913, accessed via Lexis-Nexis Academic, May/June 2004.

25. *Southern School News*, August 1956, 10. The use of pupil placement laws was common throughout the South as a method of resisting desegregation.

26. *Gibson et al. v. Dade County Board of Public Instruction et al.*, 1956, Dade County, Florida.

27. *Southern School News*, September 1955, 13. See *Papers of the NAACP* (Part 23, series A, reel 10) for materials related to the case. NAACP Papers-Edited.

28. *Southern School News*, March 1959, 3, and November 1955, 11.

29. Mohl, *South of the South*, 194.

30. H. Dixon to W. White, August 21, 1954, A226, Group II. *Papers of the NAACP*. Manuscript Division, Library of Congress, Washington, DC.

31. Ibid.

32. Glenda Rabby, *The Pain and the Promise: The Struggle for Civil Rights in Tallahassee, Florida* (Athens: University of Georgia Press, 1999), 34.

33. FLIC Transcripts, February 4, 1957, S1486, Carton 3. FLIC Records, State Archives of Florida, Tallahassee.

34. Rabby, *The Pain and the Promise*, 212; Emmons, *Flame of Resistance*, 225.

35. FLIC Transcripts, February 4, 1957, S1486, Carton 3. FLIC Records, State Archives of Florida, Tallahassee.

36. FLIC Transcripts, February 25, 1957, S1486, Carton 4. FLIC Records, State Archives of Florida, Tallahassee.

37. Rabby, *The Pain and the Promise*, 71.

38. Ruby Hurley to Lucille Black, November 5, 1957. Part III: C171, Papers of the NAACP. Library of Congress, Washington, DC.

39. *Southern School News*, December 1957, 12.

40. *Holland v. Board of Public Instruction of Palm Beach County et al.*

41. *Southern School News,* December 1959, 11.

42. Rabby, *The Pain and the Promise,* 107.

43. *Southern School News,* June 1957, 11.

44. Colburn, "Florida's Governors Confront the *Brown* Decision," 341.

45. *Southern School News,* May 1961, 6.

46. *Southern School News,* September 1961, 7.

47. *New York Times,* August 18, 1961, 18.

48. *Southern School News,* November 1961, 10.

49. Rabby, *The Pain and the Promise,* 226.

50. *Southern School News,* December 1961, 3.

51. *Southern School News*l, September 1962, 1.

52. *Southern School News,* January 1963, 10.

53. Rabby, *The Pain and the Promise,* 228.

54. Colburn, "Florida's Governors Confront the *Brown* Decision," 341.

55. Ibid., 342.

56. Ibid., 343.

57. *Southern School News,* August 1964, 7.

58. Colburn, "Florida's Governors Confront the *Brown* Decision," 34.

59. Burns served only a two-year term as the Florida Constitution had been changed so that gubernatorial elections did not coincide with presidential election years.

60. *Southern School News,* February 1965, 3.

61. *Southern School News,* May 1965, 6.

62. Colburn, "Florida's Governors Confront the *Brown* Decision," 343–44.

63. Ibid., 345.

64. Letter from Claude Kirk to attorneys for the County School Board of Leon County, 7/16/70. Papers of Claude Kirk, S926, box 9. Florida State Archives, Tallahassee.

65. Evelyn Rupp, "Investigation of Media Coverage of a Local Crisis: The Courts, the Orange County School Board and the Community" (M.A. thesis, University of Central Florida, 1974), 21.

66. Ibid., 22.

67. Marjorie Arnaud, Comments at the University of South Florida Conference on the Civil Rights Movement in Florida, June 5, 2004, St. Petersburg, Florida.

68. Federal Education Progress Reports, S1129, box 1. Florida State Archives, Tallahassee.

69. Marvin Davies, 1968 Annual Report of the Florida NAACP, Part 29, series A, reel 3. NAACP Papers-Edited.

70. Colburn, "Florida's Governors Confront the *Brown* Decision," 346; *New York Times,* April 7, 1970, 28.

71. Papers of Claude Kirk, S929, RG102, box 15. Florida State Archives, Tallahassee.

72. Colburn, "Florida's Governors Confront the *Brown* Decision," 347.

73. Ibid.

74. *New York Times,* January 22, 1971, 39.

75. John Yun and Sean Reardon, "Trends in Public School Segregation in the South, 1987–2000." Paper Presented at the Resegregation of Public School Conference, University of North Carolina, Chapel Hill, August 2002.

76. "Desegregating Florida's Schools: The *Brown* Decision and Its Legacy in the Sunshine State." Panel discussion at the *Civil Rights Movement in Florida Conference.* University of South Florida-St. Petersburg, June 2004.

Promises of *Brown*: Desegregating Education in Delaware, 1950–1968

1. *Parker v. University of Delaware,* 75 A. 2d 225 (Del. Ch. 1950).

2. Louis L. Reading, "Desegregation in Higher Education in Delaware," *Journal of Negro Education* 27 (November 1958): 254–55.

3. *Belton v. Gebhart,* 87 A. 2d 862 (Del. Ch. 1952); *Belton v. Gebhart,* 91 A. 2d 137 (Del. 1952); Doll Test handwritten notes, Kenneth Clark Papers, Manuscripts Division, Library of Congress, Washington, DC.

4. *Brown v. Board of Education I,* 347 U.S. 483 (1954); *Brown v. Board of Education II,* 349 U.S. 294 (1955).

5. Bradley Skelcher, *African American Education in Delaware* (Wilmington: Heritage Press of Delaware, 1999), 109; James D. Anderson, *The Education of Blacks in the South, 1860–1935* (Chapel Hill: University of North Carolina Press, 1988), 21; *Debates and Proceedings of the Constitutional Convention of the State of Delaware, Volume II, 1897* (Dover: Supreme Court of the State of Delaware, 1959), 1283–84; Richard Kluger, *Simple Justice* (New York: Vintage Books, 1977; 2004 Reprint), see sections on Delaware.

6. Attorney General Files, School Segregation Records, 1952–1954, Delaware Public Archive, Dover, Delaware.

7. Ibid.

8. James T. Patterson, *Brown v. Board of Education: A Civil Rights Milestone and Its Troubled Legacy* (New York: Oxford University Press, 2001), 221–22.

9. Michael J. Klarman, *From Jim Crow to Civil Rights: The Supreme Court and the Struggle for Racial Equality* (New York: Oxford University Press, 2004), 193.

10. Klarman, *From Jim Crow to Civil Rights,* 193.

11. Frederic Wertham, "Psychiatric Observations on Abolition of School Segregation," *Journal of Educational Sociology* 26 (March 1953).

12. Wertham, "Psychiatric Observations."

13. William Peters, "The Schools That Broke the Color Line," *Red Book Magazine* (October 1954).

14. Selwyn James, "The Town That Surrendered to Hate," *Red Book Magazine* (April 1955); Klarman, *From Jim Crow to Civil Rights,* 346.

15. Ed Kee, "The *Brown* Decision and Milford, Delaware, 1954–1965," *Delaware History* (Fall–Winter 1997): 205–44; Kenneth Clark Observations of Milford, Kenneth Clark Papers, Manuscript Division, Library of Congress, Washington, DC.

16. Ed Kee, "The *Brown* Decision and Milford, Delaware, 1954–1965," *Delaware History* (Fall–Winter 1997–1998): 208–10.

17. Attorney General Files, Delaware Public Archive, Dover, Delaware.

18. Louis L. Redding to J. Caleb Boggs, Governor of Delaware, Redding Telegraph (September 24, 1954), RG 1302.7, Delaware Public Archive; Clark Observations.

19. Selwyn James, "Town That Surrendered to Hate," *Red Book Magazine* (April 1955): 35.

20. June Shagaloff, NAACP Field Representative, to NAACP Headquarters in Washington, DC. November 1954, NAACP Files, Manuscript Division, Library of Congress, Washington, DC.

21. Derrick Bell, *Silent Covenants: Brown v. Board of Education and the Unfulfilled Hopes for Racial Reform* (New York: Oxford University Press, 2004), 40–68; "Delaware Hears Nixon Fight Bias," *New York Times,* October 1, 1954.

22. "Delaware Hears Nixon Fight Bias"; Jack Beach, "Attendance Increases at Milford School: Four Per Cent Hike Is Noted This Morning; Boycott Lincoln School," *Delaware State News,* September 28, 1954.

23. U.S. Attorney General, *Amicus Curai* brief, *Brown v. Board of Education* (1952).

24. Charles J. Ogletree Jr., *All Deliberate Speed: Reflections for the First Half-Century of Brown v. Board of Education* (New York: W. W. Norton, 2004), 307.

25. Clark Observations; State Board of Education, *Suggested Policies for Opening of School* (August 19, 1954), Delaware Board of Education Files, Public Archive of Delaware, Dover.

26. "Move to Stop Spread of School Terror: Dover Board Member Calls Meet Tonight," *Delaware State News,* October 1, 1954; Clark Observations; George R. Miller, Superintendent of Public Instruction, to Students, ten black students at Milford High School, October 2, 1954, NAACP Papers, Manuscript Division, Library of Congress, Washington, DC.

27. "Expect Negro Students Back at Milford High"; Press Release, "Expect Negro Students Back at Milford High," October 14, 1956, NAACP Papers, Manuscript Division, Library of Congress, Washington, DC.

28. "Court Bans Negro Pupils in Milford: Delaware High Tribunal Says Students Have No Immediate Legal Rights," *Delaware State News,* February 8, 1955.

29. John W. Flamer, NAACP Field Secretary, "Summary of the Milford Incident," September 17–October 4, 1954, NAACP Papers, Manuscript Division, Library of Congress, Washington, DC.

30. Clark Papers, Manuscript Division, Library of Congress, Washington, DC; John P. Jackson Jr., *Social Scientists for Social Justice: Making the Case against Segregation* (New York: New York University Press), 199–203.

31. Kenneth Clark, "Statement to be issued in connection with the situation in Milford, Delaware, schools," September 27, 1954, Clark Papers, Manuscript Division, Library of Congress, Washington, DC.

32. "Governor Blamed for Setback in Delaware," *Los Angeles Herald,* October 14, 1954.

33. Kenneth Clark, "Suggested Statement on Milford, Delaware," September 27, 1954, Clark Papers, Manuscript Division, Library of Congress, Washington, DC.

34. Flamer, "Summary of the Milford Incident"; "Four Towns Plan Integration Poll: Georgetown, Harrington, Milford and Greenwood Citizens Vote Saturday," *Delaware State News,* November 18, 1954; "Five Towns Favor Segregation: Public Opinion Polls Show Strong Sentiment Opposing Integration," *Delaware State News,* November 22, 1954: "Governor Plans Human Relations Commission for Integration Study," *Delaware State News,* November 29, 1954.

35. "Fifteen Schools in State to Integrate This Year," *Delaware State News,* August 19, 1955; John Flamer, NAACP Field Secretary, to Gloster B. Current, Director of NAACP Branches, September 30, 1954, NAACP Papers, Manuscript Division, Library of Congress, Washington, DC; June Shagaloff, NAACP Field Representative, to Thurgood Marshall, December 20, 1954, NAACP Papers, Manuscript Division, Library of Congress, Washington, DC.

36. H. Albert Young, "State Board of Education Policies regarding Desegregation of Schools of the State," June 11, 1954, Attorney General Files, State Public Archive, Dover, Delaware.

37. "Supreme Court Begins Segregation Hearings," *Delaware State News,* April 11, 1955; "Delaware Asks Time to End Racial Segregation in State School System," *Delaware State News,* April 12, 1955; Irving Morris, "The Role of Delaware Lawyers in the Desegregation of Delaware's Public Schools: A Memoir," *Widener Law Symposium Journal* 9 (2002): 16; "States Request Additional Time to Integrate," *Delaware State News,* April 13, 1955.

38. "Millsboro Will Keep Segregation; Cites Danger," *Delaware State News,* August 18, 1955.

39. Morris, "The Role of Delaware Lawyers," 16.

40. *Brown II,* 349 U.S., 297; "Court Asks Segregation End as Soon as

Locally Feasible," *Delaware State News*, May 31, 1955; "State Likely to Act Cautiously on Integration," *Delaware State News*, June 1, 1955; "Delaware Asks Time to End Racial Segregation in State School System," *Delaware State News*, April 12, 1955; Peters, "The Schools That Broke the Color Line"; Kenneth Clark, *Daedalus*, Drafts, Undated, The Papers of Kenneth B. Clark, Manuscript Division, Library of Congress, Washington, DC; Leland Ware, "Setting the Stage for *Brown*: The Development and Implementation of the NAACP's School Desegregation Campaign, 1930–1950," *Mercer Law Review* 52 (Winter 2001): 672; Robert J. Cottrol, Raymond T. Diamond, and Leland B. Ware, *Brown v. Board of Education: Caste, Culture, and the Constitution* (Lawrence: University Press of Kansas, 2003), 211; "Integration Not Political Issue—Williams: Delaware Senator Says Candidates Are Helpless to Alter Court Decision," *Delaware State News*, October 7, 1954.

41. Ogletree Jr., *All Deliberate Speed*, 307.

42. Ibid., 307.

43. "Never Before Has Politics Been Brought into a City Election," *Delaware State News*, January 11, 1956.

44. "Executive Body of Milford PTA Resigns *En Masse*," *Delaware State News*, March 12, 1956; "Charge against Cobbs Was Withdrawn Today," *Delaware State News*, March 7, 1955; "Cobbs Declines to Consider Staying in Milford School," *Delaware State News*, March 16, 1955.

45. "Milton Meeting Set Tonight to Fight Integration," *Delaware State News*, June 28, 1956.

46. Nancy Gates, "Milton Segregation Rally Asks Board to Resign," *Delaware State News*, June 29, 1956.

47. Gates, "Milton Segregation."

48. "Milford Board Fires Student Council Advisor," *Delaware State News*, May 2, 1956.

49. Jack Greenberg, *Crusaders in the Courts: How a Dedicated Band of Lawyers Fought for the Civil Rights Revolution* (New York: Basic Books, 1994), 214.

50. "Seaford Ends Athletic Relations with Dover High," *Delaware State News*, March 16, 1956; "State Board Rejects Prompt Desegregation for Eight More Schools," *Delaware State News*, March 16, 1956.

51. Kenneth Clark, "Psychological Aspects of Desegregation: An Evaluation of Social Science Predictions, Presidential Address Society for the Psychological Study of Social Issues," *Chicago* (September 5, 1960), 7, Kenneth Clark Papers, Manuscript Division, Library of Congress, Washington, DC.

52. Steve J. Crossland, "Brown's Companions: Briggs, Belton, and Davis," *Washburn Law Journal* 43, no. 2 (Winter 2004): 411.

53. Morris, "The Role of Delaware Lawyers," 17–20.

54. *Evans, et al. v. Buchanan, et al.* 522.Dela 1 (1957); Morris, "The Role of Delaware Lawyers," 20.

55. Raymond Wolters, *The Burden of Brown: Thirty Years of School Desegregation* (Knoxville: University of Tennessee Press, 1984), 201.

56. Morris, "The Role of Delaware Lawyers," 21–23; Crossland, "Brown's Companions," 411; *Staten, et al. v. Buchanan, et al.* (522.Dela 8).

57. *Evans v. Ennis,* 281 F. 2d 385, 389 (3d Cir. 1960).

58. Morris, "The Role of Delaware Lawyers," 21–23; Wolters, *The Burden of Brown,* 202–3.

59. *Green v. New Kent County School Board, Virginia,* 391 U.S. 430 (1968).

60. *Griffin v. County School Board of Prince Edward County,* 377 U.S. 218 (1964).

61. U.S. Civil Rights Act of 1965 (PL 88–352).

62. Interview with Howard Row, April 1999; Elementary and Secondary Education Act 20 U.S.C. § 6301 et seq. (1965).

63. Richard P. Gousha, "A Constructive Criticism of Guidelines," Unpublished Report, Undated, Department of Public Instruction Files, Public Archives of Delaware, Dover; Interview with Howard Row, April 1999; Letter to Eleanor Tucker, President of William Henry High School Board, November 9, 1965.

64. Gousha, "A Construction Criticism."

65. *Green v. New Kent County School Board, Virginia,* 391 U.S. 430 (1968).

66. U.S. Commission on Civil Right, *Survey of School Desegregation in the Southern and Border States, 1965–1966,* quoted in *Green v. New Kent County,* 391 U.S. (1968), footnote 5.

67. Educational Advancement Act, 14 Del. C. 1001.2 (1968).

68. Ibid.; "Carper Looks Forward to Reopening Export Markets," *Delmarva Farmer Newspaper,* February 17, 2005.

69. Bureau of the Census, *City of Wilmington,* U.S. Department of Commerce (Washington, DC: U.S. Government Printing Office, 1960–1970).

70. *Buchanan v. Evans,* 439 U.S. 1360 (1978), footnote 5.

71. *Buchanan v. Evans,* 439 U.S. 1360 (1978).

72. Ware, "Setting the Stage for *Brown,*" 672; Cottrol, Diamond, and Ware, *Brown v. Board of Education,* 211.

73. Greenberg, *Crusaders in the Courts,* 509–12.

Border State Ebb and Flow: School Desegregation in Missouri, 1954–1999

1. *Missouri ex rel. Gaines v. Canada,* 305 U.S. 337 (1938).

2. *Shelley v. Kraemer,* 334 U.S. 1 (1948).

3. United States Bureau of the Census, *U.S. Census of Population: 1950,* vol. II, *Characteristics of the Population,* Part 25, Missouri (Washington, DC: U.S. Government Printing Office, 1952): Table 13.

4. *Missouri Constitution,* art. 9, sec. 1; *Revised Statutes of the State of Missouri, 1949,* sec. 163.130.

5. Gunnar Myrdal, *An American Dilemma: The Negro Problem and Modern Democracy,* 2d ed. (New York: Harper and Row, 1962), 338–39; Jessie Parkhurst Guzman and Lewis W. Jones, eds., *The Negro Yearbook, 1952,* 11th ed. (New York: Wise and Co., 1952), 201–16; Alethea H. Washington, "The Availability of Education for Negroes in the Elementary School," *Journal of Negro Education* 16, no. 3 (Summer 1947): 439–49.

6. Arthur Benson, "School Segregation and Desegregation in Kansas City, Missouri," unpublished manuscript. Benson and Associates, Kansas City, Missouri.

7. Myrdal, *An American Dilemma,* 1263; Guzman and Jones, eds., *The Negro Yearbook, 1952,* 201–16; Hubert Wheeler, State Commissioner of Education, *100th Report of the Public Schools of the State of Missouri for the School Year Ending June 30, 1949* (Jefferson City, MO: Mid-State Printing, 1949), 281, 305, 333, 361, 382; Office of the Superintendent, *Statistical Data for the Public Schools of Kansas City, Missouri, 1946–47,* 60–72; *Hobby v. Disman, Transcript of the Record on Appeal of the Relators, From the Circuit Court of Jackson County, Missouri, Number 3, Judge Thomas J. Seehorn, Presiding,* 129–44.

8. Alvin W. Rose, "The Impending Crisis," *Antioch Review* 14, no. 4 (December 1954): 421–30; Reid E. Jackson, "The Development and Character of Permissive and Partly Segregated Schools," *Journal of Negro Education* 15, no. 3 (Summer 1947): 301–10; Leon Jones, *From Brown to Boston: Desegregation in Education, 1954–1974,* 2 vols. (Metuchen, NJ: Scarecrow Press, 1979), 1–11; Anthony Lewis, *Portrait of a Decade: The Second American Revolution* (New York: Random House, 1964), 15–31.

9. *Kansas City Star,* May 17, 1954; May 24, 1954.

10. Ibid., June 3, 1954.

11. Dalton to Ray Joslyn, President of Kansas City Board of Education, June 30, 1954, Integration File, KCMSD Archives.

12. George D. Brantley, "Present Status of Integration in the Public Schools of Missouri," *Journal of Negro Education* 24, no. 3 (Summer 1955): 293–309; Albert P. Marshall, "Racial Integration in Missouri," *Journal of Negro Education* 25, no. 3 (Summer 1956): 289–98; Monroe Billington, "Public School Integration in Missouri, 1954–64," *Journal of Negro Education* 33, no. 3 (Summer 1964): 252–62.

13. Brantley, "Present Status of Integration in the Public Schools of Missouri," 302.

14. *Missouri Schools,* November 1954, 8, quoted in Brantley, "Present Status of Integration in the Public Schools of Missouri," 302.

15. *Time Magazine* 66, no. 12 (September 19, 1955), 25.

16. Brantley, "Present Status of Integration in the Public Schools of Missouri," 307.

17. David Henderson, *Integration in Missouri Public Schools: Faculty and Students Twenty Years after Brown* (Jefferson City: Missouri Commission on Human Rights, 1974), 33–34.

18. *Brooks, et al. v. School District of Moberly, et al.* 267 F. 2d 733 (8th Cir. 1959).

19. Henderson, *Integration in Missouri Public Schools,* 30–31.

20. Ibid., 29–41, 55–57, Appendix A.

21. Ibid., 36–41.

22. Benjamin Muse, *Ten Years of Prelude: The Story of Integration since the Supreme Court's 1954 Decision* (New York: Viking, 1964), 33.

23. Ibid., 20–23, 30–37; *Kansas City Times,* June 4, 1954; Preston Valien, "The Desegregation Decision—One Year Afterward—A Critical Summary," *Journal of Negro Education* 24, no. 3 (Summer 1955): 388–96; C. H. Parrish, "Desegregation in Public Education—A Critical Summary," *Journal of Negro Education* 24, no. 3 (Summer 1955): 382–87.

24. Brantley, "Present Status of Integration in the Public Schools of Missouri," 298–300, 304–6.

25. KCMSD, *Board of Education Meeting Minutes,* May 20, 1954, Doc. No. 250319; June 3, 1954, Doc. No. 252604, 252610.

26. Kansas City, Missouri School District (KCMSD), "Policies for the Transition from System of Segregated Schools to a Desegregated School System," March 3, 1955, Desegregation Policy for Transition File, KCMSD Archives; Missouri Advisory Committee to the U.S. Commission on Civil Rights, *School Desegregation in the St. Louis and Kansas City Areas: Metropolitan Interdistrict Options* (Washington, DC: U.S. Commission on Civil Rights, 1981), 16–17.

27. Office of the Superintendent, "Desegregation Report, 1955," Integrated Pupils, Schools and Faculties File, KCMSD Archives; KCMSD, "Enrollment by School: 1954–55—1983–84," Integrated Pupils, Schools and Faculties File, KCMSD Archives.

28. KCMSD Research Department, "Integration Data: Actual Occurrence Compared with Predicted Occurrence," Integration Data File, KCMSD Archives; KCMSD, "Enrollment by School."

29. Henderson, *Integration in Missouri Public Schools,* 45.

30. Daniel J. Monti, *A Semblance of Justice: St. Louis School Desegregation and Order in Urban America* (Columbia: University of Missouri Press, 1985), 130–32; KCMSD, *Board of Education Meeting*

Minutes, October 18, 1964, Doc. No. 299737; *Kansas City Times,* October 29, 1964.

31. KCMSD, "Enrollment by School"; *Kansas City Times,* August 8, 1963.

32. United States Bureau of the Census, *U.S. Census of Population: 1960,* Vol. I, *Characteristics of the Population,* Part 27, Missouri (Washington, DC: U.S. Government Printing Office, 1963): Tables 17, 32; *U.S. Census of Population: 1970,* Vol. I, *Characteristics of the Population,* Part 27, Missouri (Washington, DC: U.S. Government Printing Office, 1973): Tables 21, 91; *U.S. Census of Population: 1980,* Vol. I, *Characteristics of the Population,* Part 27, Missouri (Washington, DC: U.S. Government Printing Office, 1982): Table 15; KCMSD, "Enrollment by School."

33. Bureau of the Census, *Census Tracts: Kansas City SMSA, 1950,* Table 1; *Census Tracts: Kansas City SMSA, 1960,* Table P-1; *Census Tracts: Kansas City SMSA, 1970,* Table P-1; *Census Tracts: Kansas City SMSA, 1980,* Table P-7; *Census Tracts: St. Louis SMSA, 1950,* Table 1; *Census Tracts: St. Louis SMSA, 1960,* Table P-1; *Census Tracts: St. Louis SMSA, 1970,* Table P-1; *Census Tracts: St. Louis SMSA, 1980,* Table P-7.

34. KCMSD, "Enrollment by School"; Henderson, *Integration in Missouri Public Schools,* Appendix C.

35. J. Glenn Travis, "Historic Report," unpublished manuscript, 112–15, KCMSD Archives.

36. KCMSD, "Enrollment by School"; Henderson, *Integration in Missouri Public Schools,* Appendix A.

37. *Green v. County School Board of New Kent County,* 391 U.S. 430 (1968); *Alexander v. Holmes County Board of Education,* 396 U.S. 19 (1969); *Swann v. Charlotte-Mecklenberg Board of Education,* 402 U.S. 1 (1971).

38. "Administrative Proceedings in the Department of Health, Education and Welfare, Proceedings Under Title VI of the Civil Rights Act of 1964, Kansas City, Missouri School District and Missouri State Department of Education, Respondents, Decision of Administrative Law Judge Rollie D. Thedford," HEW Administrative Decision File, KCMSD Archives.

39. KCMSD, "Plan 6-C," Plan 6-C File, KCMSD Archives.

40. James Hazlett, "Concepts for Changing Times," Hazlett Concepts File, KCMSD Archives; Benson, "School Segregation and Desegregation in Kansas City, Missouri."

41. Missouri School District Reorganization Commission (Spainhower Commission), "Equal Treatment to Equals: A New Structure for Public Schools in the Kansas City and St. Louis Metropolitan Areas," June 1969, Spainhower Report File, KCMSD Archives.

42. KCMSD, "Enrollment by School."

43. *School District of Kansas City, Missouri v. State of Missouri et al.* 438 F. Supp. 830 (W.D. Mo. 1977).

44. *Jenkins v. Missouri* 593 F. Supp. 1485 (W.D. Mo. 1984); *Jenkins v. Missouri* 639 F. Supp. 19 (1985); *Jenkins v. Missouri,* unreported slip opinion, November 12, 1986; *Jenkins v. Missouri* 855 F. 2d 1295 (8th Cir. 1988); *Jenkins v. Missouri* 672 F. Supp. 400 (W.D. Mo. 1987).

45. *Jenkins* 672 F. Supp. 400 (W.D. Mo. 1987).

46. *Missouri v. Jenkins* 491 U.S. 274 (1989); *Missouri v. Jenkins* 495 U.S. 33 (1990); *Missouri v. Jenkins* 515 U.S. 70 (1995).

47. Gary Orfield and Susan Eaton, *Dismantling Desegregation: The Quiet Reversal of Brown v. Board of Education* (New York: New Press, 1996).

48. *Kansas City Star,* November 17, 1999.

49. Monti, *A Semblance of Justice,* 132–35.

50. *Adams v. United States* 620 F. 2d 1277 (8th Cir. 1980), cert. denied, 449 U.S. 826 (1980); William H. Freivogel, "St. Louis: Desegregation and School Choice in the Land of Dred Scott," in Century Foundation Task Force on the Common School, *Divided We Fail: Coming Together through Public School Choice* (New York: Century Foundation Press, 2002): 209–35.

51. Freivogel, "St. Louis: Desegregation and School Choice in the Land of Dred Scott," 211–15; *"Liddell v. Missouri,"* in Jones-Wilson et al. (eds.), *Encyclopedia of African-American Education* (Westport, CT: Greenwood Press, 1996), 262–65.

52. *Liddell v. State of Missouri* 567 F. Supp. 1037 (E.D. Mo. 1983); *Liddell v. State of Missouri* 717 F. 2d 1180 (8th Cir. 1983).

53. Freivogel, "St. Louis: Desegregation and School Choice in the Land of Dred Scott," 211–15.

54. Monti, *A Semblance of Justice,* 131–35.

55. *Adams v. United States* 620 F. 2d 1277 (8th Cir. 1980).

56. *Board of Education of Oklahoma City v. Dowell* 498 U.S. 237 (1991); *Freeman v. Pitts* 503 U.S. 467 (1992).

The Complexity of School Desegregation in the Borderland: The Case of Indiana

1. Gordon Parks, *The Learning Tree* (New York: Fawcett Books, 1963), 20.

2. For a broader discussion of midwestern racial attitudes at mid-nineteenth century, see V. Jacque Voegeli, *Free but Not Equal: The Midwest and the Negro during the Civil War* (Chicago: University of Chicago Press, 1967).

3. Leon Litwack, *North of Slavery: The Negro in the Free States, 1790–1860* (Chicago: University of Chicago Press, 1961), 114–15.

4. Emma Lou Thornbrough, *The Negro in Indiana before 1900: A Study of a Minority* (reprint, Bloomington: Indiana University Press, 1993), 167. After the passage of the Fourteenth Amendment to the Constitution in 1866, five states "outside the old Confederacy either directly or by implication

excluded colored children entirely from their public schools (Delaware, Indiana, Illinois, Kentucky, and Maryland). Richard Kluger, *Simple Justice: The History of Brown v. Board of Education and Black America's Struggle for Equality* (New York: Vintage Books, 1977), 633–34.

5. Maureen A. Reynolds, "The Challenge of Racial Equality," in *Hoosier Schools Past and Present,* ed. William J. Reese (Bloomington: Indiana University Press, 1998), 174.

6. Ibid., 175–76.

7. Emma Lou Thornbrough, *Indiana Blacks in the Twentieth Century,* edited and with a final chapter by Lana Ruegamer (Bloomington: Indiana University Press, 2000), 48. According to Voegeli, "Except for the South, the Middle West—Ohio, Indiana, Illinois, Iowa, Michigan, Wisconsin, and Minnesota—was the region most firmly committed to white supremacy" (*Free but Not Equal,* 1).

8. Thornbrough, *The Negro in Indiana before 1900,* 140.

9. Ibid., 141.

10. Ibid., 141–42.

11. Ibid., 142.

12. Ibid., 142.

13. Ibid., 145.

14. Women's History Moment [Roselyn Comer Richardson]. *The Bridge* 11 (2) Indiana Historical Society (Indianapolis, Indiana, March/April 2005), 5.

15. Thornbrough and Ruegamer, *Indiana Blacks in the Twentieth Century,* 145.

16. Indiana Laws (1949), 604–7.

17. Ibid., 604–7.

18. Thornbrough and Ruegamer, *Indiana Blacks in the Twentieth Century,* 150.

19. Ibid., 150.

20. Reynolds, "The Challenge of Racial Equality," 181. See also Ronald D. Cohen, *Children of the Mill: Schooling and Society in Gary, Indiana, 1906–1960* (New York: Routledge Falmer, 2002), 232–34.

21. Thornbrough and Ruegamer, *Indiana Blacks in the Twentieth Century,* 154.

22. Richard B. Pierce, *Polite Protest: The Political Economy of Race in Indianapolis, 1920–1970* (Bloomington: Indiana University Press, 2005), 127. For a more specific study of Indianapolis schooling, see also Eric R. Jackson, "The Endless Journey: The Black Struggle for Quality Public Schools in Indianapolis, Indiana, 1900–1949" (Ed.D. dissertation, University of Cincinnati, 2000).

23. Lynn Ford, "Crispus Attucks High School: Despite Protests, City

Created All-Black School," *Indianapolis Star.* Retrieved August 31, 2004, from <http://www2.indystar.com/library/factfiles/>.

24. Thornbrough and Ruegamer, *Indiana Blacks in the Twentieth Century,* 155.

25. James T. Patterson, *Brown v. Board of Education: A Civil Rights Milestone and Its Troubled Legacy* (Oxford: Oxford University Press, 2001), 155–56.

26. *United States v. Board of School Commissioners, Indianapolis, Indiana,* 332 D. Supp. 655–60, 680.

27. Pierce, *Polite Protest,* 112.

28. Ibid., 113.

29. Emma Lou Thornbrough, "The Indianapolis School Busing Case," in *We the People: Indiana and the United States Constitution,* ed. Patrick J. Furlong et al. (Indianapolis: Indiana Historical Society, 1987), 79.

30. Ibid., 80.

31. Pierce, *Polite Protest,* 54.

32. Frank D. Aquila, "U.S. Board of School Commissioners, Indianapolis: A Case in Point," in *School Desegregation: A Model at Work,* ed. Frank D. Aquila (Bloomington: Indiana University School of Education, 1978), 110.

33. Reynolds, "The Challenge of Racial Equality," 186; Thornbrough and Ruegamer, *Indiana Blacks in the Twentieth Century,* 156.

34. Aquila, "U.S. Board of School Commissioners, Indianapolis," 111.

35. Thornbrough and Ruegamer, *Indiana Blacks in the Twentieth Century,* 158.

36. Patterson, *Brown v. Board of Education,* 178–82.

37. Rob Schneider, "Desegregation Order Transformed IPS," *Indianapolis Star,* December 28, 1999. Retrieved from <http://www2.indystar.com/library/factfiles/>.

38. Aquila, "U.S. Board of School Commissioners, Indianapolis," 108.

39. Thornbrough and Ruegamer, *Indiana Blacks in the Twentieth Century,* 160.

40. Ibid., 160.

41. Ibid., 160–61.

42. Ibid., 161.

43. *Banks v. Muncie Community Schools,* 433 F. 2d 292 (7th Cir. 1970)

44. Ibid., 293–94.

45. Ibid., 293–95.

46. Hurley C. Goodall, "A Chronological History of the Muncie Southside Racial Outbreak That Occurred on March 6, 1968, Recorded by Hurley C. Goodall, Chair of the Muncie Human Rights Commission Education Committee," in Hurley C. Goodall, *The Other Side of Town in Middletown* (Muncie: Center for Middletown Studies, 1994), 167. See also Hurley Goodall

and J. Paul Mitchell, *A History of Negroes in Muncie* (Muncie: Ball State University, 1976); Taylor A. Marrow III, *Reconciling the Past: A Brief History of Race Relations in Muncie, 1827–2004* (Muncie: TEAMwork for Quality Living, 2004).

47. *Banks v. Muncie Community Schools*, 433 F. 2d 292 (7th Cir. 1970); Indiana State Advisory Committee to the U.S. Commission on Civil Rights, *Student Friction and Racial Unrest at Southside High School, Muncie, Indiana* (April 1968), 3, 10–12.

48. Thornbrough and Ruegamer, *Indiana Blacks in the Twentieth Century*, 4.

49. Reynolds, "The Challenge of Racial Equality," 173–74.

50. Carl F. Kaestle, *Pillars of the Republic: Common Schools and American Society, 1780–1860* (New York: Hill and Wang, 1983), 183.

Northern Desegregation and the Racial Politics of Magnet Schools in Milwaukee, Wisconsin

1. Richard Kluger, *Simple Justice: The History of Brown v. Board of Education and Black America's Struggle for Equality* (New York: Vintage, 1975), 768, 770–72, 777.

2. *Roberts v. City of Boston*, 5 Cushing Reports 198 (1849); J. Morgan Kousser, *Dead End: The Development of Nineteenth-Century Litigation on Racial Discrimination in Schools* (New York: Oxford University Press, 1986); Davison M. Douglas, "The Limits of Law in Accomplishing Racial Change: School Segregation in the Pre-*Brown* North," *UCLA Law Review* 44 (February 1997): 685.

3. Douglas, "The Limits of Law," 719–31. See also Davison M. Douglas, *Law and Culture: The Desegregation of Northern Schools, 1865–1954* (Unpublished book manuscript, 2004.)

4. Adina Back, "Up South in New York: The 1950s School Desegregation Struggles" (Ph.D. thesis, New York University, 1997); Clarence Taylor, *Knocking at Our Own Door: Milton A. Galamison and the Struggle to Integrate New York City Schools* (New York: Columbia University Press, 1997); "De Facto Segregation in the Chicago Public Schools," *The Crisis* (November 1957): 563.

5. *Taylor v. Board of Education of New Rochelle*, 191 F. Supp. 181 (1961); Will Maslow, "De Facto Public School Segregation," *Villanova Law Review* 6 (Spring 1961): 353–76; *The Crisis* (August–September 1961): 403; (August–September 1962): 384.

6. Robert Carter, *A Matter of Law: A Memoir of Struggle in the Cause of Equal Rights* (New York: New Press, 2005), 170; June Shagaloff, "A Review of Public School Desegregation in the North and West," *Journal of*

Educational Sociology 36 (February 1963): 292–96.

7. Jack Dougherty, *More Than One Struggle: The Evolution of Black School Reform in Milwaukee* (Chapel Hill: University of North Carolina Press, 2004), 74–75, 80–81.

8. Ibid., ch. 1.

9. Ibid., ch. 3; Doris Peyser Slesinger and Eugene Howard Grigsby, *African Americans in Wisconsin: A Statistical Overview, Population Series,* 90–6 (Madison, WI: Applied Population Laboratory, University of Wisconsin-Madison/Extension, 1997), 2–6; William F. Thompson, *The History of Wisconsin: Volume 6, Continuity and Change, 1940–1965* (Madison, WI: State Historical Society, 1988), 306–7.

10. *Milwaukee Journal,* July 9, July 12, 1963.

11. "Report of the Education Committee of the Wisconsin NAACP," 1963, box 96, folder 9, Lloyd Barbee Papers, Milwaukee Urban Archives, University of Wisconsin-Milwaukee Library; Doris Peyser Slesinger and Eugene Howard Grigsby, *African Americans in Wisconsin: A Statistical Overview, Population Series,* 90–6 (Madison, WI: Applied Population Laboratory, University of Wisconsin-Madison/Extension, 1997).

12. "History of Student Bussing Practices, 1949–1966," box 203, folder 8, Lloyd Barbee Papers; *Milwaukee Star,* July 27, 1963, February 15, 1964; *Milwaukee Weekly Post,* October 23, 1963.

13. Dougherty, *More Than One Struggle,* ch. 5.

14. Lloyd Barbee to HEW Secretary Anthony Celebrezze, July 7, 1965, box 196, folder 14, Lloyd Barbee Papers; "Rights Probe by US Seen for Schools Here," *Milwaukee Journal,* July 8, 1965; Gary Orfield, *The Reconstruction of Southern Education: The Schools and the 1964 Civil Rights Act* (New York: Wiley, 1969), ch. 4.

15. Robert Carter to Lloyd Barbee, November 5, 1964, box 196, folder 13, Lloyd Barbee Papers.

16. *Milwaukee Journal,* September 8, 1969; *Milwaukee Courier,* December 2, 1972.

17. Carter, *A Matter of Law,* 199–202; Roy Wilkins to Joan Franklin, June 20, 1969, part 5, section C, box 320, "Wisconsin Amos case January–September 1969" folder, National NAACP Papers, Library of Congress, Washington, DC; *Milwaukee Journal* September 9 and 10, 1973. Morheuser later became director of the Education Law Center in Newark, New Jersey, where she served as the lead attorney who won the *Abbott v. Burke* school finance reform decision at the New Jersey State Supreme Court in 1990.

18. *Capital Times* (Madison, WI), March 2, 1972; *Keyes et al. v. Denver School District No. 1 et al.,* 413 U.S. 189 (1973); Michael Stolee, "The Milwaukee Desegregation Case," in *Seeds of Crisis: Public Schooling in*

Milwaukee since 1920, ed. John L. Rury and Frank A. Cassell (Madison: University of Wisconsin Press, 1993), 42–77, 231–32.

19. *Amos et al. v. Board of School Directors of the City of Milwaukee,* 408 F. Supp. 765 (1976); *Armstrong et al. V. O'Connell et al.,* 416 F. Supp. 1344 (1976); *Dayton Board of Education et al. v. Brinkman et al.,* 433 U.S. 406 (1977); *Brennan et al. v. Armstrong et al.,* 433 U.S. 672 (1977); *Armstrong et al. v. O'Connell et al.,* 451 F. Supp. 817 (1978).

20. *Milwaukee Journal,* October 15 and 21, 1975. On school desegregation violence in other northern cities, see Ronald P. Formisano, *Boston against Busing: Race, Class, and Ethnicity in the 1960s and 1970s* (Chapel Hill: University of North Carolina Press, 1991).

21. Mary Haywood Metz, *Different by Design: Context and Character of Three Magnet Schools* (New York: Routledge, 1986), ch. 2; David A. Bennett, "A Plan for Increasing Educational Opportunities and Improving Racial Balance in Milwaukee," in *School Desegregation Plans That Work,* ed. Charles V. Willie (Westport, CT: Greenwood Press, 1984), 80–115; Michael Barndt, Rick Janka, and Harold Rose, "The West and Midwest: Milwaukee, Wisconsin: Moblization for School and Community Cooperation," in *Community Politics and Educational Change: Ten School Systems under Court Order,* ed. Charles V. Willie and Susan L. Greenblatt (New York: Longman, 1981), 237–59.

22. Blacks for Two-Way Integration, "Blacks Forced to 'Volunteer,'" box 49, folder 1, Clement Zablocki Papers, Marquette University Library, Milwaukee, Wisconsin; *Milwaukee Community Journal,* October 19, 1977.

23. *Milwaukee Journal,* April 15, 1978; *Milwaukee Community Journal,* July 26, 1978.

24. *Milwaukee Sentinel,* September 6, 1978; *Armstrong et al. v. Board of School Directors of the City of Milwaukee,* 471 F. Supp. 800 (1979); "The History of the Matter: North Division School Board Plan vs. Community Plan," Coalition for Peaceful Schools special newsletter, 1979, box 7, folder 9, Henry Reuss Papers, Milwaukee Urban Archives, University of Wisconsin-Milwaukee Library; *Milwaukee Journal,* April 30, 1979.

25. Howard Fuller, "The Impact of the Milwaukee Public School System's Desegregation Plan on Black Students and the Black Community, 1976–1982" (Ph.D. thesis, Marquette University, 1985), 156–57.

26. Robert L. Carter, "A Reassessment of *Brown v. Board,*" in *Shades of Brown: New Perspectives on School Desegregation,* ed. Derrick Bell (New York: Teachers College Press, 1980), 21–28. Compare with his remarks fifteen years later in Carter, "The Unending Struggle for Equal Educational Opportunity," in *Brown v. Board of Education: The Challenge for Today's Schools,* ed. Ellen Condliffe Lagemann and LaMar P. Miller (New York: Teachers College Press, 1996), 19–26. See also Derrick Bell, *And We Are Not*

Saved: The Elusive Quest for Racial Justice (New York: Basic Books, 1987), ch. 4.

27. Milwaukee integrationists also supported the state-sponsored Chapter 220 desegregation program (a voluntary city-to-suburb transfer arrangement launched in 1976), and subsequent lawsuits to mandate suburban participation. See Stolee, "The Milwaukee Desegregation Case," 256–62. For competing interpretations of city desegregation statistics, compare the following: Fuller, "The Impact of the Milwaukee Public School System's Desegregation Plan"; Douglas Archbald, "Magnet Schools, Voluntary Desegregation, and Public Choice Theory: Limits and Possibilities in a Big City School System" (Ph.D. thesis, University of Wisconsin-Madison, 1989); Bennett, "A Plan for Increasing Educational Opportunities," 103.

Brown, Integration, and Nevada

1. For population statistics and the history of the state's development generally, see Russell R. Elliott and William D. Rowley, *History of Nevada,* 2d ed. (Lincoln: University of Nebraska Press, 1987), especially 404–5.

2. Ibid., for the general history of the state. On Las Vegas in particular, the outstanding scholarly work is Eugene P. Moehring, *Resort City in the Sunbelt: Las Vegas, 1930–2000* (Reno: University of Nevada Press, 2000). See also Gerald D. Nash, *The American West Transformed: The Impact of the Second World War* (Bloomington: Indiana University Press, 1985). On Nevada's political evolution, see Michael W. Bowers, *The Sagebrush State: Nevada's History, Government, and Politics,* 2d ed. (Reno and Las Vegas: University of Nevada Press, 2002). On Las Vegas and its role in postwar national trends, see also John M. Findlay, *People of Chance: Gambling in America from Jamestown to Las Vegas* (New York: Oxford University Press, 1986).

3. Elliott and Rowley, *History of Nevada,* 404–5. Moehring, *Resort City in the Sunbelt,* 173–202, is an excellent introduction to racial issues in Las Vegas. See also M. Gottdiener, Claudia C. Collins, and David R. Dickens, *Las Vegas: The Social Production of an All-American City* (Malden and London: Blackwell, 1999). The superintendent of the Humboldt County School District once wrote, "Nevada's remote areas also have multicultural concerns. Besides people of Hispanic origin, there are small clusters of Basque, Cornish, Greek, Austrian, Japanese, and other ethnic groups, as well as several tribes of Native Americans, primarily Paiutes and Shoshones." That he said nothing about blacks speaks volumes about the paucity of their numbers in rural Nevada. See Robert J. Scott, "Remote Nevada Schools: Dilemmas of Rural Education," in *Nevada Public Affairs Review: Rural Nevada: Survival and Development,* ed. Richard L. Siegel and Alice M. Good (Reno: Senator Alan

Bible Center for Applied Research, University of Nevada, Reno, 1986, Number 1), 57–59. On the specter of racial discrimination and the comparatively small size of Reno's African American population, see *Reno News and Review,* February 20, 2003. See also Elmer Rusco, *Not Like a River: The Memoir of an Activist Academic* (Reno: University of Nevada Oral History Program, 2004), and Rusco's papers housed at the Department of Special Collections, Noble Getchell Library, University of Nevada, Reno, and the Department of Special Collections, Lied Library, University of Nevada, Las Vegas. The *Nevada Law Journal,* V:1 (Fall 2004), published by the William S. Boyd School of Law at UNLV, featured several articles from a symposium, "Pursuing Equal Justice in the West." See especially Michael S. Green, "The Mississippi of the West," 57–70; Claytee White, "The March That Never Happened: Desegregating the Las Vegas Strip," 71–83; and Quintard Taylor, "'Justice Is Slow but Sure': The Civil Rights Movement in the West, 1950–1970," 84–92.

4. *Las Vegas Evening Review-Journal,* May 17 and 18, 1954; *Las Vegas Sun,* May 18, 1954; *Nevada State Journal,* May 18, 1954; *Reno Evening Gazette,* May 17 and 18, 1954; *Elko Daily Free Press,* May 18, 1954. On Nevada's press, see Jake Highton, *Nevada Newspaper Days: A History of Journalism in the Silver State* (Stockton, NV: Heritage West, 1990). The classic history of *Brown* is still Richard Kluger, *Simple Justice: The History of Brown v. Board of Education and Black America's Struggle for Equality* (New York: Alfred A. Knopf, 1976). See also Michael J. Klarman, *From Jim Crow to Civil Rights: The Supreme Court and the Struggle for Racial Equality* (New York: Oxford University Press, 2003).

5. Mary Ellen Glass, *Nevada's Turbulent '50s: Decade of Political and Economic Change* (Reno: University of Nevada Press, 1981), especially 39–60. See also Don W. Driggs, "Taxation and the Financing of Education in Nevada," in *Sagebrush and Neon: Studies in Nevada Politics,* ed. Eleanore Bushnell (Reno: Bureau of Governmental Research, 1973), 75–92; James W. Hulse, "Maude Frazier: Pioneering Educator and Lawmaker," in *The Maverick Spirit: Building the New Nevada,* ed. Richard O. Davies (Reno and Las Vegas: University of Nevada Press, 1998), 12–23.

6. Elmer R. Rusco, *"Good Time Coming?": Black Nevadans in the Nineteenth Century* (Westport, CT: Greenwood Press, 1975); *State of Nevada ex. Rel. Stoutmeyer v. Duffy,* 7 Nevada 342. See also William Hanchett, "Yankee Law and the Negro in Nevada, 1861–1869," *Western Humanities Review* 10 (Summer 1956): 241–49; Elmer R. Rusco, "Nevada Law and Race," in Elmer R. Rusco and Sue Fawn Chung, eds., *Nevada Public Affairs Review: Ethnicity and Race in Nevada* (1987, Number 2), 71–74.

7. NAACP Reno-Sparks branch papers, Department of Special Collections, Getchell Library, University of Nevada, Reno; Craig F. Swallow,

"The Ku Klux Klan in Nevada during the 1920s" (Master's thesis, University of Nevada, Las Vegas, 1978); Clarence Ray, Helen M. Blue, and Jamie Coughtry, *Clarence Ray: Black Politics and Gaming in Las Vegas, 1920s–1980s* (Reno: University of Nevada Oral History Program, 1991); Roosevelt Fitzgerald, "The Evolution of a Black Community in Las Vegas, 1905–1940," Department of Special Collections, Lied Library, UNLV; Fitzgerald, "Blacks and the Boulder Dam Project," *Nevada Historical Society Quarterly* 22, no. 3 (Fall 1981): 255–60; Elmer R. Rusco, "The Civil Rights Movement in Hawthorne," *Nevada Historical Society Quarterly* 43, no. 1 (Spring 2000): 35–73; Andrew J. Dunar and Dennis McBride, *Building Hoover Dam: An Oral History of the Great Depression* (Reno: University of Nevada Press, 2001, reprint of Norman: University of Oklahoma Press, 1993); *Las Vegas Sun, Scene,* n.d., Rev. Donald Clark mss, box 1, Department of Special Collections, Lied Library, UNLV; A. D. Hopkins, "Ernie Cragin: Flawed Vision," in *The First 100: Portraits of the Men and Women Who Shaped Las Vegas,* ed. A. D. Hopkins and K. J. Evans (Las Vegas: Huntington Press, 1999), 81–83; Moehring, *Resort City in the Sunbelt,* 23–27; Elmer R. Rusco, "The Civil Rights Movement in Nevada," in Rusco and Chung, eds., *Nevada Public Affairs Review,* 75–81.

8. Woodrow Wilson, Jamie Coughtry, and R. T. King, *Woodrow Wilson: Race, Community and Politics in Las Vegas, 1940s–1980s* (Reno: University of Nevada Oral History Program, 1990); Lubertha Johnson, Jamie Coughtry, and R. T. King, *Lubertha Johnson: Civil Rights Efforts in Las Vegas, 1940s–1960s: An Oral History Interview* (Reno: University of Nevada Oral History Program, 1988); William T. Dobbs, "Southern Nevada and the Legacy of Basic Magnesium, Inc.," *Nevada Historical Society Quarterly* 34, no. 1 (Spring 1991): 273–303; Roosevelt Fitzgerald, "A Demographic Impact of Basic Magnesium on Southern Nevada," Department of Special Collections, Lied Library, UNLV; Moehring, *Resort City in the Sunbelt,* 13–72; Earnest N. Bracey, "Anatomy of the Second Baptist Church: The First Black Baptist Church in Las Vegas," *Nevada Historical Society Quarterly* 43, no. 3 (Fall 2000): 201–13; Perry Bruce Kaufman, "The Best City of Them All: A History of Las Vegas, 1930–1960" (Ph.D. dissertation, University of California, Santa Barbara, 1974), especially 325–98; Eric N. Moody, "The Democratic Senatorial Primary of 1944: Vail Pittman Renews an Old Rivalry," *Nevada Historical Society Quarterly* 15, no. 2 (Summer 1972): 2–23; Jerome E. Edwards, *Pat McCarran: Political Boss of Nevada* (Reno: University of Nevada Press, 1982), 94–121; Mabel Hoggard Biography File, Department of Special Collections, Lied Library, UNLV; Lubertha Johnson Biography File; Ralph L. Denton and MIchael S. Green, *A Liberal Conscience: Ralph Denton, Nevadan* (Reno: University of Nevada Oral History Program, 2001); Grant Sawyer, Gary E. Elliott, and R. T. King, *Hang Tough! Grant*

Sawyer: An Activist in the Governor's Mansion (Reno: University of Nevada Oral History Program, 1993); Rusco, "Civil Rights in Hawthorne," 35–73. See also Annelise Orleck, *Storming Caesars Palace: How Black Mothers Fought Their Own War on Poverty* (Boston: Beacon Press, 2005).

9. A. D. Hopkins, "Fighting Racism: James B. McMillan," in Hopkins and Evans, eds., *The First 100*, 143–46; K. J. Evans, "Mayor Who Made His Mark: Oran Gragson," in ibid., 146–47; Hopkins, "Breaking the Color Line: Bob Bailey," ibid., 151–52; Hopkins, "Fighting the Power: Charles Kellar," ibid., 153–54; Evans, "Good Citizen Ralph: Ralph Denton," ibid., 155–56; Hopkins, "Grant Sawyer: The Hang-Tough Governor," ibid., 148–50; Earnest N. Bracey, "Ruby Duncan, Operation Life, and Welfare Rights in Nevada," *Nevada Historical Society Quarterly* 44, no. 2 (Summer 2001): 133–46; Claytee White, "'Eight Dollars a Day and Working in the Shade': An Oral History of African American Migrant Women in the Las Vegas Gaming Industry," in *African American Women Confront the West, 1600–2000*, ed. Quintard Taylor and Shirley Ann Wilson Moore (Norman: University of Oklahoma Press, 2003), 276–91; James B. McMillan, Gary E. Elliott, and R. T. King, *Fighting Back: A Life in the Struggle for Civil Rights* (Reno: University of Nevada Oral History Program, 1997); Gary E. Elliott, "James B. McMillan: The Pursuit of Equality," in Davies, ed., *The Maverick Spirit*, 44–57.

10. Wilson, Coughtry, and King, *Woodrow Wilson*; McMillan, Elliott, and King, *Fighting Back*, especially 77–116; Moehring, *Resort City in the Sunbelt*, 173–202; Sawyer, Elliott, and King, *Hang Tough!*; Denton and Green, *A Liberal Conscience*; Richard E. Lingenfelter and Karen Rix Gash, *The Newspapers of Nevada: A History and Bibliography, 1854–1979* (Reno: University of Nevada Press, 1984), 134, 209.

11. Numerous works deal with the civil rights movement and its evolution. See, for example, Maurice Isserman and Michael Kazin, *America Divided: The Civil War of the 1960s* (New York: Oxford University Press, 2000). On Nevada in this period, see Sawyer, Elliott, and King, *Hang Tough!*, 133–39; Denton and Green, *A Liberal Conscience*, 261–98.

12. On fair housing, see especially Joseph N. Crowley, "Race and Residence: The Politics of Open Housing in Nevada," in Eleanore Bushnell, ed., *Sagebrush and Neon: Studies in Nevada Politics* (Reno: Bureau of Governmental Research, 1973), 55–74. On welfare rights, see Annelise Orleck, *Storming Caesars Palace: How Black Mothers Fought Their Own War on Poverty* (Boston: Beacon Press, 2005).

13. See generally Todd Gitlin, *The Sixties: Years of Hope, Days of Rage* (New York: Bantam Books, 1987); David Farber, *The Age of Great Dreams: America in the 1960s* (New York: Hill and Wang, 1994).

14. Hopkins, "Fighting the Power: Charles Kellar," in Hopkins and Evans,

eds., *The First* 100, 153–54; *Las Vegas Review-Journal,* July 10, 2002; *Las Vegas Sun,* June 14, 1999; Leslie B. Gray, "Nevada Beginnings in Civil Rights: A Memoir," in Rusco and Chung, eds., *Nevada Public Affairs Review,* 87–88. Because Nevada had a one-year residency requirement before taking the bar, Kellar, to make a living, ended up becoming Nevada's first licensed African American real estate broker.

15. Hopkins, "Kellar," in Hopkins and Evans, eds., *The First 100,* 153–54; Hopkins, "Al Bramlet: The Organizer," in ibid., 196–97; *Las Vegas Review-Journal,* July 10, 2002; Jeffrey J. Sallaz, "Civil Rights and Employment Equity in Las Vegas: The Failed Enforcement of the Casino Consent Decree, 1971–1986" (Article accepted for publication in *Nevada Historical Society Quarterly,* in author's possession); Moehring, *Resort City in the Sunbelt,* 189–91.

16. *Las Vegas Sun,* February 15, 1969; November 17, 2000.

17. Moehring, *Resort City in the Sunbelt,* 191.

18. Ibid., 191–94. See also Mike Davis, "The Racial Cauldron," in Hal K. Rothman and Mike Davis, eds., *The Grit beneath the Glitter: Tales from the Real Las Vegas* (Berkeley: University of California Press, 2002), 260–67; Robert E. Parker, "The Social Costs of Rapid Urbanization in Southern Nevada," in ibid., 126–44; Nefertiti Makenta, "A View from West Las Vegas," in *The Real Las Vegas: Life beyond the Strip,* ed. David Littlejohn (New York: Oxford University Press, 1999), 109–31.

19. *Bureau of Governmental Research Newsletter,* University of Nevada, Reno 12, no. 4 (December 1973): 1–2. Moehring, *Resort City in the Sunbelt,* deals with the history of local schools at various points throughout the book. See also Nevada State Retired Teachers Association, *Inside Nevada Schools: A Challenge for the Future* (Carson City: Nevada State Retired Teachers Association, 1976), 25–52; "To Bus or Not to Bus: An Investigation of the Sixth Grade Plan to Achieve Racial Integration in Clark County, Nevada" (Student paper, 1972, Department of Special Collections, Lied Library, University of Nevada, Las Vegas).

20. Moehring, *Resort City in the Sunbelt,* 194–95; Virginia Alleman, "Education and Integration in Las Vegas" (Student paper, Department of Special Collections, Lied Library, UNLV), 5–6.

21. Moehring, *Resort City in the Sunbelt,* 194–95; Alleman, "Education and Integration in Las Vegas," 7–8; Clark County School District, "Interim Position on Integration," July 1966 (Department of Special Collections, Lied Library, UNLV), 4; Clark County School District, "Integration Policy and Action Plan: An Abstract of the Original Documents" (Department of Special Collections, Lied Library, UNLV); Clark County School District, "Status Report on the District's Integration Policy," ibid.; *Las Vegas Review-Journal,* December 17, 20, and 23, 1966; *Las Vegas Voice,* December 22, 1966.

22. Moehring, *Resort City in the Sunbelt*, 194–95. See also Jack Greenberg, *Crusaders in the Courts: How a Dedicated Band of Lawyers Fought for the Civil Rights Revolution* (New York: Basic Books, 1994).

23. *Reno Gazette-Journal*, February 11–12, 1992; *Las Vegas Review-Journal*, February 11–12, 1992; A. D. Hopkins, "The Foley Family: A Most Judicious Clan," in Hopkins and Evans, eds., *The First 100*, 173–74; J. Dee Kille, *Academic Freedom Imperiled: The McCarthy Era at the University of Nevada* (Reno: University of Nevada Press, 2004), discusses Thompson throughout. See also Glass, *Nevada's Turbulent '50s*, 61–72; Moehring, *Resort City in the Sunbelt*, 173–202.

24. *Kelly v. Mason, et al.*, CV-LV-1146 (D. Nev. 1968); *Governmental Research Newsletter*, 2; "To Bus or Not to Bus," 10; L. Steven Demaree, Donna M. Mendoza-Mitchell, and Africa A. Sanchez, "Equality by Law: *Brown v. Board of Education* Fifty Years Later," *Communiqué* 25, no. 2 (February 2004).

25. *Kelly v. Mason*, CV-LV-1146; *Kelly v. Brown*, CV-LV-1146; "To Bus or Not to Bus," 10–11; Clark County School District, "Report of Task Force on Integration," February 27, 1969, Department of Special Collections, Lied Library, UNLV.

26. *Kelly v. Mason*, CV-LV-1146; "To Bus or Not to Bus," 10–11.

27. *Kelly v. Mason*, CV-LV-1146; *Las Vegas Sun*, May 28, 1970.

28. *Governmental Research Newsletter*, 2; Judgment and Decree of U.S. District Judge Bruce Thompson, U.S. District Court, District of Nevada, December 2, 1970, 2; "To Bus or Not to Bus," 11.

29. *Governmental Research Newsletter*, 2–3; "To Bus or Not to Bus," 11; McMillan, Elliott, and King, *Fighting Back*, 130.

30. *Governmental Research Newsletter*, 3; Charles A. Fleming to Elmer R. Rusco, Las Vegas, n.d., Elmer R. Rusco Papers, Department of Special Collections, Lied Library, UNLV.

31. *Kelly v. Guinn*, 456 F. 2d 100 (9th Cir. 1972), cert. denied, 413 U.S. 919: Demaree, Mendoza-Mitchell, and Sanchez, "Equality by Law"; "To Bus or Not to Bus," 12–13, 30–33; *Governmental Research Newsletter*, 3; Bowers, *The Sagebrush State*, 105–13, 191; *Las Vegas Review-Journal*, September 17, 1972.

32. *Governmental Research Newsletter*, 4–6. The author would add that he was an elementary school student at the time and can vouch for the need for newer, better buses.

33. *Governmental Research Newsletter*, 6–7; *Las Vegas Review-Journal*, August 30, 1972; September 17, 1972; "To Bus or Not to Bus," 13, 22, 30–33.

34. <www.inclusiveschools.org>; <www.ccsd.net>; Demaree, Mendoza-Mitchell, and Sanchez, "Equality by Law"; *Las Vegas Review-Journal*, June 11, 2000; August 12, 2001; McMillan, Elliott, and King, *Fighting Back*, 131.

35. McMillan, Elliott, and King, *Fighting Back,* 137–38; *Las Vegas Review-Journal,* July 10, 2002; *Las Vegas Sun,* July 10, 2002; <www.ccsd.net>; Earnest N. Bracey, "The Political Participation of Blacks in an Open Society: The Changing Political Climate in Nevada," *Nevada Historical Society Quarterly* 42, no. 3 (Fall 1999): 140–59; Bracey, "The African Americans," in *The Peoples of Las Vegas: One City, Many Faces,* ed. Jerry L. Simich and Thomas C. Wright (Reno: University of Nevada Press, 2005).

Contributors

Jayne R. Beilke is a professor of Secondary and Social Foundations of Education in the Department of Educational Studies at Ball State University, Muncie, Indiana. Her research interests focus on educational philanthropy (particularly the Julius Rosenwald Fund) and African American educational history in general.

Charles C. Bolton is professor and head of History at the University of North Carolina Greensboro. He is the author of *The Hardest Deal of All: The Battle over School Integration in Mississippi, 1870–1980.*

Vernon Burton is University Distinguished Teacher/Scholar at the University of Illinois at Urbana-Champaign, where he is also the director of the Illinois Center for Computing in Humanities, Arts, and Social Science. Burton is the author of more than one hundred articles and the author or editor of fourteen books; his most recent publication is *The Age of Lincoln* (New York: Hill and Wang, 2007).

Brian J. Daugherity is a collateral instructor of History and the assistant to the chair of the History Department at Virginia Commonwealth University in Richmond, Virginia. His research interests include the civil rights movement, southern race relations, and the history of Virginia. He is currently working on a manuscript examining the NAACP and the implementation of *Brown v. Board of Education* in Virginia and co-producing a documentary film on the historic but little-known *Green v. New Kent County, Virginia,* United States Supreme Court decision (1968).

Jack Dougherty is an associate professor and director of the Educational Studies Program at Trinity College in Hartford, Connecticut. His prize-winning book, *More Than One Struggle: The Evolution of Black School Reform in Milwaukee* explores how three generations of civil rights activism changed in the urban Midwest from the 1930s to 2004. His current research examines how housing markets and education politics shaped cities, suburbs, and schooling during the twentieth century.

Caroline Emmons is associate professor of History at Hampden-Sydney College in Hampden-Sydney, Virginia, where she teaches courses on American and African American history. She has published articles on Harry T. Moore and the civil rights movement in Florida. She is currently at work on a biography of Ruby Hurley, head of the Southeastern Regional NAACP office from 1951 to 1978.

Michael S. Green is a professor of History at the Community College of Southern Nevada. He has published several books on Nevada and Las Vegas history, including *Freedom, Union, and Power: The Republican Party During the Civil War,* and a number of articles on ethnicity and civil rights in southern Nevada. He is now writing a history of the politics of the 1850s and co-writing the autobiography of a pioneer Las Vegas gaming figure.

Johanna Miller Lewis is professor of History and graduate coordinator of Public History at the University of Arkansas at Little Rock. In addition to a book and numerous publications, she has led award-winning history projects, including the traveling exhibit, "'The Finest High School for Negro Boys and Girls': Dunbar High School of Little Rock, Arkansas, 1929–1955," the Central High Museum and Visitor Center, the National Historic Landmark designation for the Daisy Bates House, and "Life Interrupted: The Japanese American Experience in World War II Arkansas."

J. Michael McElreath is an assistant professor of History at Meredith College in Raleigh, North Carolina. He completed his dissertation, "The Cost of Opportunity: School Desegregation and Changing Race Relations in the Triangle," in 2002, at the University of Pennsylvania. He has taught at public and private high schools in New Jersey and North Carolina and is the on-site director of the North Carolina Governor's School East.

Peter William Moran is an associate professor of Education at the University of Wyoming. His research focuses broadly on the history of education generally with particular interest in school desegregation. Moran is the author of *Race, Law and the Desegregation of Public Schools*, a case study of Kansas City, Missouri's fifty-year struggle to integrate their schools.

Thomas V. O'Brien is an associate professor of Education and director of Educational Studies at The Ohio State University at Mansfield. His research interests are in the foundations of education with a specialty in the history of race and education. He has published numerous journal articles and reviews as well as two books: *The Politics of Race and Schooling: Public Education in Georgia, 1900–1961* and *Bridging Theory and Practice in Teacher Education*, co-edited with Mordechai Gordon.

Lewie Reece is an assistant professor of History at Anderson University, South Carolina. The focus of Dr. Reece's work is on Reconstruction, Civil War, and Gilded Age History with an emphasis on politics, law, and race.

Bradley Skelcher is currently a professor of History specializing in historic preservation and African American history at Delaware State University. He is also serving as acting dean of the College of Humanities and Social Sciences. Skelcher is the author of several works in historic preservation and African American history with a focus on the preservation and history of education in Delaware.

Index